NIGHT OF THE BEASTS

1

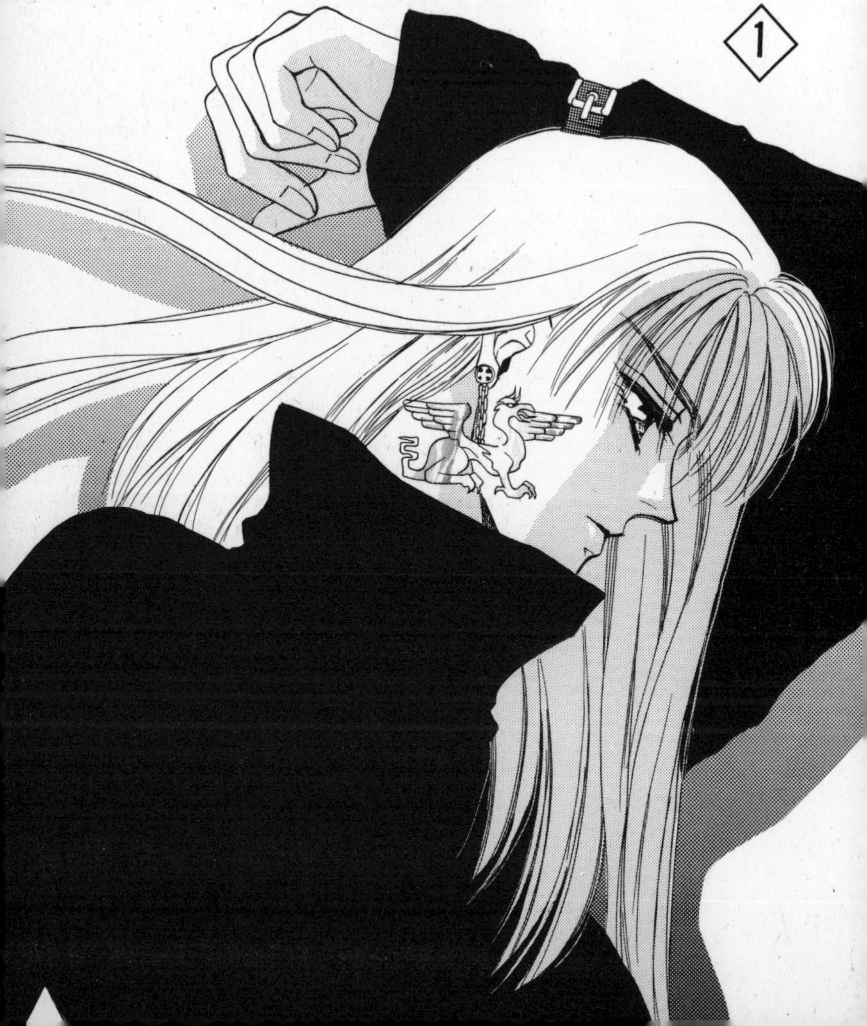

Translation – Kathy Schilling
Adaptation – Jake Forbes
Lettering & Design – Jihye Hong
Production Manager - James Dashiell
Editor -- Audry Taylor

A Go! Comi manga

Published by Go! Media Entertainment, LLC

Night of the Beasts Volume 1
© CHIKA SHIOMI 1996
Originally published in Japan in 1996 by Akita Publishing Co., Ltd., Tokyo.
English translation rights arranged with Akita Publishing Co., Ltd.
through TOHAN CORPORATION, Tokyo.

Visit us online at www.gocomi.com
e-mail: info@gocomi.com

ISBN 1-933617-14-4

First printed in August 2006

1 2 3 4 5 6 7 8 9

Manufactured in the United States of America

NIGHT OF THE BEASTS

STORY AND ART BY

CHIKA SHIOMI

VOLUME 1

go!comi

Concerning Honorifics

At Go! Comi, we do our best to ensure that our translations read seamlessly in English while respecting the original Japanese language and culture. To this end, the original honorifics (the suffixes found at the end of characters' names) remain intact. In Japan, where politeness and formality are more integrated into every aspect of the language, honorifics give a better understanding of character relationships. They can be used to indicate both respect and affection. Whether a person addresses someone by first name or last name also indicates how close their relationship is.

Here are some of the honorifics you might encounter in reading this book:

-san: This is the most common and neutral of honorifics. The polite way to address someone you're not on close terms with is to use "-san." It's kind of like Mr. or Ms., except you can use "-san" with first names as easily as family names.

-chan: Used for friendly familiarity, mostly applied towards young girls. "-chan" also carries a connotation of cuteness with it, so it is frequently used with nicknames towards both boys and girls (such as "Na-chan" for "Natsu").

-kun: Like "-chan," it's an informal suffix for friends and classmates, only "-kun" is usually associated with boys. It can also be used in a professional environment by someone addressing a subordinate.

-sama: Indicates a great deal of respect or admiration.

Sempai: In school, "sempai" is used to refer to an upperclassman or club leader. It can also be used in the workplace by a new employee to address a mentor or staff member with seniority.

Sensei: Teachers, doctors, writers or any master of a trade are referred to as "sensei." When addressing a manga creator, the polite thing to do is attach "-sensei" to the manga-ka's name (as in Shiomi-sensei).

Onii: This is the more casual term for an older brother. Usually you'll see it with an honorific attached, such as "onii-chan."

Onee: The casual term for older sister, it's used like "onii" with honorifics.

[blank]: Not using an honorific when addressing someone indicates that the speaker has permission to speak intimately with the other person. This relationship is usually reserved for close friends and family.

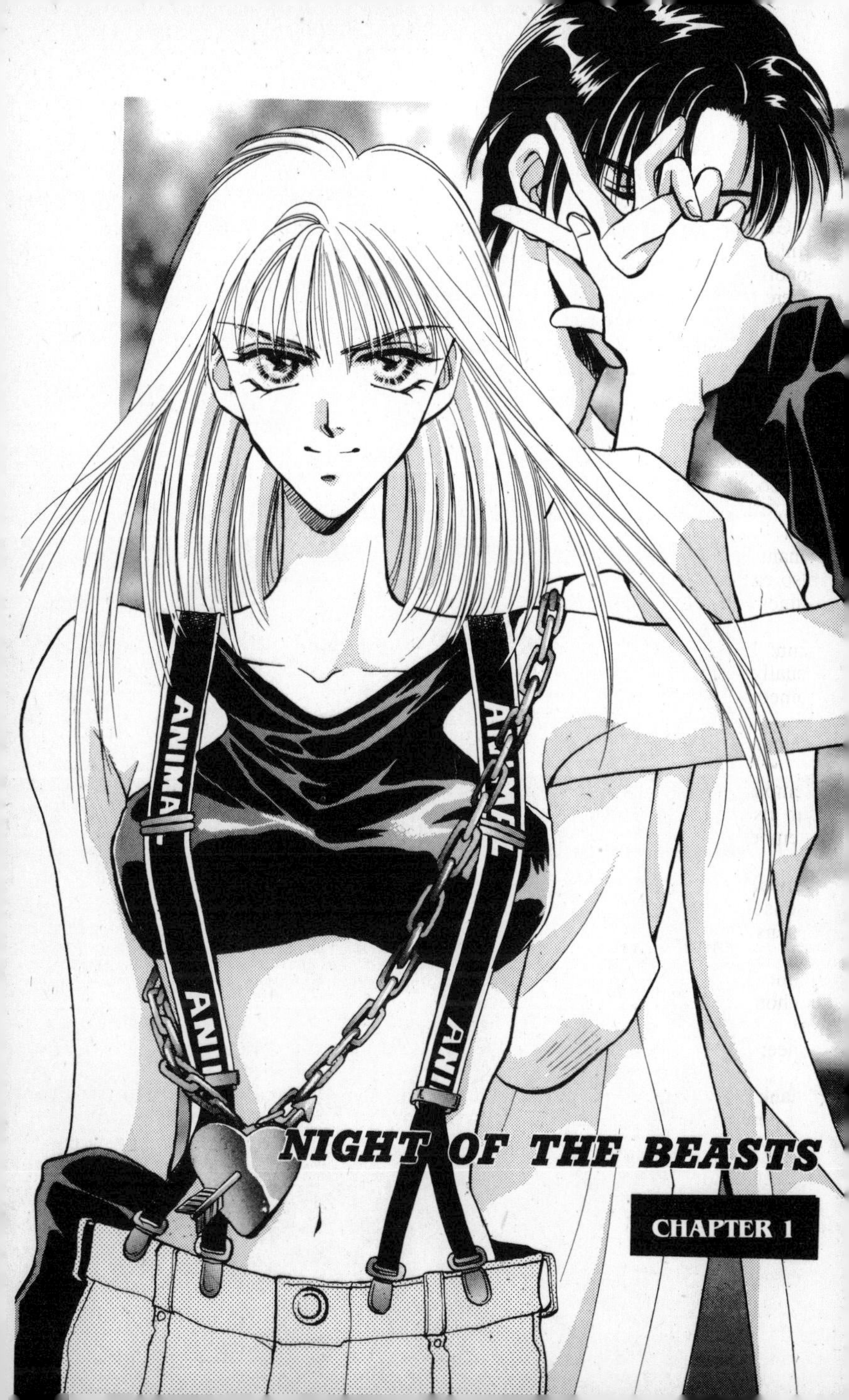
NIGHT OF THE BEASTS
CHAPTER 1

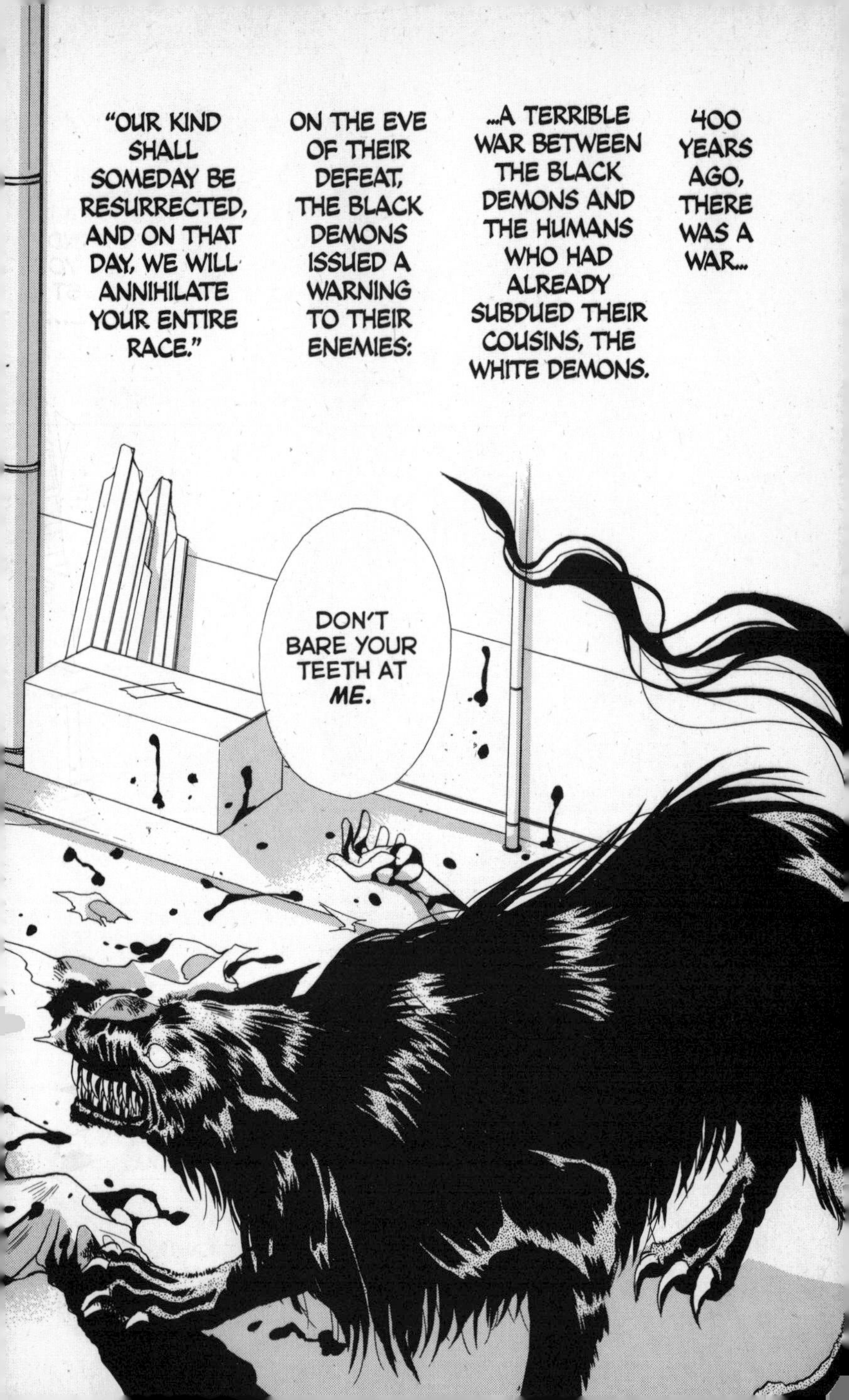
400 YEARS AGO, THERE WAS A WAR...
...A TERRIBLE WAR BETWEEN THE BLACK DEMONS AND THE HUMANS WHO HAD ALREADY SUBDUED THEIR COUSINS, THE WHITE DEMONS.
ON THE EVE OF THEIR DEFEAT, THE BLACK DEMONS ISSUED A WARNING TO THEIR ENEMIES:
"OUR KIND SHALL SOMEDAY BE RESURRECTED, AND ON THAT DAY, WE WILL ANNIHILATE YOUR ENTIRE RACE."
DON'T BARE YOUR TEETH AT *ME.*

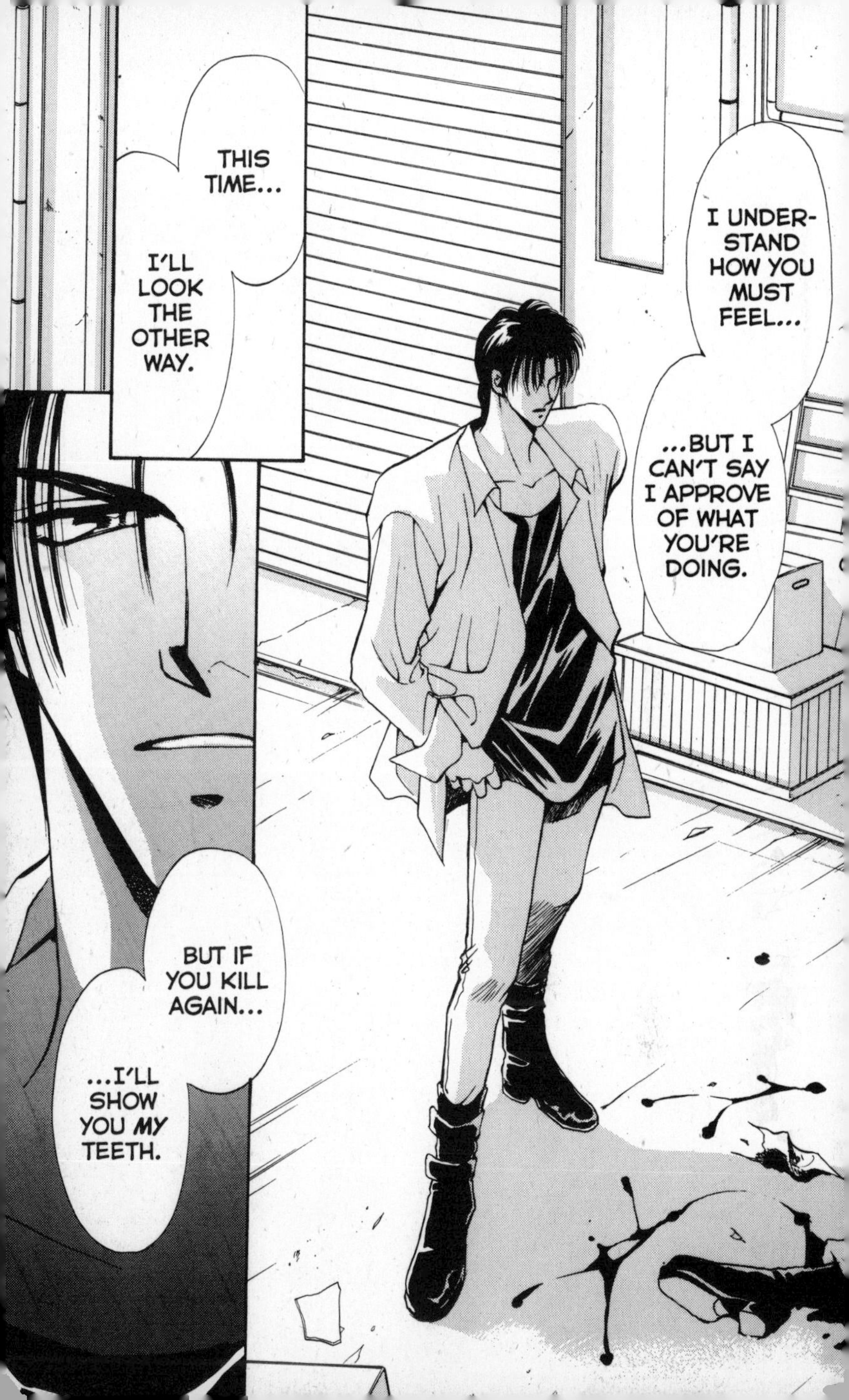
I UNDER-STAND HOW YOU MUST FEEL...
...BUT I CAN'T SAY I APPROVE OF WHAT YOU'RE DOING.
THIS TIME...
I'LL LOOK THE OTHER WAY.
BUT IF YOU KILL AGAIN...
...I'LL SHOW YOU *MY* TEETH.

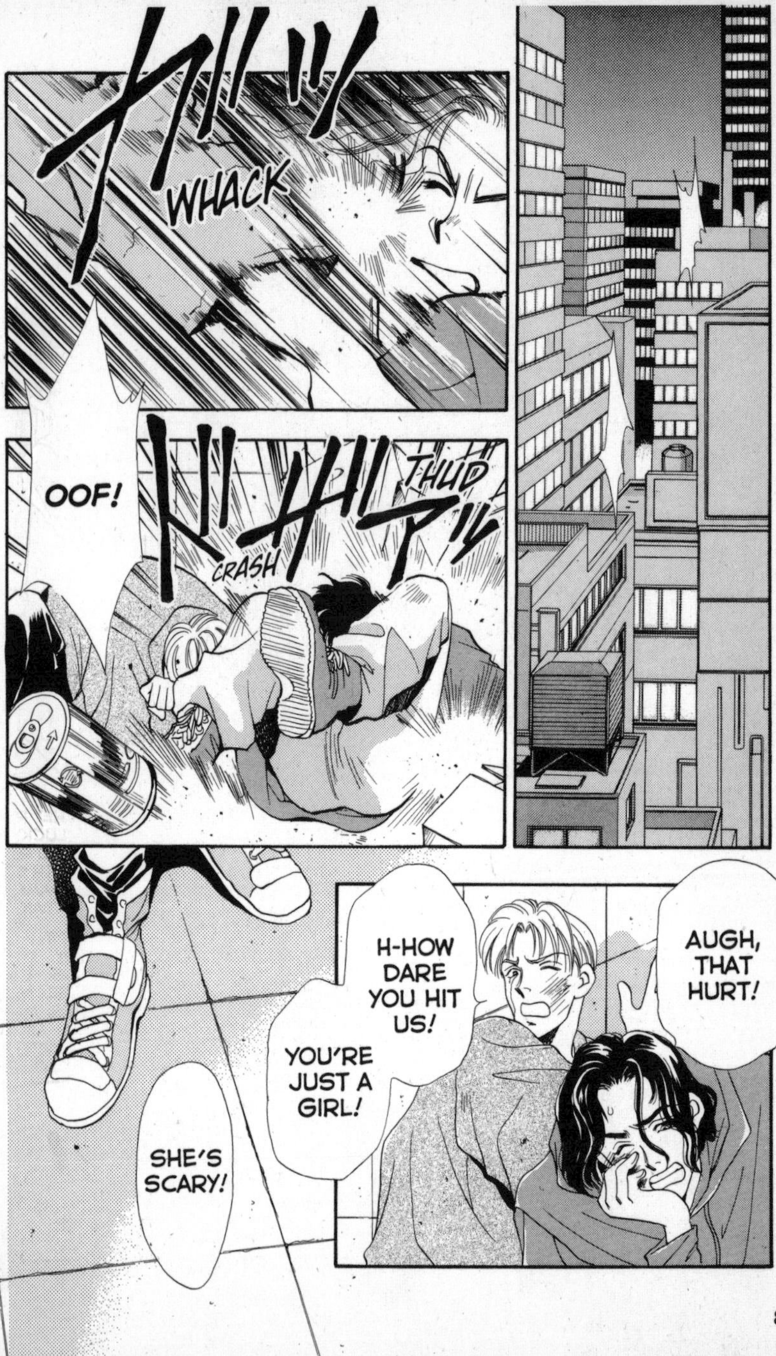
WHACK
THUD
OOF!
CRASH
AUGH, THAT HURT!
H-HOW DARE YOU HIT US!
YOU'RE JUST A GIRL!
SHE'S SCARY!

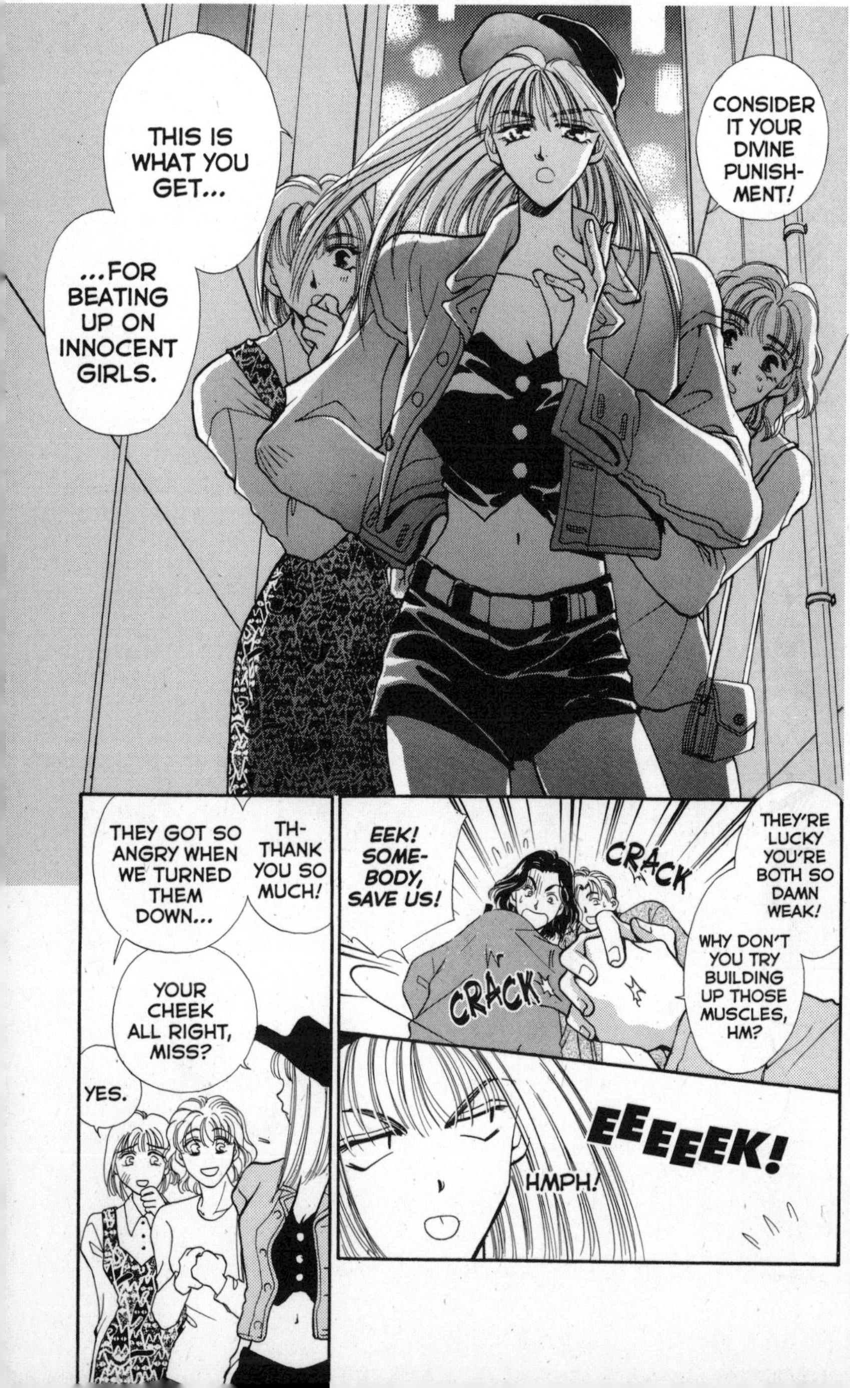
THIS IS WHAT YOU GET...
...FOR BEATING UP ON INNOCENT GIRLS.
CONSIDER IT YOUR DIVINE PUNISH-MENT!
THEY'RE LUCKY YOU'RE BOTH SO DAMN WEAK!
WHY DON'T YOU TRY BUILDING UP THOSE MUSCLES, HM?
CRACK
EEK! SOME-BODY, SAVE US!
CRACK
EEEEEK!
HMPH!
TH-THANK YOU SO MUCH!
THEY GOT SO ANGRY WHEN WE TURNED THEM DOWN...
YOUR CHEEK ALL RIGHT, MISS?
YES.

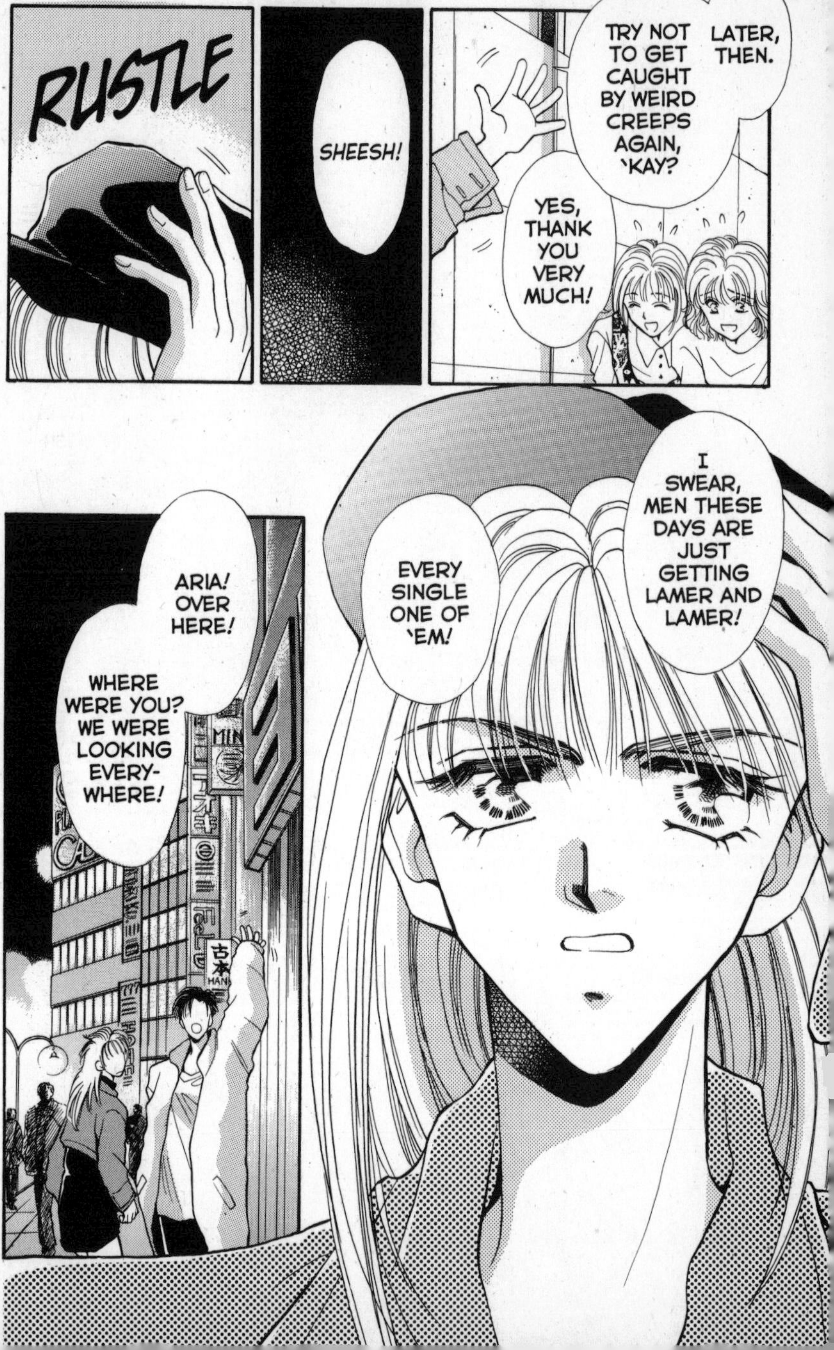
LATER, THEN.
TRY NOT TO GET CAUGHT BY WEIRD CREEPS AGAIN, 'KAY?
YES, THANK YOU VERY MUCH!
SHEESH!
RUSTLE
I SWEAR, MEN THESE DAYS ARE JUST GETTING LAMER AND LAMER!
EVERY SINGLE ONE OF 'EM!
ARIA! OVER HERE!
WHERE WERE YOU? WE WERE LOOKING EVERY-WHERE!

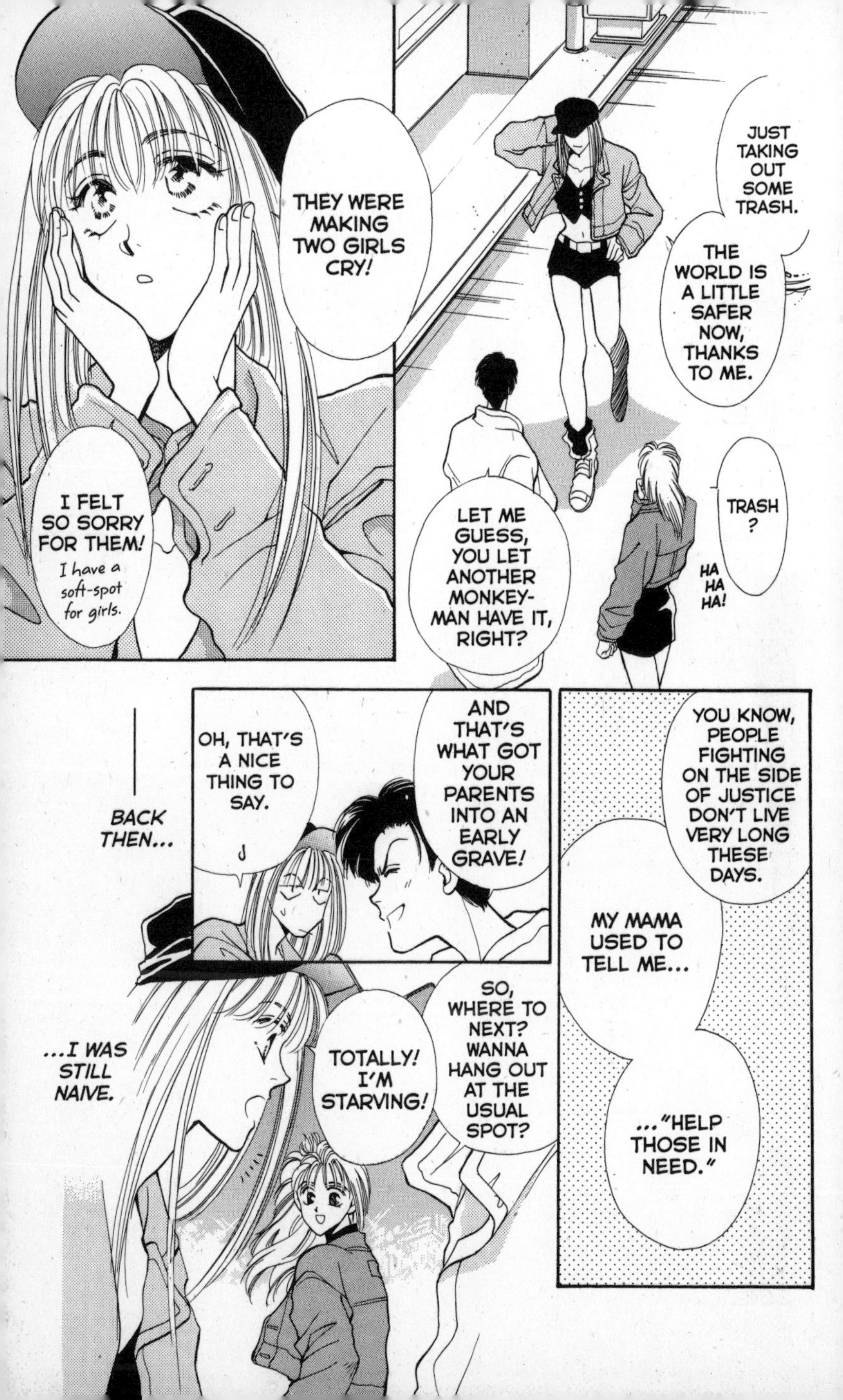

JUST TAKING OUT SOME TRASH.
THE WORLD IS A LITTLE SAFER NOW, THANKS TO ME.
TRASH?
HA HA HA!
LET ME GUESS, YOU LET ANOTHER MONKEY-MAN HAVE IT, RIGHT?
THEY WERE MAKING TWO GIRLS CRY!
I FELT SO SORRY FOR THEM!
I have a soft-spot for girls.
YOU KNOW, PEOPLE FIGHTING ON THE SIDE OF JUSTICE DON'T LIVE VERY LONG THESE DAYS.
MY MAMA USED TO TELL ME...
..."HELP THOSE IN NEED."
AND THAT'S WHAT GOT YOUR PARENTS INTO AN EARLY GRAVE!
OH, THAT'S A NICE THING TO SAY.
BACK THEN...
SO, WHERE TO NEXT? WANNA HANG OUT AT THE USUAL SPOT?
TOTALLY! I'M STARVING!
...I WAS STILL NAIVE.

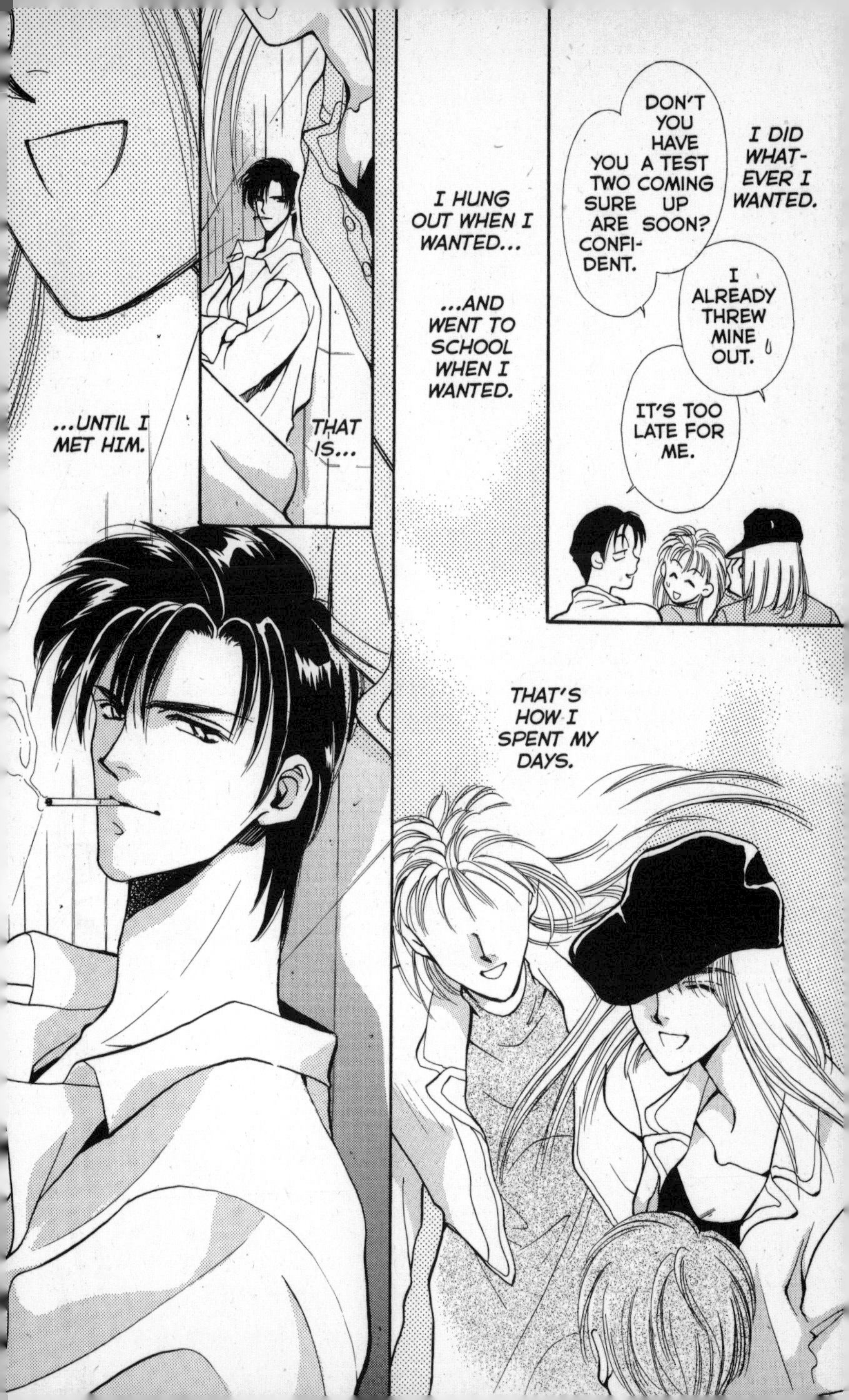
I DID WHATEVER I WANTED.
DON'T YOU HAVE A TEST COMING UP SOON?
YOU TWO SURE ARE CONFIDENT.
I ALREADY THREW MINE OUT.
IT'S TOO LATE FOR ME.
I HUNG OUT WHEN I WANTED...
...AND WENT TO SCHOOL WHEN I WANTED.
THAT'S HOW I SPENT MY DAYS.
THAT IS...
...UNTIL I MET HIM.

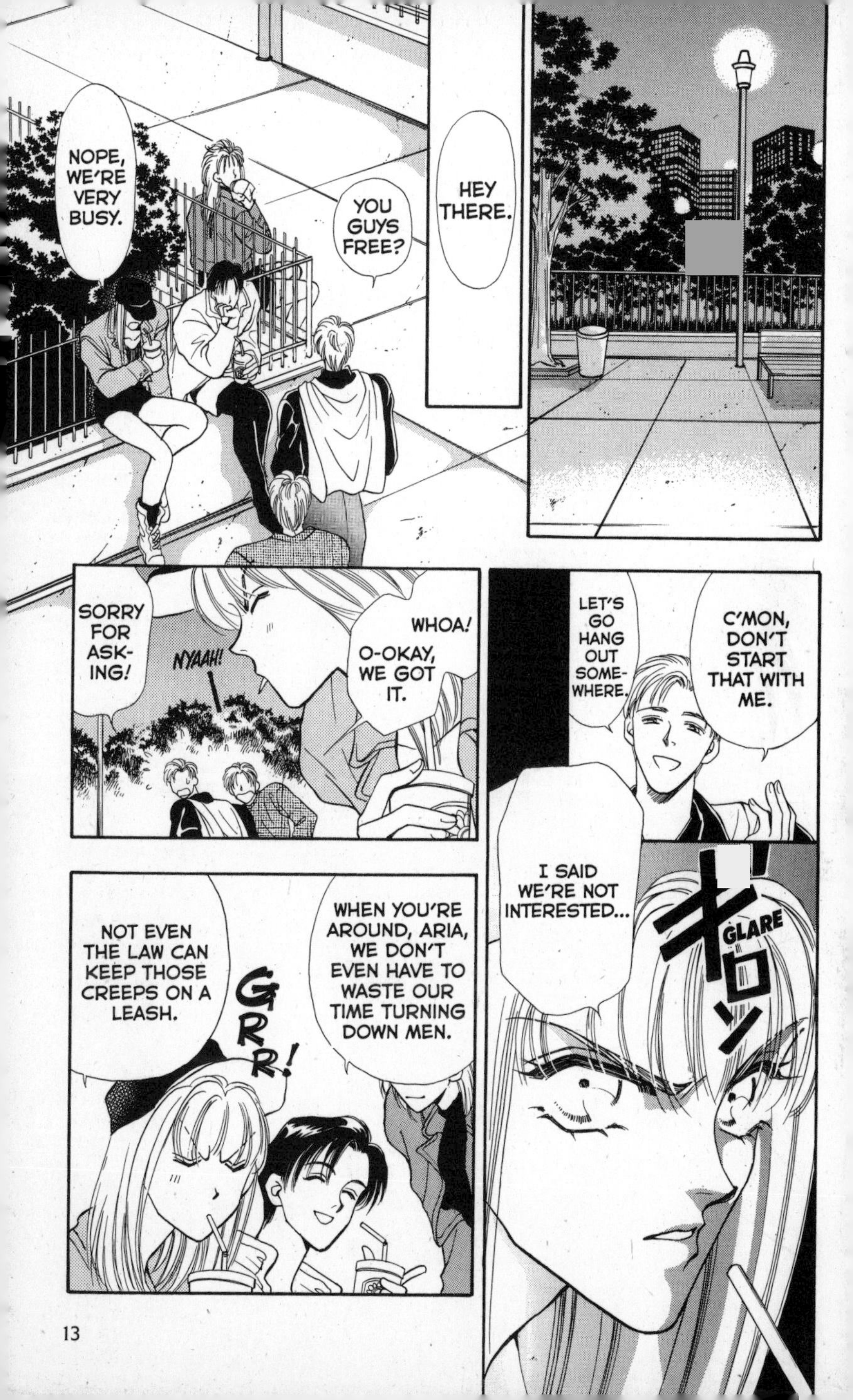
HEY THERE.
YOU GUYS FREE?
NOPE, WE'RE VERY BUSY.
C'MON, DON'T START THAT WITH ME.
LET'S GO HANG OUT SOME-WHERE.
WHOA!
O-OKAY, WE GOT IT.
SORRY FOR ASK-ING!
NYAAH!
I SAID WE'RE NOT INTERESTED...
GLARE
WHEN YOU'RE AROUND, ARIA, WE DON'T EVEN HAVE TO WASTE OUR TIME TURNING DOWN MEN.
GRR!
NOT EVEN THE LAW CAN KEEP THOSE CREEPS ON A LEASH.

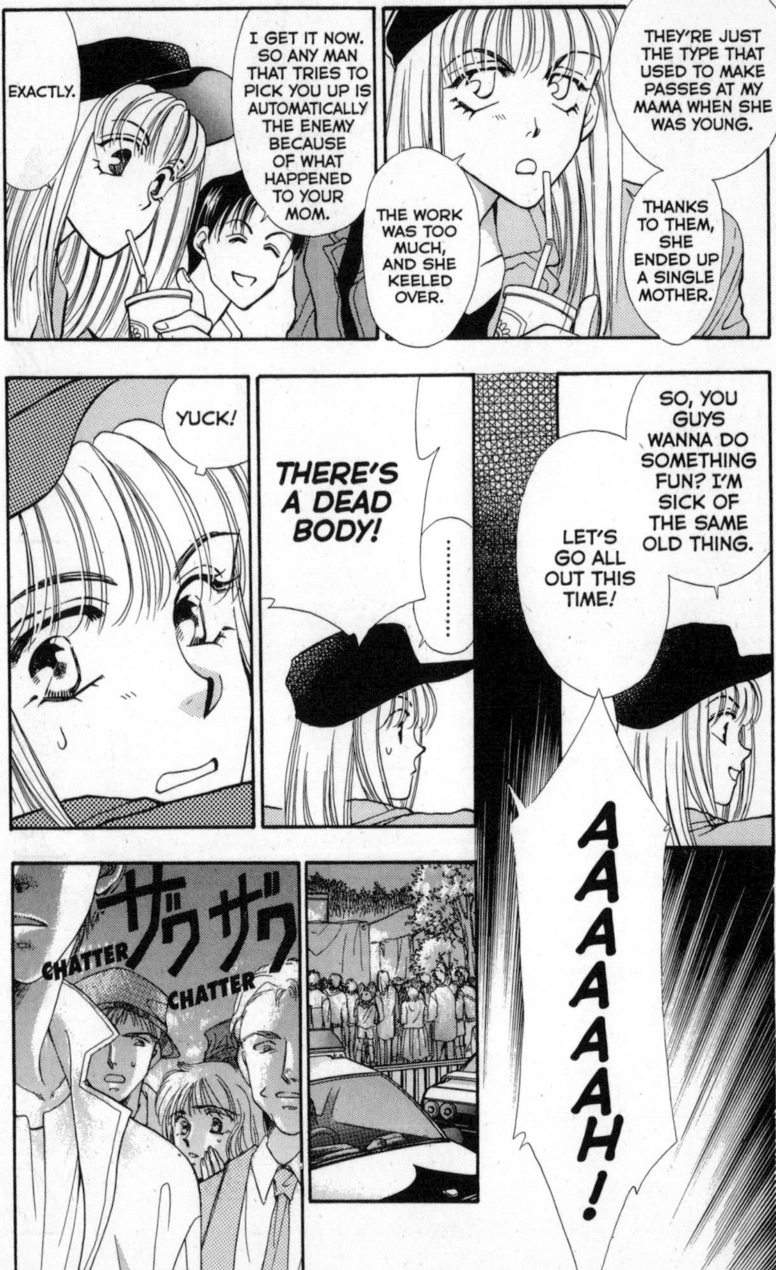
THEY'RE JUST THE TYPE THAT USED TO MAKE PASSES AT MY MAMA WHEN SHE WAS YOUNG.
THANKS TO THEM, SHE ENDED UP A SINGLE MOTHER.
THE WORK WAS TOO MUCH, AND SHE KEELED OVER.
I GET IT NOW. SO ANY MAN THAT TRIES TO PICK YOU UP IS AUTOMATICALLY THE ENEMY BECAUSE OF WHAT HAPPENED TO YOUR MOM.
EXACTLY.
SO, YOU GUYS WANNA DO SOMETHING FUN? I'M SICK OF THE SAME OLD THING.
LET'S GO ALL OUT THIS TIME!
AAAAAAH!
THERE'S A DEAD BODY!
....
YUCK!
ザワザワ
CHATTER
CHATTER

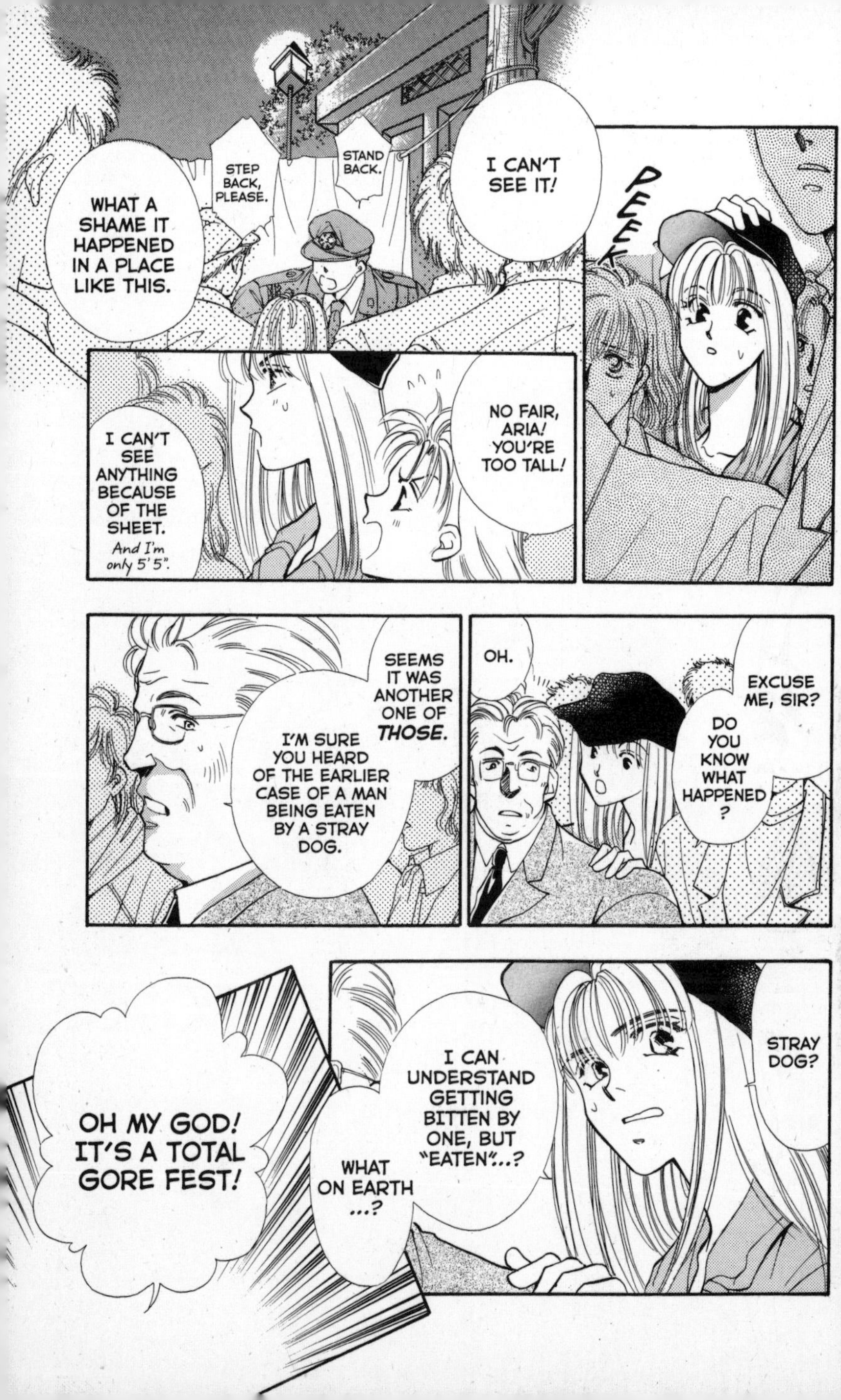
I CAN'T SEE IT!
STAND BACK.
STEP BACK, PLEASE.
WHAT A SHAME IT HAPPENED IN A PLACE LIKE THIS.
PEEK
NO FAIR, ARIA! YOU'RE TOO TALL!
I CAN'T SEE ANYTHING BECAUSE OF THE SHEET.
And I'm only 5'5".
EXCUSE ME, SIR?
DO YOU KNOW WHAT HAPPENED?
OH.
SEEMS IT WAS ANOTHER ONE OF *THOSE.*
I'M SURE YOU HEARD OF THE EARLIER CASE OF A MAN BEING EATEN BY A STRAY DOG.
STRAY DOG?
I CAN UNDERSTAND GETTING BITTEN BY ONE, BUT "EATEN"...?
WHAT ON EARTH ...?
OH MY GOD! IT'S A TOTAL GORE FEST!

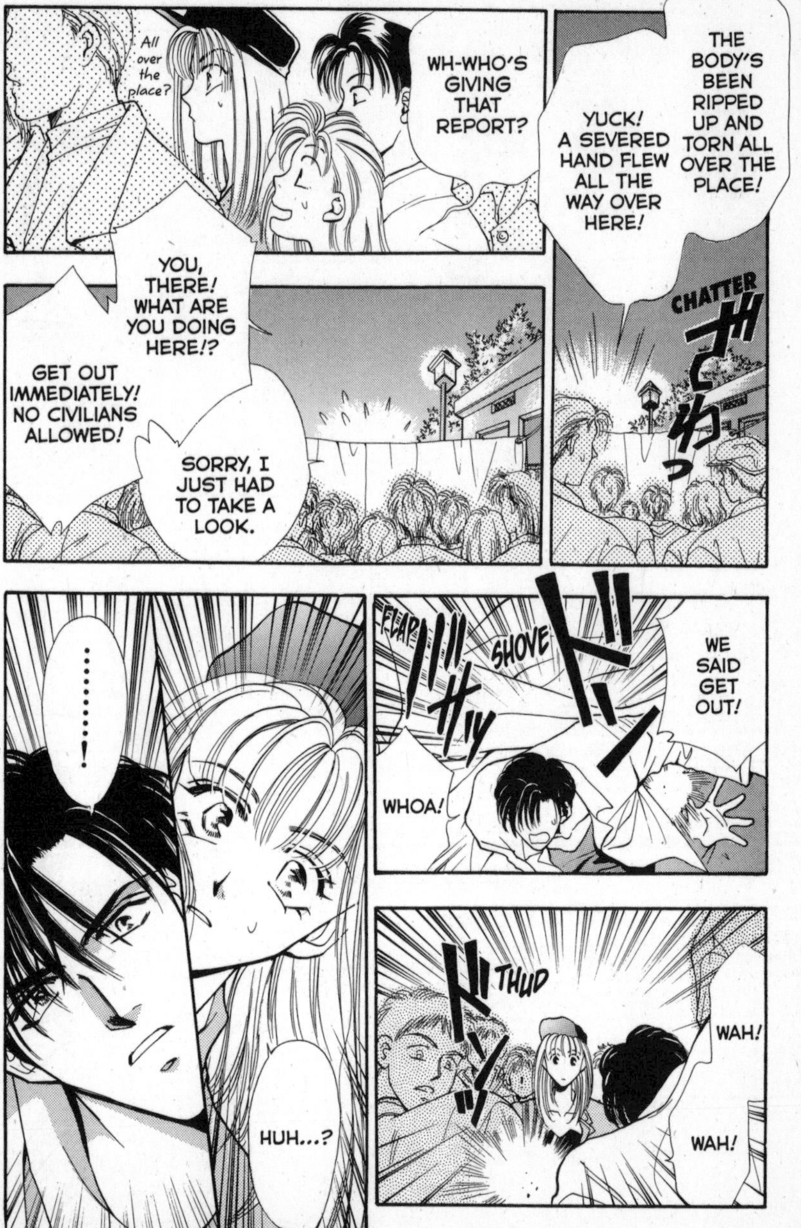
THE BODY'S BEEN RIPPED UP AND TORN ALL OVER THE PLACE!
YUCK! A SEVERED HAND FLEW ALL THE WAY OVER HERE!
CHATTER
ざわっ
WH-WHO'S GIVING THAT REPORT?
All over the place?
YOU, THERE! WHAT ARE YOU DOING HERE!?
SORRY, I JUST HAD TO TAKE A LOOK.
GET OUT IMMEDIATELY! NO CIVILIANS ALLOWED!
WE SAID GET OUT!
SHOVE
ドン
FLAP
バサッ
WHOA!
WAH!
WAH!
THUD
ドン
......!
HUH...?

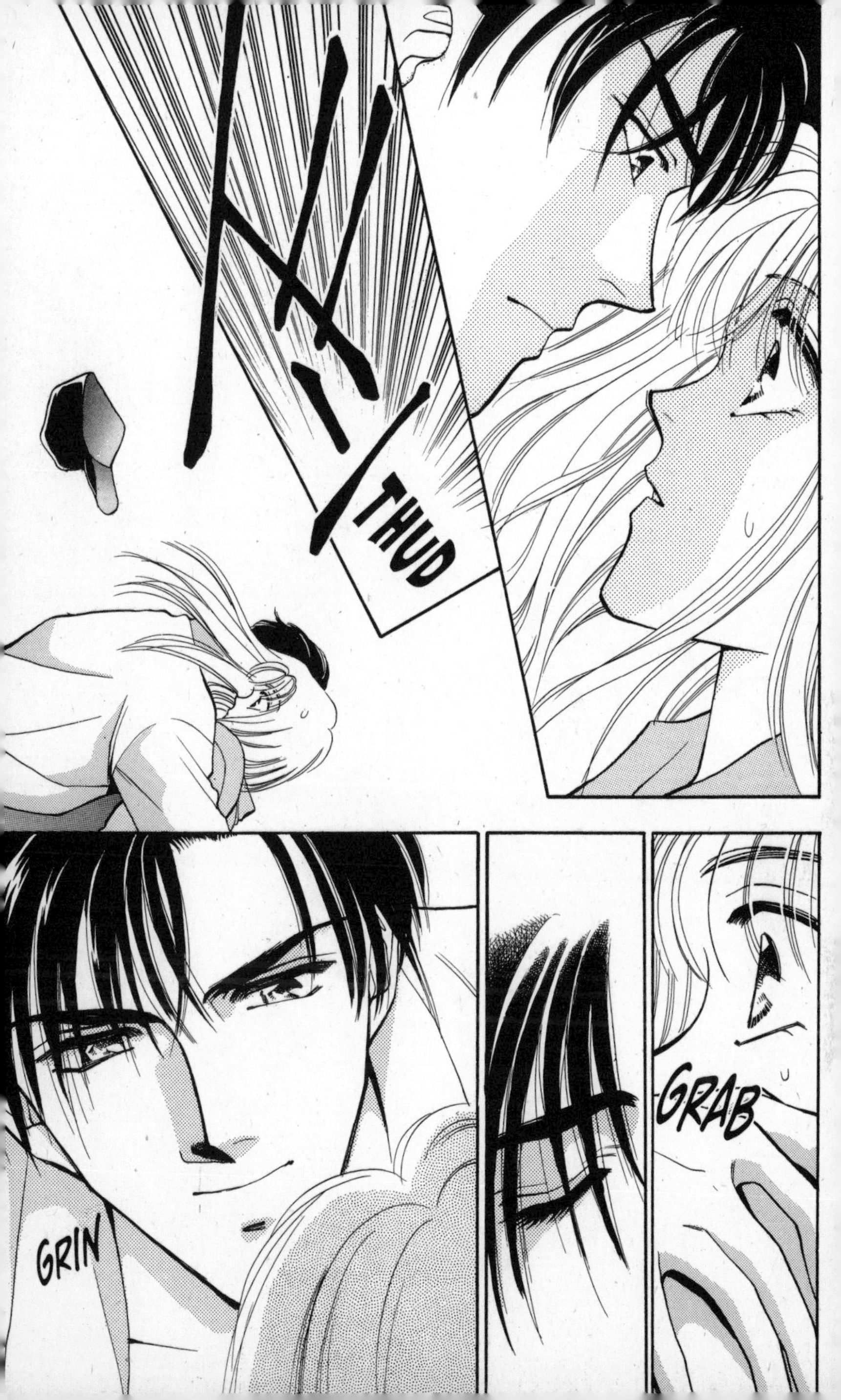
THUD
GRAB
GRIN

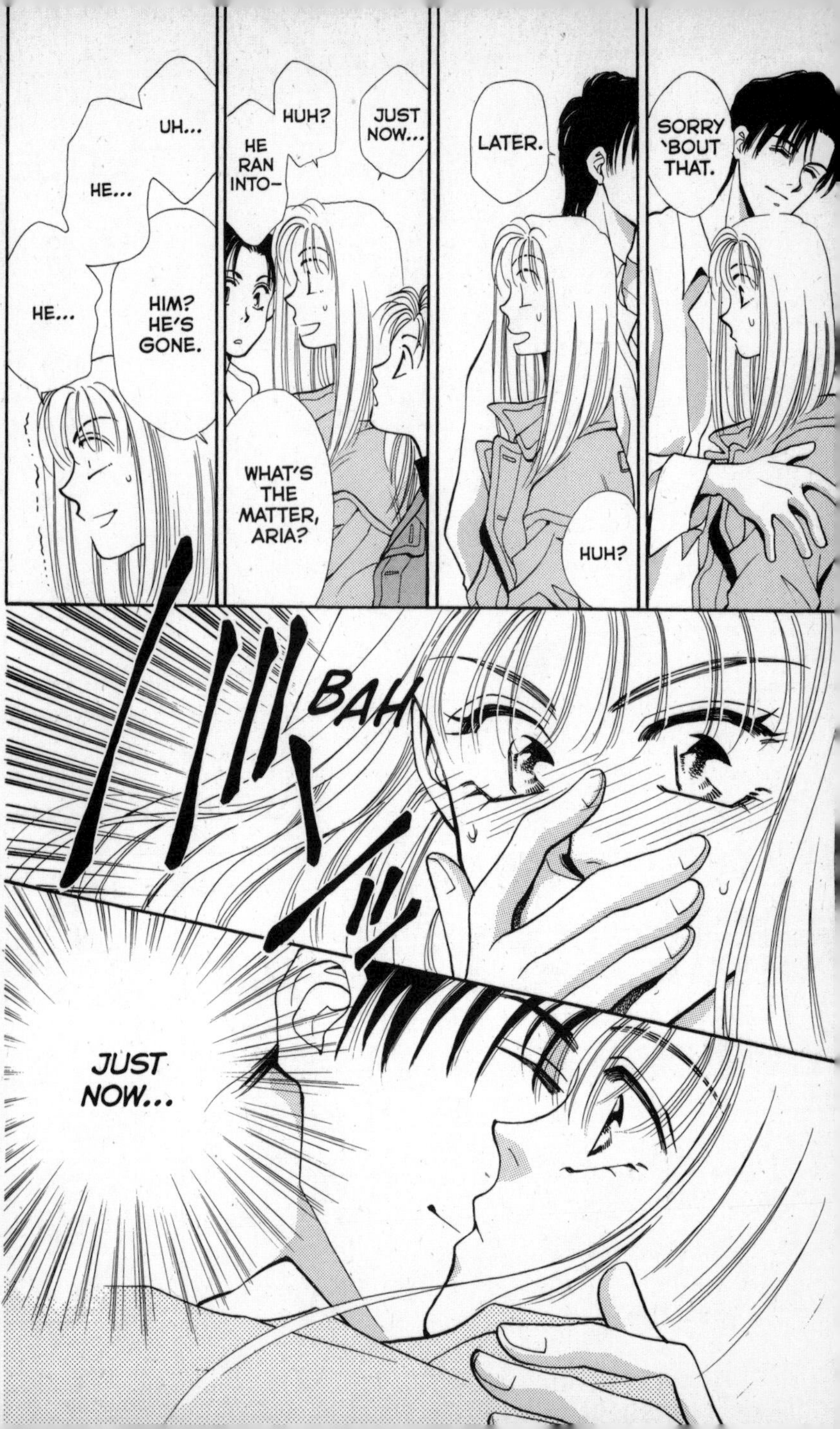
SORRY 'BOUT THAT.
LATER.
HUH?
JUST NOW...
HUH?
HE RAN INTO–
WHAT'S THE MATTER, ARIA?
UH...
HE...
HIM? HE'S GONE.
HE...
BAH
JUST NOW...

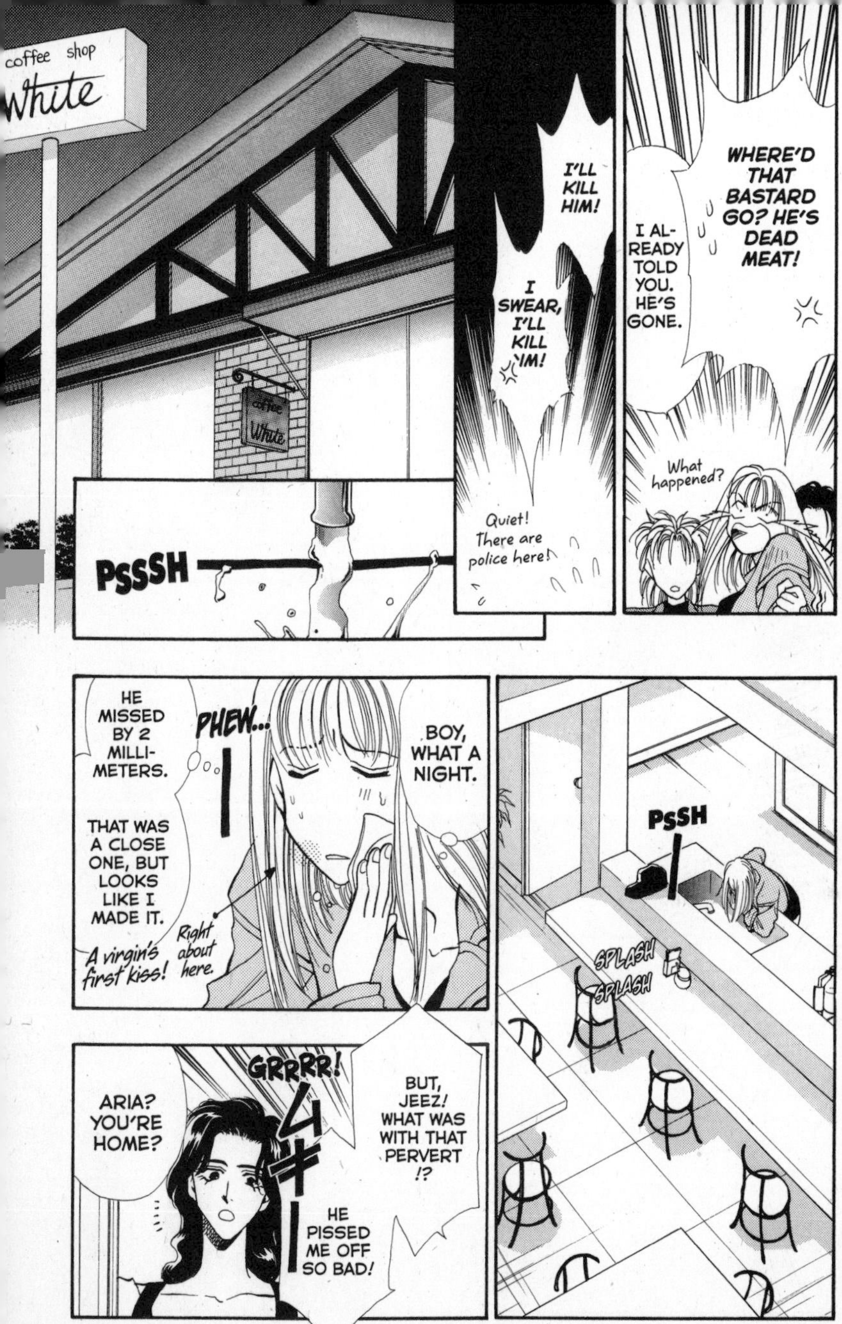
WHERE'D THAT BASTARD GO? HE'S DEAD MEAT!
I ALREADY TOLD YOU. HE'S GONE.
What happened?
I'LL KILL HIM!
I SWEAR, I'LL KILL 'IM!
Quiet! There are police here!
coffee shop White
coffee White
PSSSH
PSSH
SPLASH
SPLASH
BOY, WHAT A NIGHT.
PHEW...
HE MISSED BY 2 MILLIMETERS.
THAT WAS A CLOSE ONE, BUT LOOKS LIKE I MADE IT.
A virgin's first kiss!
Right about here.
BUT, JEEZ! WHAT WAS WITH THAT PERVERT!?
GRRRR!
HE PISSED ME OFF SO BAD!
ARIA? YOU'RE HOME?

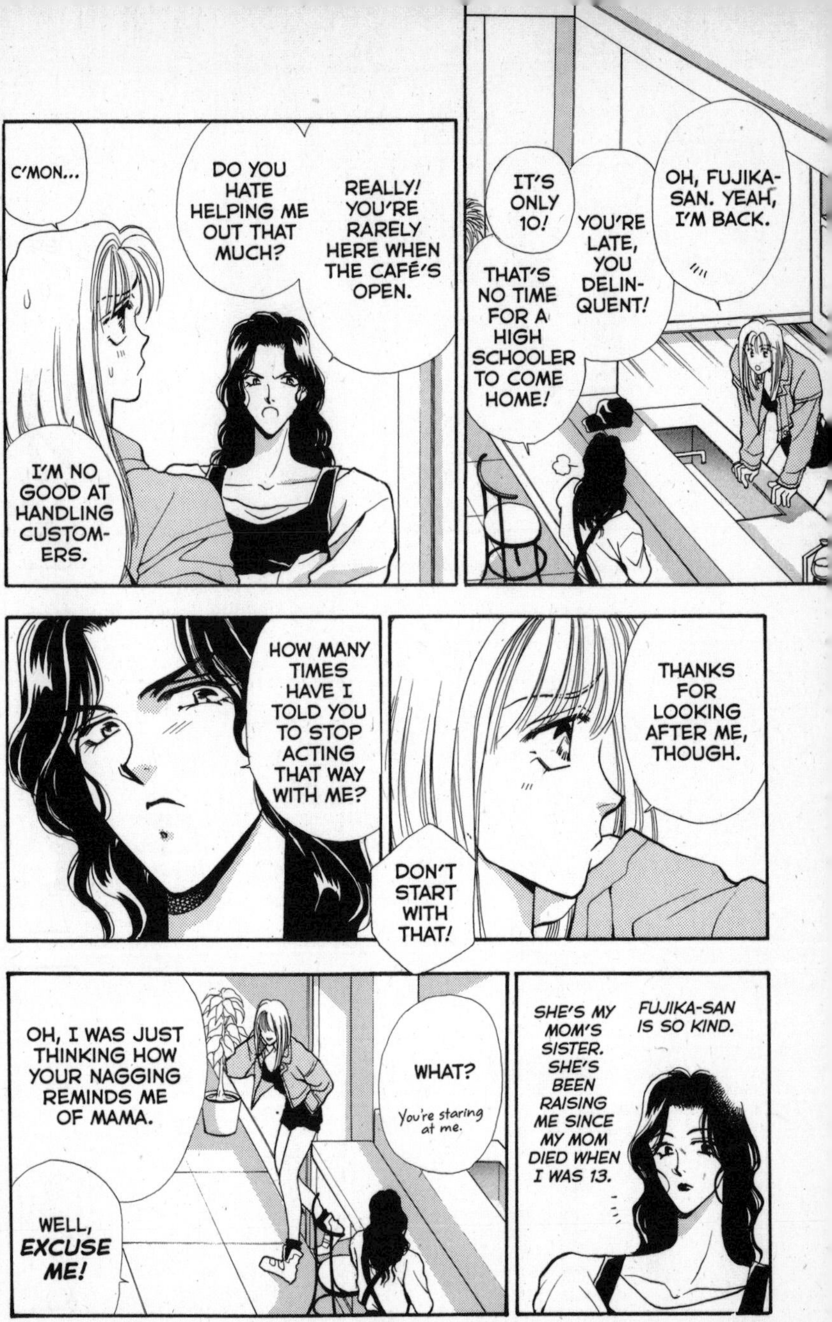

OH, FUJIKA-SAN. YEAH, I'M BACK.
YOU'RE LATE, YOU DELINQUENT!
IT'S ONLY 10!
THAT'S NO TIME FOR A HIGH SCHOOLER TO COME HOME!
REALLY! YOU'RE RARELY HERE WHEN THE CAFÉ'S OPEN.
DO YOU HATE HELPING ME OUT THAT MUCH?
C'MON...
I'M NO GOOD AT HANDLING CUSTOMERS.
THANKS FOR LOOKING AFTER ME, THOUGH.
DON'T START WITH THAT!
HOW MANY TIMES HAVE I TOLD YOU TO STOP ACTING THAT WAY WITH ME?
FUJIKA-SAN IS SO KIND.
SHE'S MY MOM'S SISTER. SHE'S BEEN RAISING ME SINCE MY MOM DIED WHEN I WAS 13.
WHAT?
You're staring at me.
OH, I WAS JUST THINKING HOW YOUR NAGGING REMINDS ME OF MAMA.
WELL, EXCUSE ME!

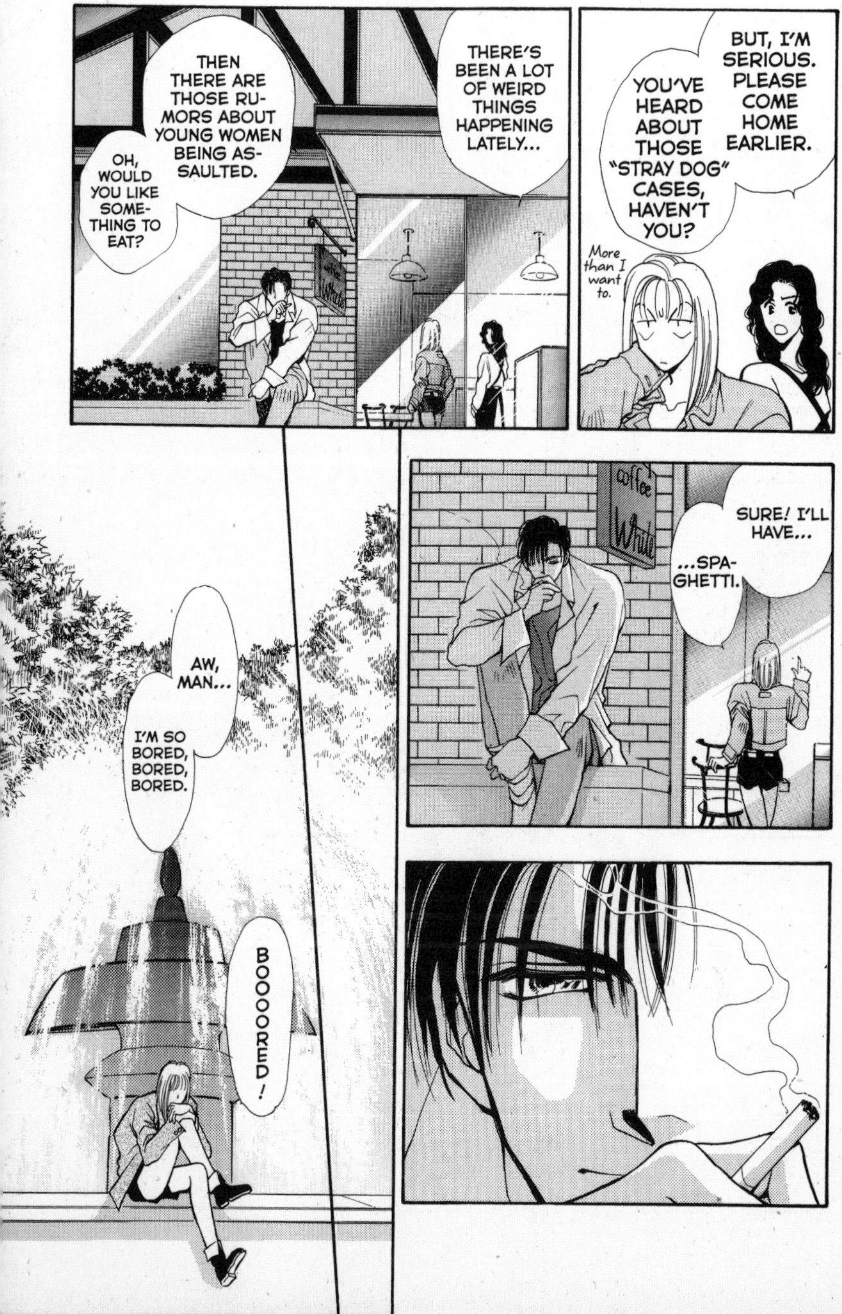
BUT, I'M SERIOUS. PLEASE COME HOME EARLIER.
YOU'VE HEARD ABOUT THOSE "STRAY DOG" CASES, HAVEN'T YOU?
More than I want to.
THERE'S BEEN A LOT OF WEIRD THINGS HAPPENING LATELY...
THEN THERE ARE THOSE RU-MORS ABOUT YOUNG WOMEN BEING AS-SAULTED.
OH, WOULD YOU LIKE SOME-THING TO EAT?
SURE! I'LL HAVE...
...SPA-GHETTI.
AW, MAN...
I'M SO BORED, BORED, BORED.
BOOOOORED!

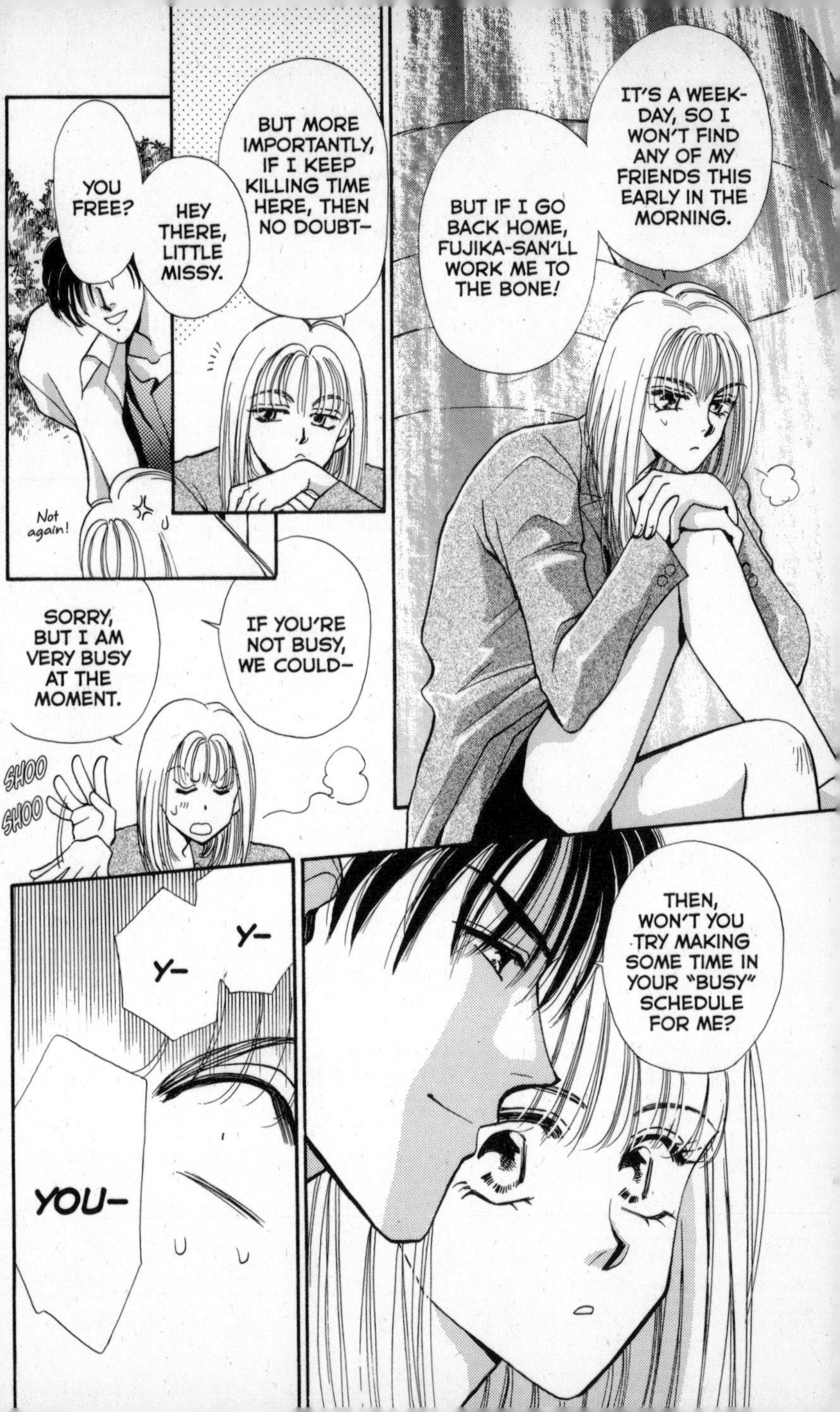
IT'S A WEEK-DAY, SO I WON'T FIND ANY OF MY FRIENDS THIS EARLY IN THE MORNING.
BUT IF I GO BACK HOME, FUJIKA-SAN'LL WORK ME TO THE BONE!
BUT MORE IMPORTANTLY, IF I KEEP KILLING TIME HERE, THEN NO DOUBT–
HEY THERE, LITTLE MISSY.
YOU FREE?
Not again!
IF YOU'RE NOT BUSY, WE COULD–
SORRY, BUT I AM VERY BUSY AT THE MOMENT.
SHOO
SHOO
THEN, WON'T YOU TRY MAKING SOME TIME IN YOUR "BUSY" SCHEDULE FOR ME?
Y–
Y–
YOU–

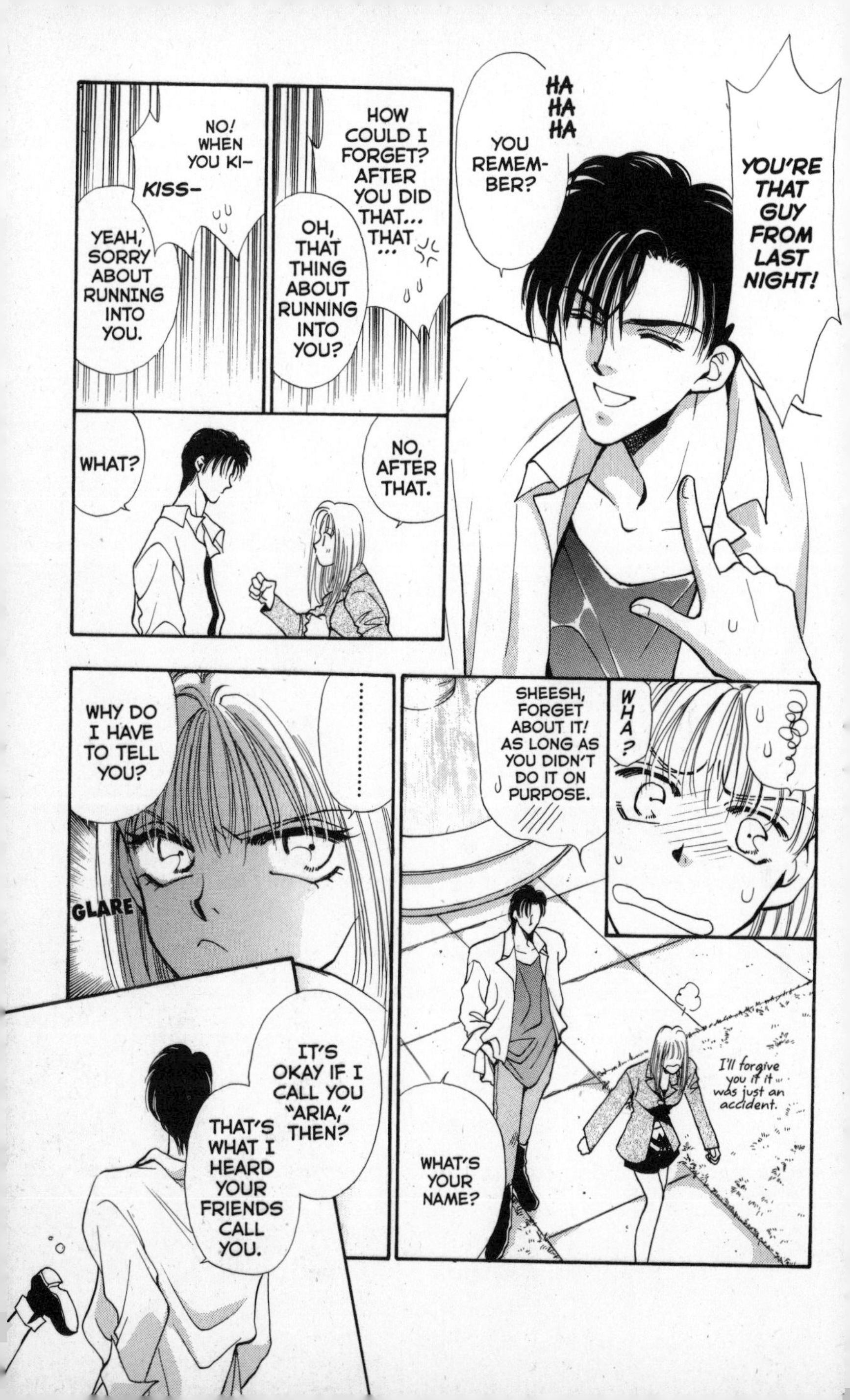

YOU'RE THAT GUY FROM LAST NIGHT!
HA HA HA
YOU REMEMBER?
HOW COULD I FORGET? AFTER YOU DID THAT... THAT ...
OH, THAT THING ABOUT RUNNING INTO YOU?
NO! WHEN YOU KI- KISS-
YEAH, SORRY ABOUT RUNNING INTO YOU.
NO, AFTER THAT.
WHAT?
WHA?
SHEESH, FORGET ABOUT IT! AS LONG AS YOU DIDN'T DO IT ON PURPOSE.
I'll forgive you if it was just an accident.
WHAT'S YOUR NAME?
......
WHY DO I HAVE TO TELL YOU?
GLARE
IT'S OKAY IF I CALL YOU "ARIA," THEN?
THAT'S WHAT I HEARD YOUR FRIENDS CALL YOU.

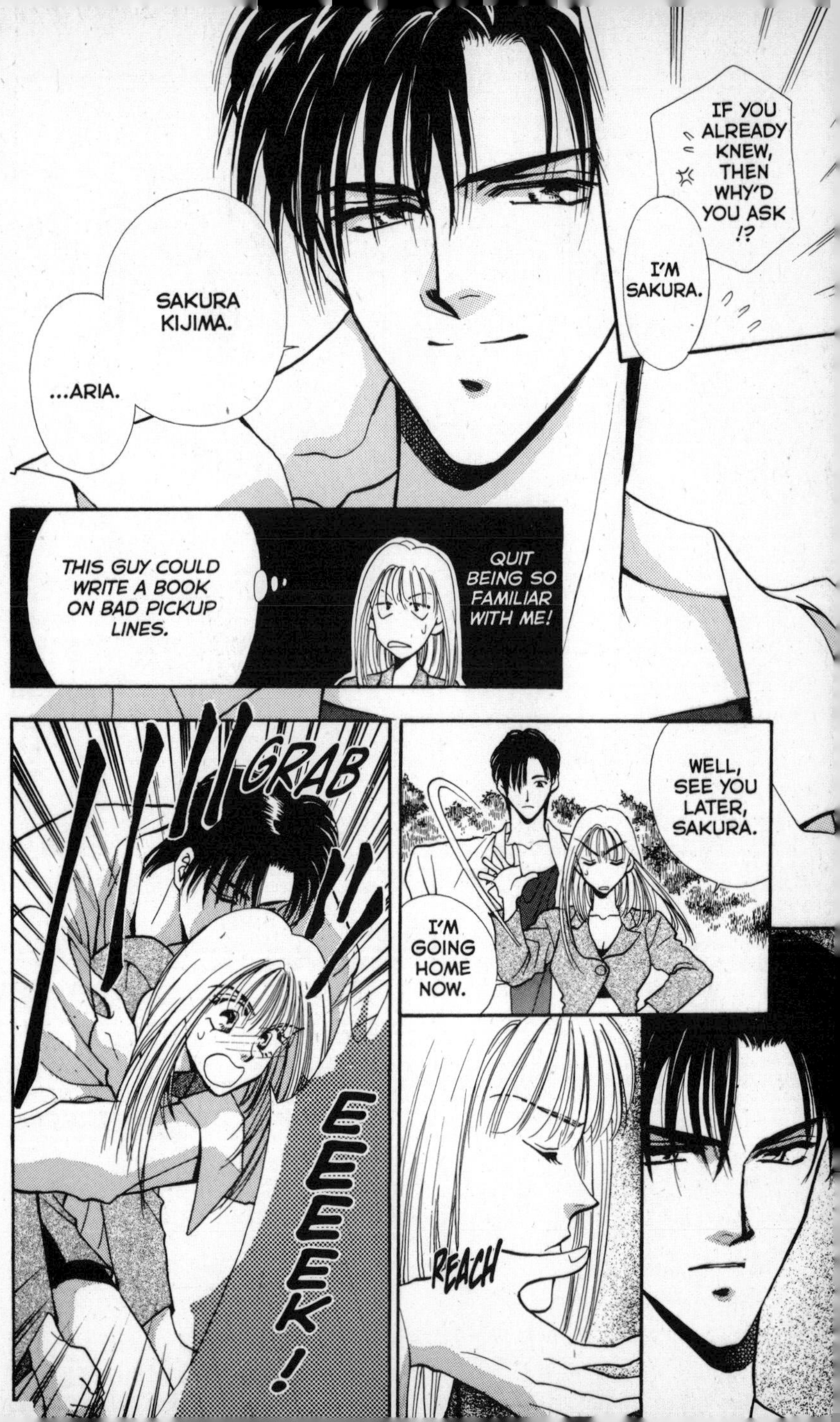
IF YOU ALREADY KNEW, THEN WHY'D YOU ASK !?
I'M SAKURA.
SAKURA KIJIMA.
...ARIA.
QUIT BEING SO FAMILIAR WITH ME!
THIS GUY COULD WRITE A BOOK ON BAD PICKUP LINES.
WELL, SEE YOU LATER, SAKURA.
I'M GOING HOME NOW.
REACH
GRAB
EEEEEEK!

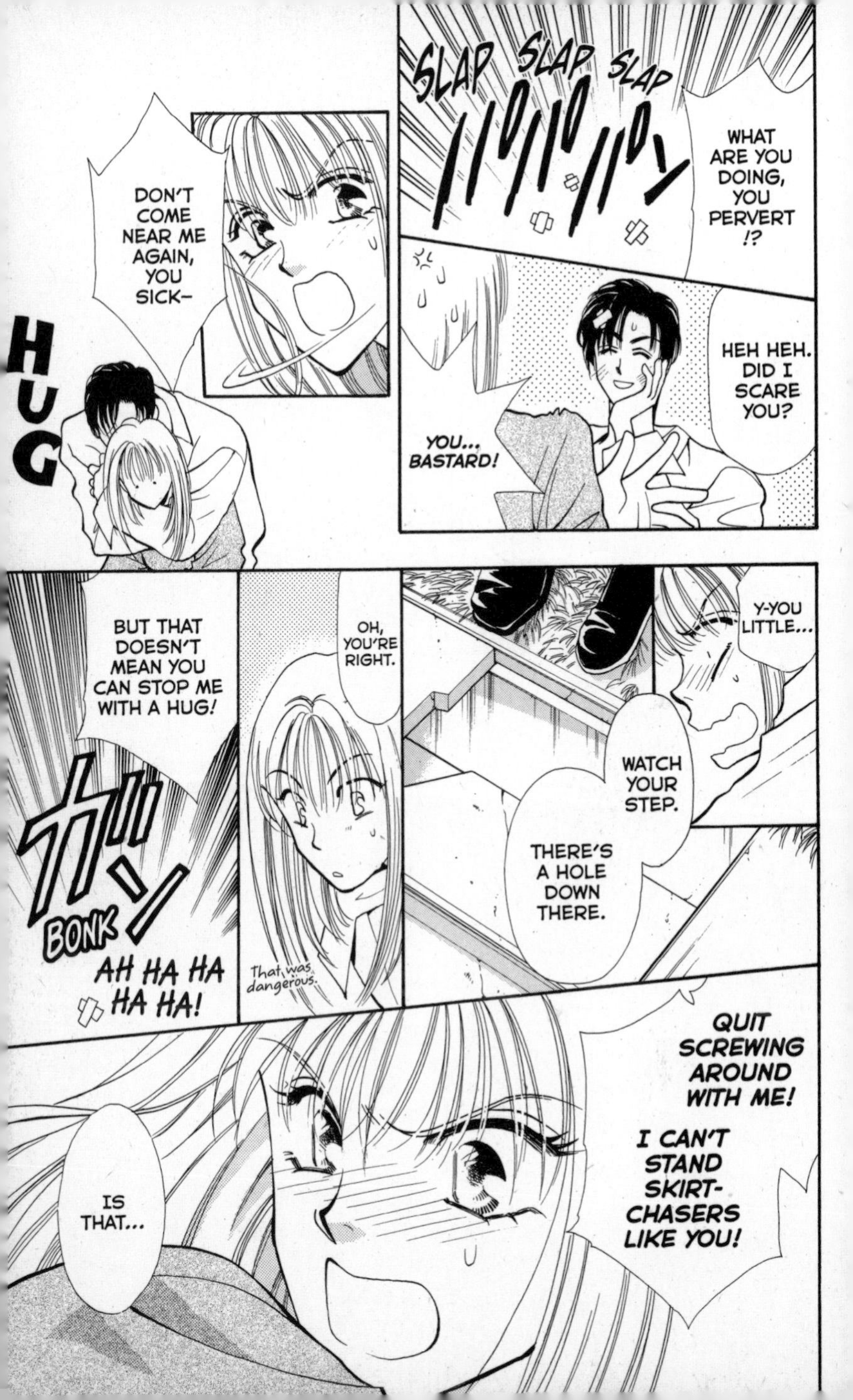
SLAP SLAP SLAP
WHAT ARE YOU DOING, YOU PERVERT!?
HEH HEH. DID I SCARE YOU?
YOU... BASTARD!
DON'T COME NEAR ME AGAIN, YOU SICK–
HUG
Y-YOU LITTLE...
WATCH YOUR STEP.
THERE'S A HOLE DOWN THERE.
OH, YOU'RE RIGHT.
That was dangerous.
BUT THAT DOESN'T MEAN YOU CAN STOP ME WITH A HUG!
BONK
AH HA HA HA HA!
QUIT SCREWING AROUND WITH ME!
I CAN'T STAND SKIRT-CHASERS LIKE YOU!
IS THAT...

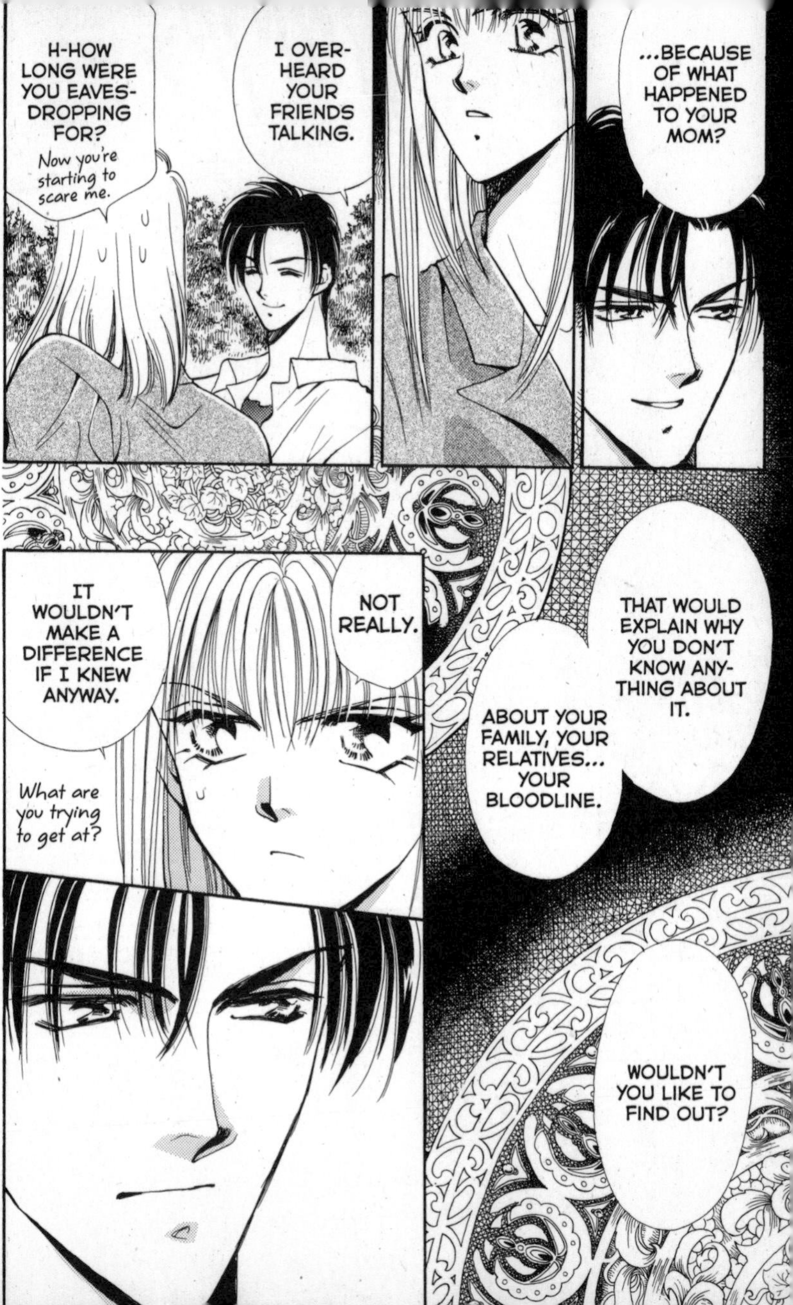
...BECAUSE OF WHAT HAPPENED TO YOUR MOM?
I OVER-HEARD YOUR FRIENDS TALKING.
H-HOW LONG WERE YOU EAVES-DROPPING FOR?
Now you're starting to scare me.
THAT WOULD EXPLAIN WHY YOU DON'T KNOW ANY-THING ABOUT IT.
ABOUT YOUR FAMILY, YOUR RELATIVES... YOUR BLOODLINE.
NOT REALLY.
IT WOULDN'T MAKE A DIFFERENCE IF I KNEW ANYWAY.
What are you trying to get at?
WOULDN'T YOU LIKE TO FIND OUT?

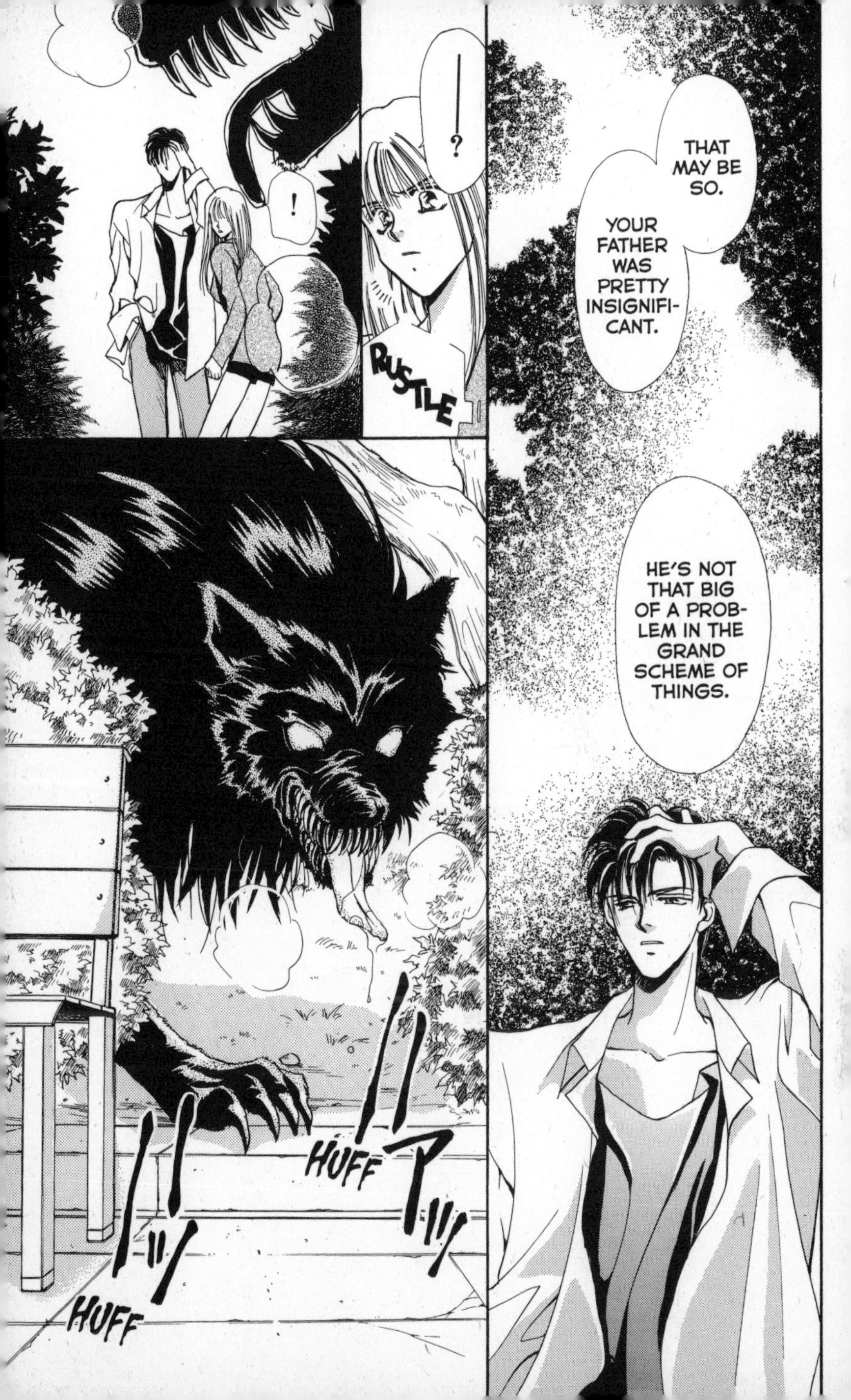
THAT MAY BE SO.
YOUR FATHER WAS PRETTY INSIGNIFICANT.
HE'S NOT THAT BIG OF A PROBLEM IN THE GRAND SCHEME OF THINGS.
—?
RUSTLE
!
HUFF
HUFF

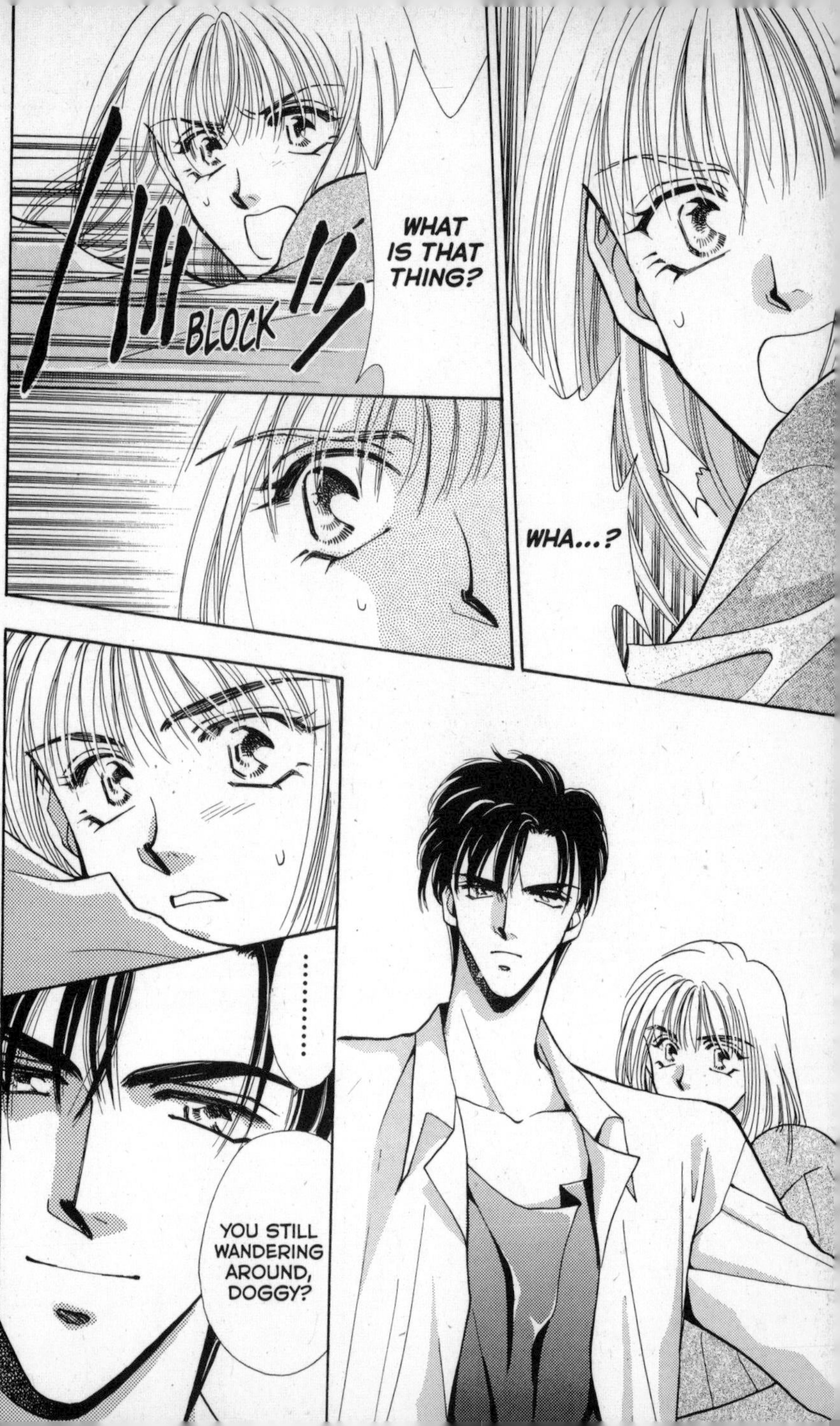
WHAT IS THAT THING?
BLOCK
WHA...?
......
YOU STILL WANDERING AROUND, DOGGY?

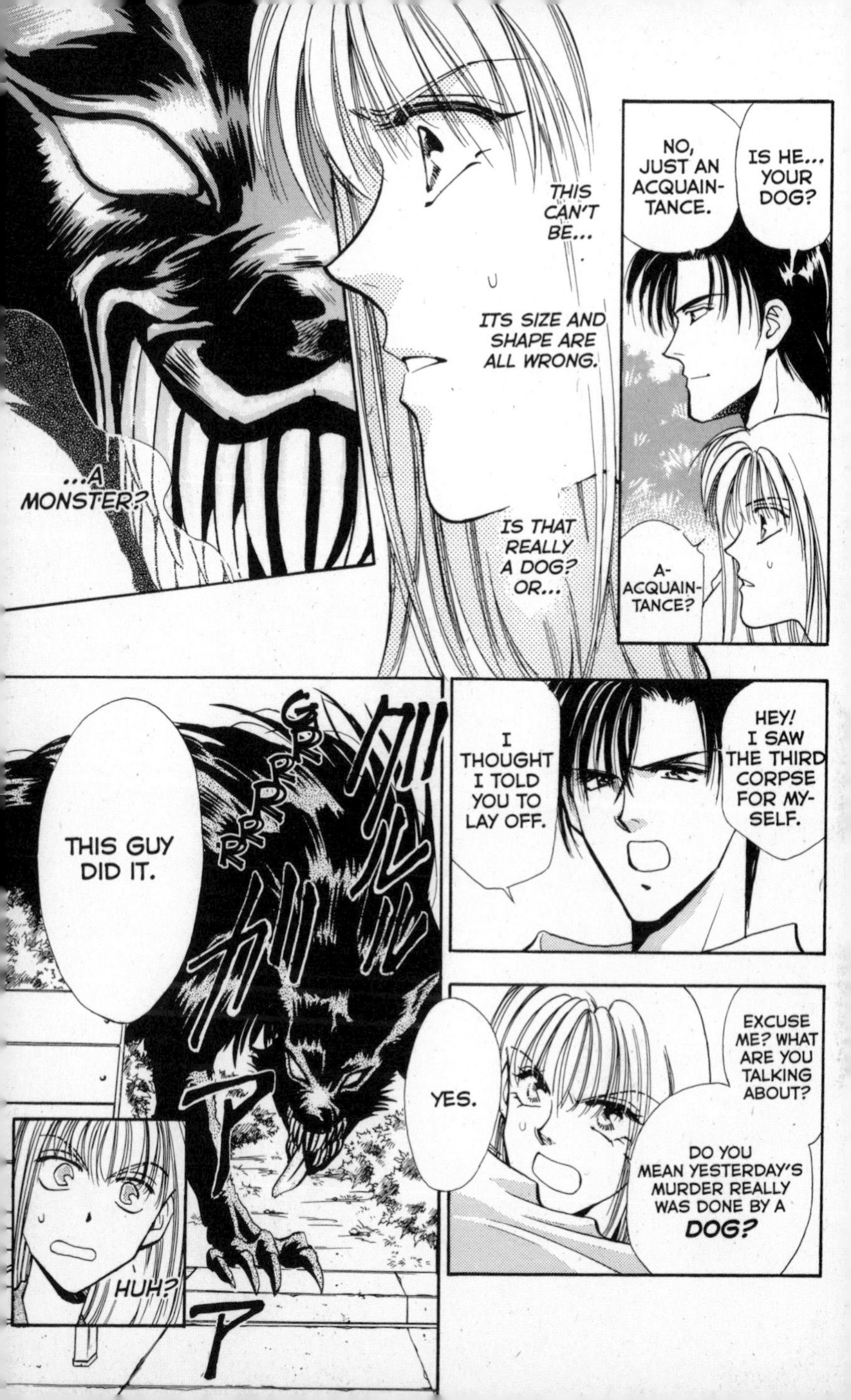
IS HE... YOUR DOG?
NO, JUST AN ACQUAINTANCE.
A-ACQUAINTANCE?
THIS CAN'T BE...
ITS SIZE AND SHAPE ARE ALL WRONG.
IS THAT REALLY A DOG? OR...
...A MONSTER?
HEY! I SAW THE THIRD CORPSE FOR MYSELF.
I THOUGHT I TOLD YOU TO LAY OFF.
EXCUSE ME? WHAT ARE YOU TALKING ABOUT?
DO YOU MEAN YESTERDAY'S MURDER REALLY WAS DONE BY A **DOG?**
YES.
THIS GUY DID IT.
HUH?

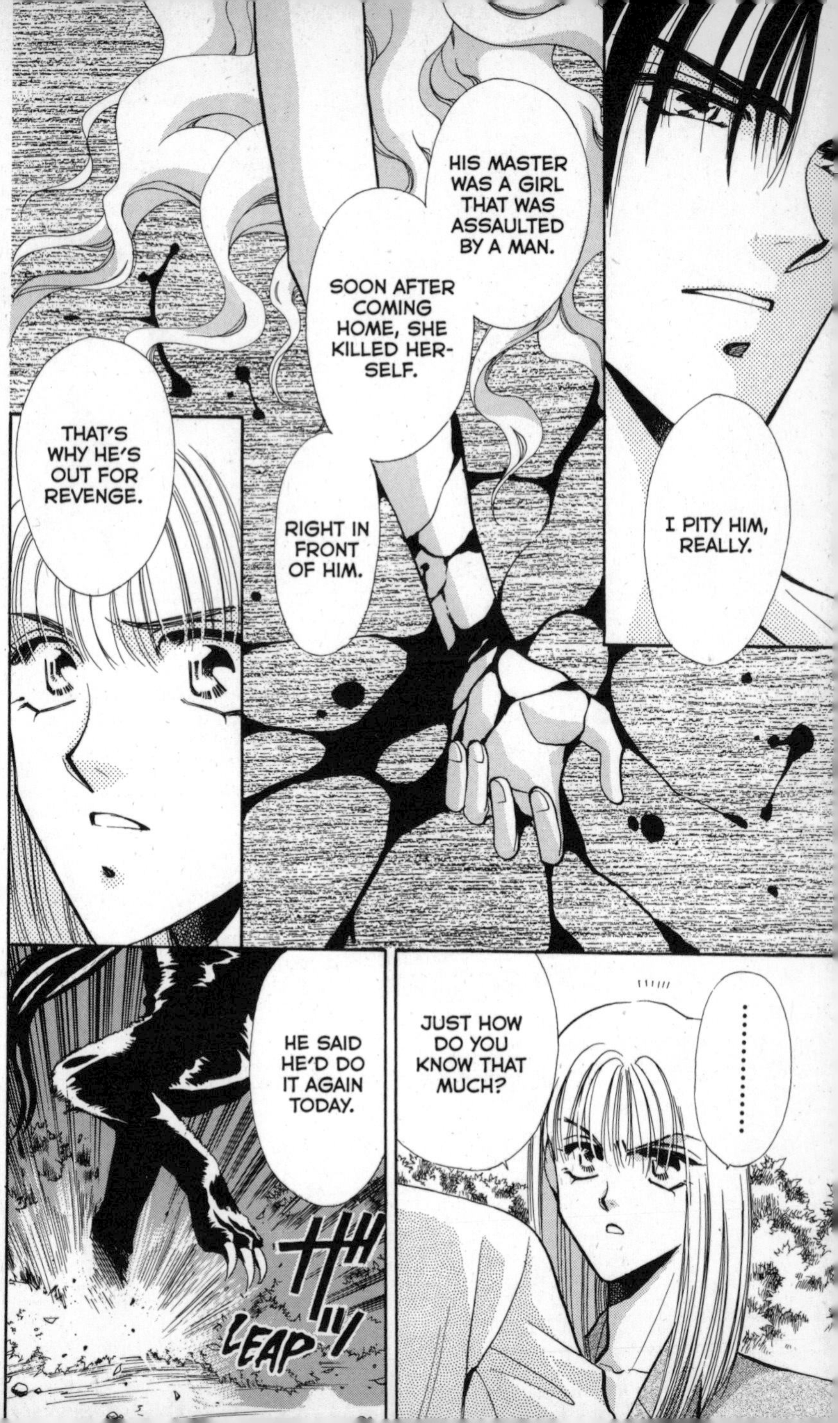
HIS MASTER WAS A GIRL THAT WAS ASSAULTED BY A MAN.
SOON AFTER COMING HOME, SHE KILLED HER-SELF.
RIGHT IN FRONT OF HIM.
THAT'S WHY HE'S OUT FOR REVENGE.
I PITY HIM, REALLY.
......
JUST HOW DO YOU KNOW THAT MUCH?
HE SAID HE'D DO IT AGAIN TODAY.
LEAP

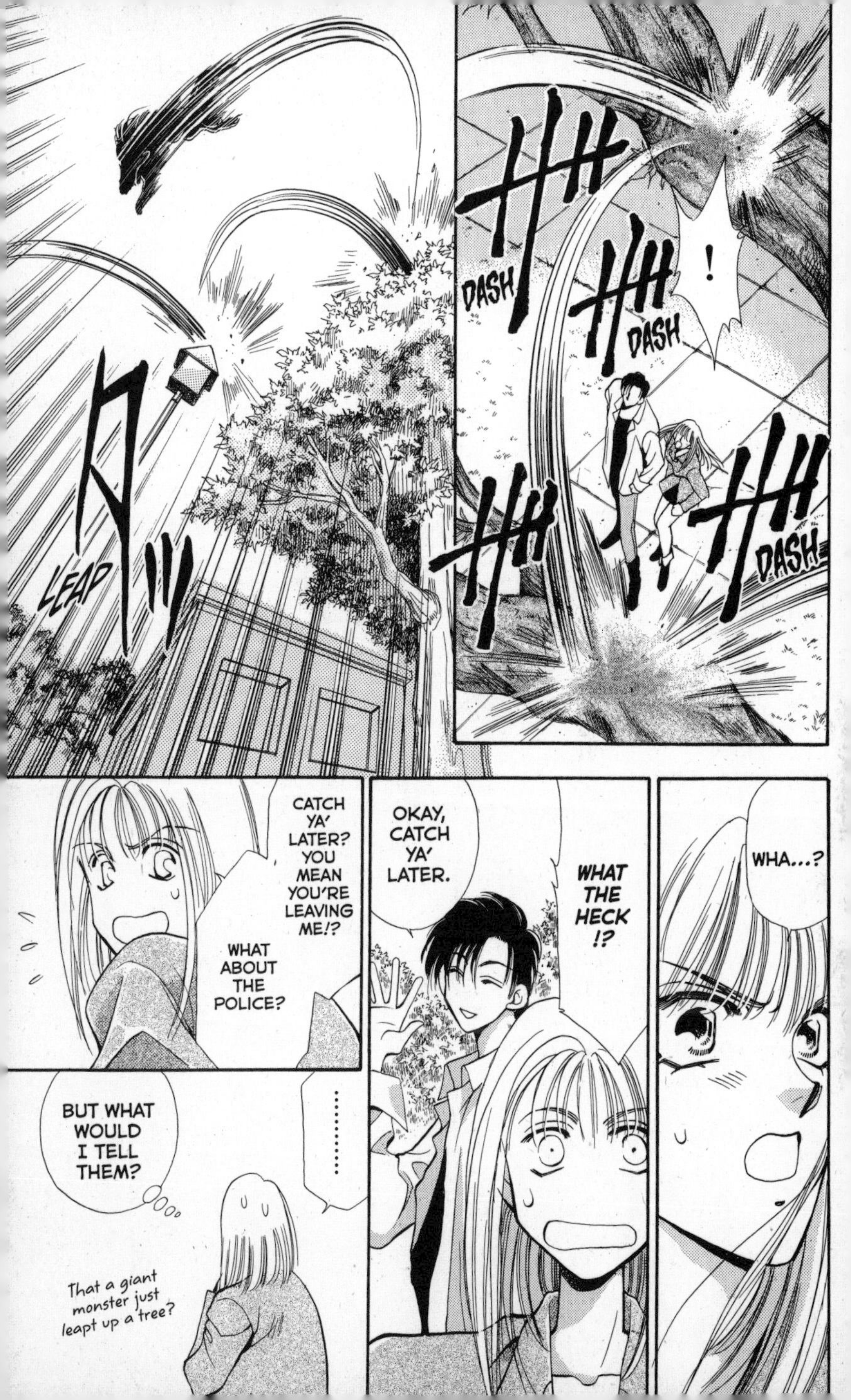
DASH
DASH
!
DASH
LEAP
WHA...?
OKAY, CATCH YA' LATER.
WHAT THE HECK!?
CATCH YA' LATER? YOU MEAN YOU'RE LEAVING ME!?
WHAT ABOUT THE POLICE?
....
BUT WHAT WOULD I TELL THEM?
That a giant monster just leapt up a tree?

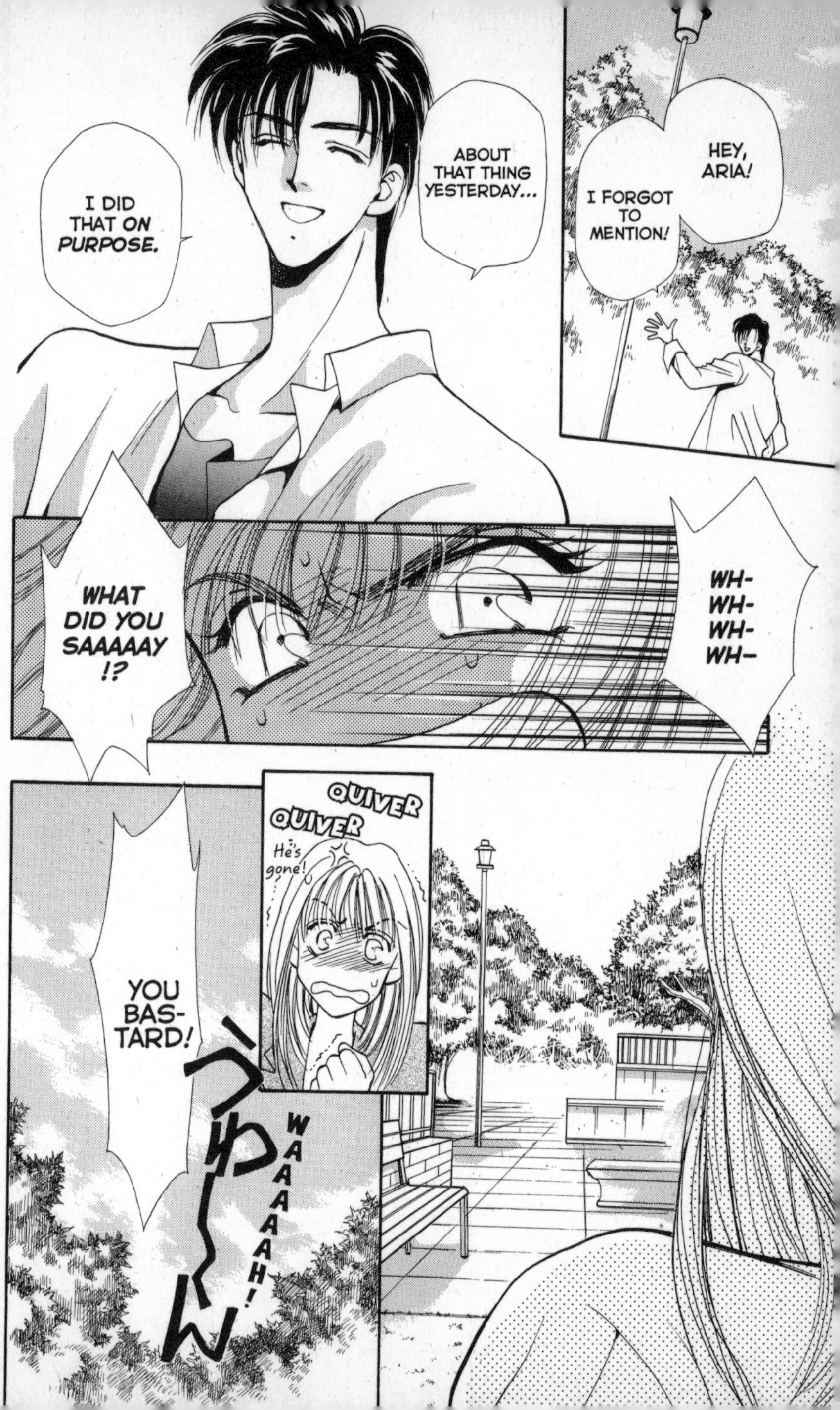
HEY, ARIA!
I FORGOT TO MENTION!
ABOUT THAT THING YESTERDAY...
I DID THAT ON PURPOSE.
WH- WH- WH- WH-
WHAT DID YOU SAAAAAY !?
QUIVER
QUIVER
He's gone!
YOU BAS- TARD!
WAAAAAAH!

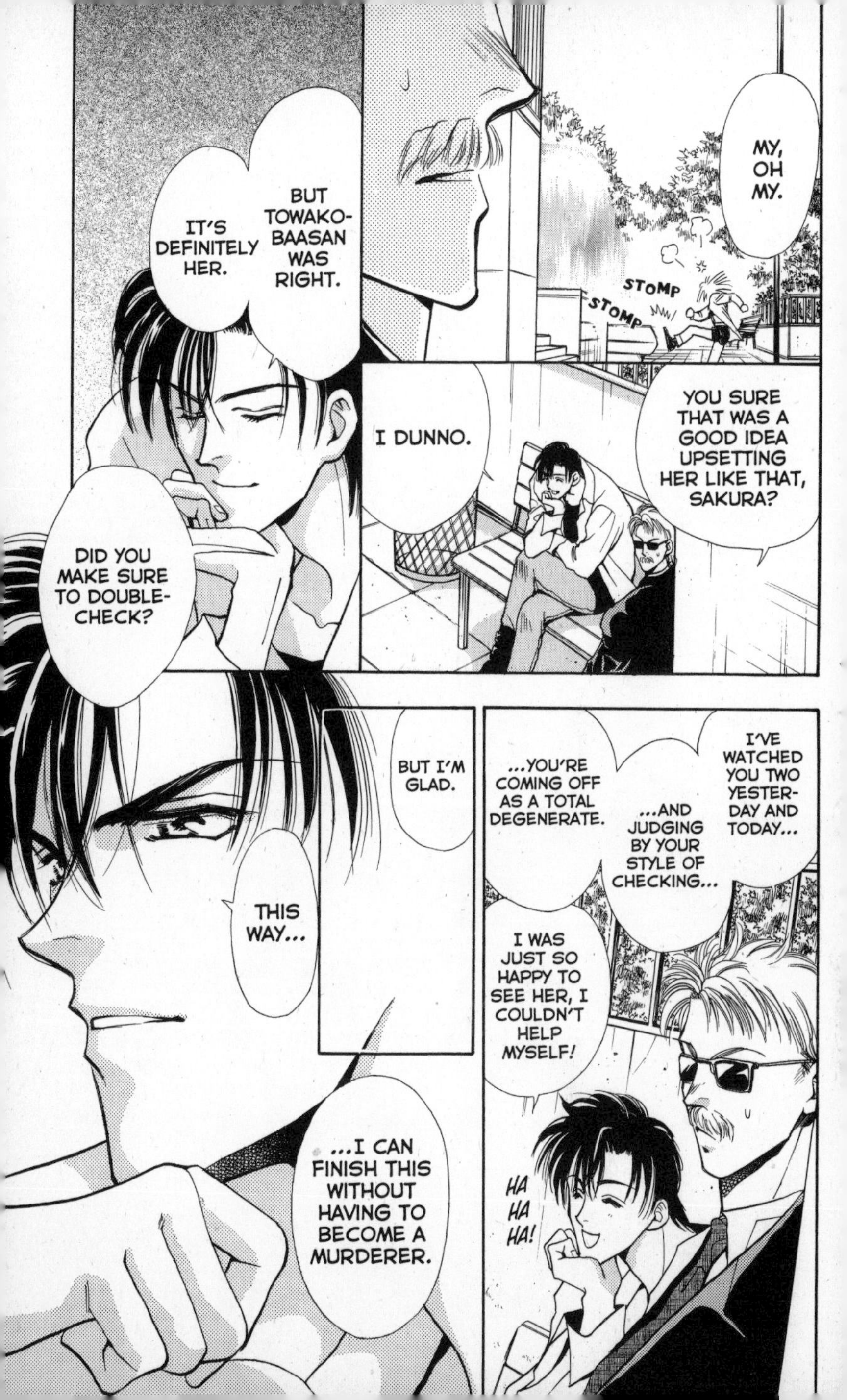
MY, OH MY.
STOMP
STOMP
YOU SURE THAT WAS A GOOD IDEA UPSETTING HER LIKE THAT, SAKURA?
I DUNNO.
BUT TOWAKO-BAASAN WAS RIGHT.
IT'S DEFINITELY HER.
DID YOU MAKE SURE TO DOUBLE-CHECK?
I'VE WATCHED YOU TWO YESTER-DAY AND TODAY...
...AND JUDGING BY YOUR STYLE OF CHECKING...
...YOU'RE COMING OFF AS A TOTAL DEGENERATE.
I WAS JUST SO HAPPY TO SEE HER, I COULDN'T HELP MYSELF!
HA HA HA!
BUT I'M GLAD.
THIS WAY...
...I CAN FINISH THIS WITHOUT HAVING TO BECOME A MURDERER.

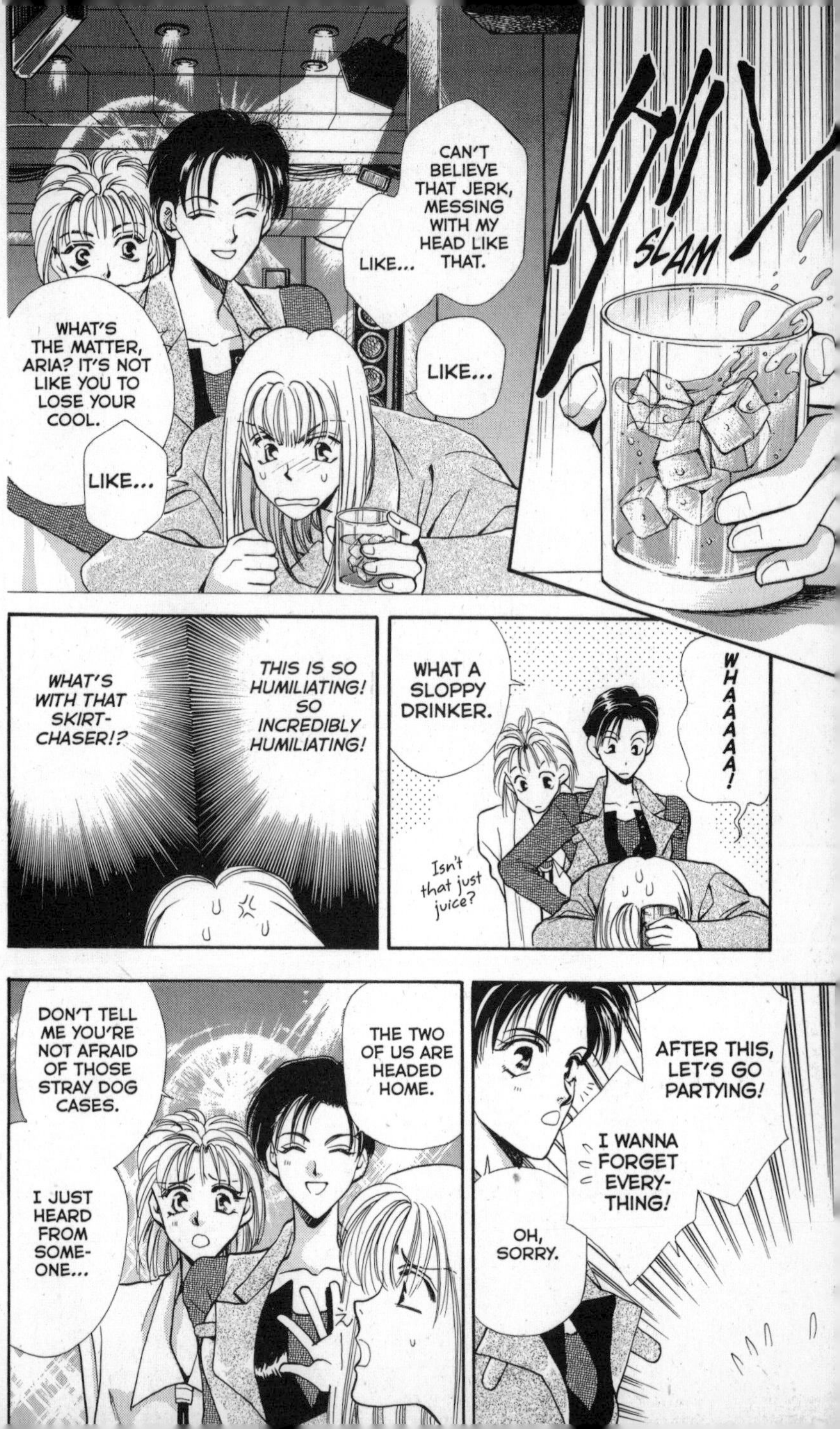
SLAM
CAN'T BELIEVE THAT JERK, MESSING WITH MY HEAD LIKE THAT.
LIKE...
LIKE...
WHAT'S THE MATTER, ARIA? IT'S NOT LIKE YOU TO LOSE YOUR COOL.
LIKE...
WHAAAAAA!
WHAT A SLOPPY DRINKER.
Isn't that just juice?
THIS IS SO HUMILIATING! SO INCREDIBLY HUMILIATING!
WHAT'S WITH THAT SKIRT-CHASER!?
AFTER THIS, LET'S GO PARTYING!
I WANNA FORGET EVERY-THING!
OH, SORRY.
THE TWO OF US ARE HEADED HOME.
DON'T TELL ME YOU'RE NOT AFRAID OF THOSE STRAY DOG CASES.
I JUST HEARD FROM SOME-ONE...

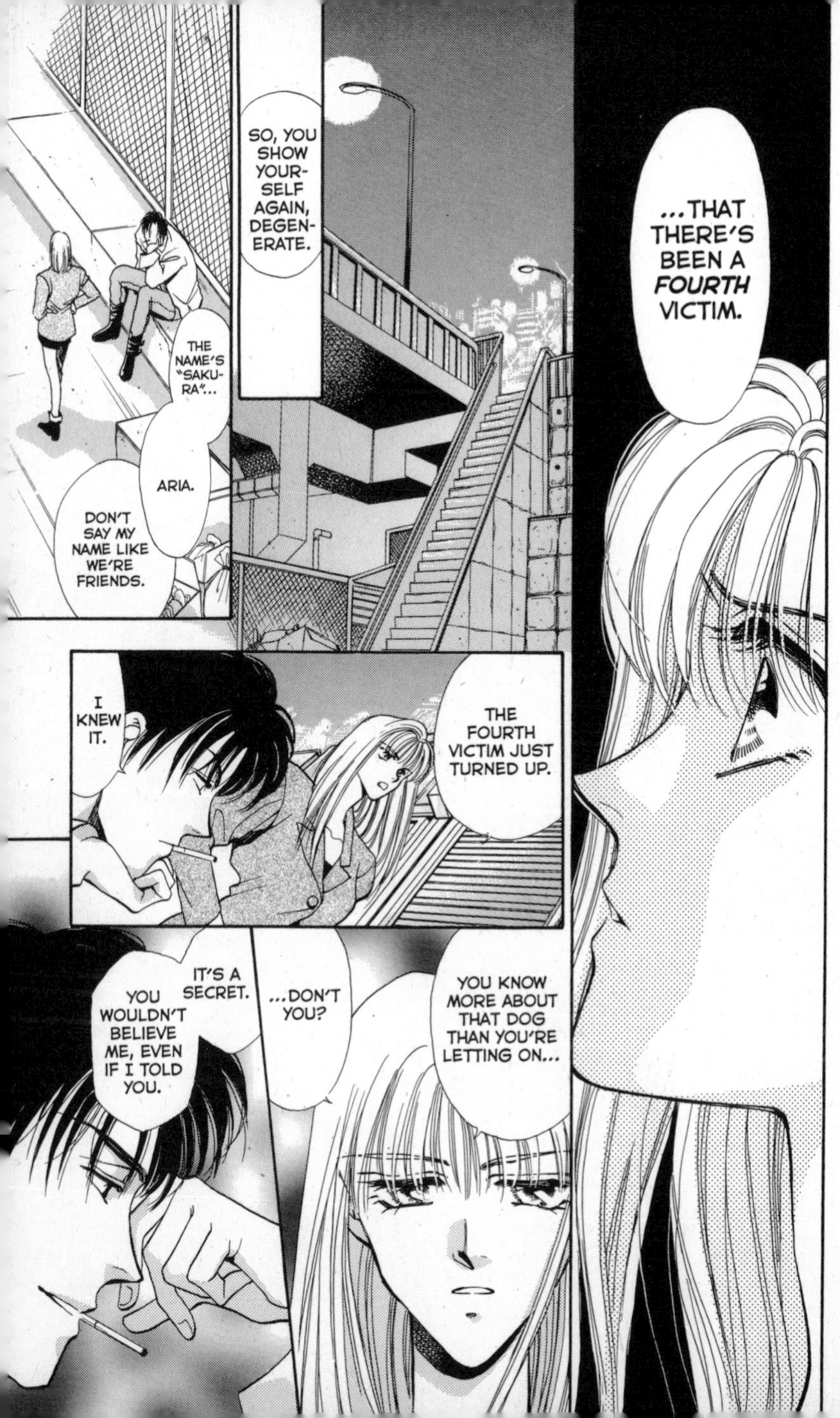
...THAT THERE'S BEEN A *FOURTH* VICTIM.
SO, YOU SHOW YOURSELF AGAIN, DEGENERATE.
THE NAME'S "SAKURA"...
ARIA.
DON'T SAY MY NAME LIKE WE'RE FRIENDS.
THE FOURTH VICTIM JUST TURNED UP.
I KNEW IT.
YOU KNOW MORE ABOUT THAT DOG THAN YOU'RE LETTING ON...
...DON'T YOU?
IT'S A SECRET.
YOU WOULDN'T BELIEVE ME, EVEN IF I TOLD YOU.

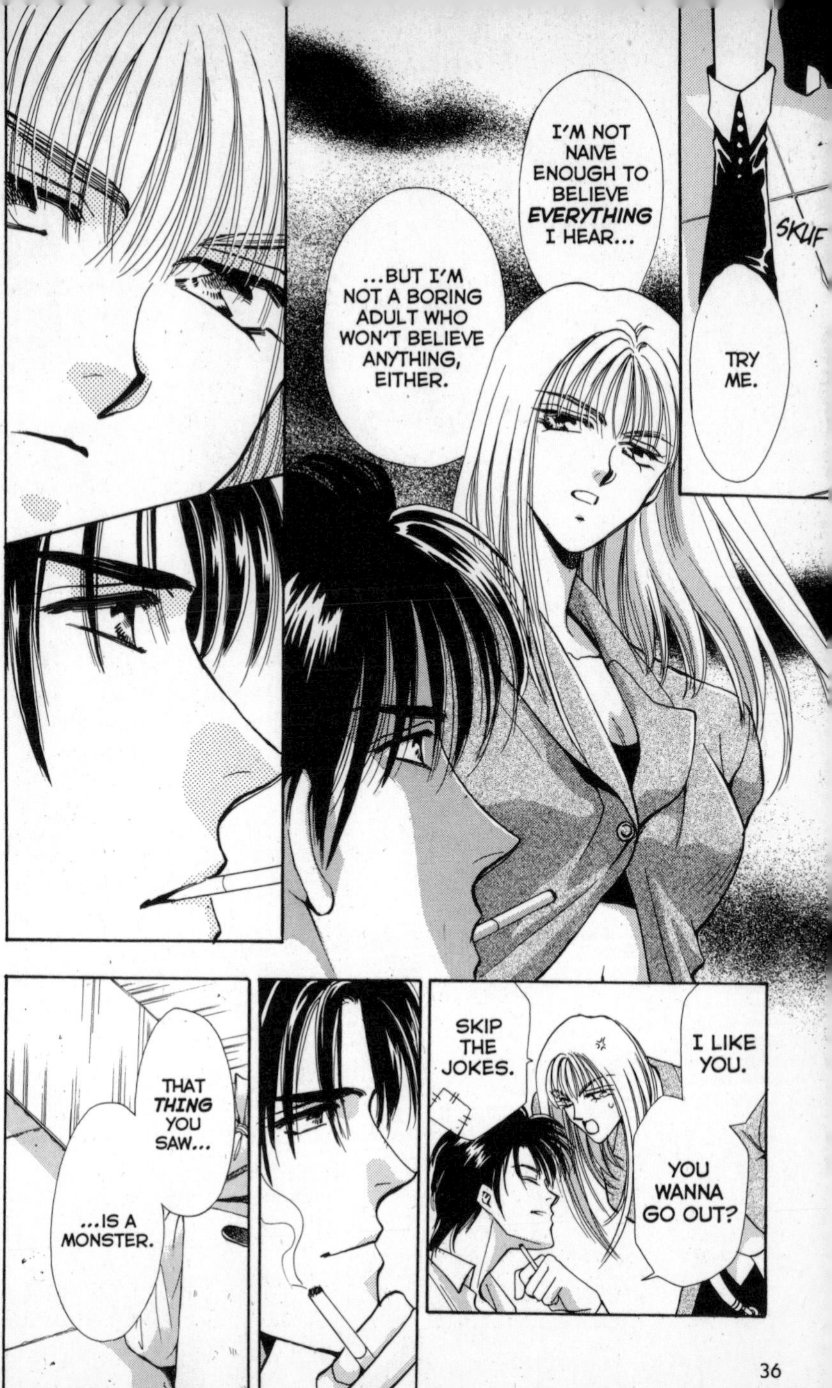
SKUF
TRY ME.
I'M NOT NAIVE ENOUGH TO BELIEVE *EVERYTHING* I HEAR...
...BUT I'M NOT A BORING ADULT WHO WON'T BELIEVE ANYTHING, EITHER.
I LIKE YOU.
YOU WANNA GO OUT?
SKIP THE JOKES.
THAT *THING* YOU SAW...
...IS A MONSTER.

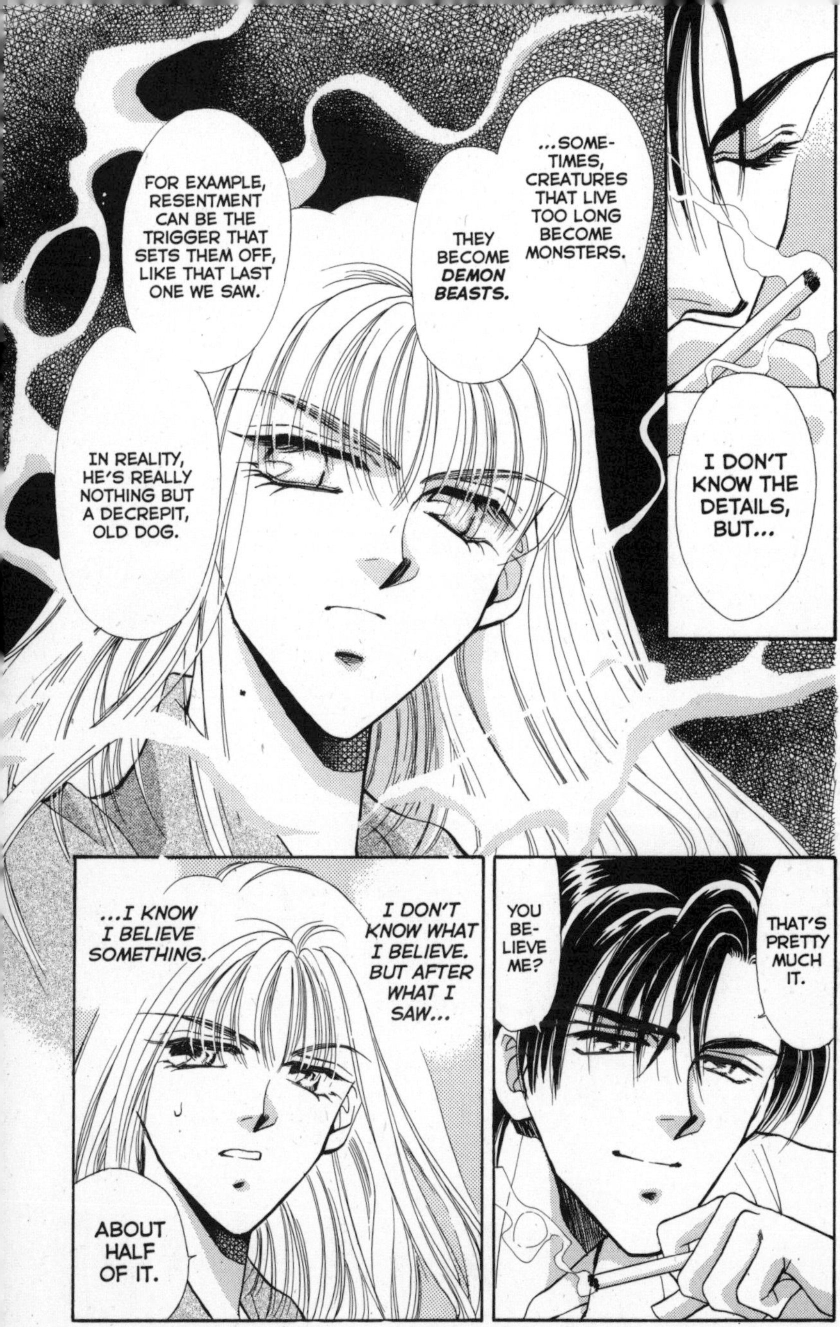
I DON'T KNOW THE DETAILS, BUT...
...SOME-TIMES, CREATURES THAT LIVE TOO LONG BECOME MONSTERS.
THEY BECOME *DEMON BEASTS.*
FOR EXAMPLE, RESENTMENT CAN BE THE TRIGGER THAT SETS THEM OFF, LIKE THAT LAST ONE WE SAW.
IN REALITY, HE'S REALLY NOTHING BUT A DECREPIT, OLD DOG.
THAT'S PRETTY MUCH IT.
YOU BE-LIEVE ME?
I DON'T KNOW WHAT I BELIEVE. BUT AFTER WHAT I SAW...
...I KNOW I BELIEVE SOMETHING.
ABOUT HALF OF IT.

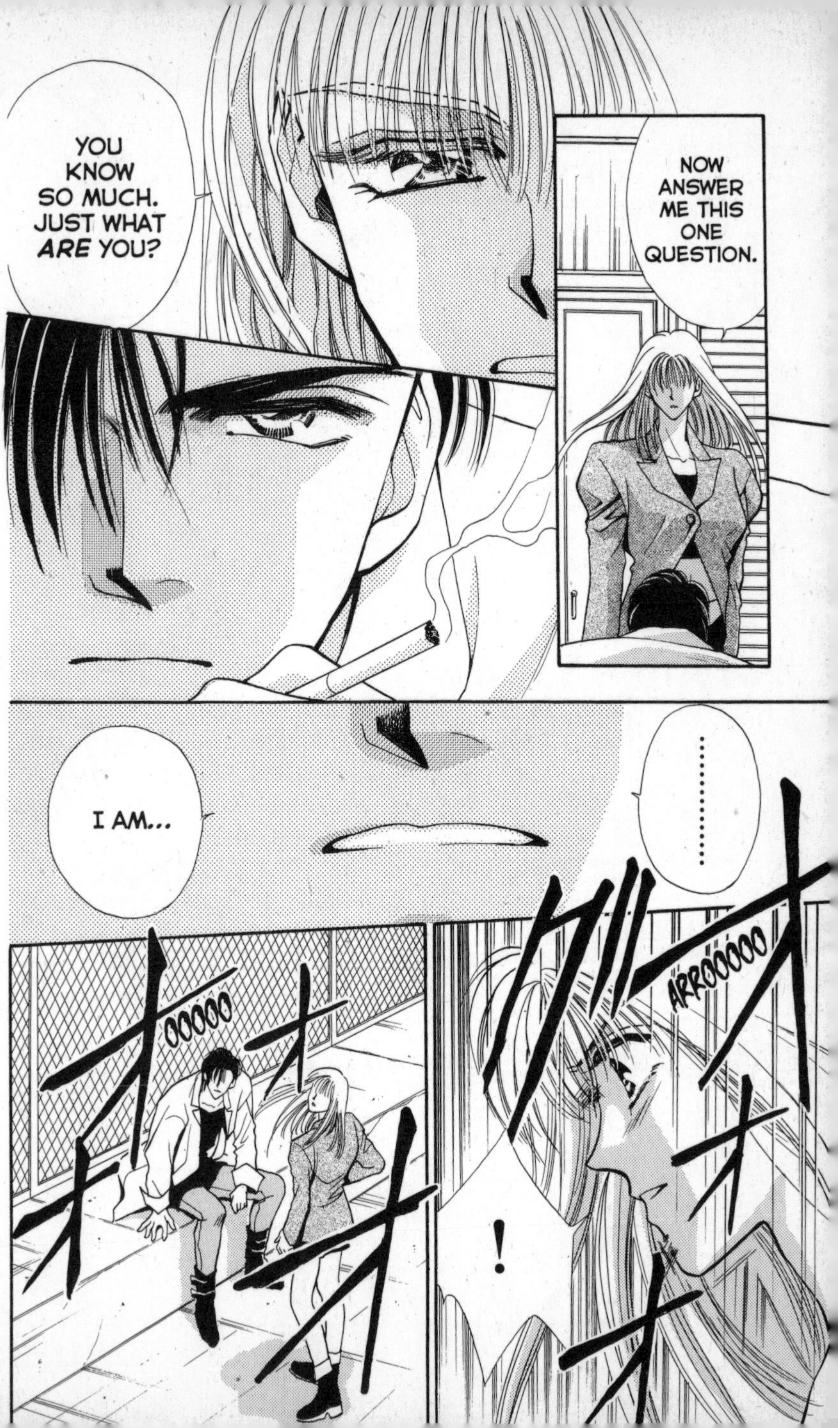
NOW ANSWER ME THIS ONE QUESTION.
YOU KNOW SO MUCH. JUST WHAT *ARE* YOU?
......
I AM...
ARROOOOO
!
OOOOO

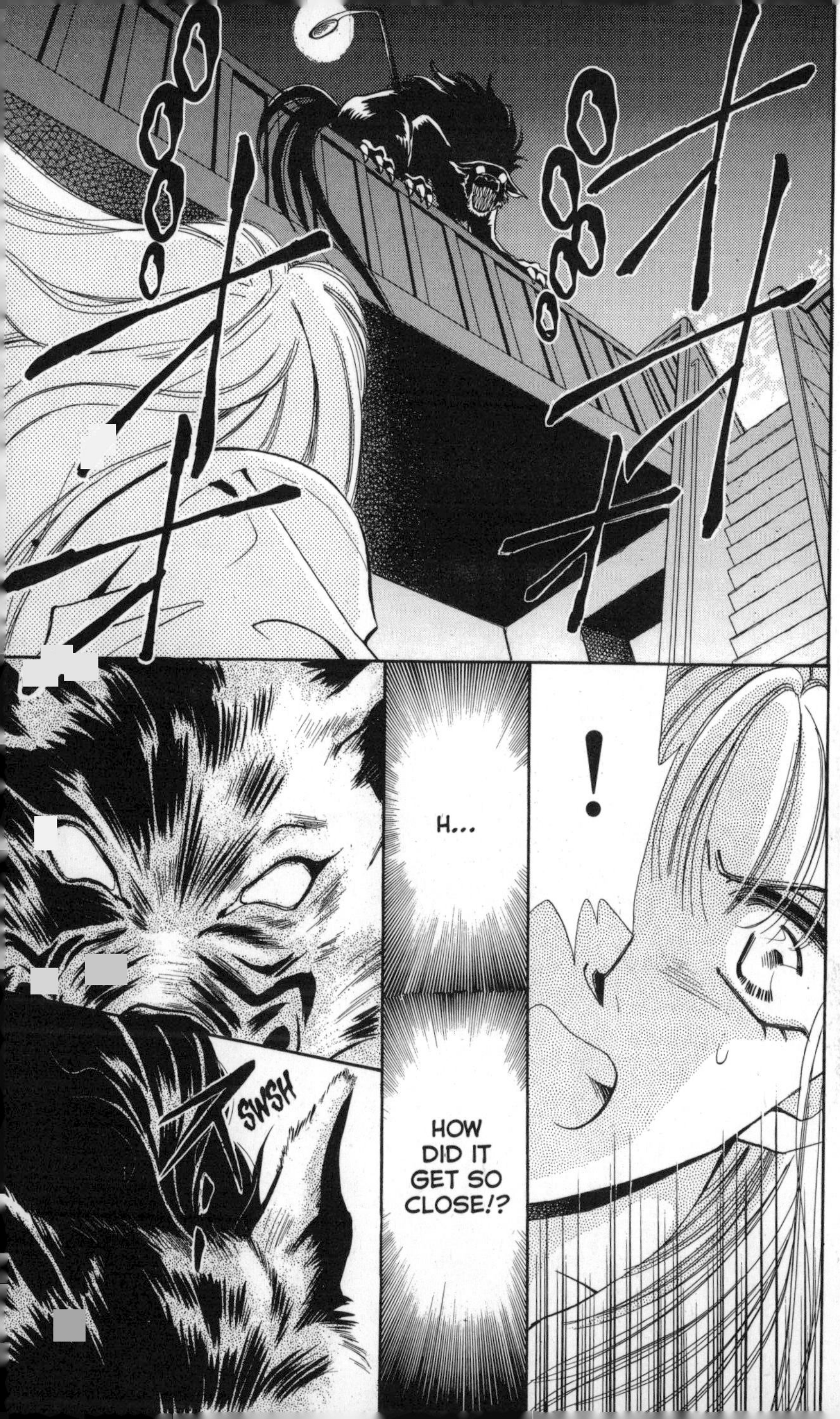
!
H...
HOW DID IT GET SO CLOSE!?
SWSH

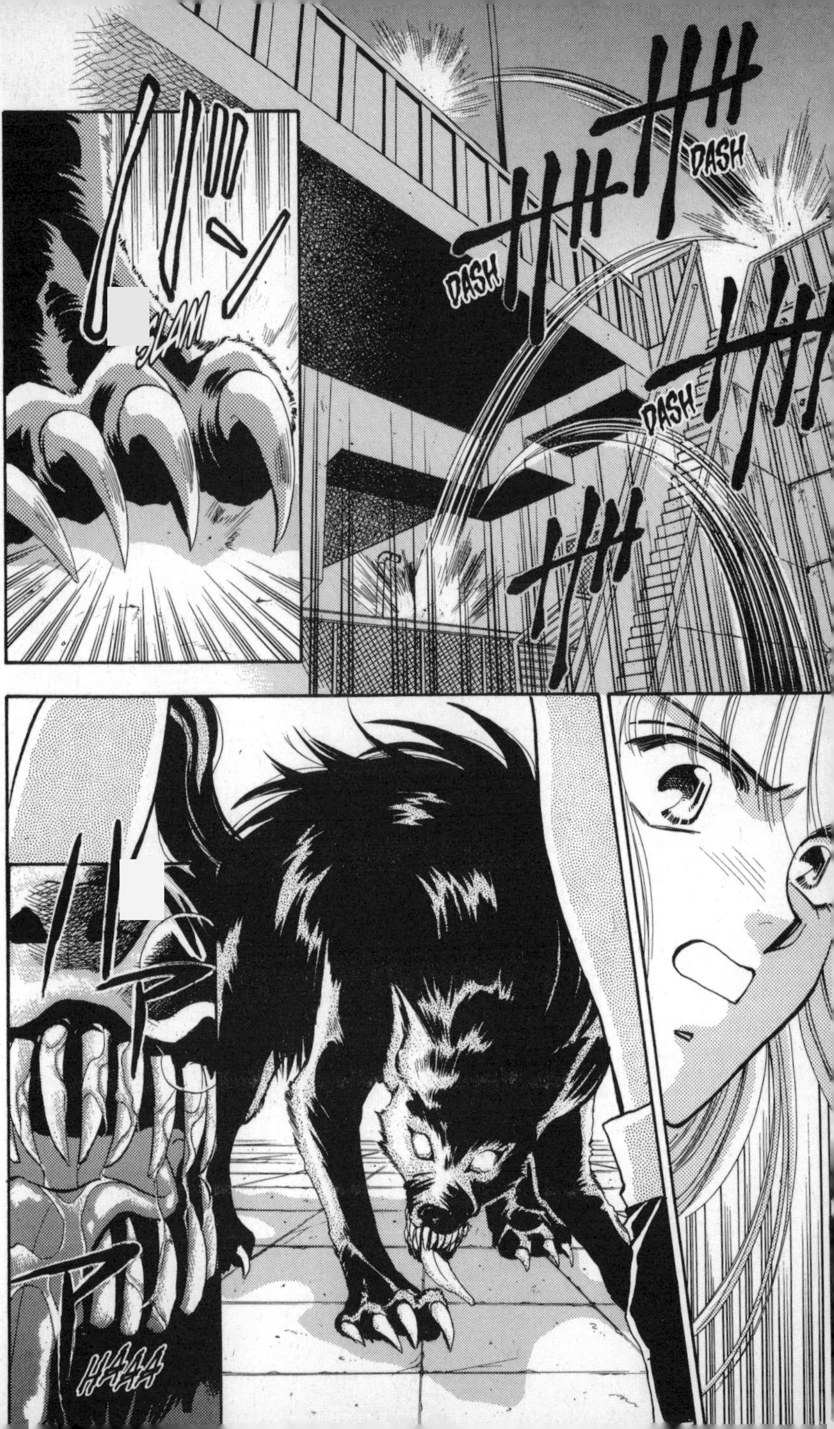
DASH
DASH
DASH
SLAM
HAAA

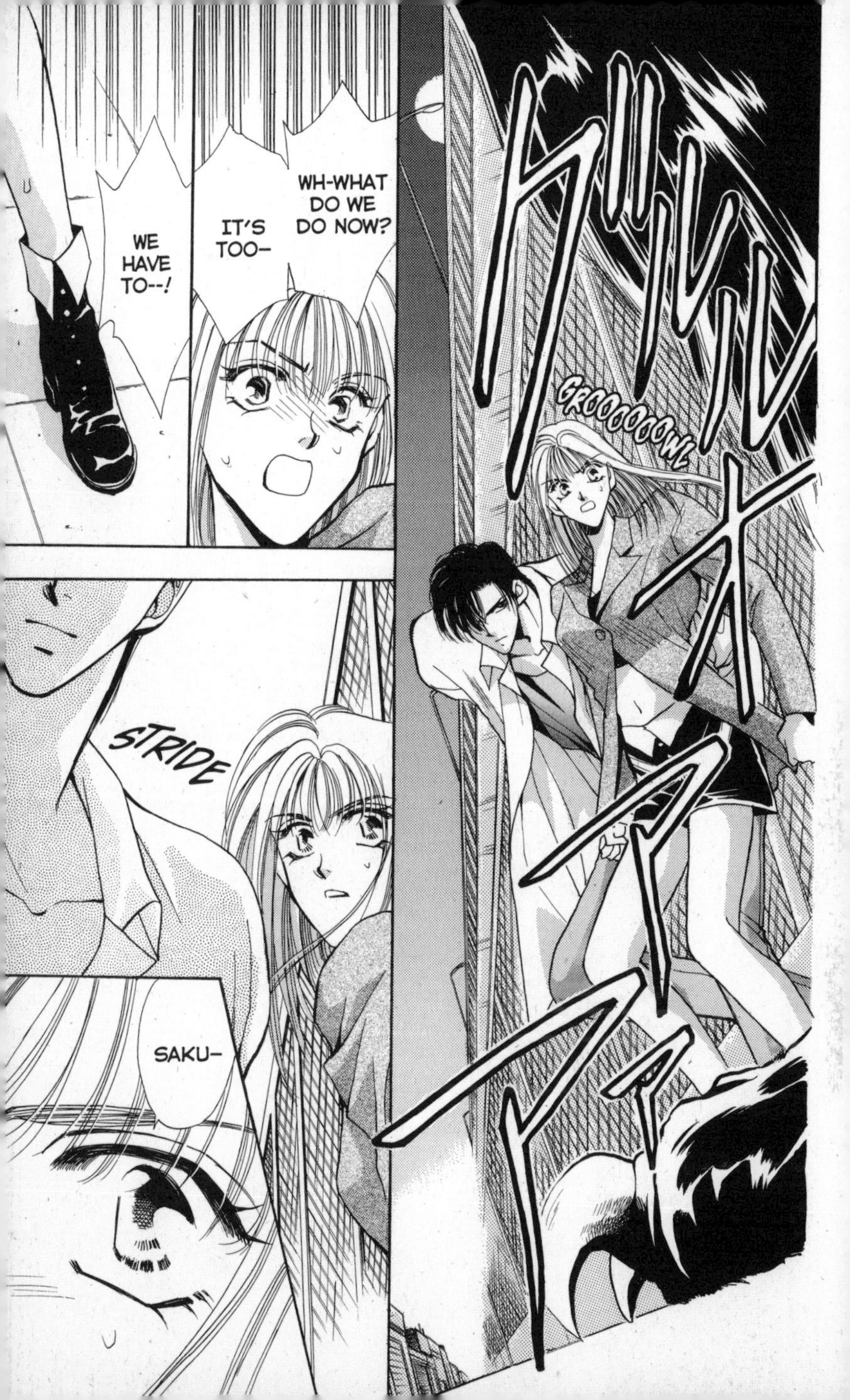
GROOOOOOWL
WH-WHAT DO WE DO NOW?
IT'S TOO–
WE HAVE TO--!
STRIDE
SAKU–

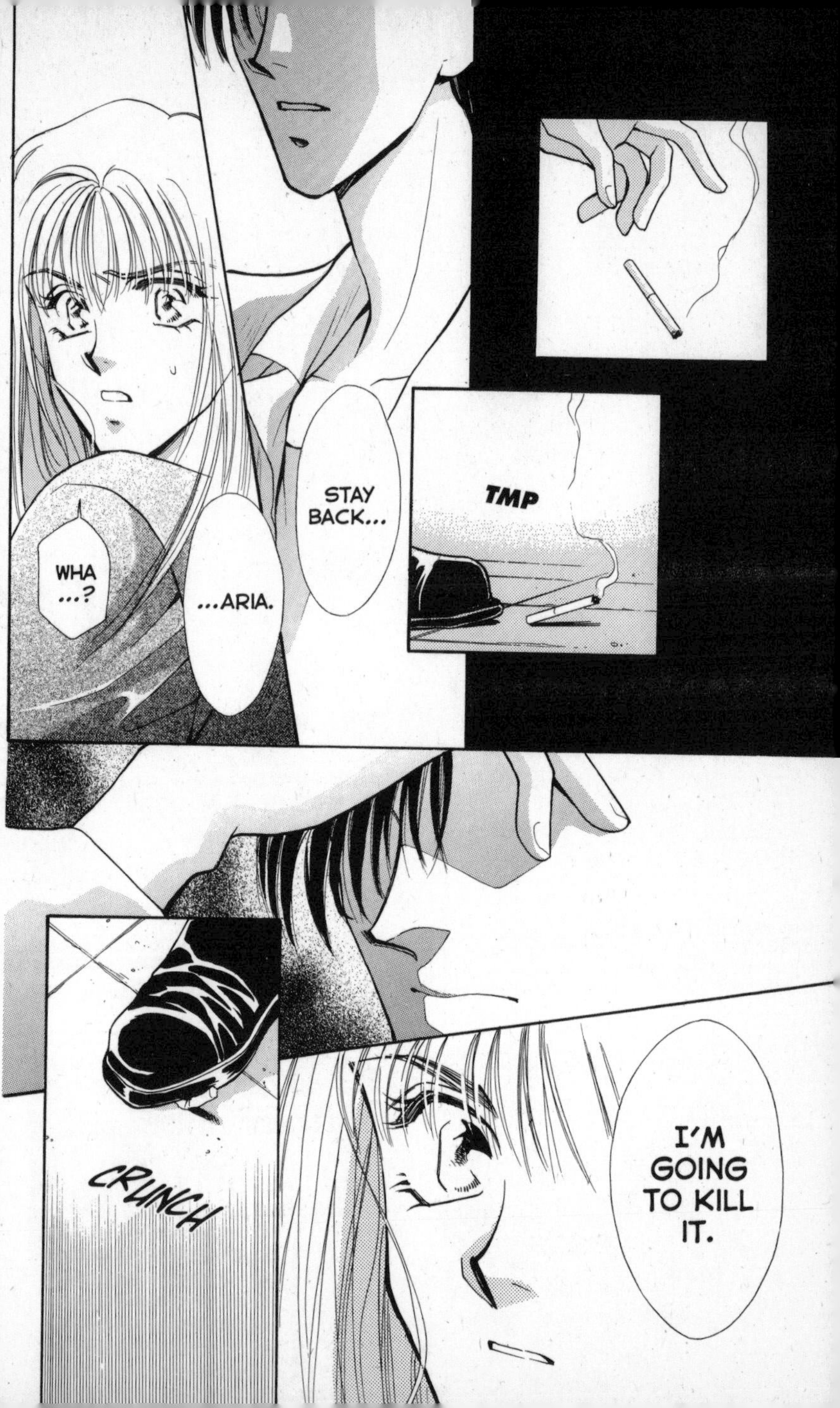
TMP
STAY BACK...
...ARIA.
WHA ...?
I'M GOING TO KILL IT.
CRUNCH

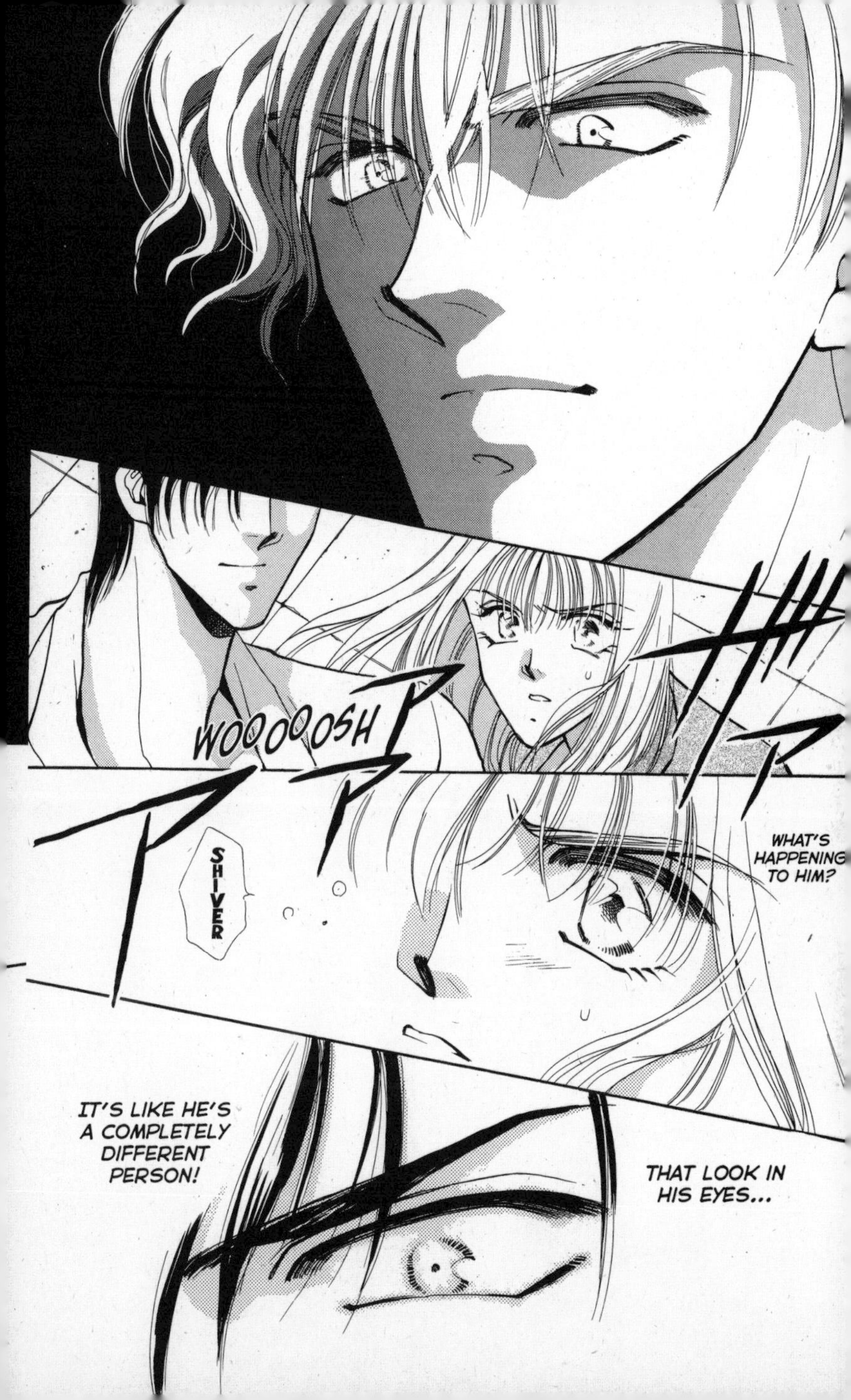
WOOOOOSH
WHAT'S HAPPENING TO HIM?
SHIVER
THAT LOOK IN HIS EYES...
IT'S LIKE HE'S A COMPLETELY DIFFERENT PERSON!

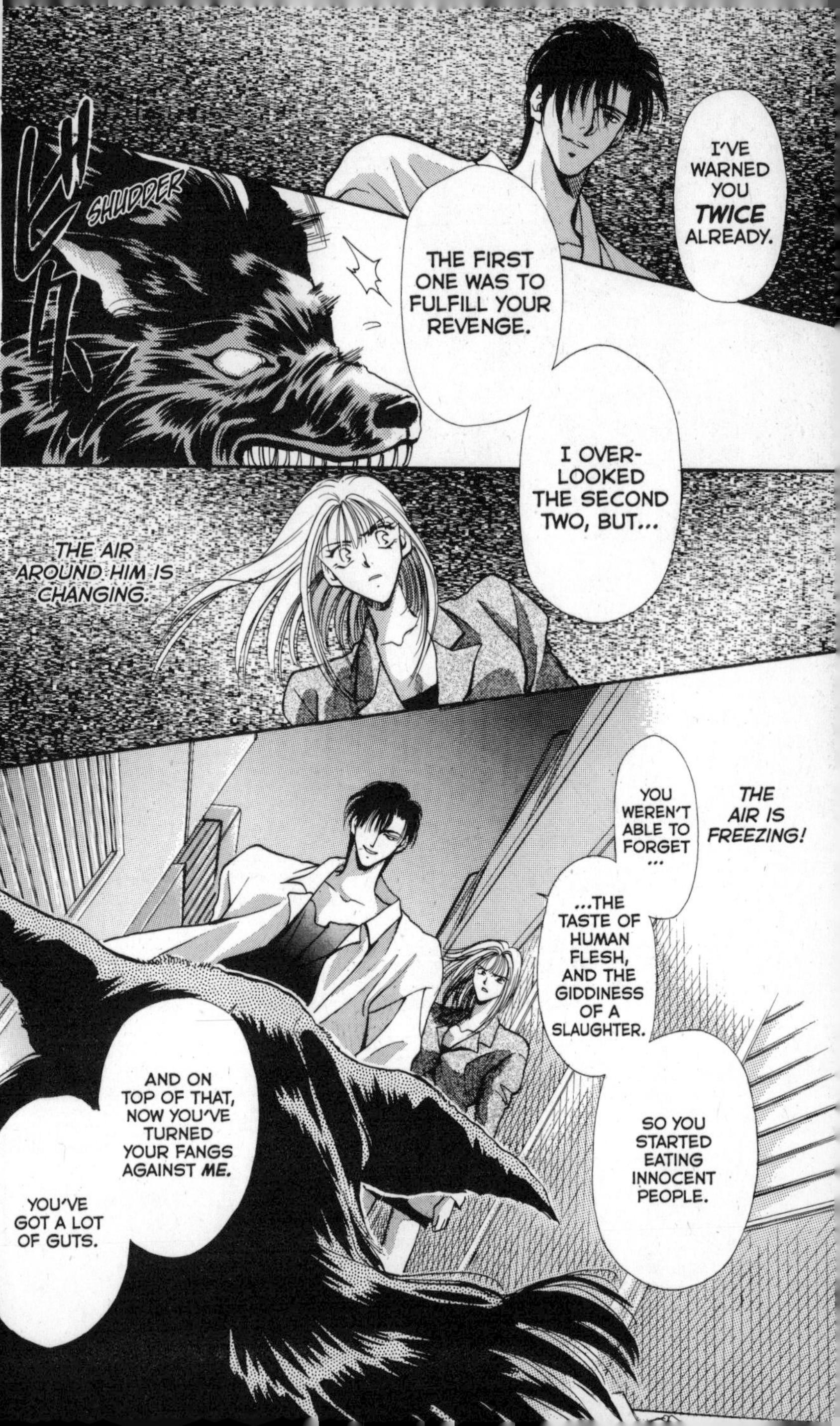
I'VE WARNED YOU **TWICE** ALREADY.
THE FIRST ONE WAS TO FULFILL YOUR REVENGE.
SHUDDER
I OVER-LOOKED THE SECOND TWO, BUT...
THE AIR AROUND HIM IS CHANGING.
THE AIR IS FREEZING!
YOU WEREN'T ABLE TO FORGET ...
...THE TASTE OF HUMAN FLESH, AND THE GIDDINESS OF A SLAUGHTER.
SO YOU STARTED EATING INNOCENT PEOPLE.
AND ON TOP OF THAT, NOW YOU'VE TURNED YOUR FANGS AGAINST *ME.*
YOU'VE GOT A LOT OF GUTS.

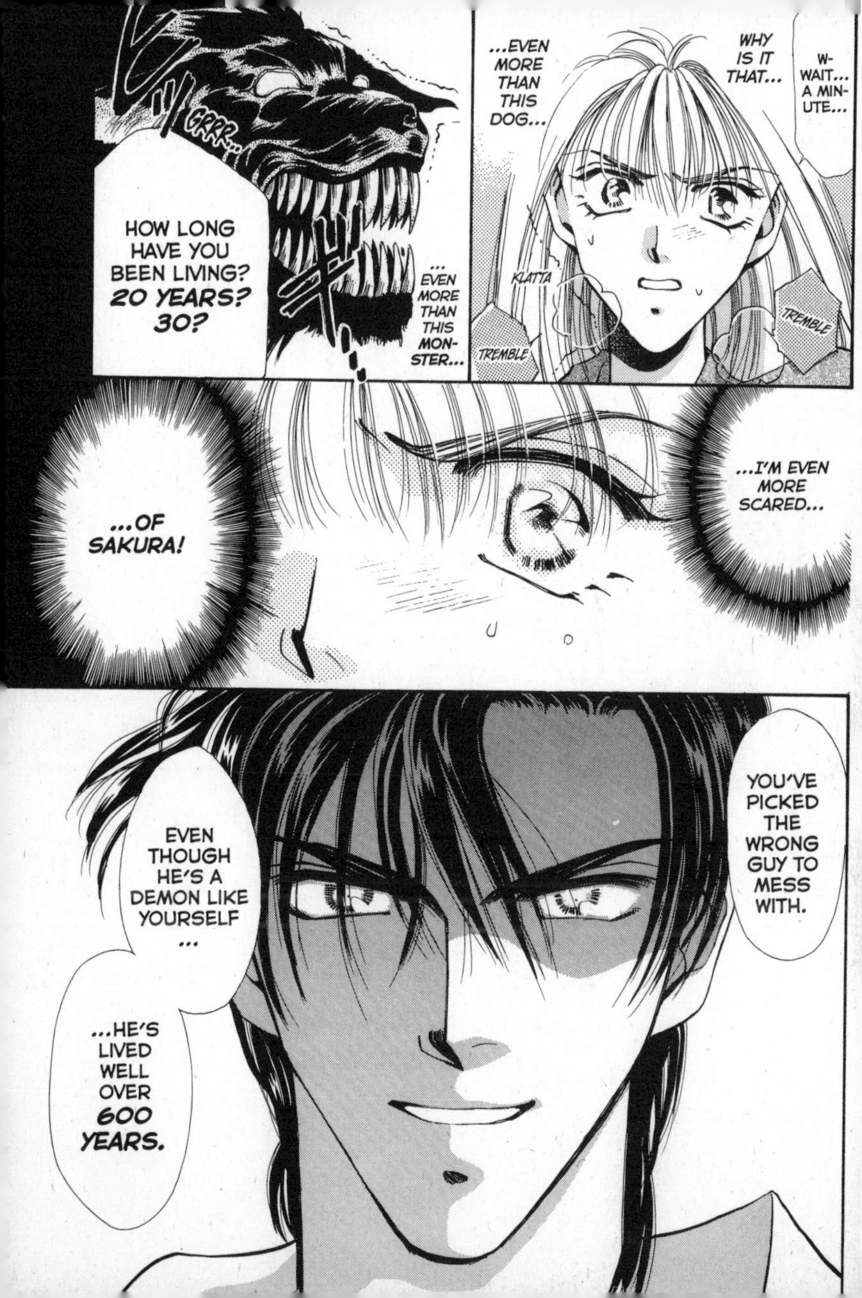
W-WAIT... A MINUTE...
WHY IS IT THAT...
...EVEN MORE THAN THIS DOG...
KLATTA
TREMBLE
TREMBLE
GRRR...
...EVEN MORE THAN THIS MONSTER...
HOW LONG HAVE YOU BEEN LIVING? 20 YEARS? 30?
...I'M EVEN MORE SCARED...
...OF SAKURA!
YOU'VE PICKED THE WRONG GUY TO MESS WITH.
EVEN THOUGH HE'S A DEMON LIKE YOURSELF...
...HE'S LIVED WELL OVER 600 YEARS.

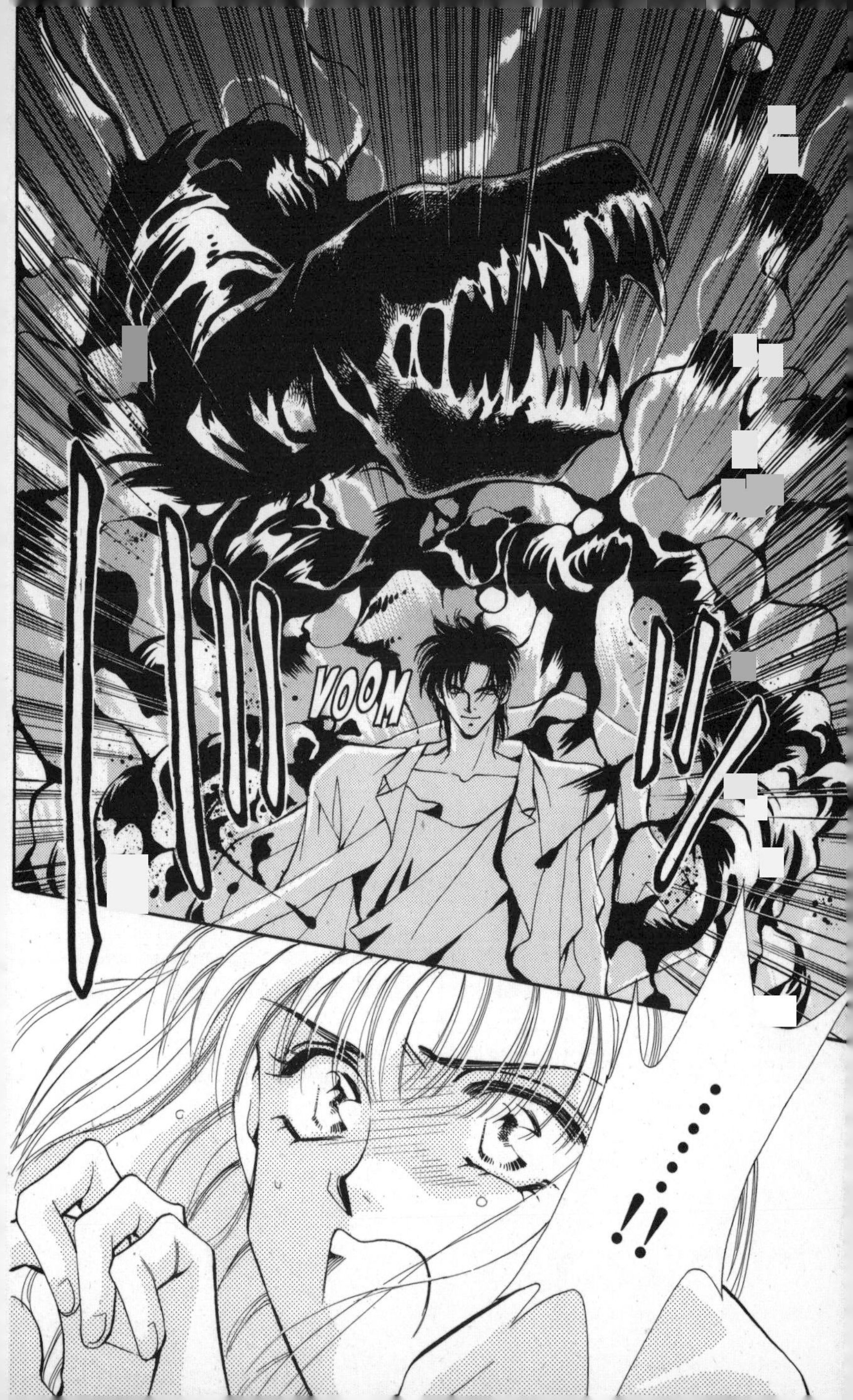
VOOM
......!!

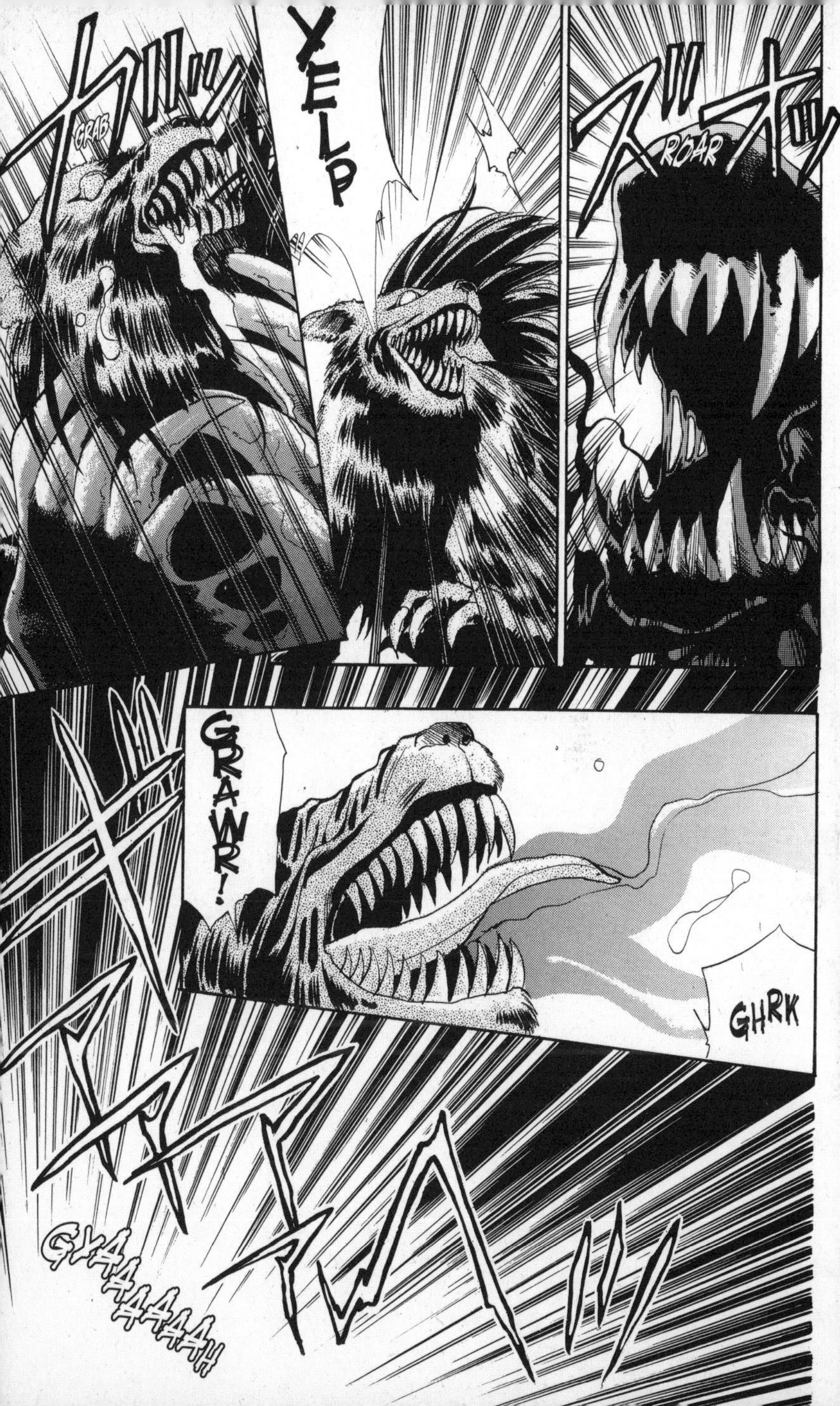
ROAR
YELP
GRAB
GRAWR!
GHRK
GYAAAAAAH

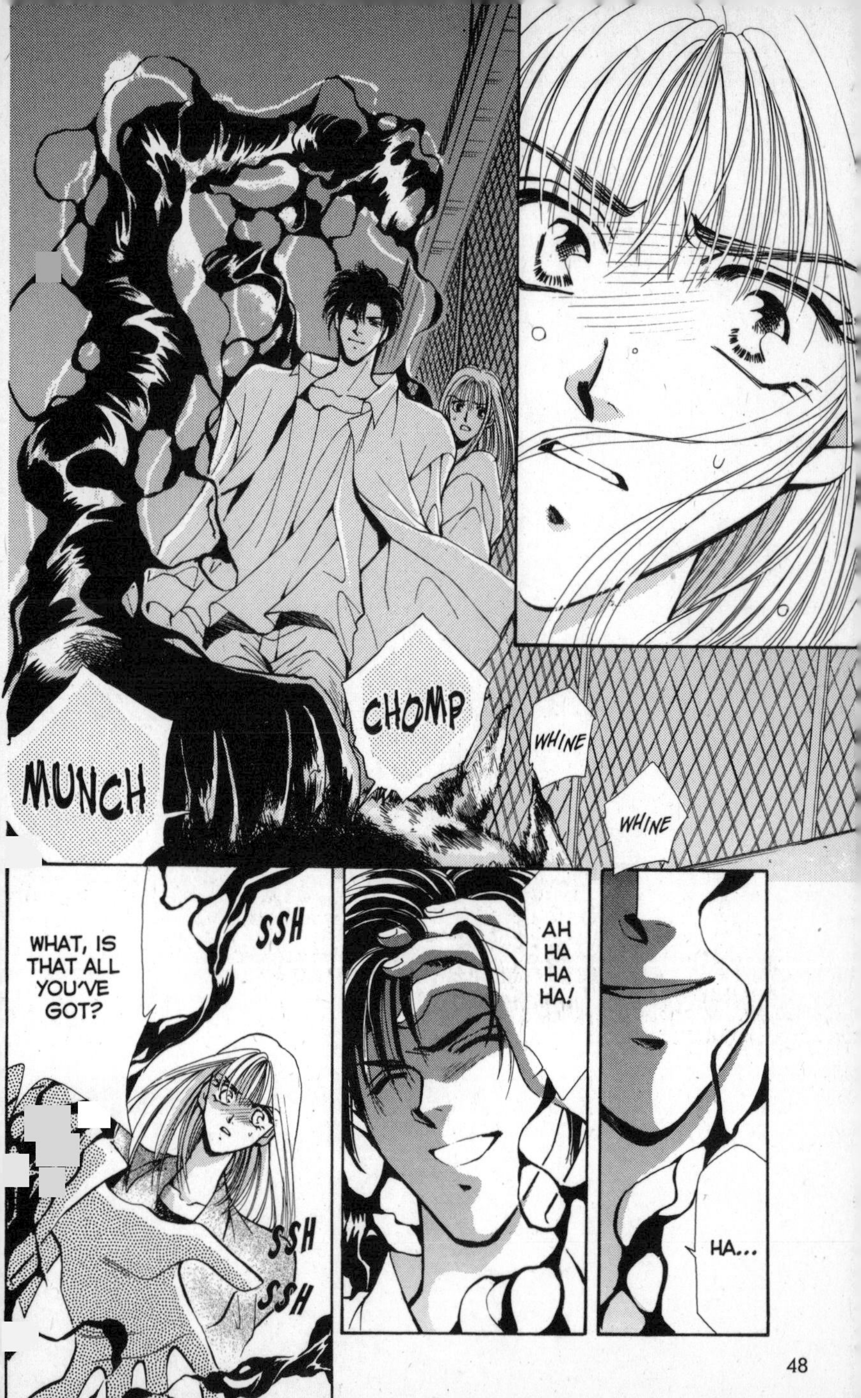
WHINE
WHINE
CHOMP
MUNCH
HA...
AH HA HA HA!
SSH
WHAT, IS THAT ALL YOU'VE GOT?
SSH
SSH

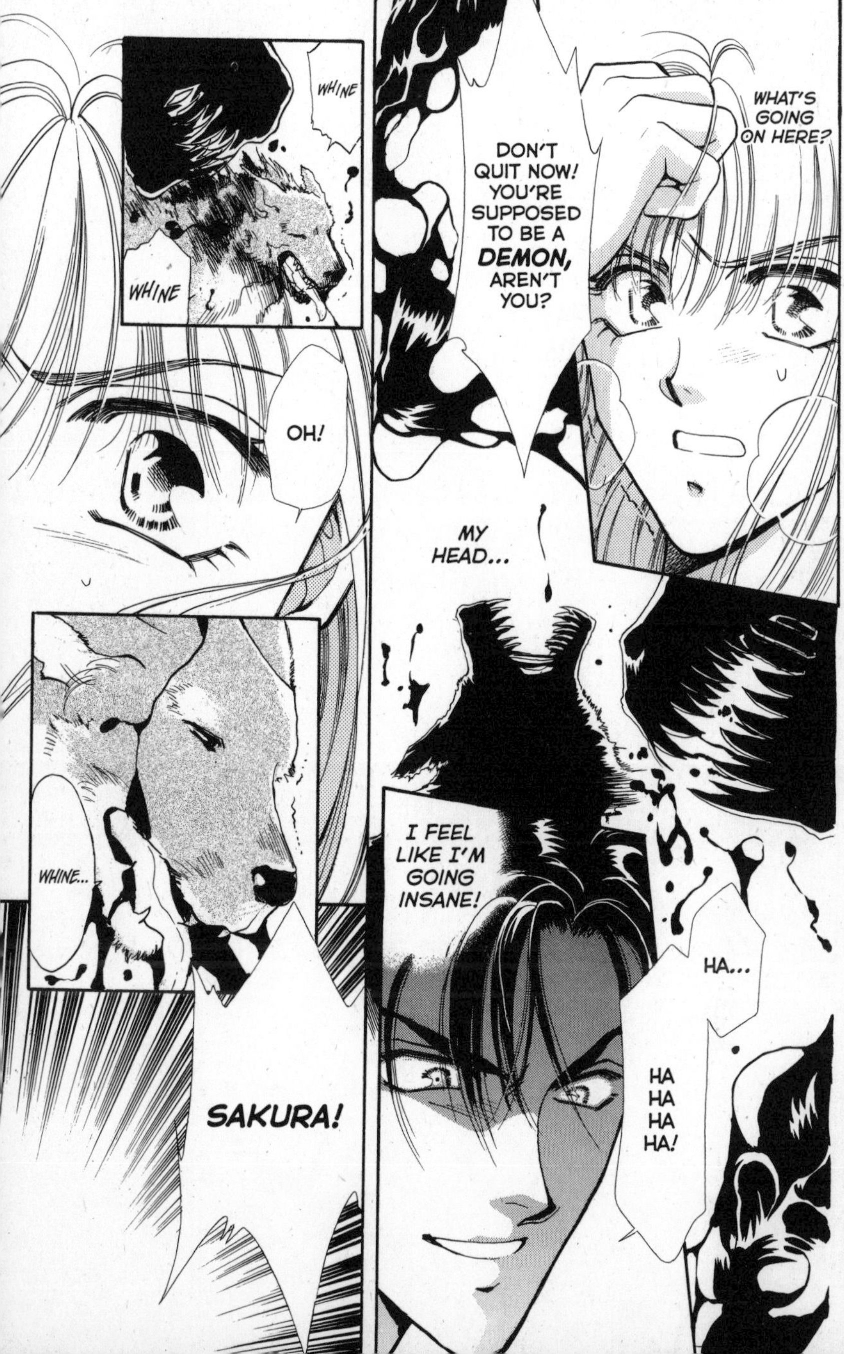
WHAT'S GOING ON HERE?
DON'T QUIT NOW! YOU'RE SUPPOSED TO BE A **DEMON,** AREN'T YOU?
MY HEAD...
I FEEL LIKE I'M GOING INSANE!
HA...
HA HA HA HA!
WHINE
WHINE
OH!
WHINE...
SAKURA!

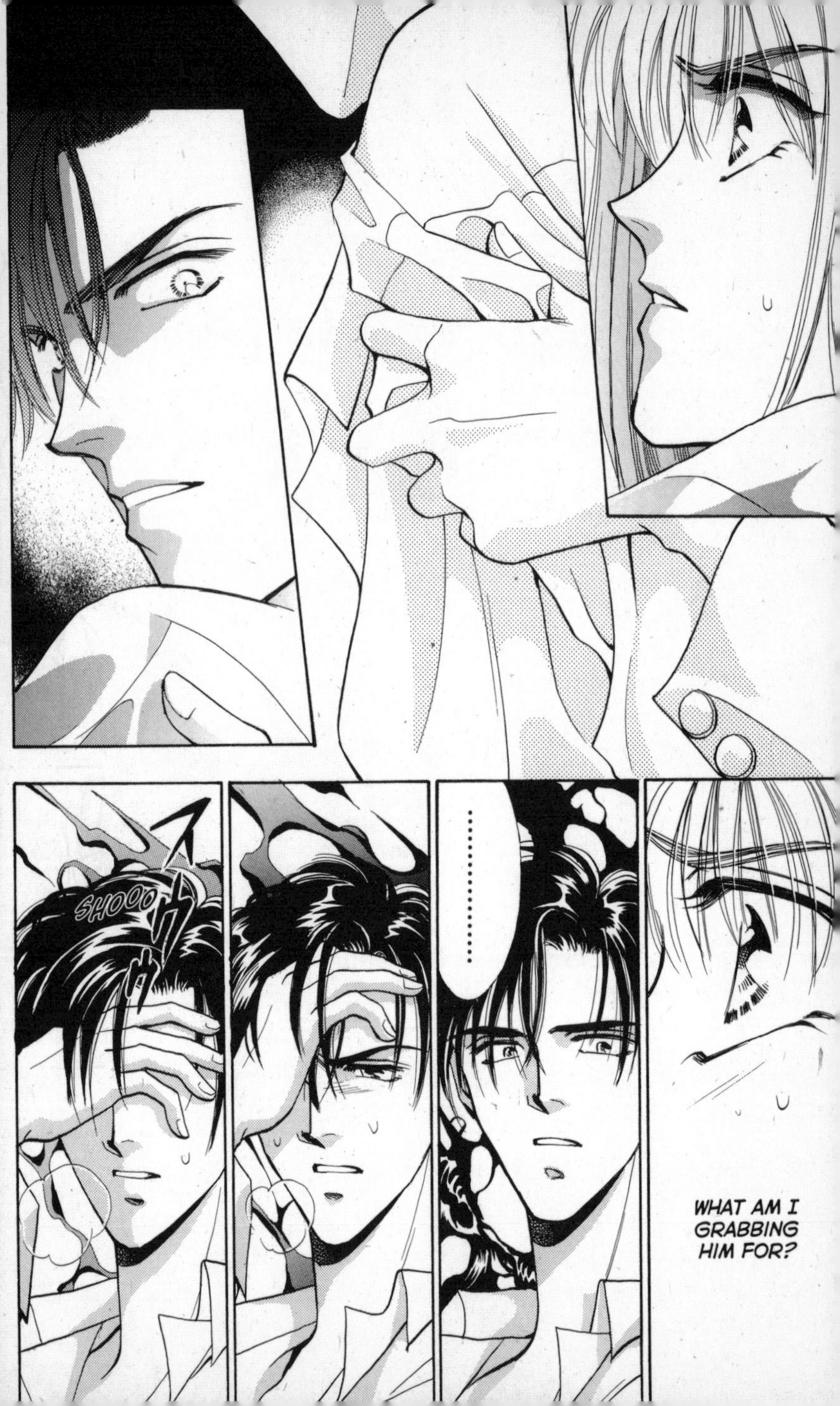
WHAT AM I GRABBING HIM FOR?
......
SHOOO

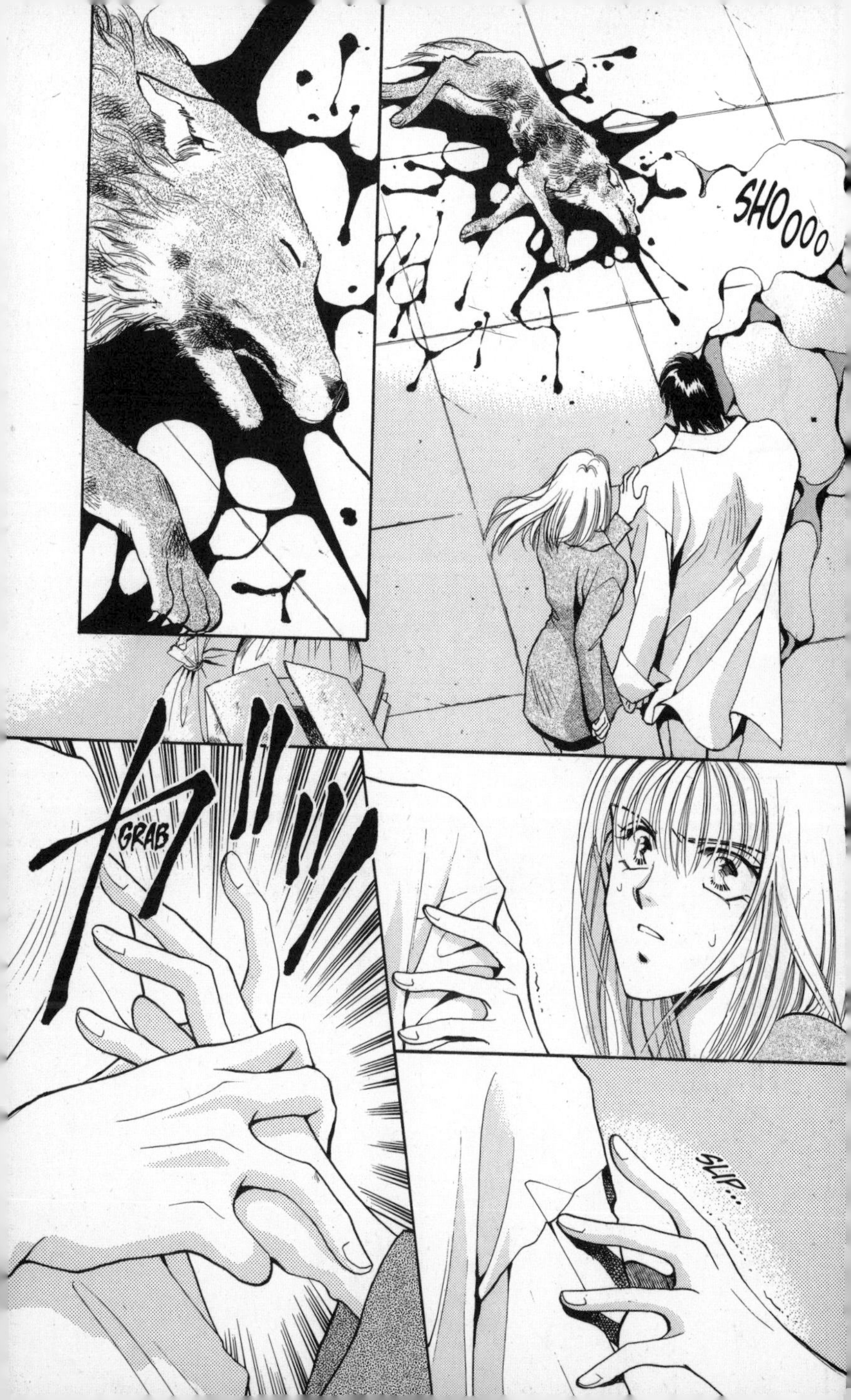
SHOOOO
SLIP...
GRAB

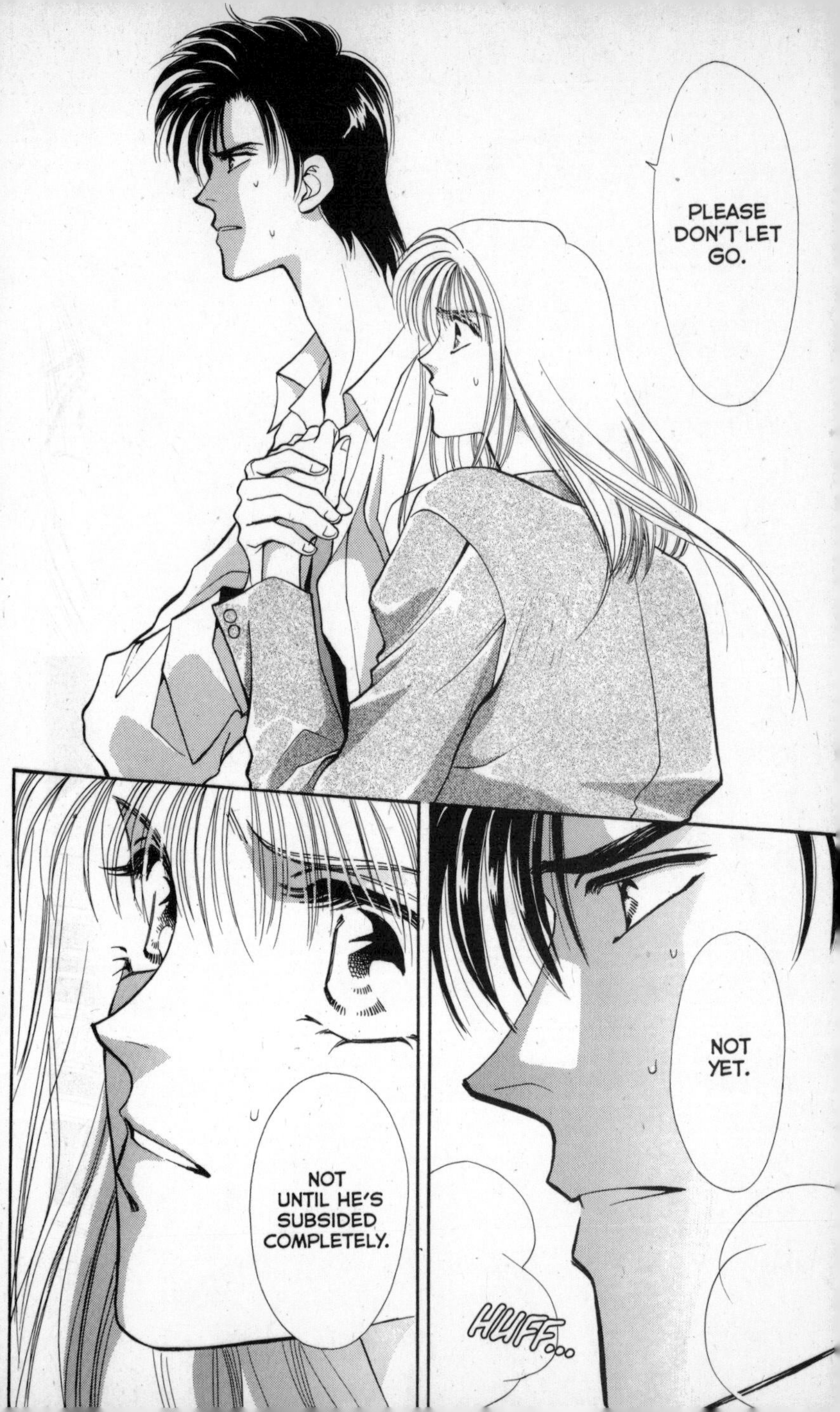
PLEASE DON'T LET GO.
NOT YET.
HUFF...
NOT UNTIL HE'S SUBSIDED COMPLETELY.

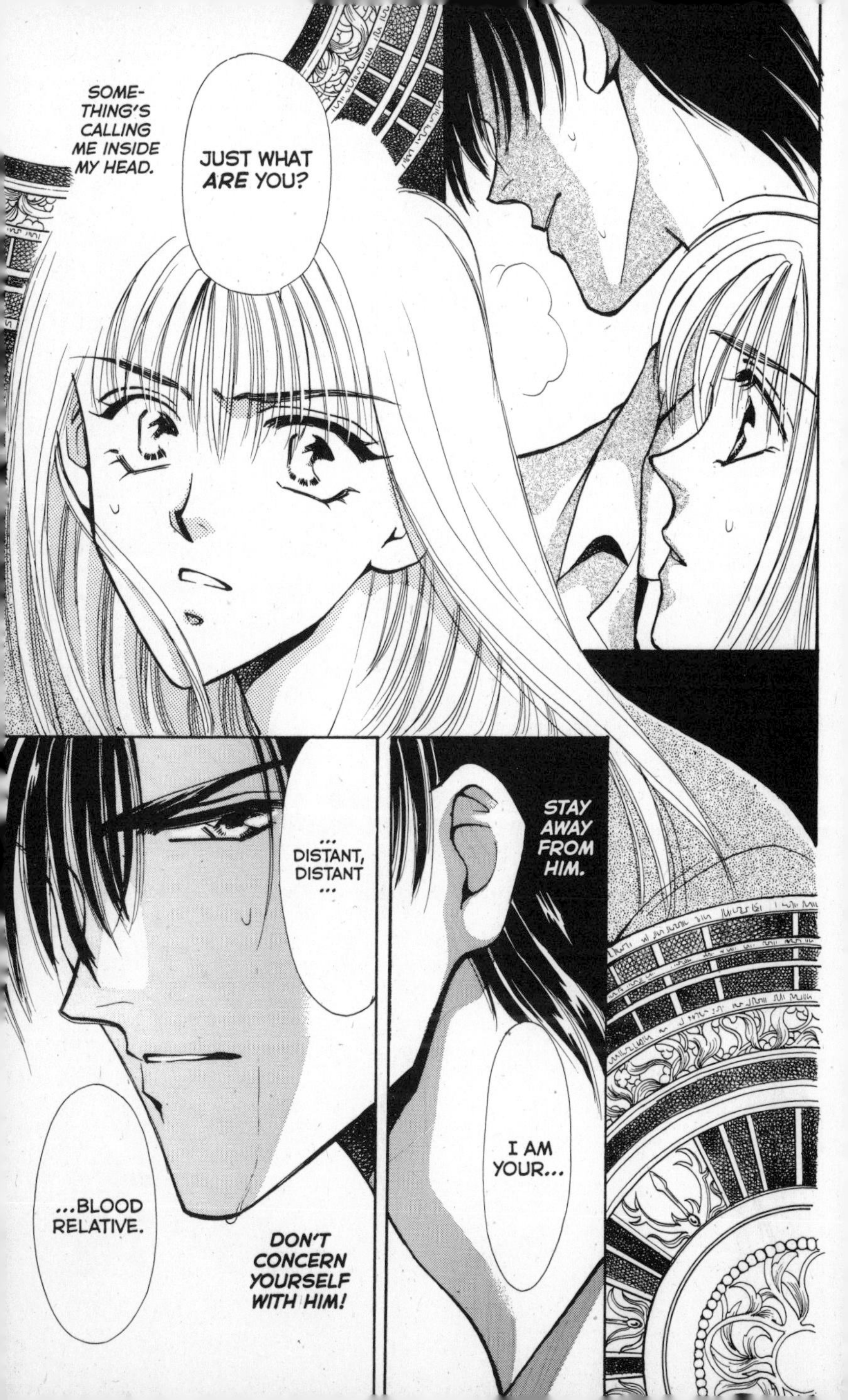
JUST WHAT *ARE* YOU?
SOME-THING'S CALLING ME INSIDE MY HEAD.
STAY AWAY FROM HIM.
I AM YOUR...
...DISTANT, DISTANT...
DON'T CONCERN YOURSELF WITH HIM!
...BLOOD RELATIVE.

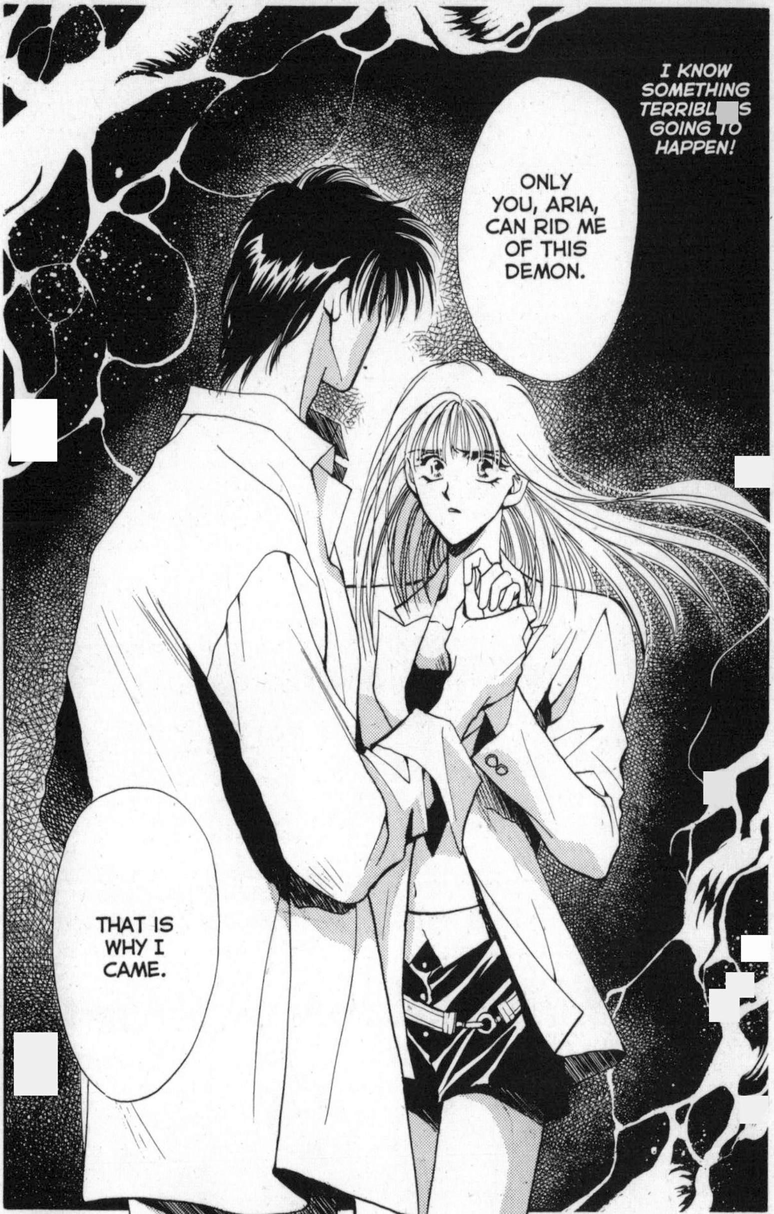
I KNOW SOMETHING TERRIBLE IS GOING TO HAPPEN!
ONLY YOU, ARIA, CAN RID ME OF THIS DEMON.
THAT IS WHY I CAME.

獣たちの夜

獣たちの夜

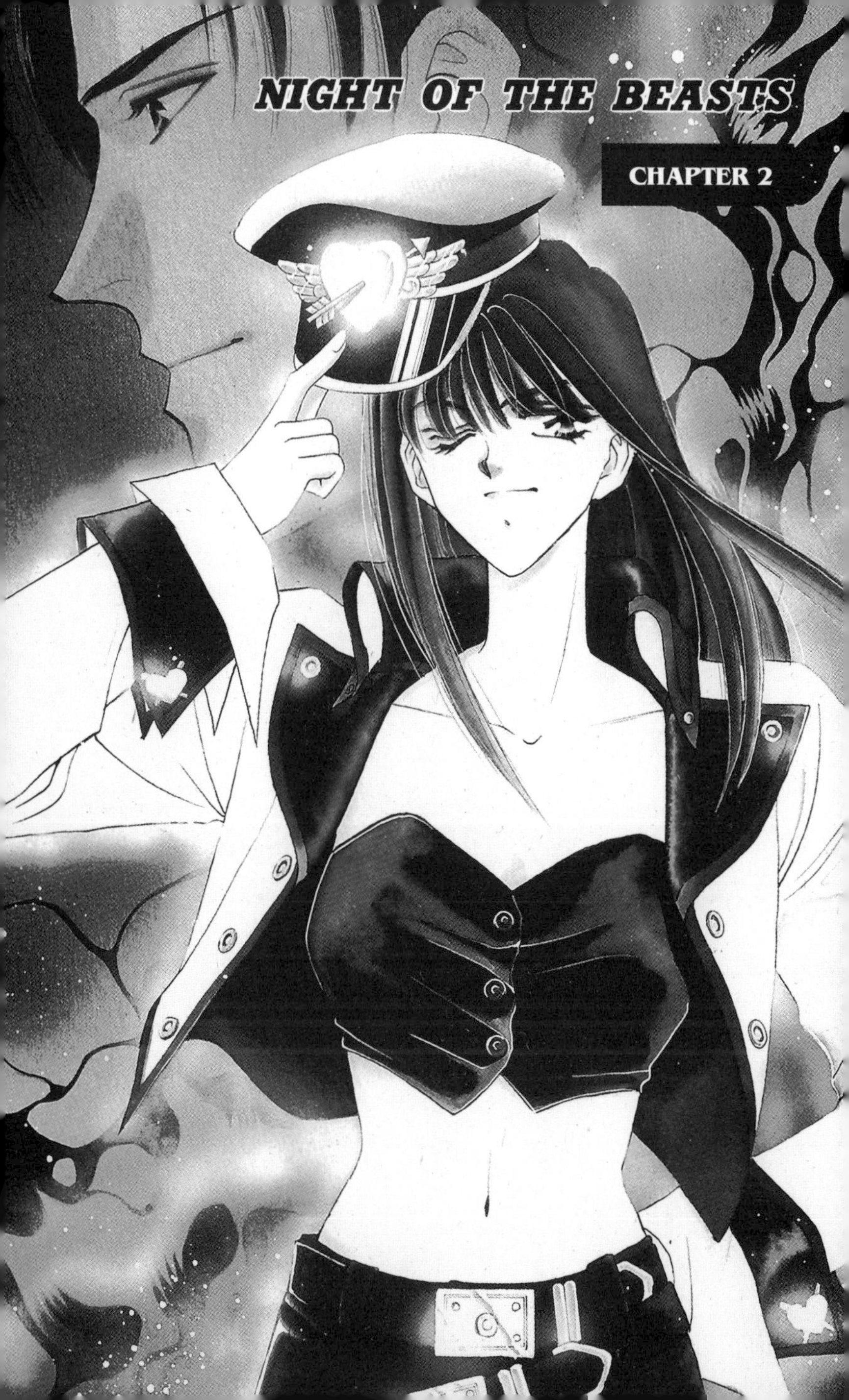
NIGHT OF THE BEASTS
CHAPTER 2

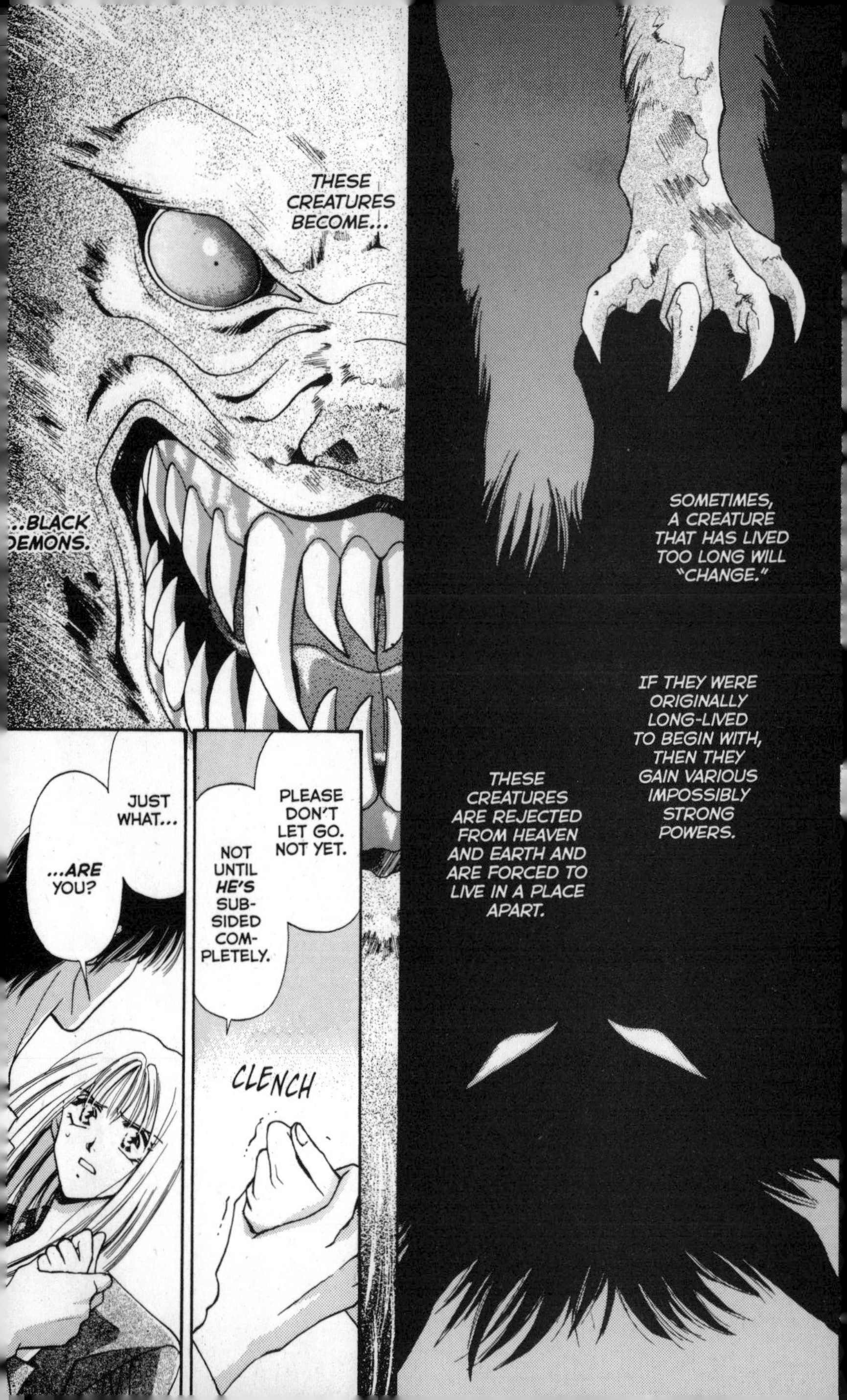
SOMETIMES, A CREATURE THAT HAS LIVED TOO LONG WILL "CHANGE."
IF THEY WERE ORIGINALLY LONG-LIVED TO BEGIN WITH, THEN THEY GAIN VARIOUS IMPOSSIBLY STRONG POWERS.
THESE CREATURES ARE REJECTED FROM HEAVEN AND EARTH AND ARE FORCED TO LIVE IN A PLACE APART.
THESE CREATURES BECOME...
...BLACK DEMONS.
PLEASE DON'T LET GO. NOT YET.
NOT UNTIL *HE'S* SUB-SIDED COM-PLETELY.
CLENCH
JUST WHAT...
...*ARE* YOU?

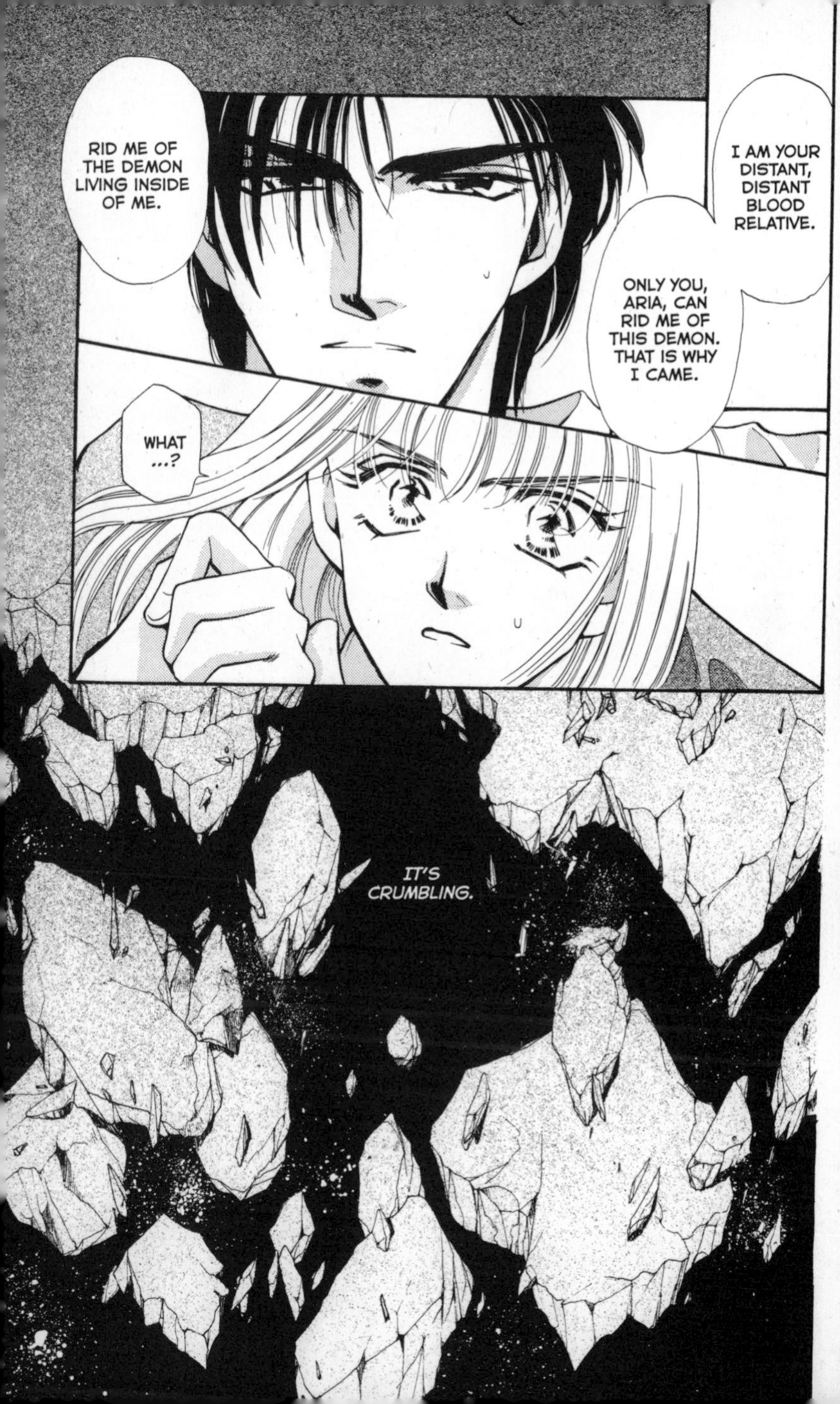
I AM YOUR DISTANT, DISTANT BLOOD RELATIVE.
RID ME OF THE DEMON LIVING INSIDE OF ME.
ONLY YOU, ARIA, CAN RID ME OF THIS DEMON. THAT IS WHY I CAME.
WHAT ...?
IT'S CRUMBLING.

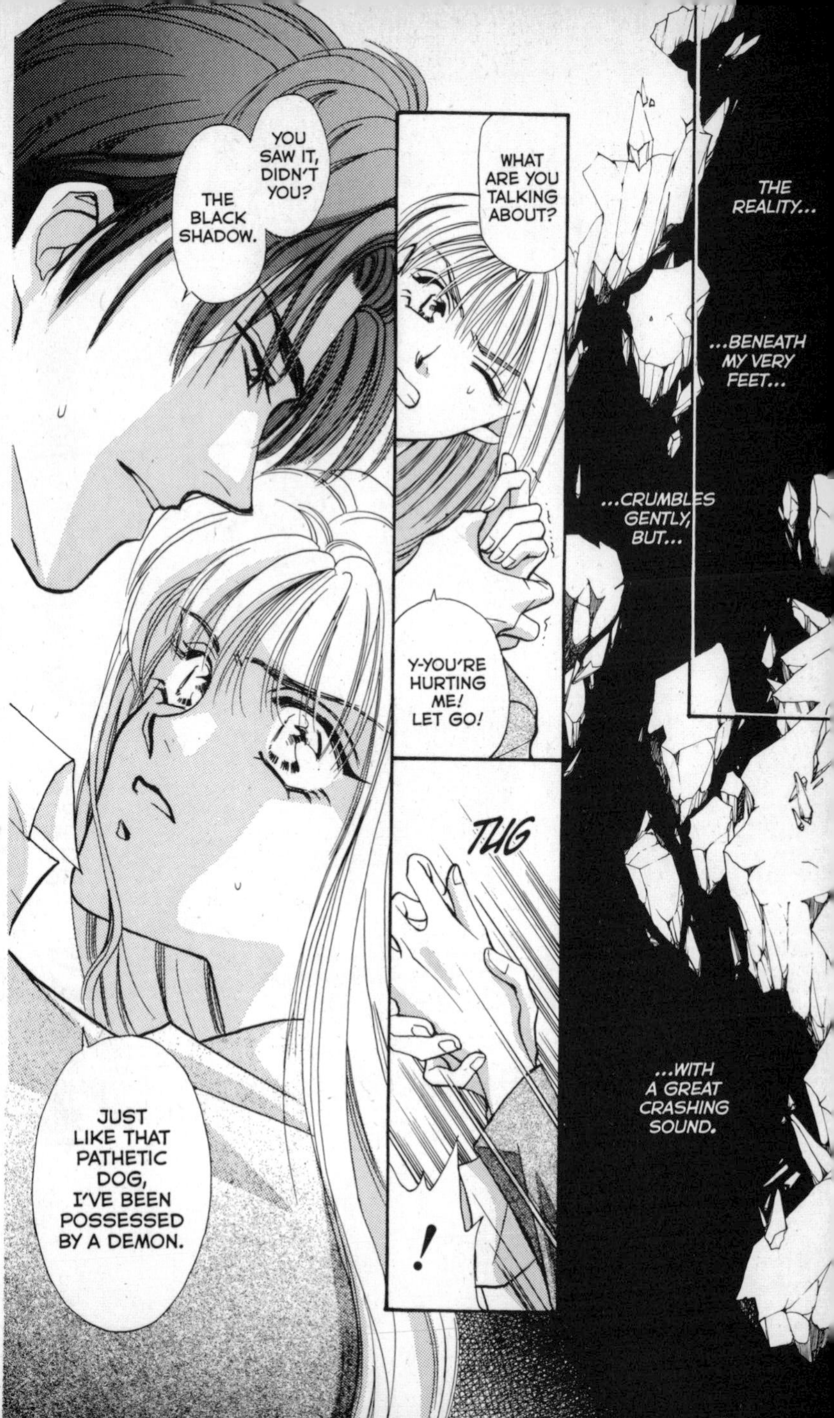
THE REALITY...
...BENEATH MY VERY FEET...
...CRUMBLES GENTLY, BUT...
...WITH A GREAT CRASHING SOUND.
WHAT ARE YOU TALKING ABOUT?
Y-YOU'RE HURTING ME! LET GO!
TUG
!
YOU SAW IT, DIDN'T YOU?
THE BLACK SHADOW.
JUST LIKE THAT PATHETIC DOG, I'VE BEEN POSSESSED BY A DEMON.

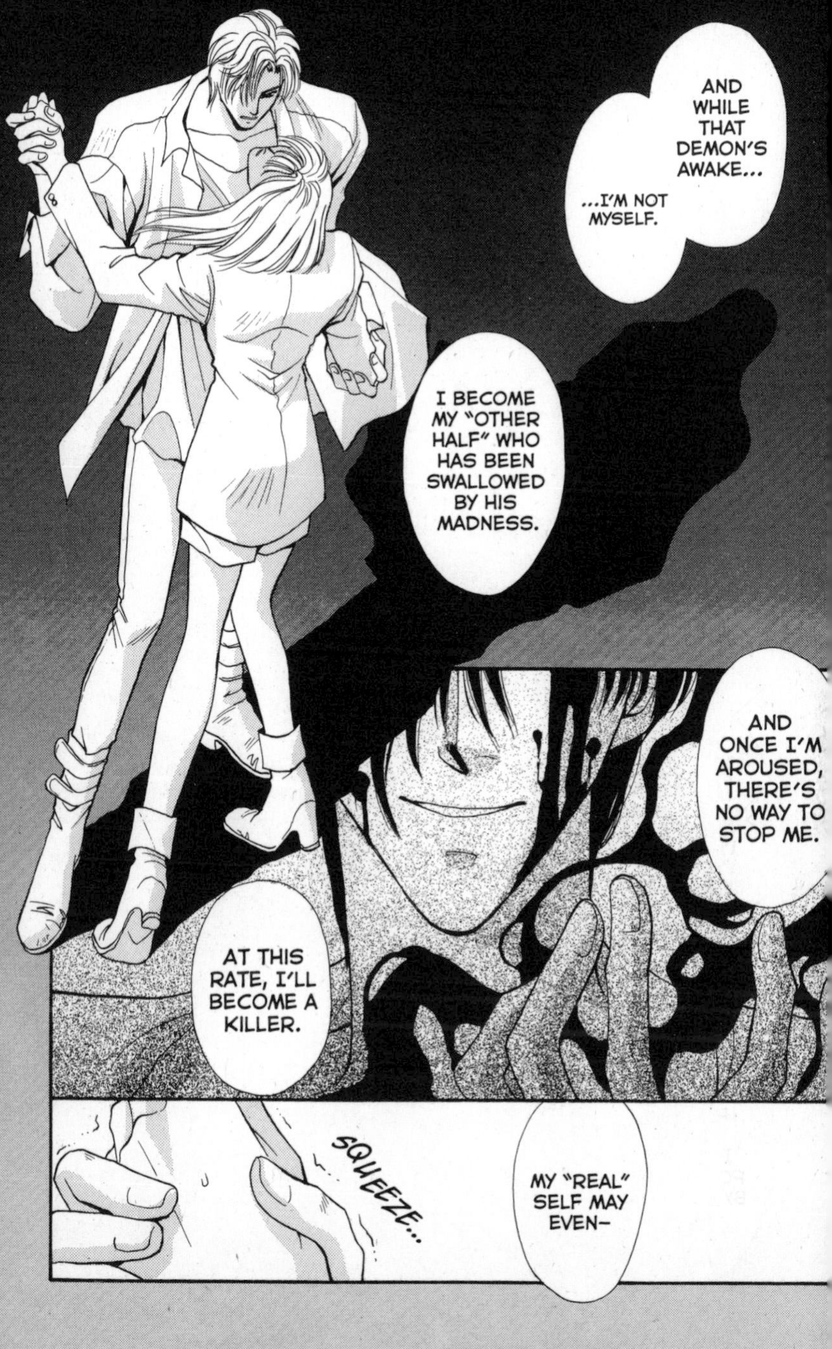
AND WHILE THAT DEMON'S AWAKE...
...I'M NOT MYSELF.
I BECOME MY "OTHER HALF" WHO HAS BEEN SWALLOWED BY HIS MADNESS.
AND ONCE I'M AROUSED, THERE'S NO WAY TO STOP ME.
AT THIS RATE, I'LL BECOME A KILLER.
MY "REAL" SELF MAY EVEN–
SQUEEZE...

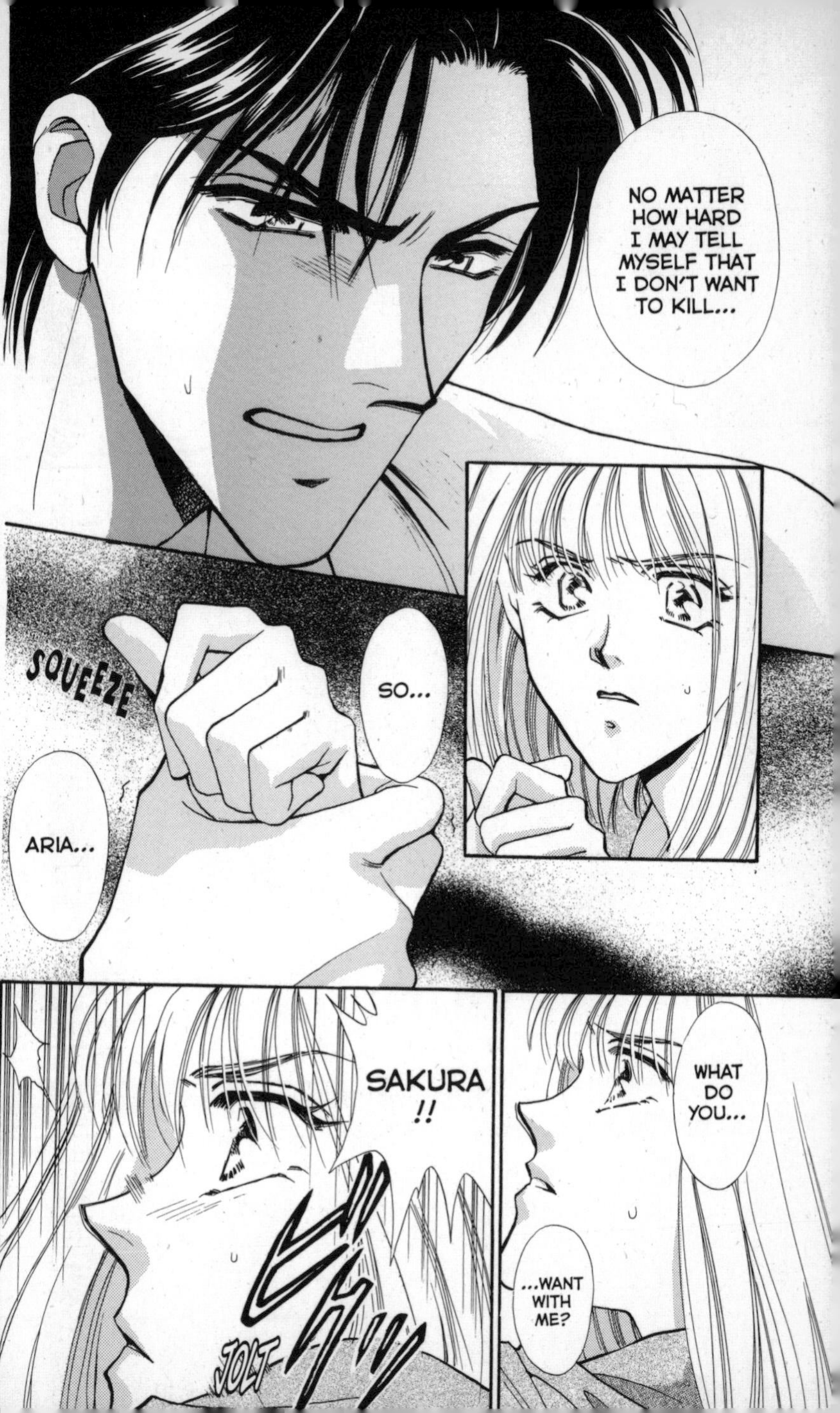
NO MATTER HOW HARD I MAY TELL MYSELF THAT I DON'T WANT TO KILL...
SO...
SQUEEZE
ARIA...
WHAT DO YOU...
...WANT WITH ME?
SAKURA!!
JOLT

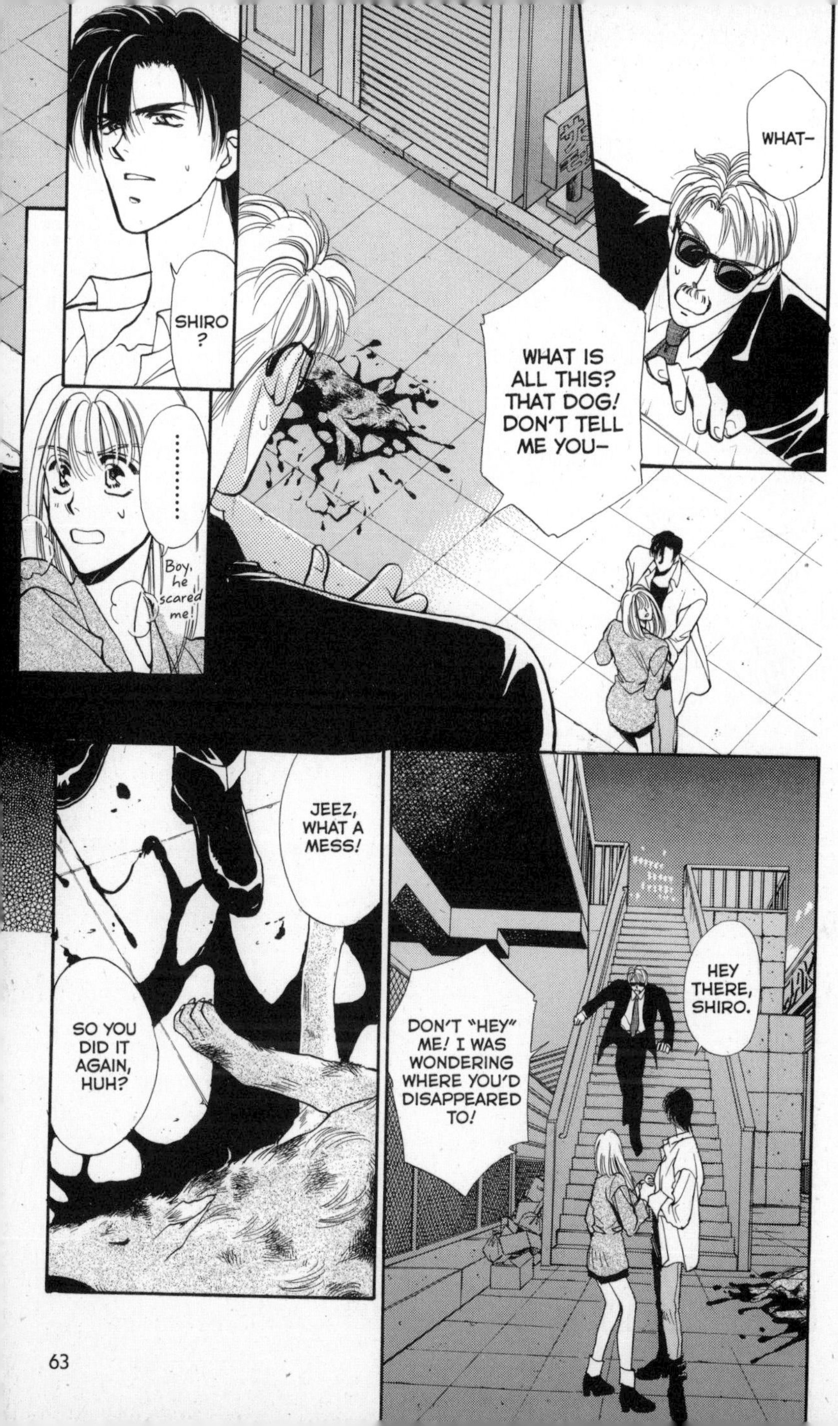
WHAT–
WHAT IS ALL THIS? THAT DOG! DON'T TELL ME YOU–
SHIRO?
......
Boy, he scared me!
HEY THERE, SHIRO.
DON'T "HEY" ME! I WAS WONDERING WHERE YOU'D DISAPPEARED TO!
JEEZ, WHAT A MESS!
SO YOU DID IT AGAIN, HUH?

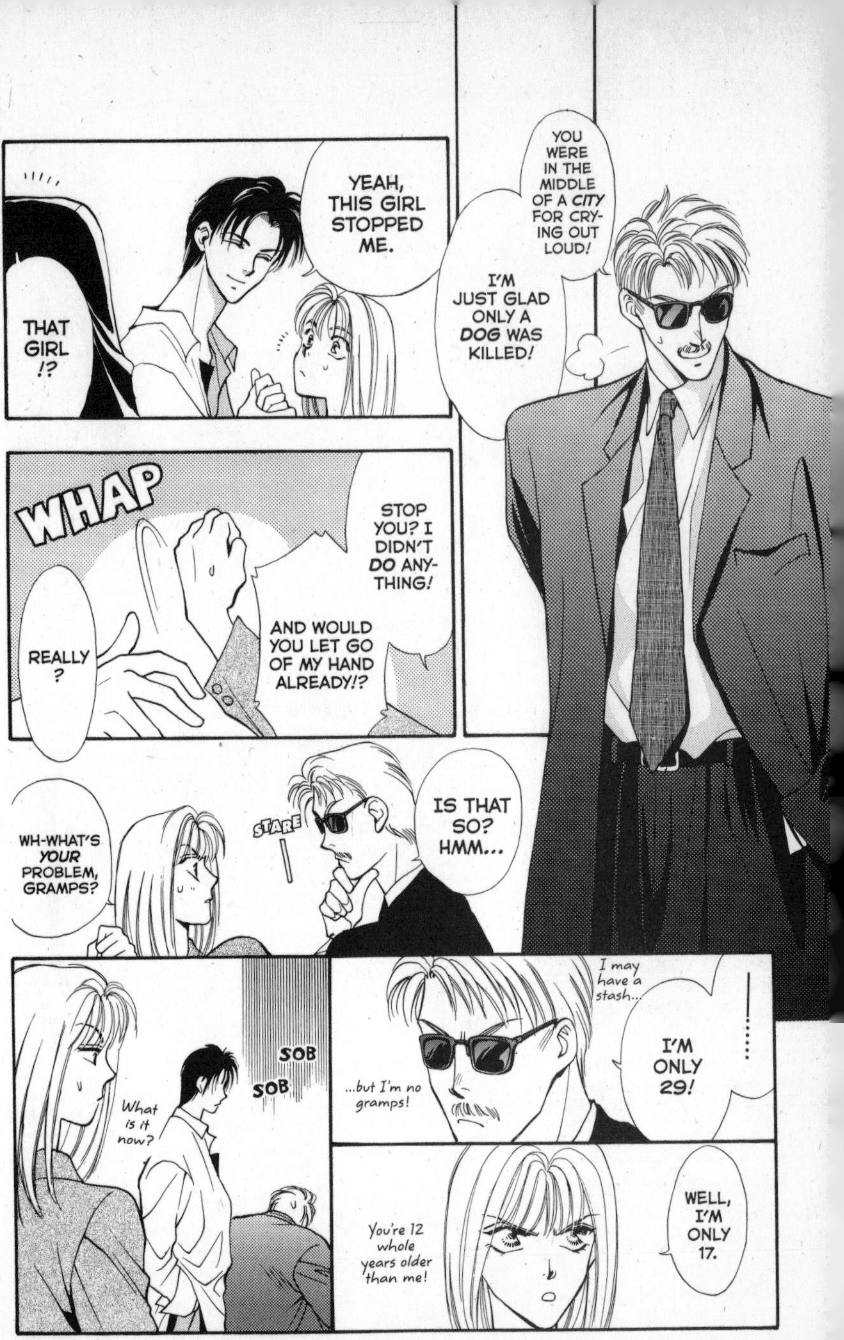
YOU WERE IN THE MIDDLE OF A *CITY* FOR CRYING OUT LOUD!
I'M JUST GLAD ONLY A *DOG* WAS KILLED!
YEAH, THIS GIRL STOPPED ME.
THAT GIRL !?
WHAP
STOP YOU? I DIDN'T *DO* ANYTHING!
AND WOULD YOU LET GO OF MY HAND ALREADY!?
REALLY ?
IS THAT SO? HMM...
STARE
WH-WHAT'S *YOUR* PROBLEM, GRAMPS?
......
I'M ONLY 29!
I may have a stash...
...but I'm no gramps!
WELL, I'M ONLY 17.
You're 12 whole years older than me!
SOB
SOB
What is it now?

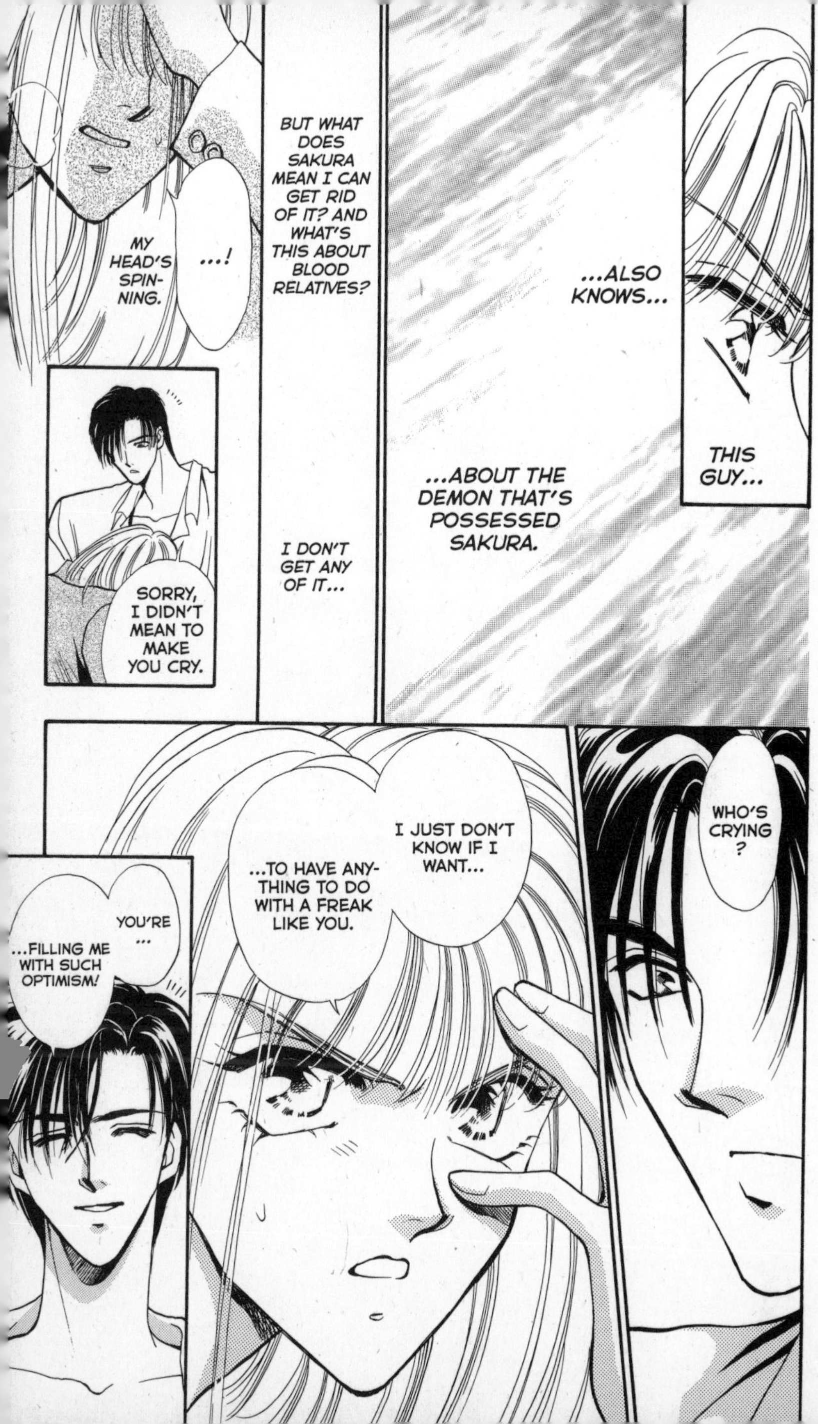
THIS GUY...
...ALSO KNOWS...
...ABOUT THE DEMON THAT'S POSSESSED SAKURA.
BUT WHAT DOES SAKURA MEAN I CAN GET RID OF IT? AND WHAT'S THIS ABOUT BLOOD RELATIVES?
I DON'T GET ANY OF IT...
...!
MY HEAD'S SPIN-NING.
SORRY, I DIDN'T MEAN TO MAKE YOU CRY.
WHO'S CRYING?
I JUST DON'T KNOW IF I WANT...
...TO HAVE ANY-THING TO DO WITH A FREAK LIKE YOU.
YOU'RE ...
...FILLING ME WITH SUCH OPTIMISM!

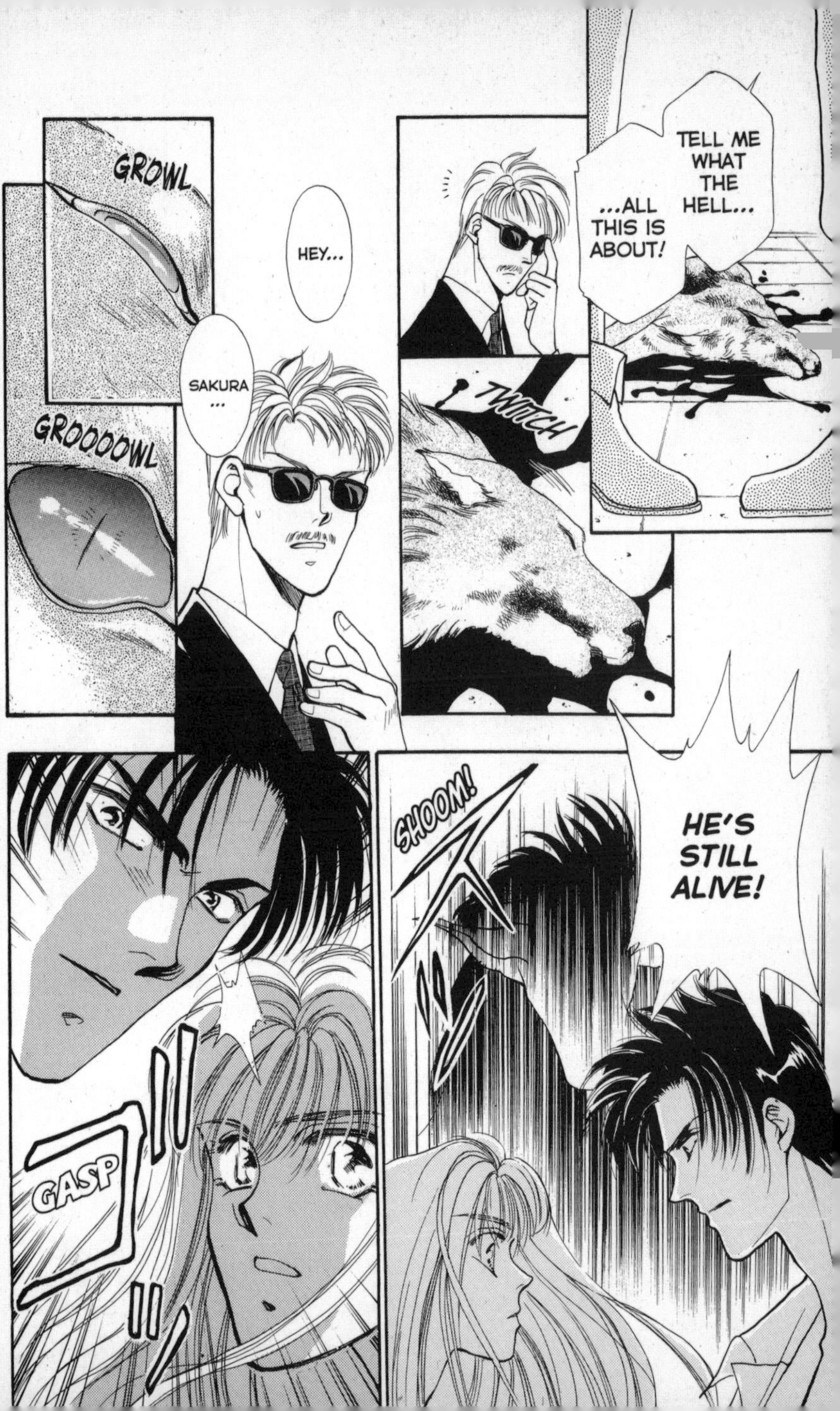

TELL ME WHAT THE HELL...
...ALL THIS IS ABOUT!
TWITCH
HEY...
SAKURA...
GROWL
GROOOOWL
SHOOM!
HE'S STILL ALIVE!
GASP

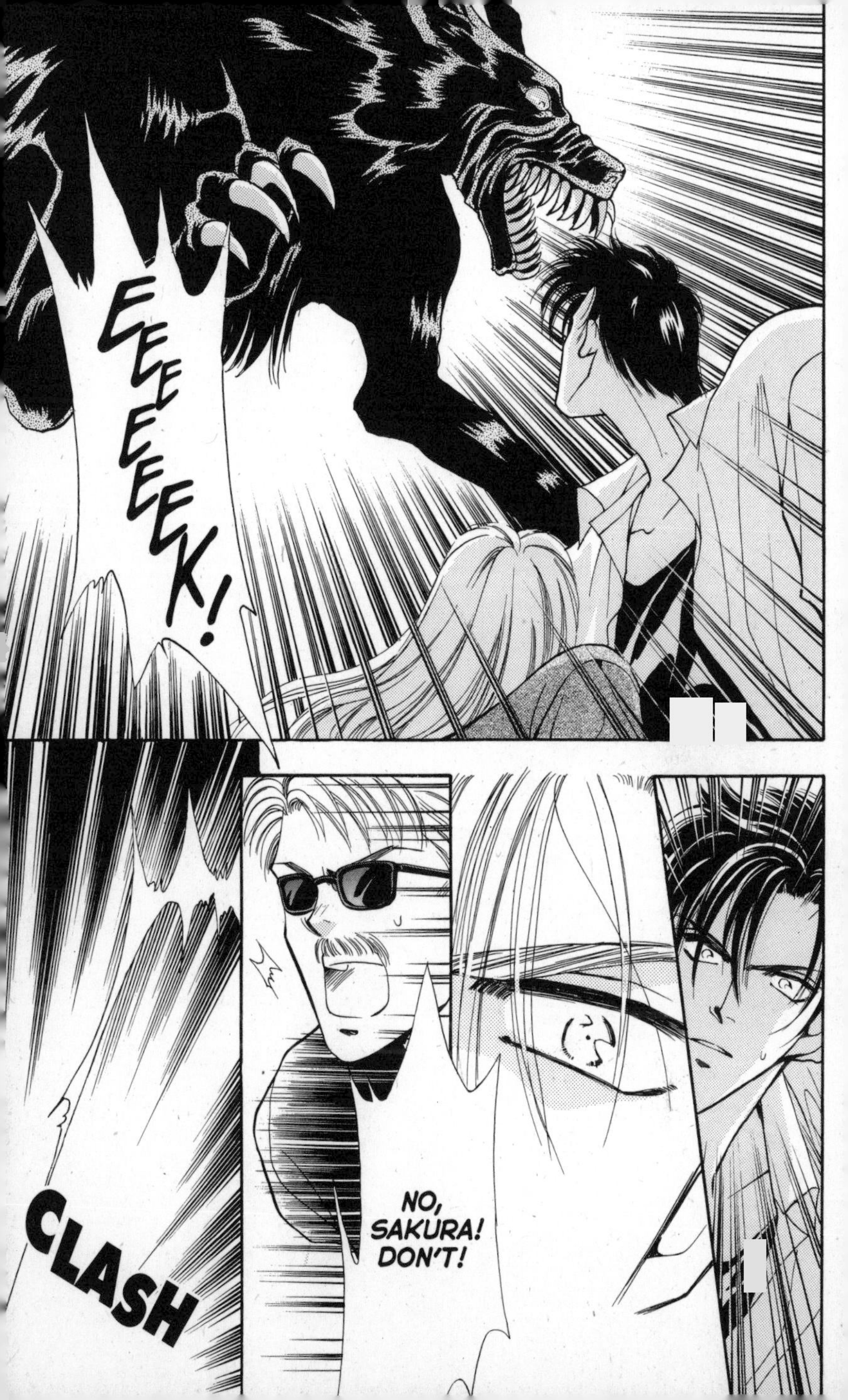
EEEEEEK!
NO, SAKURA! DON'T!
CLASH

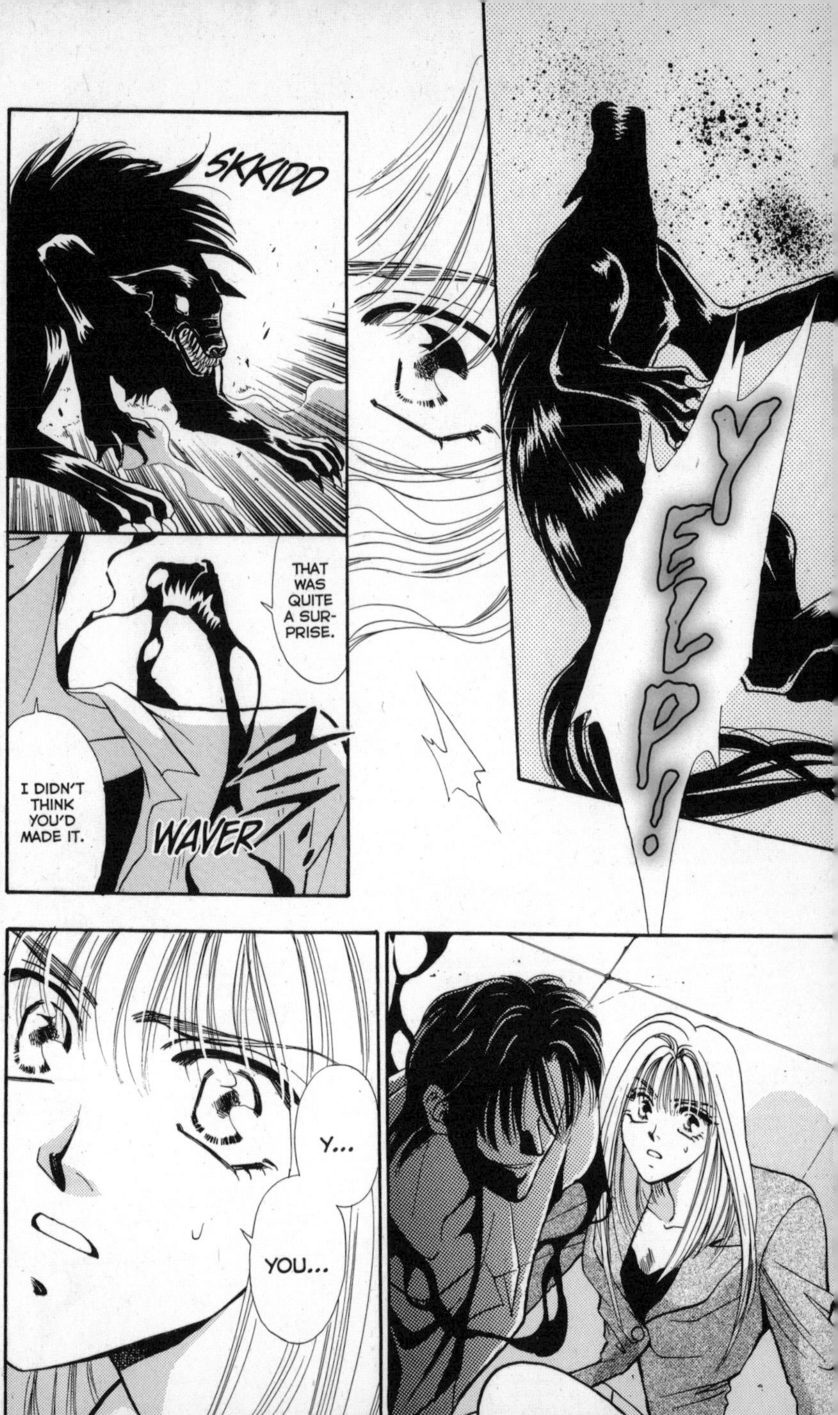
YELP!
SKKIDD
THAT WAS QUITE A SUR-PRISE.
I DIDN'T THINK YOU'D MADE IT.
WAVER
Y...
YOU...

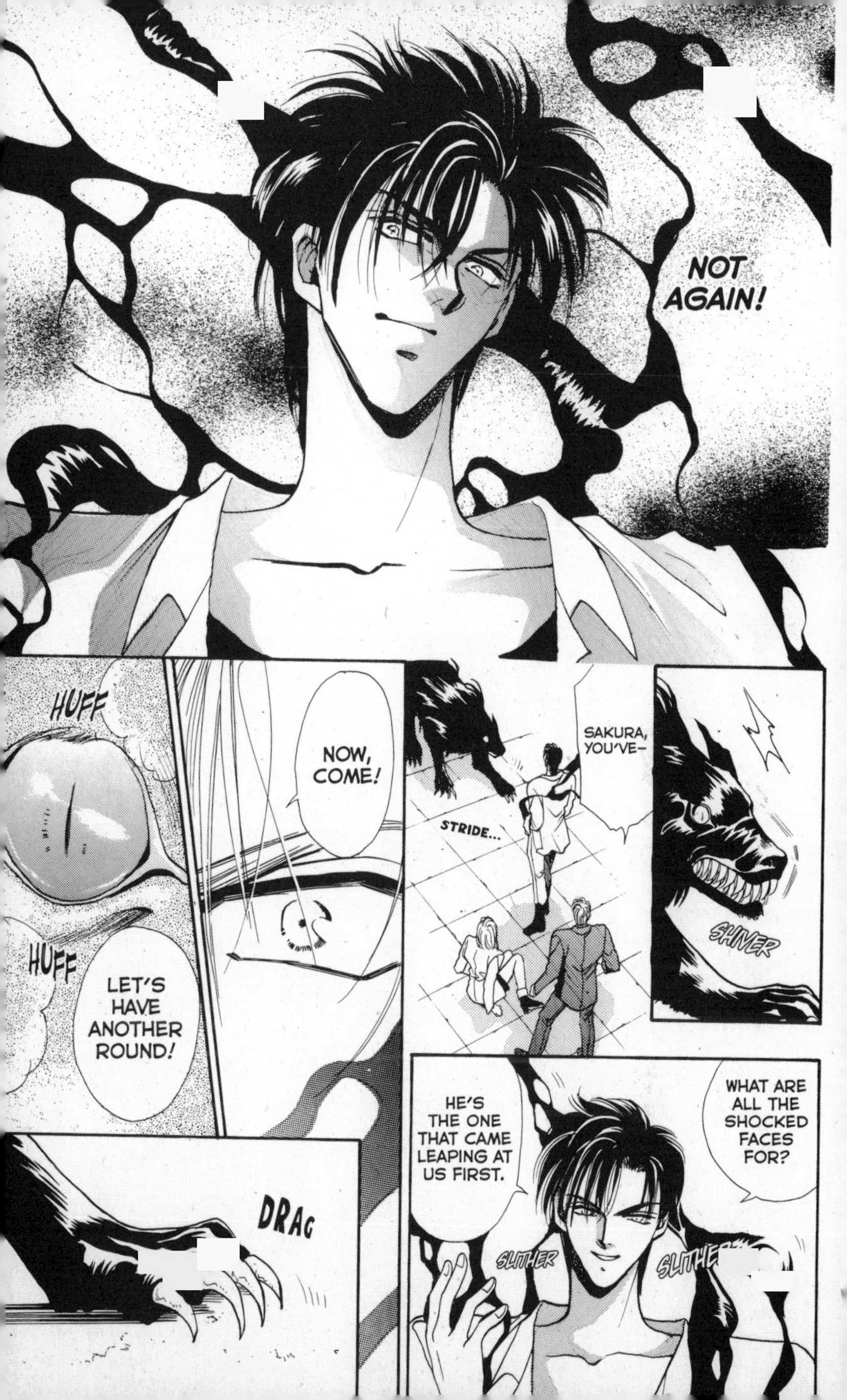
NOT AGAIN!
SHIVER
SAKURA, YOU'VE–
STRIDE...
NOW, COME!
HUFF
HUFF
LET'S HAVE ANOTHER ROUND!
WHAT ARE ALL THE SHOCKED FACES FOR?
HE'S THE ONE THAT CAME LEAPING AT US FIRST.
SLITHER
SLITHER
DRAG

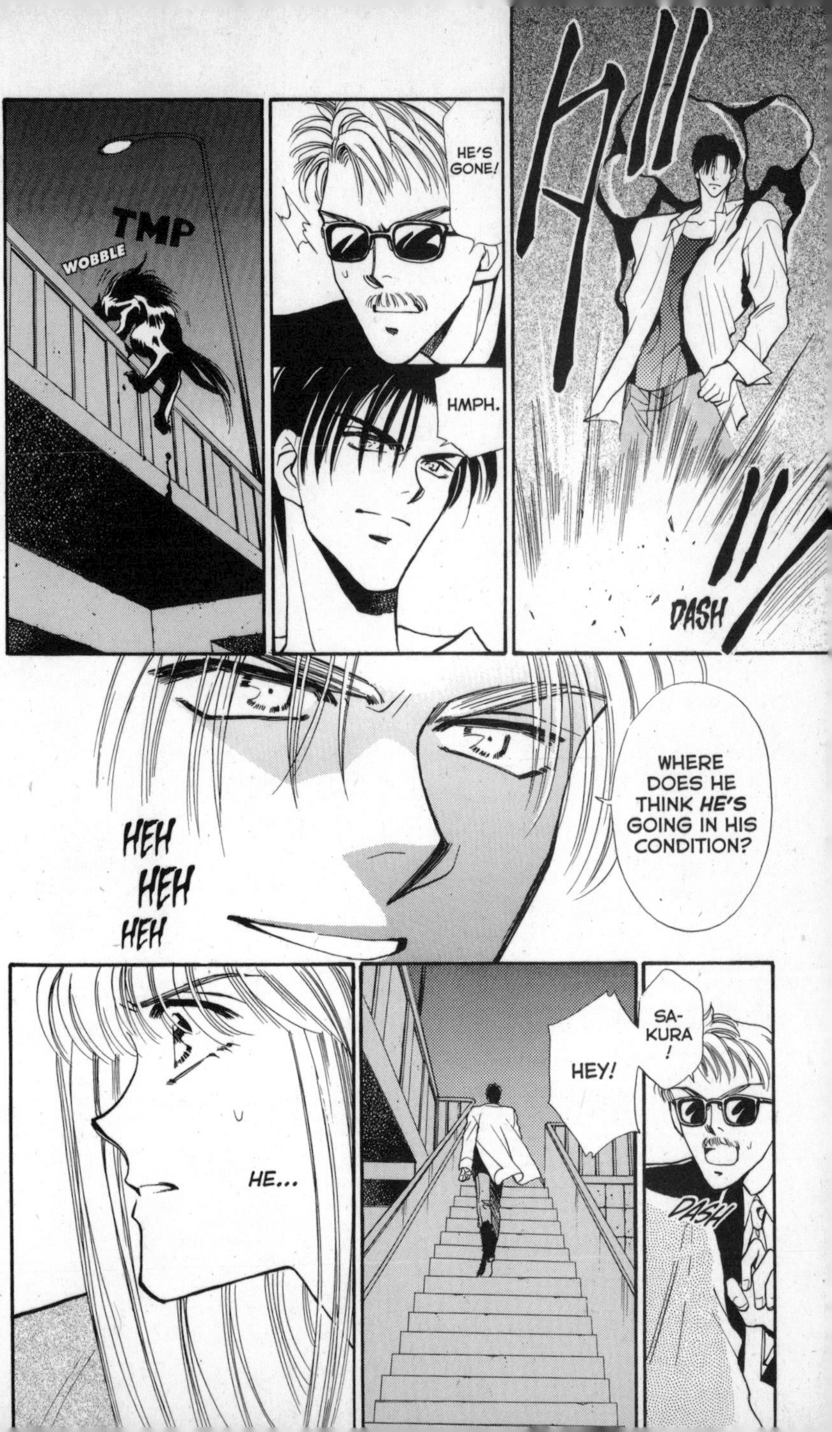
DASH
HE'S GONE!
HMPH.
TMP
WOBBLE
WHERE DOES HE THINK HE'S GOING IN HIS CONDITION?
HEH HEH HEH
SA-KURA!
HEY!
DASH
HE...

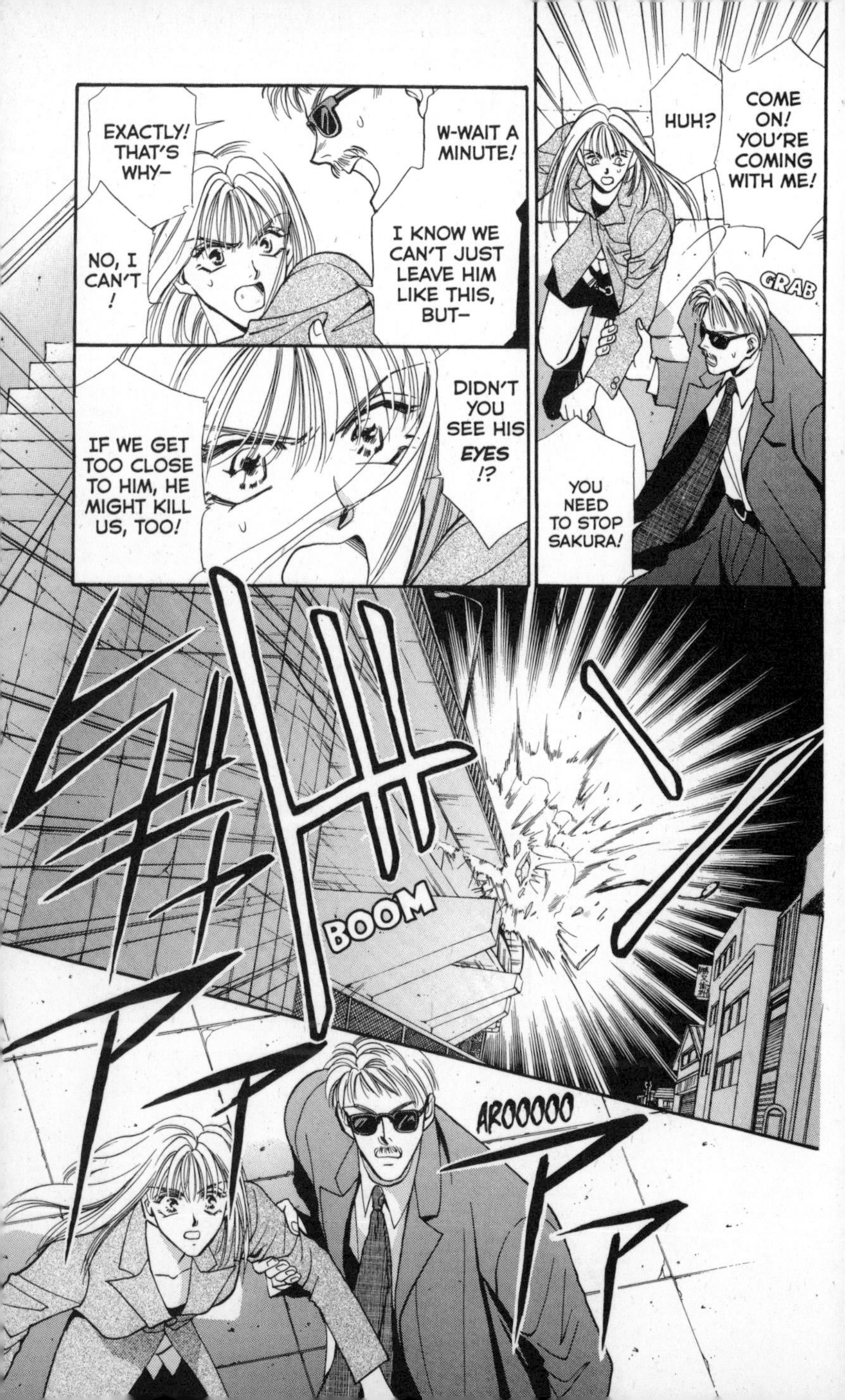
COME ON! YOU'RE COMING WITH ME!
HUH?
GRAB
YOU NEED TO STOP SAKURA!
W-WAIT A MINUTE!
EXACTLY! THAT'S WHY–
I KNOW WE CAN'T JUST LEAVE HIM LIKE THIS, BUT–
NO, I CAN'T!
DIDN'T YOU SEE HIS *EYES* !?
IF WE GET TOO CLOSE TO HIM, HE MIGHT KILL US, TOO!
BOOM
AROOOOO

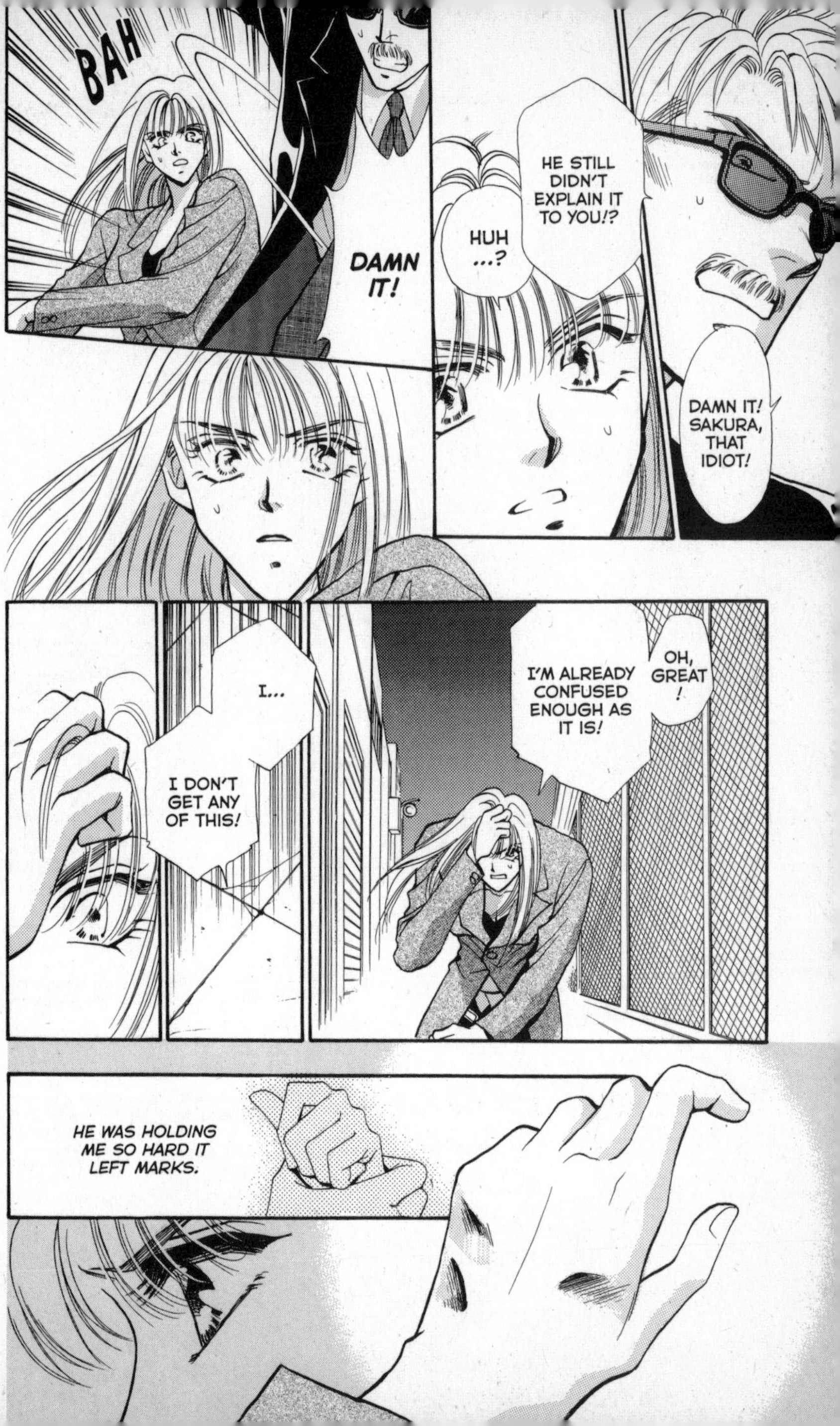
HE STILL DIDN'T EXPLAIN IT TO YOU!?
HUH ...?
DAMN IT! SAKURA, THAT IDIOT!
BAH
DAMN IT!
OH, GREAT!
I'M ALREADY CONFUSED ENOUGH AS IT IS!
I...
I DON'T GET ANY OF THIS!
HE WAS HOLDING ME SO HARD IT LEFT MARKS.

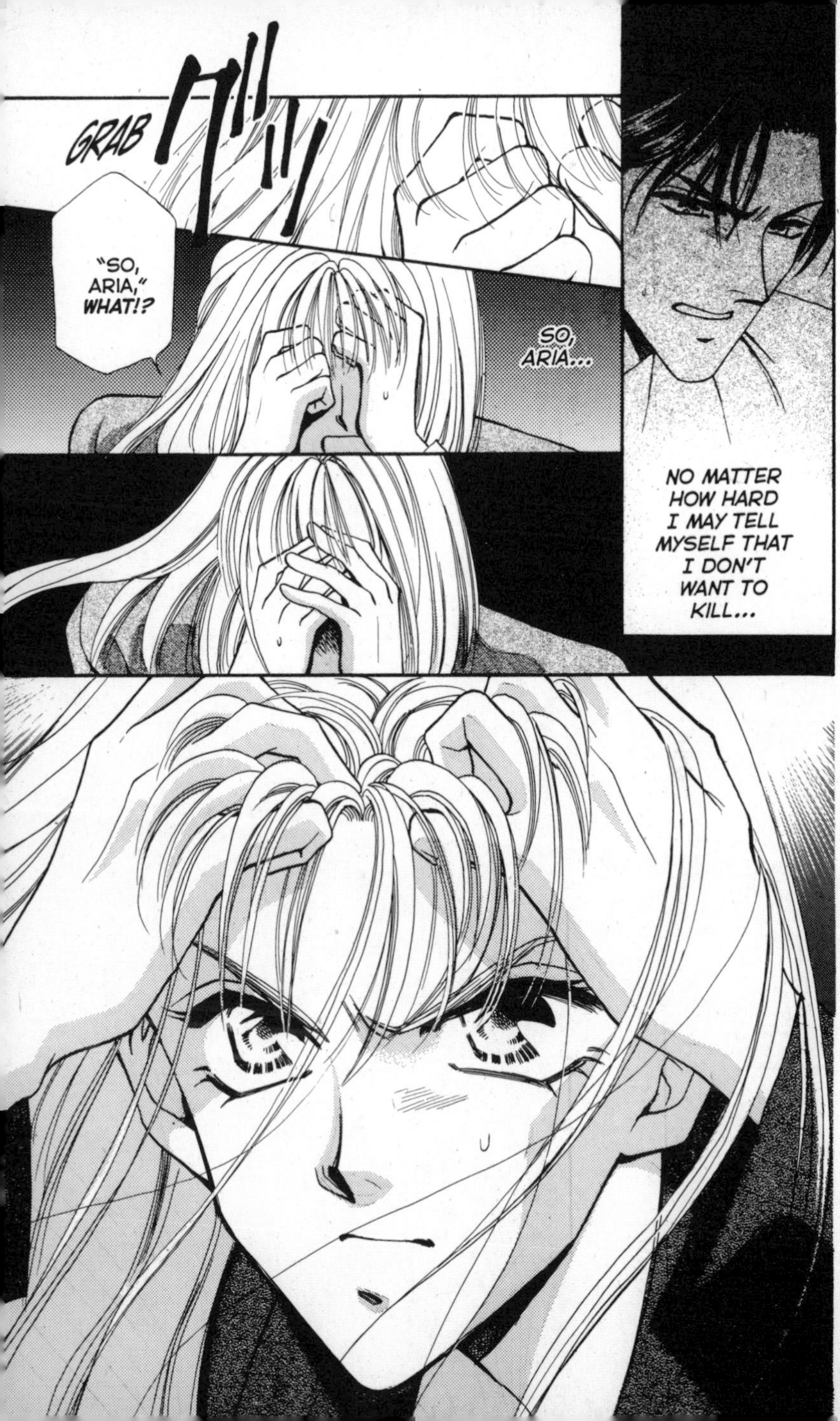
NO MATTER HOW HARD I MAY TELL MYSELF THAT I DON'T WANT TO KILL...
GRAB
SO, ARIA...
"SO, ARIA," WHAT!?

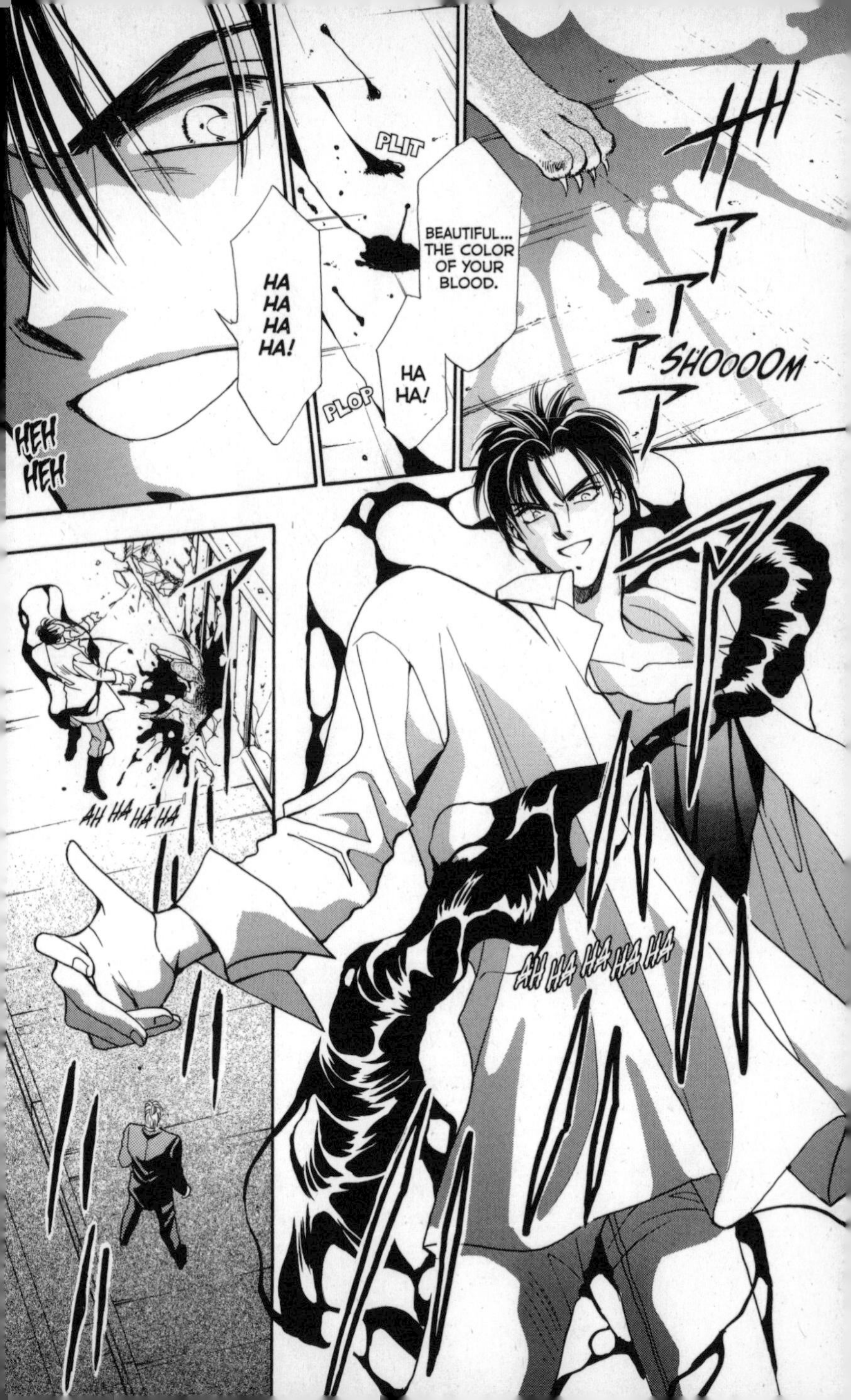

SHOOOOM
PLIT
BEAUTIFUL... THE COLOR OF YOUR BLOOD.
PLOP
HA HA!
HA HA HA HA!
HEH HEH
AH HA HA HA HA
AH HA HA HA

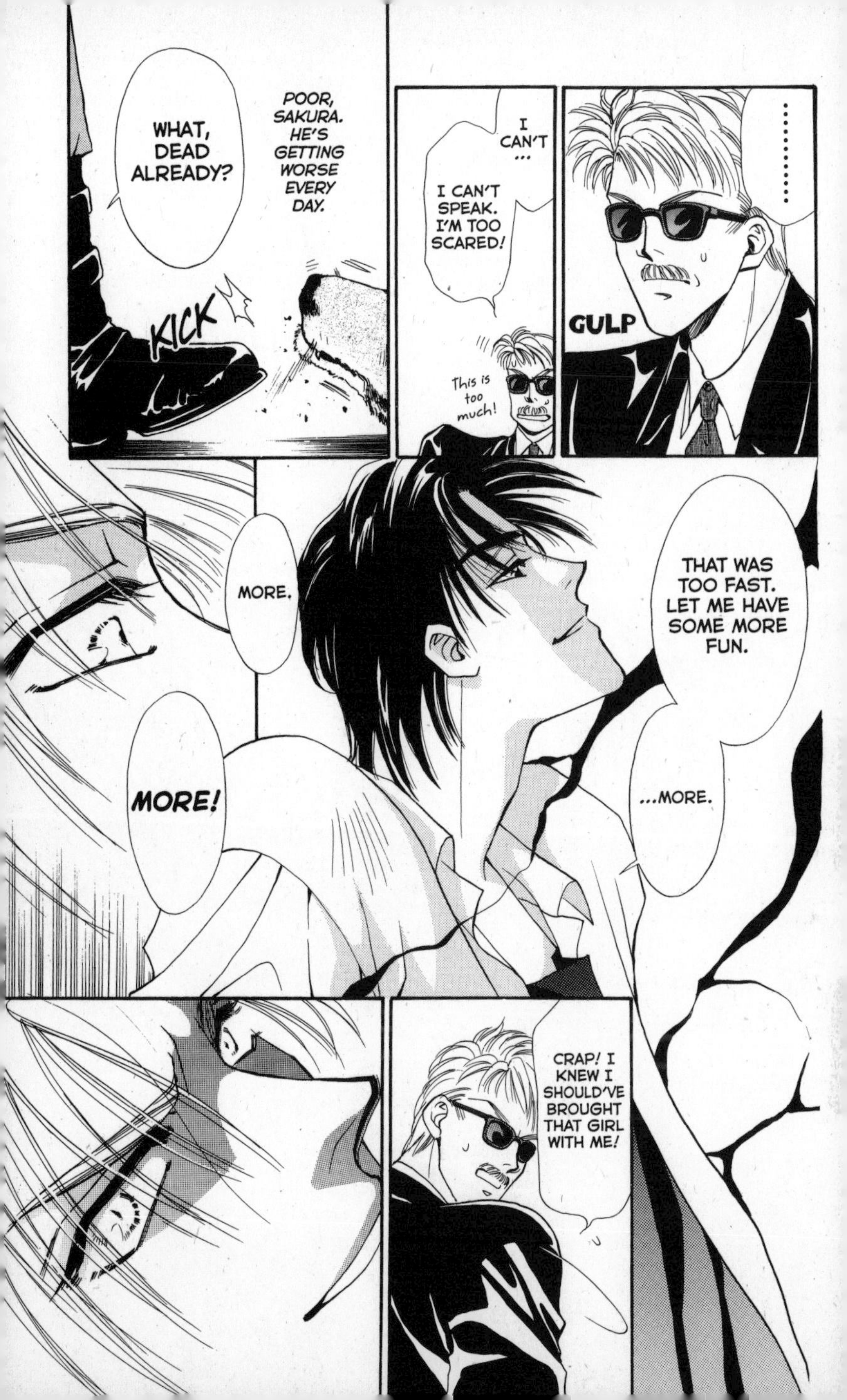

......
GULP
I CAN'T ...
I CAN'T SPEAK. I'M TOO SCARED!
This is too much!
POOR, SAKURA. HE'S GETTING WORSE EVERY DAY.
WHAT, DEAD ALREADY?
KICK
THAT WAS TOO FAST. LET ME HAVE SOME MORE FUN.
...MORE.
MORE.
MORE!
CRAP! I KNEW I SHOULD'VE BROUGHT THAT GIRL WITH ME!

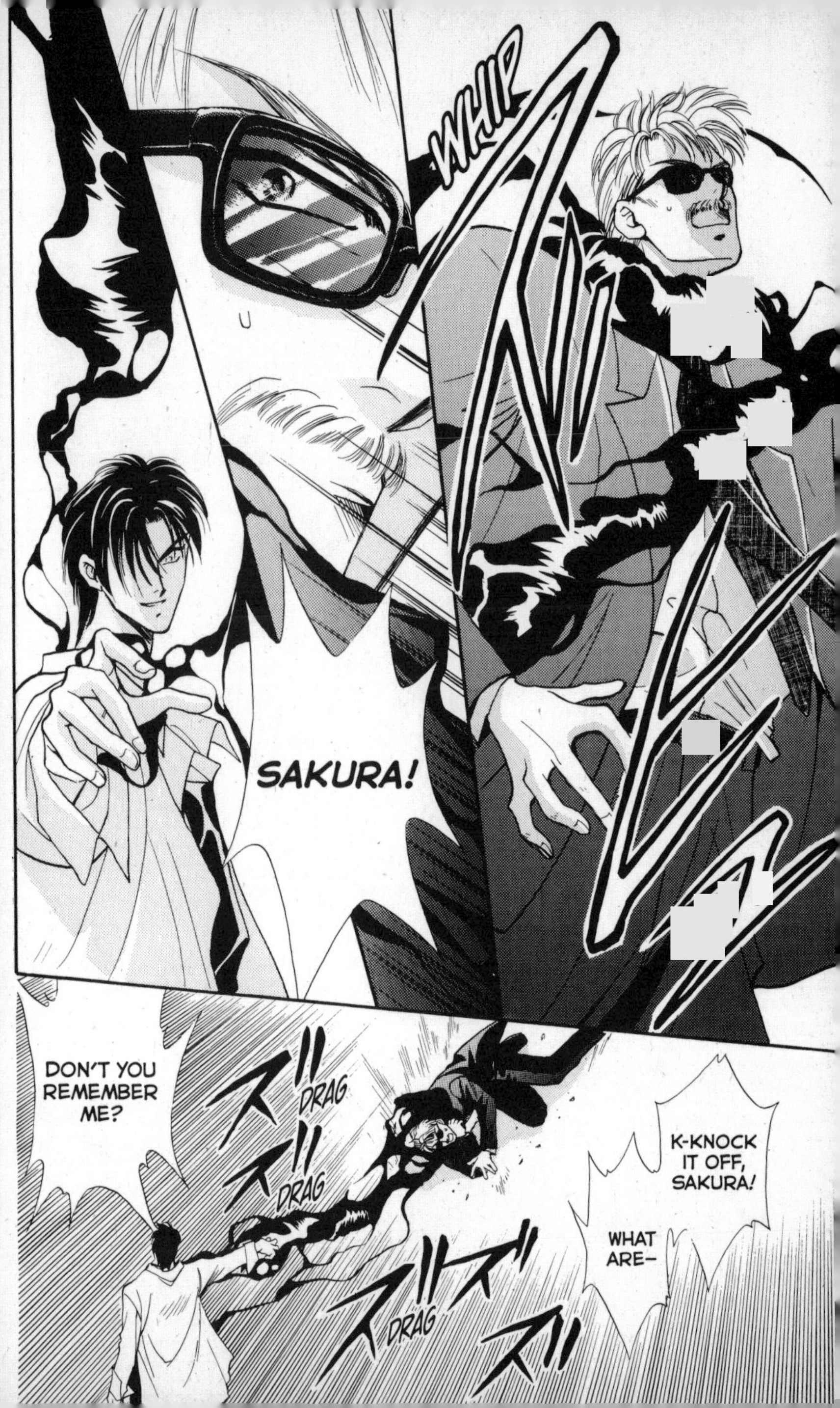
WHIP
SAKURA!
K-KNOCK IT OFF, SAKURA!
WHAT ARE—
DRAG
DRAG
DRAG
DON'T YOU REMEMBER ME?

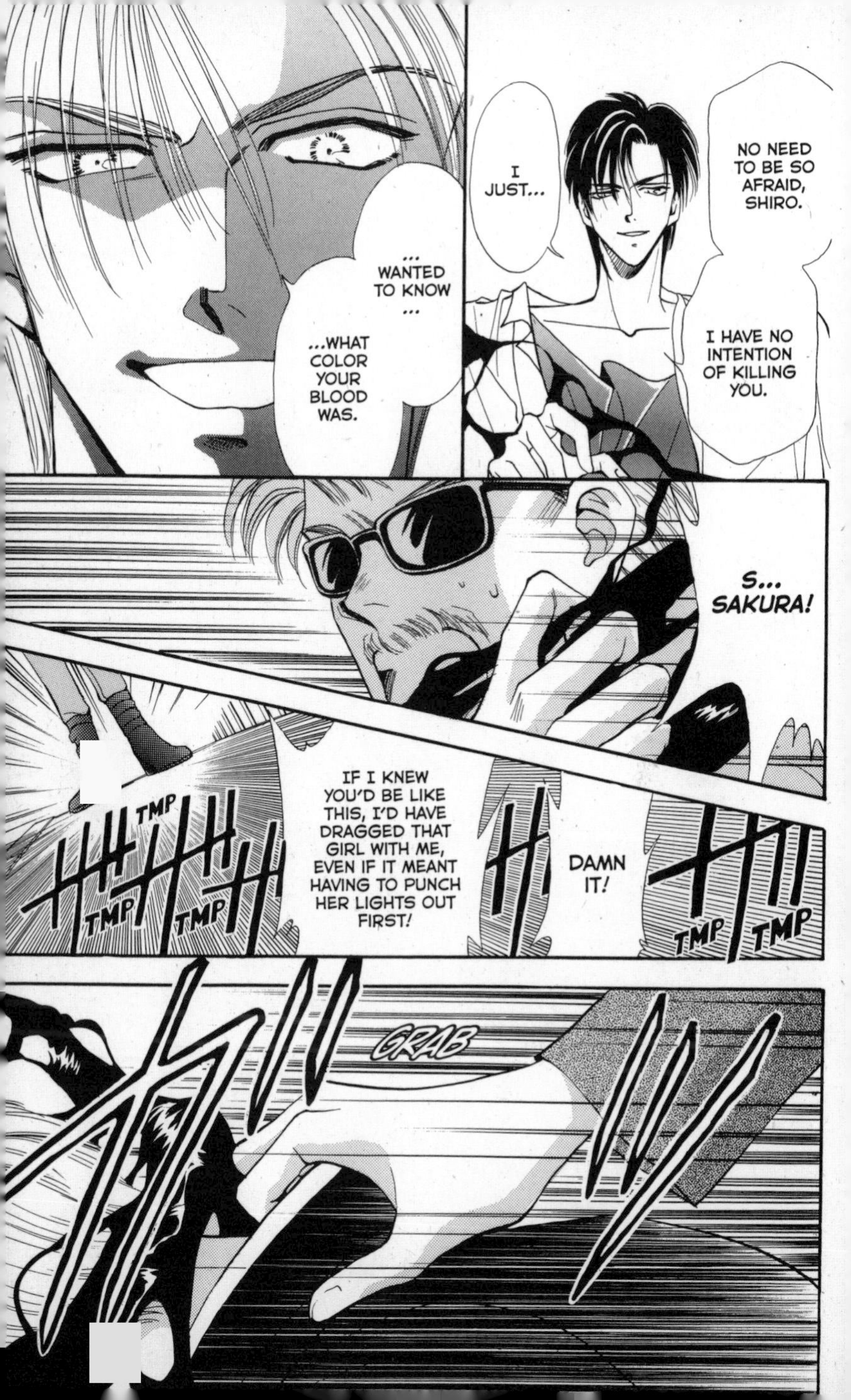
NO NEED TO BE SO AFRAID, SHIRO.
I HAVE NO INTENTION OF KILLING YOU.
I JUST...
...WANTED TO KNOW...
...WHAT COLOR YOUR BLOOD WAS.
S... SAKURA!
TMP TMP
DAMN IT!
IF I KNEW YOU'D BE LIKE THIS, I'D HAVE DRAGGED THAT GIRL WITH ME, EVEN IF IT MEANT HAVING TO PUNCH HER LIGHTS OUT FIRST!
TMP TMP TMP
GRAB

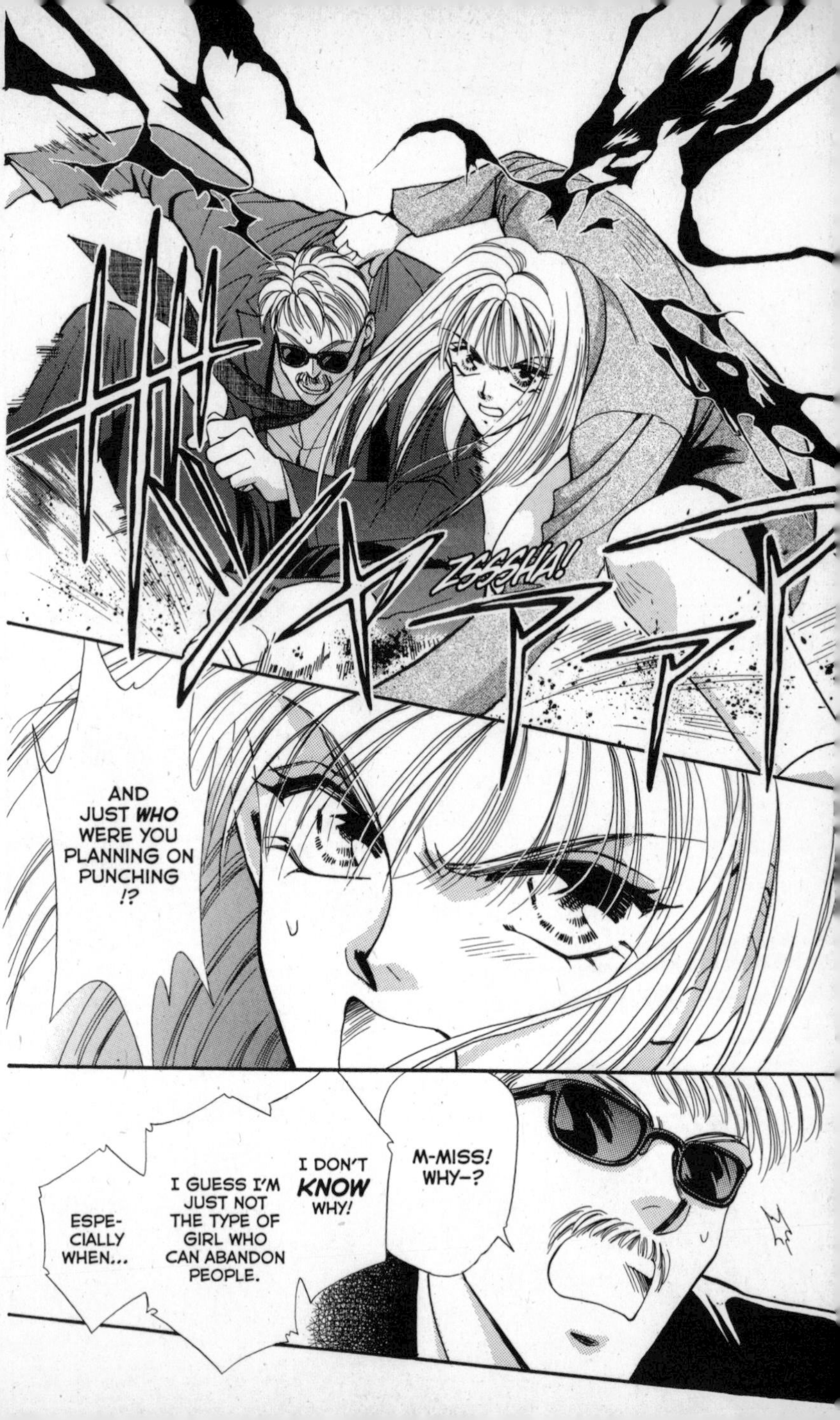
ZSSHA!
AND JUST WHO WERE YOU PLANNING ON PUNCHING !?
M-MISS! WHY–?
I DON'T KNOW WHY!
I GUESS I'M JUST NOT THE TYPE OF GIRL WHO CAN ABANDON PEOPLE.
ESPE- CIALLY WHEN...

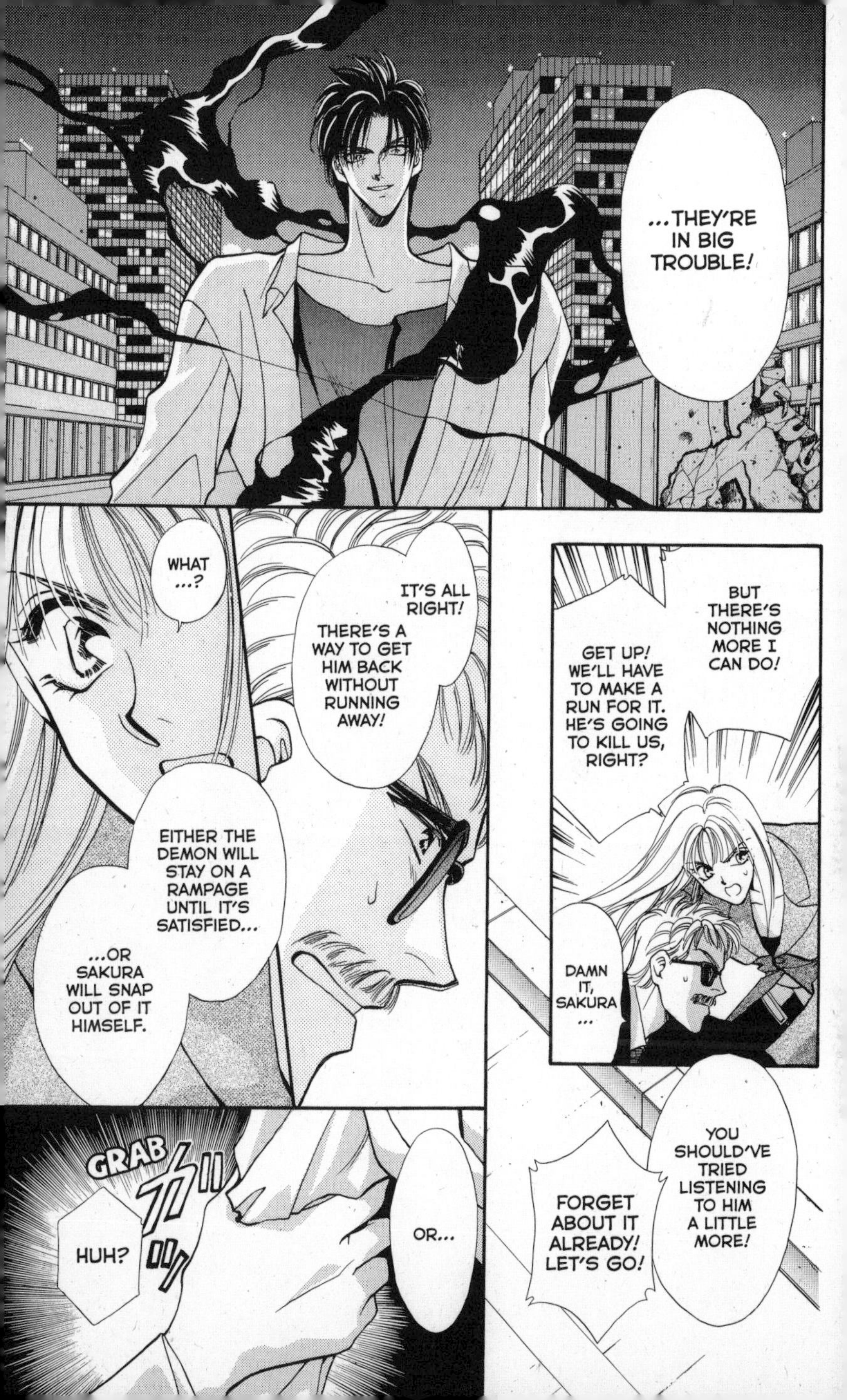
...THEY'RE IN BIG TROUBLE!
BUT THERE'S NOTHING MORE I CAN DO!
GET UP! WE'LL HAVE TO MAKE A RUN FOR IT. HE'S GOING TO KILL US, RIGHT?
DAMN IT, SAKURA ...
YOU SHOULD'VE TRIED LISTENING TO HIM A LITTLE MORE!
FORGET ABOUT IT ALREADY! LET'S GO!
IT'S ALL RIGHT!
THERE'S A WAY TO GET HIM BACK WITHOUT RUNNING AWAY!
WHAT ...?
EITHER THE DEMON WILL STAY ON A RAMPAGE UNTIL IT'S SATISFIED...
...OR SAKURA WILL SNAP OUT OF IT HIMSELF.
OR...
GRAB
HUH?

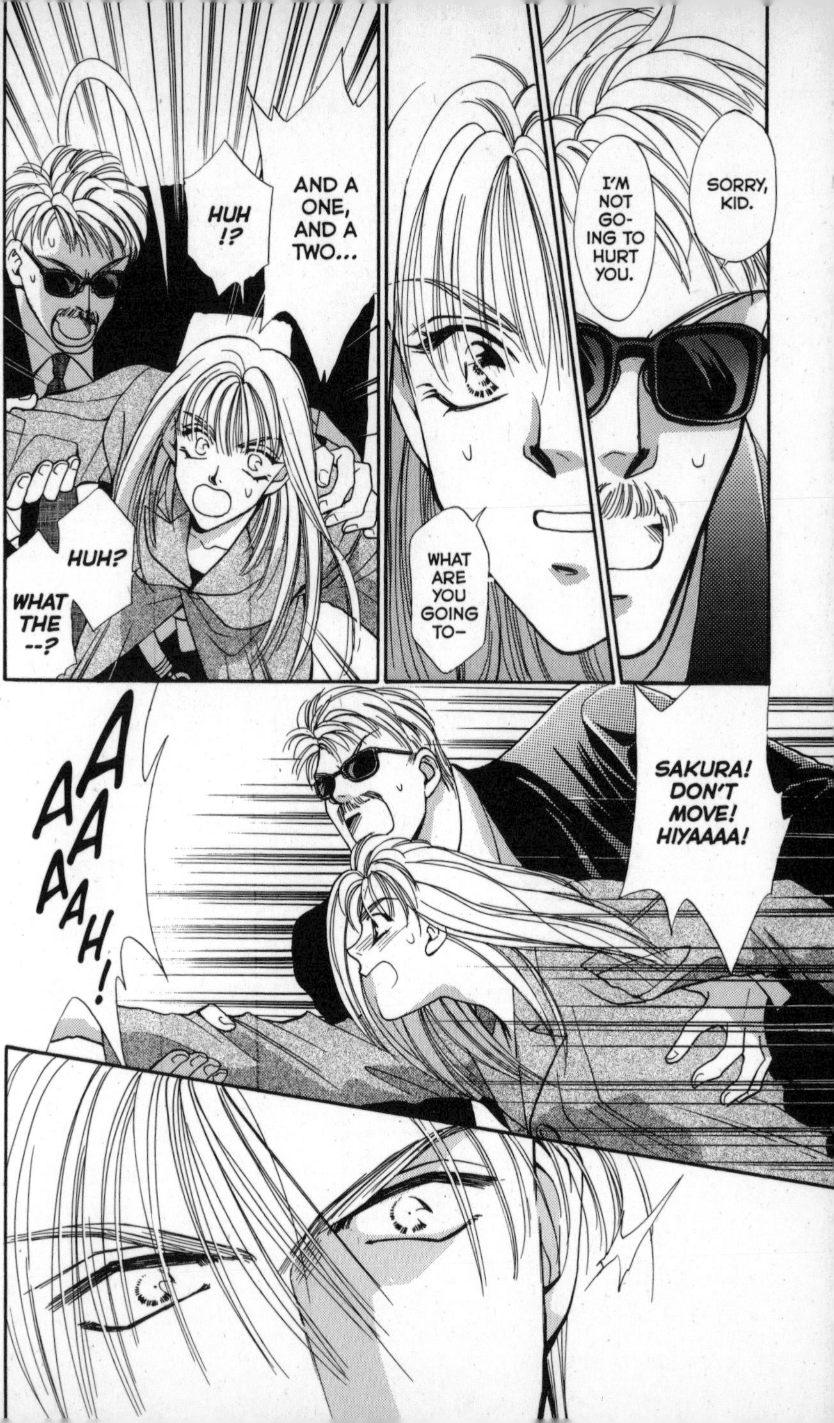
SORRY, KID.
I'M NOT GOING TO HURT YOU.
WHAT ARE YOU GOING TO–
AND A ONE, AND A TWO...
HUH !?
HUH? WHAT THE --?
SAKURA! DON'T MOVE! HIYAAAA!
AAAAAAH!

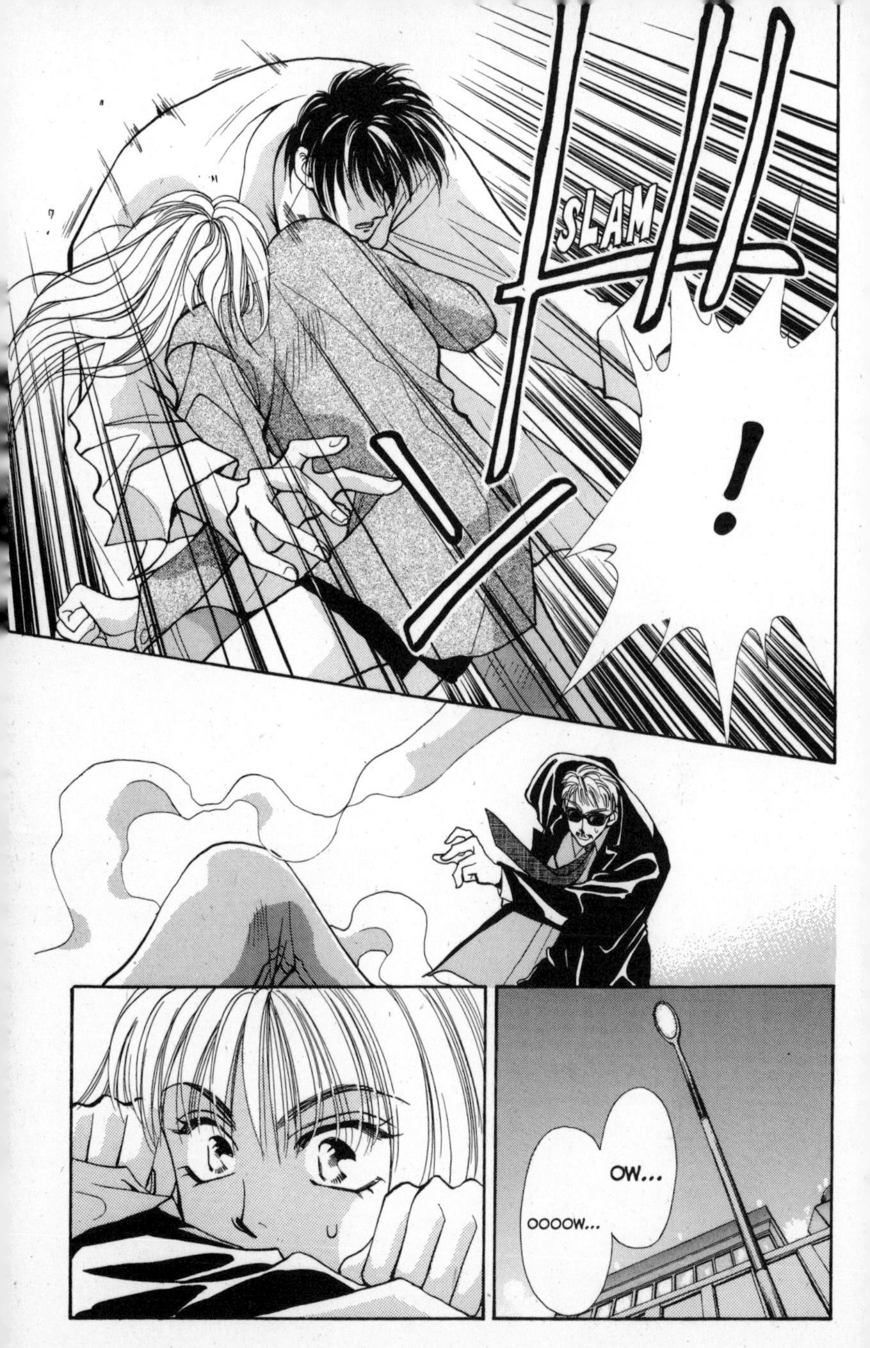
SLAM
!
OW...
OOOOW...

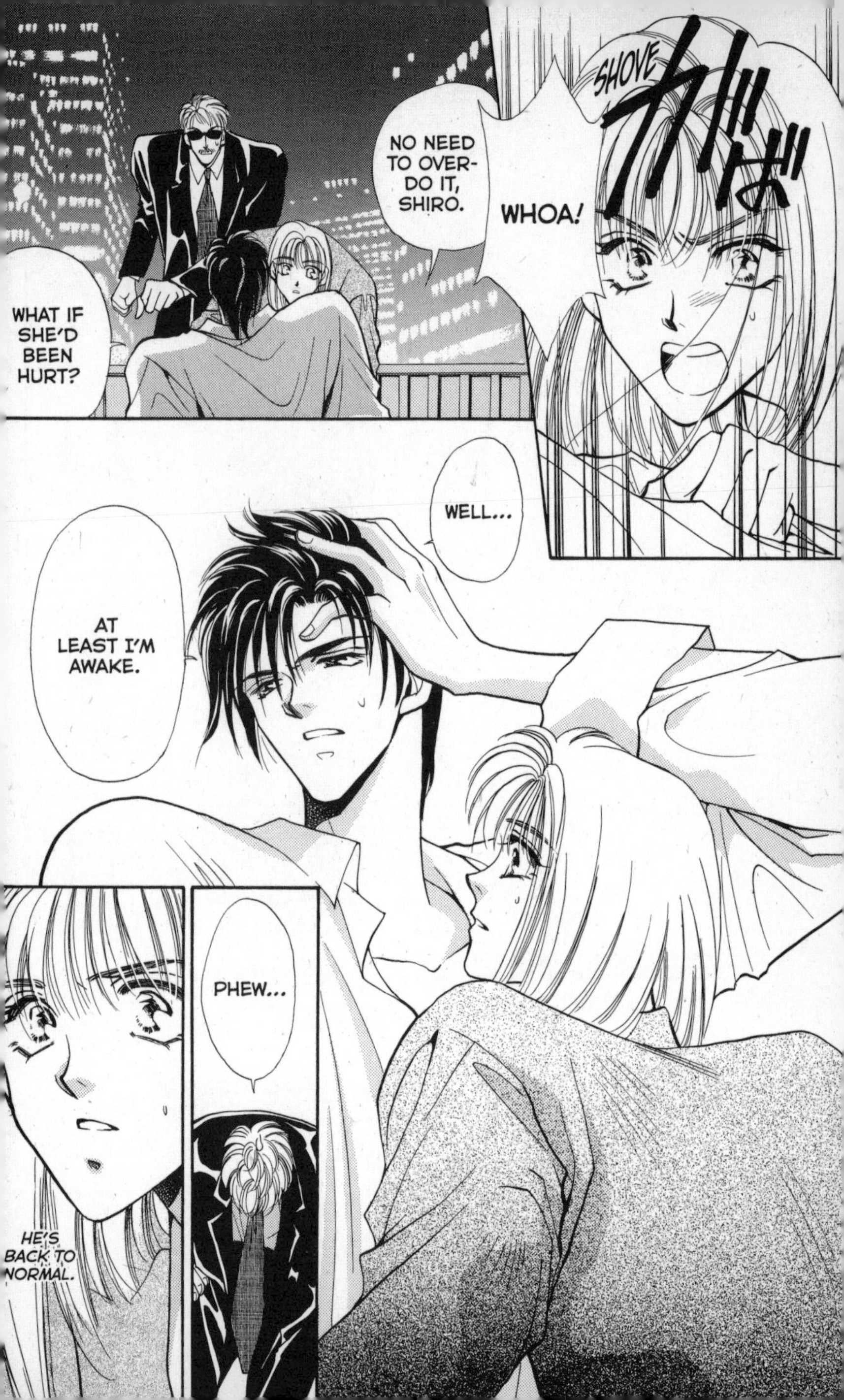
SHOVE
WHOA!
NO NEED TO OVER-DO IT, SHIRO.
WHAT IF SHE'D BEEN HURT?
WELL...
AT LEAST I'M AWAKE.
PHEW...
HE'S BACK TO NORMAL.

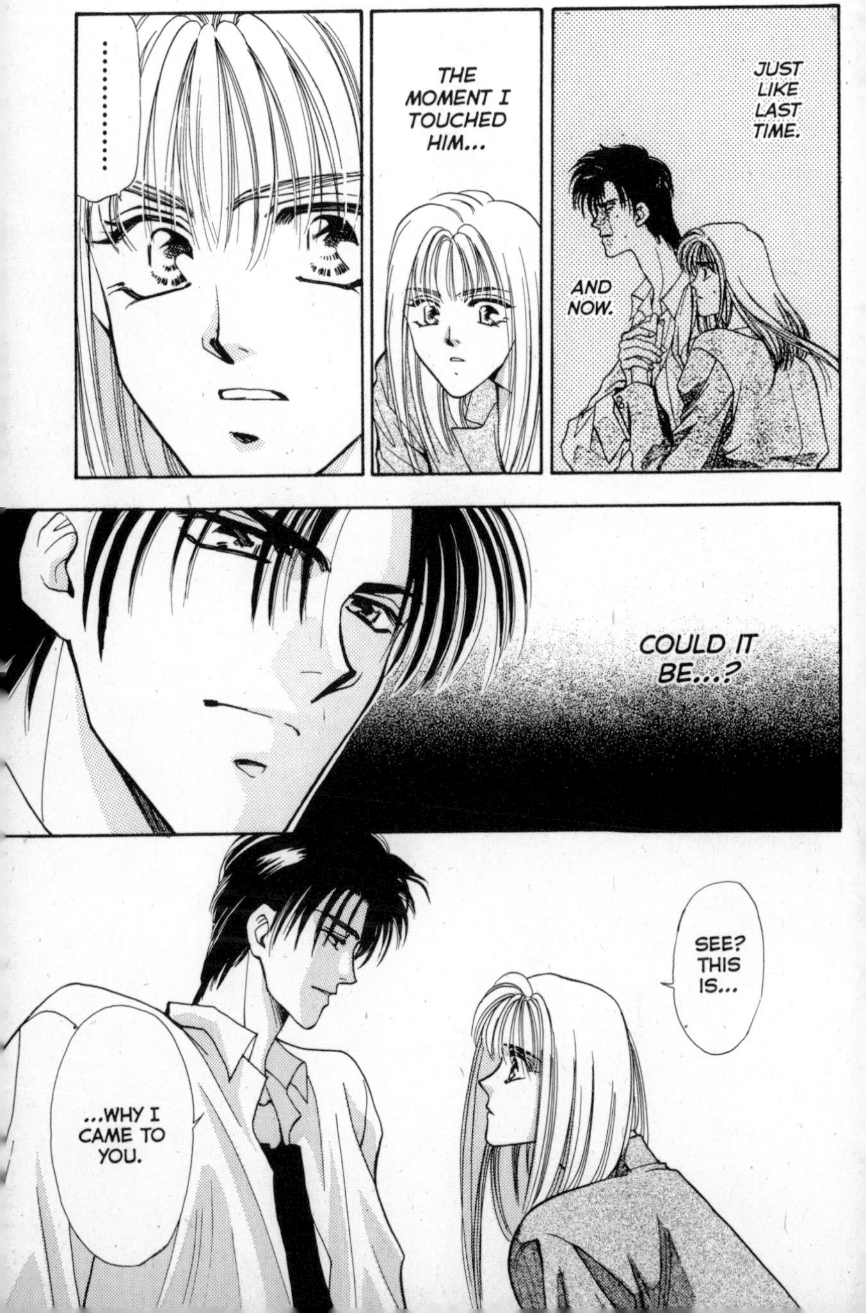
JUST LIKE LAST TIME.
AND NOW.
THE MOMENT I TOUCHED HIM...
......
COULD IT BE...?
SEE? THIS IS...
...WHY I CAME TO YOU.

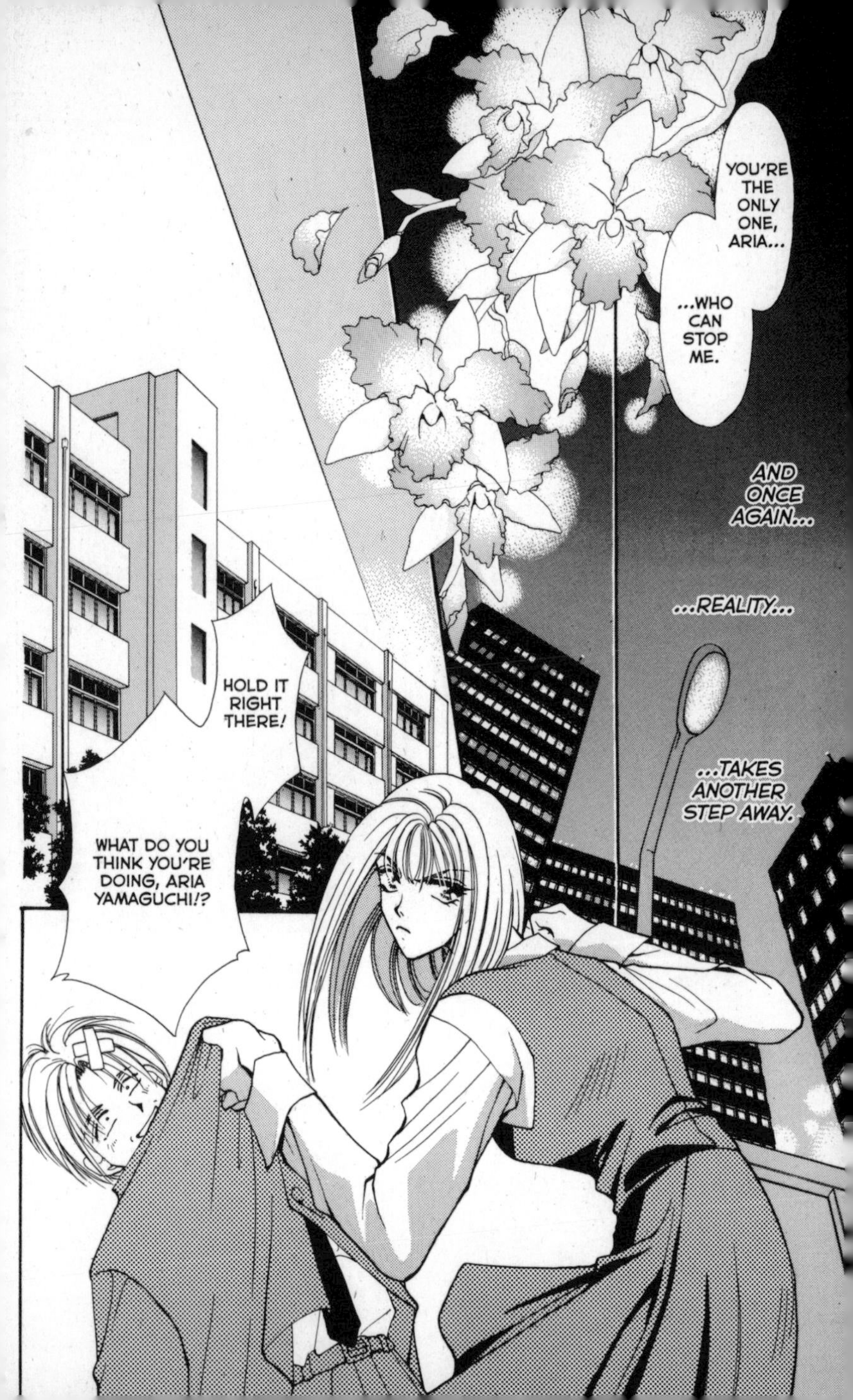
YOU'RE THE ONLY ONE, ARIA...
...WHO CAN STOP ME.
AND ONCE AGAIN...
...REALITY...
...TAKES ANOTHER STEP AWAY.
HOLD IT RIGHT THERE!
WHAT DO YOU THINK YOU'RE DOING, ARIA YAMAGUCHI!?

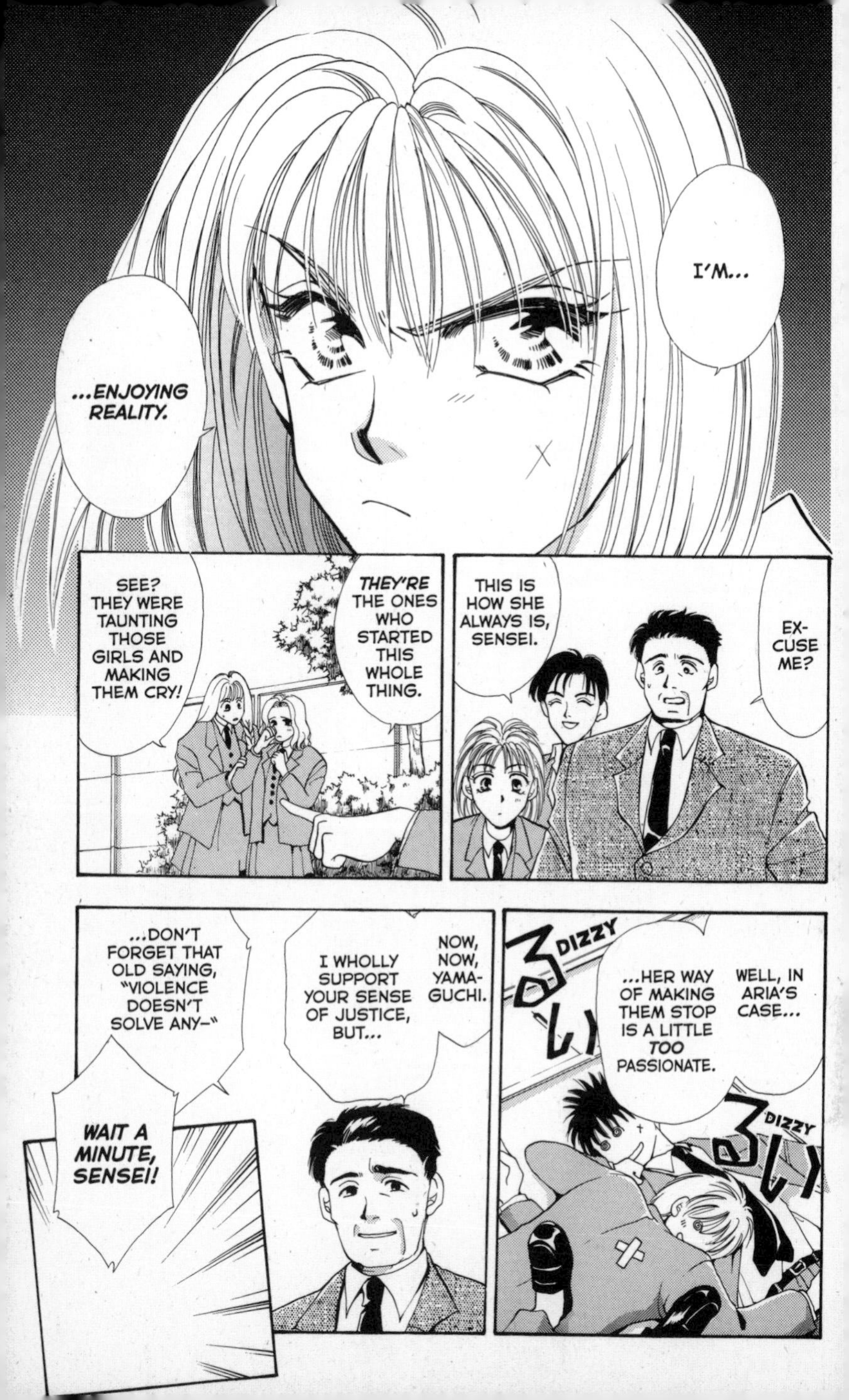
I'M...
...ENJOYING REALITY.
EX-CUSE ME?
THIS IS HOW SHE ALWAYS IS, SENSEI.
THEY'RE THE ONES WHO STARTED THIS WHOLE THING.
SEE? THEY WERE TAUNTING THOSE GIRLS AND MAKING THEM CRY!
WELL, IN ARIA'S CASE...
...HER WAY OF MAKING THEM STOP IS A LITTLE *TOO* PASSIONATE.
DIZZY
DIZZY
NOW, NOW, YAMA-GUCHI.
I WHOLLY SUPPORT YOUR SENSE OF JUSTICE, BUT...
...DON'T FORGET THAT OLD SAYING, "VIOLENCE DOESN'T SOLVE ANY–"
WAIT A MINUTE, SENSEI!

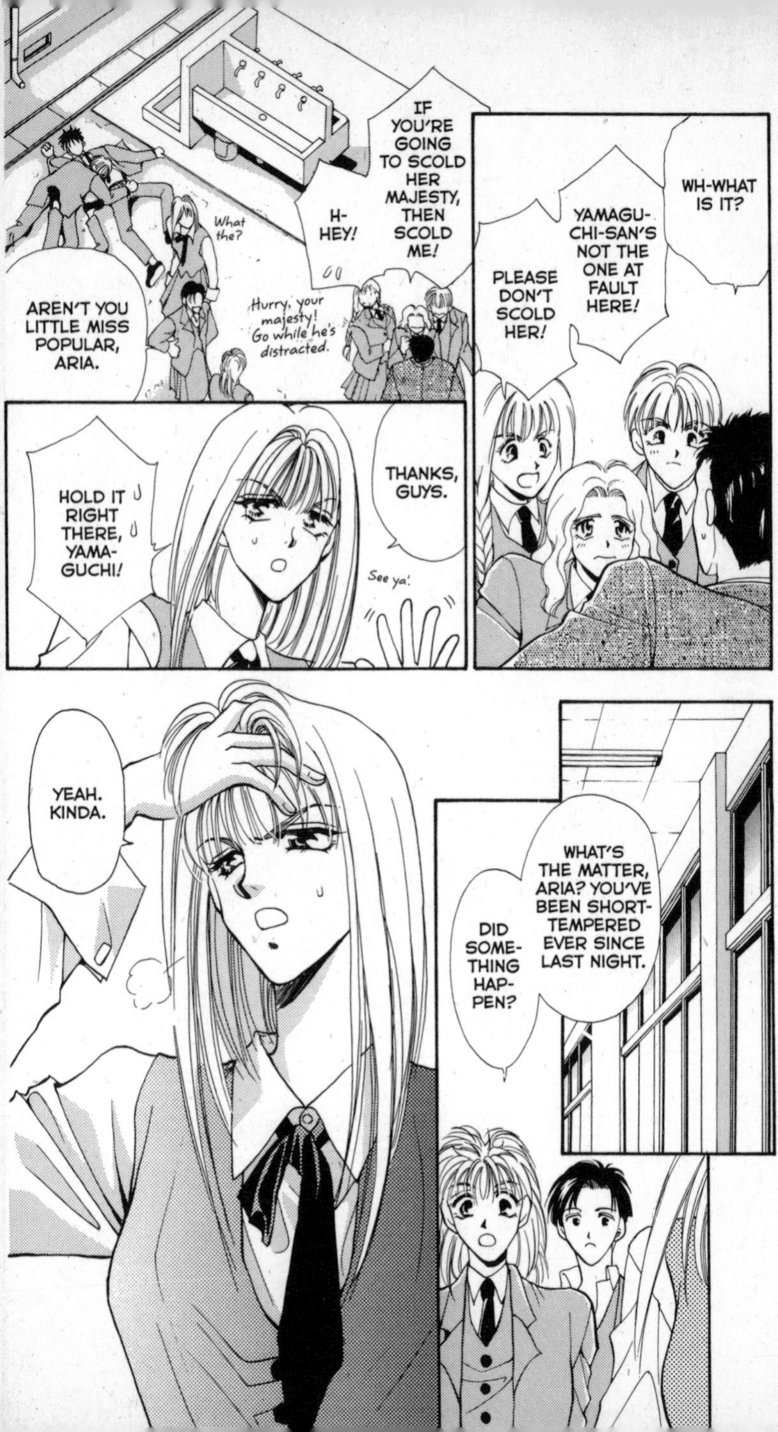

WH-WHAT IS IT?
YAMAGUCHI-SAN'S NOT THE ONE AT FAULT HERE!
PLEASE DON'T SCOLD HER!
IF YOU'RE GOING TO SCOLD HER MAJESTY, THEN SCOLD ME!
H-HEY!
What the?
Hurry, your majesty! Go while he's distracted.
AREN'T YOU LITTLE MISS POPULAR, ARIA.
THANKS, GUYS.
See ya!
HOLD IT RIGHT THERE, YAMAGUCHI!
WHAT'S THE MATTER, ARIA? YOU'VE BEEN SHORT-TEMPERED EVER SINCE LAST NIGHT.
DID SOMETHING HAPPEN?
YEAH. KINDA.

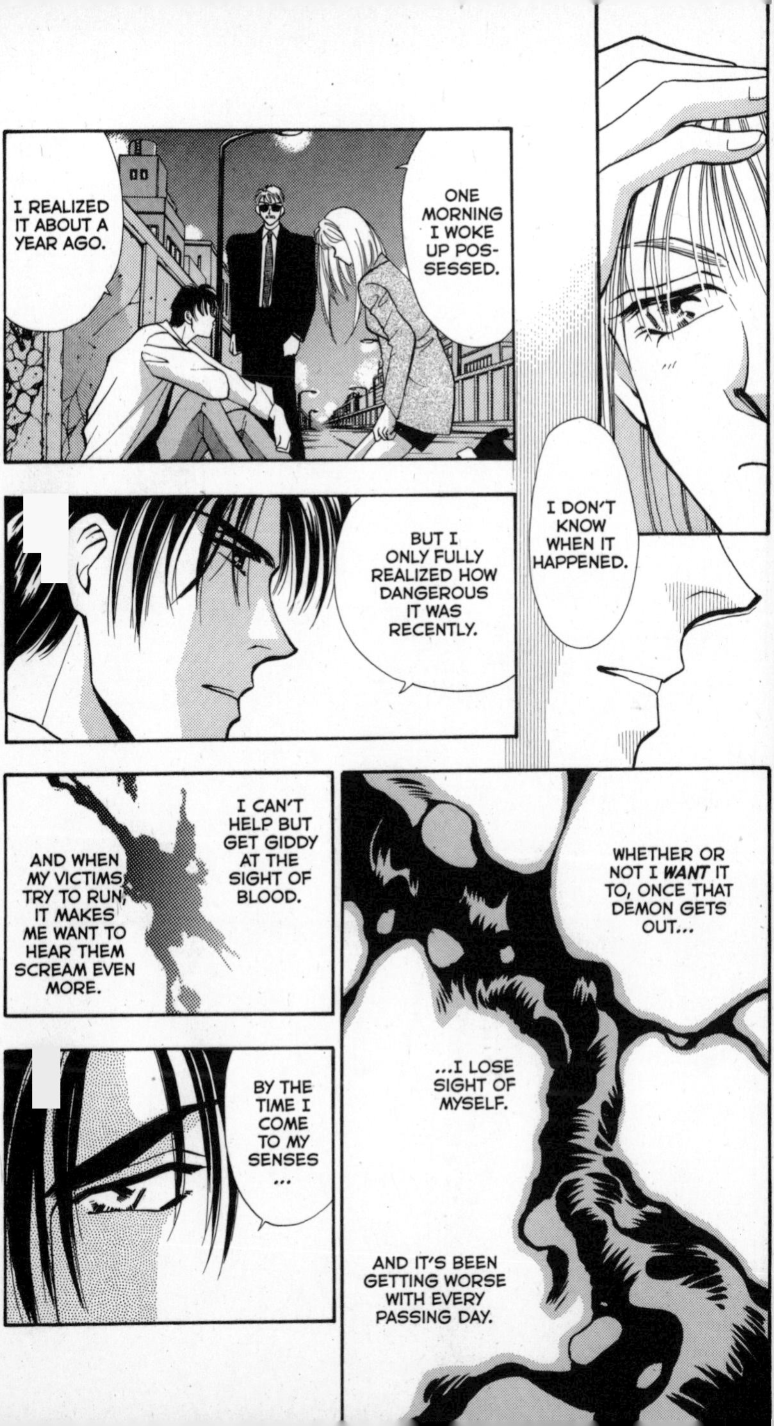
I DON'T KNOW WHEN IT HAPPENED.
ONE MORNING I WOKE UP POSSESSED.
I REALIZED IT ABOUT A YEAR AGO.
BUT I ONLY FULLY REALIZED HOW DANGEROUS IT WAS RECENTLY.
WHETHER OR NOT I *WANT* IT TO, ONCE THAT DEMON GETS OUT...
...I LOSE SIGHT OF MYSELF.
AND IT'S BEEN GETTING WORSE WITH EVERY PASSING DAY.
I CAN'T HELP BUT GET GIDDY AT THE SIGHT OF BLOOD.
AND WHEN MY VICTIMS TRY TO RUN, IT MAKES ME WANT TO HEAR THEM SCREAM EVEN MORE.
BY THE TIME I COME TO MY SENSES ...

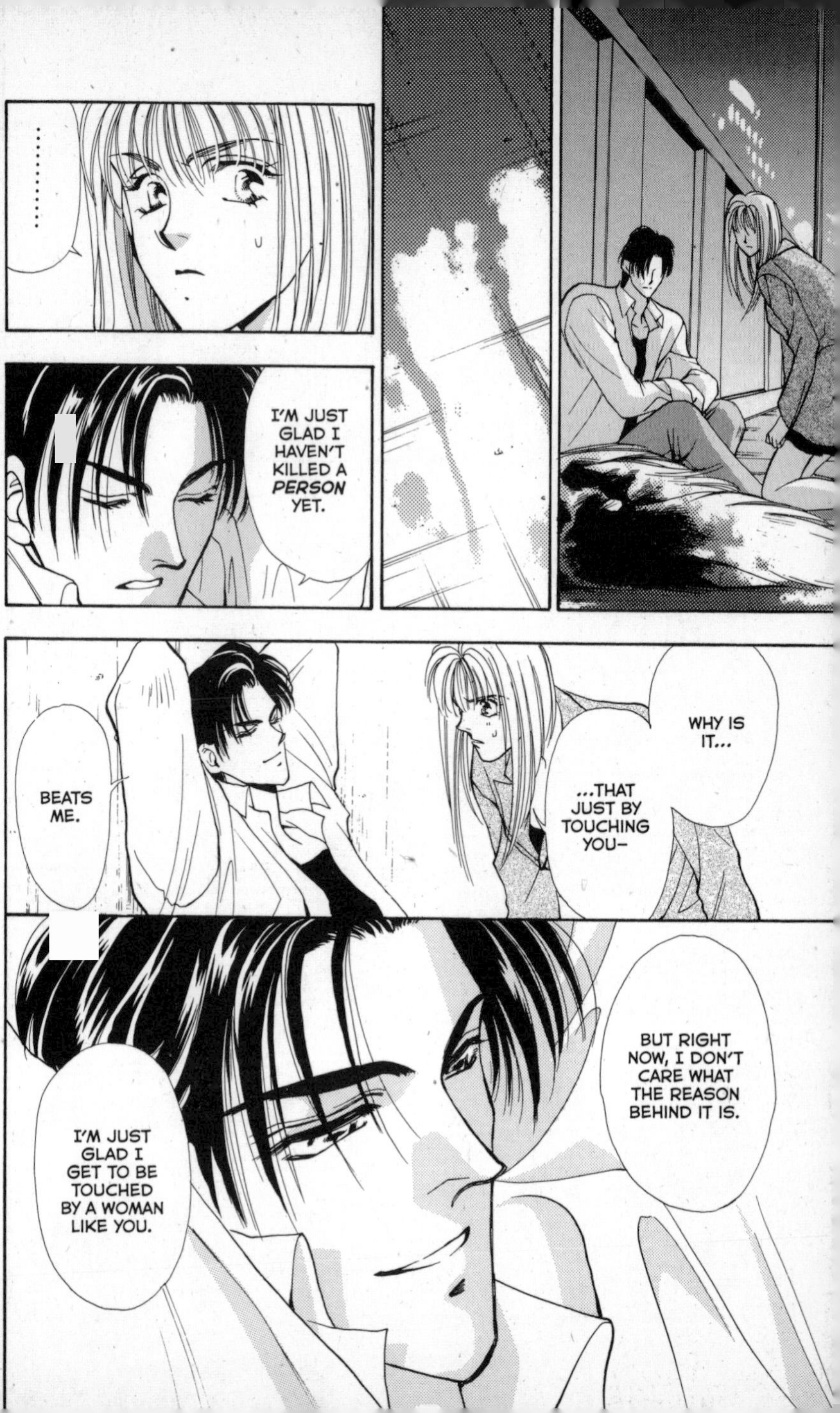
……
I'M JUST GLAD I HAVEN'T KILLED A *PERSON* YET.
WHY IS IT...
...THAT JUST BY TOUCHING YOU–
BEATS ME.
BUT RIGHT NOW, I DON'T CARE WHAT THE REASON BEHIND IT IS.
I'M JUST GLAD I GET TO BE TOUCHED BY A WOMAN LIKE YOU.

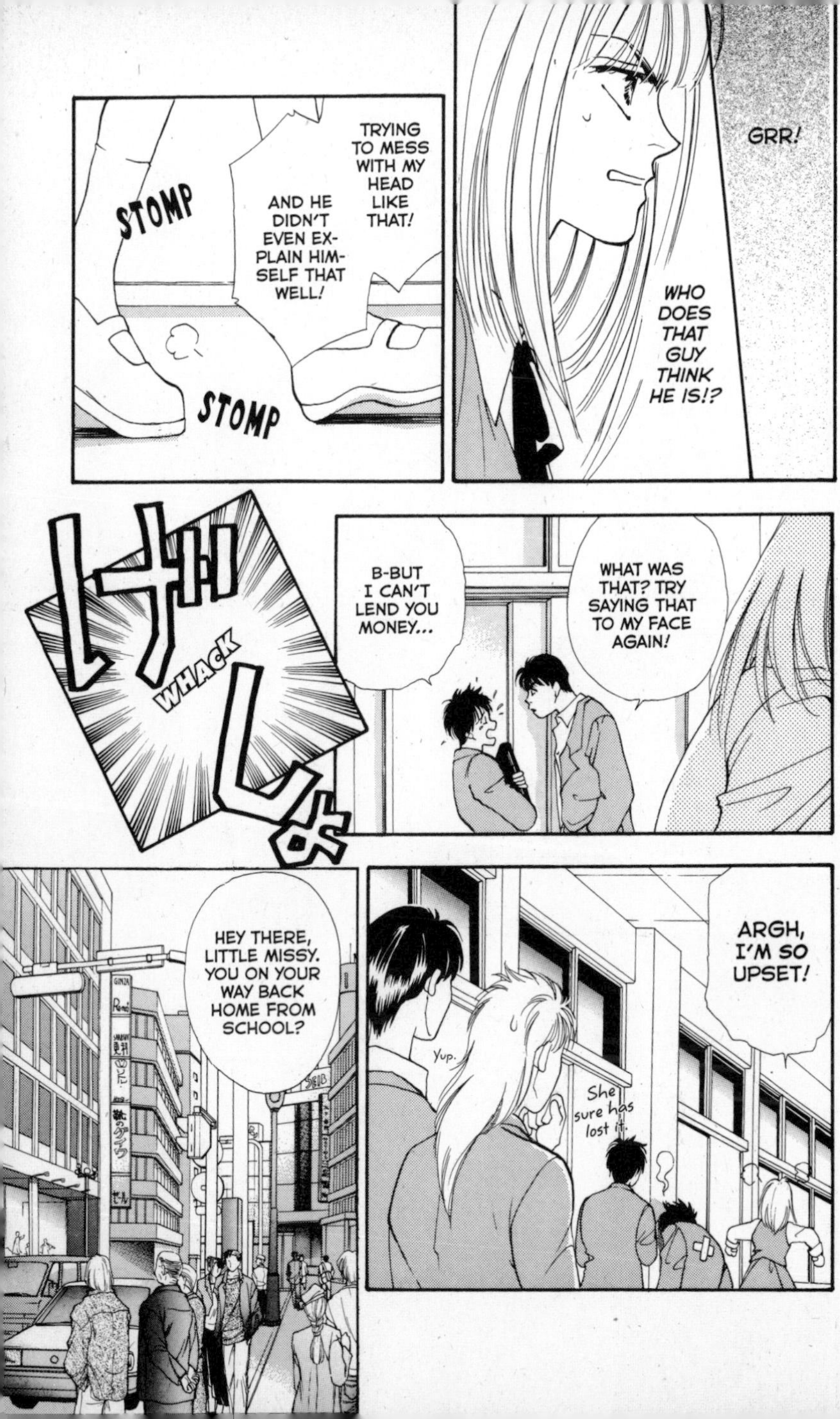
GRR!
WHO DOES THAT GUY THINK HE IS!?
TRYING TO MESS WITH MY HEAD LIKE THAT!
AND HE DIDN'T EVEN EX-PLAIN HIM-SELF THAT WELL!
STOMP
STOMP
WHAT WAS THAT? TRY SAYING THAT TO MY FACE AGAIN!
B-BUT I CAN'T LEND YOU MONEY...
WHACK
ARGH, I'M SO UPSET!
She sure has lost it.
Yup.
HEY THERE, LITTLE MISSY. YOU ON YOUR WAY BACK HOME FROM SCHOOL?

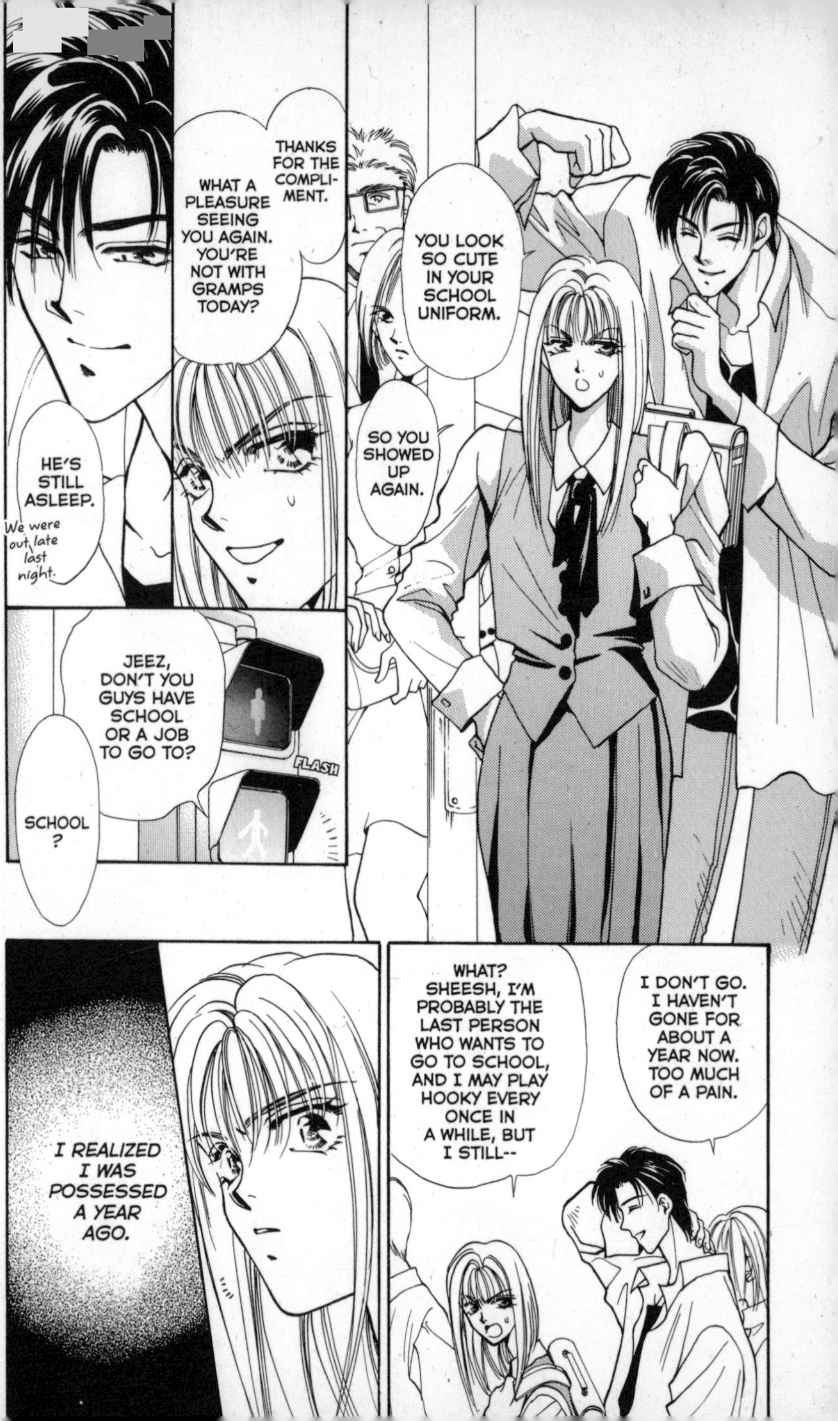

YOU LOOK SO CUTE IN YOUR SCHOOL UNIFORM.
SO YOU SHOWED UP AGAIN.
THANKS FOR THE COMPLIMENT.
WHAT A PLEASURE SEEING YOU AGAIN. YOU'RE NOT WITH GRAMPS TODAY?
HE'S STILL ASLEEP.
We were out late last night.
JEEZ, DON'T YOU GUYS HAVE SCHOOL OR A JOB TO GO TO?
FLASH
SCHOOL?
I DON'T GO. I HAVEN'T GONE FOR ABOUT A YEAR NOW. TOO MUCH OF A PAIN.
WHAT? SHEESH, I'M PROBABLY THE LAST PERSON WHO WANTS TO GO TO SCHOOL, AND I MAY PLAY HOOKY EVERY ONCE IN A WHILE, BUT I STILL--
I REALIZED I WAS POSSESSED A YEAR AGO.

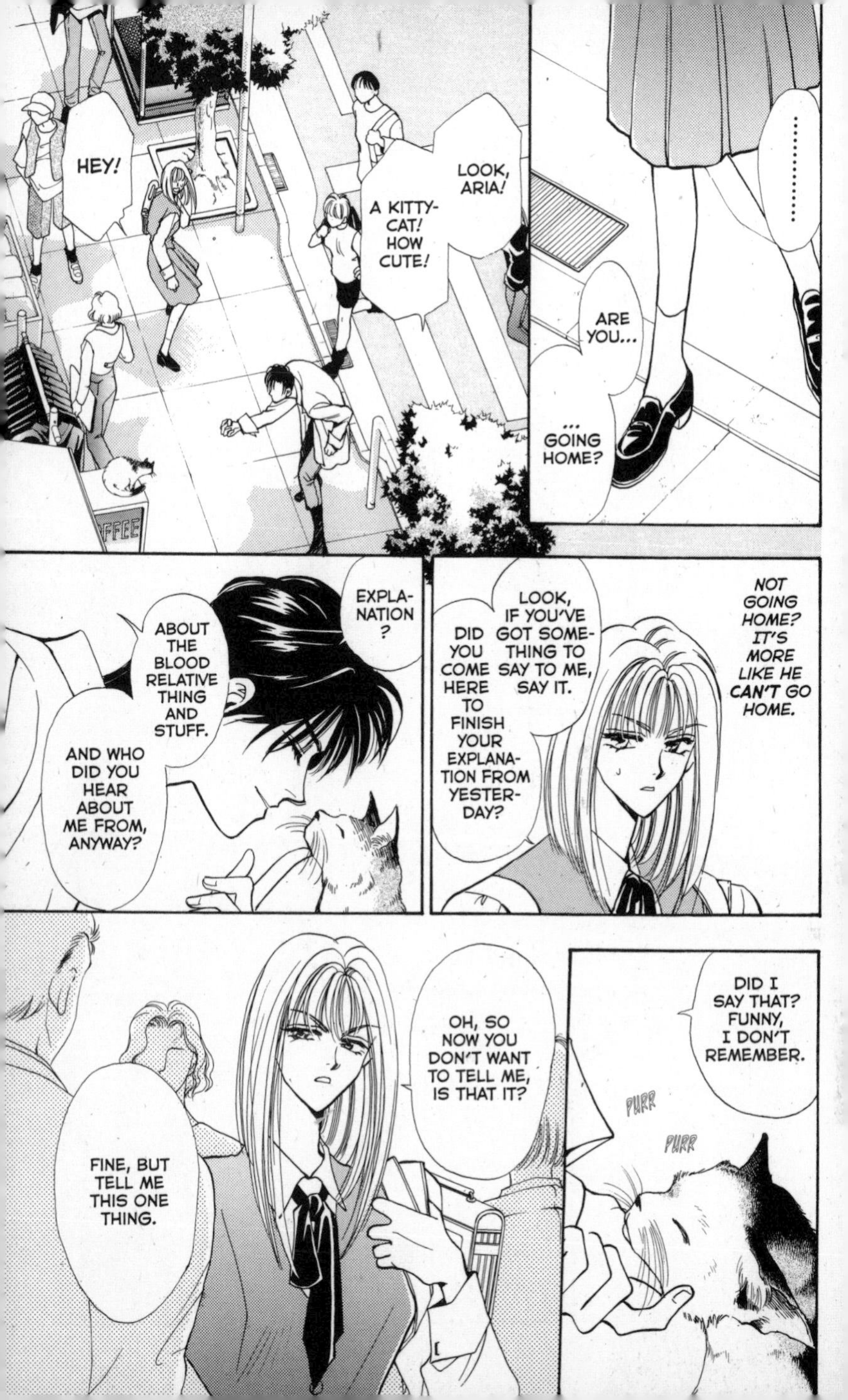
......
ARE YOU...
...GOING HOME?
LOOK, ARIA!
A KITTY-CAT! HOW CUTE!
HEY!
NOT GOING HOME? IT'S MORE LIKE HE CAN'T GO HOME.
LOOK, IF YOU'VE GOT SOMETHING TO SAY TO ME, SAY IT.
DID YOU COME HERE TO FINISH YOUR EXPLANATION FROM YESTERDAY?
EXPLANATION?
ABOUT THE BLOOD RELATIVE THING AND STUFF.
AND WHO DID YOU HEAR ABOUT ME FROM, ANYWAY?
DID I SAY THAT? FUNNY, I DON'T REMEMBER.
PURR
PURR
OH, SO NOW YOU DON'T WANT TO TELL ME, IS THAT IT?
FINE, BUT TELL ME THIS ONE THING.

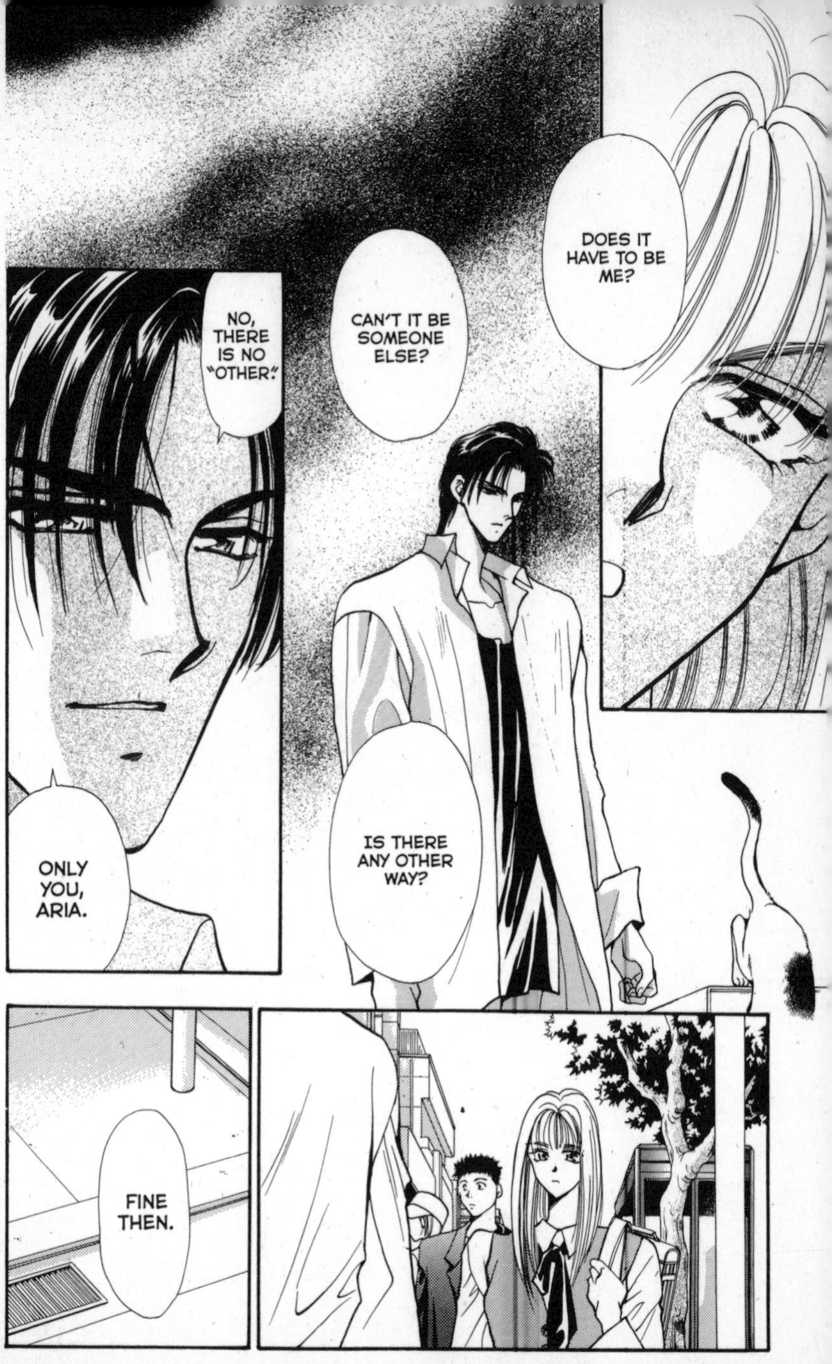
DOES IT HAVE TO BE ME?
CAN'T IT BE SOMEONE ELSE?
IS THERE ANY OTHER WAY?
NO, THERE IS NO "OTHER."
ONLY YOU, ARIA.
FINE THEN.

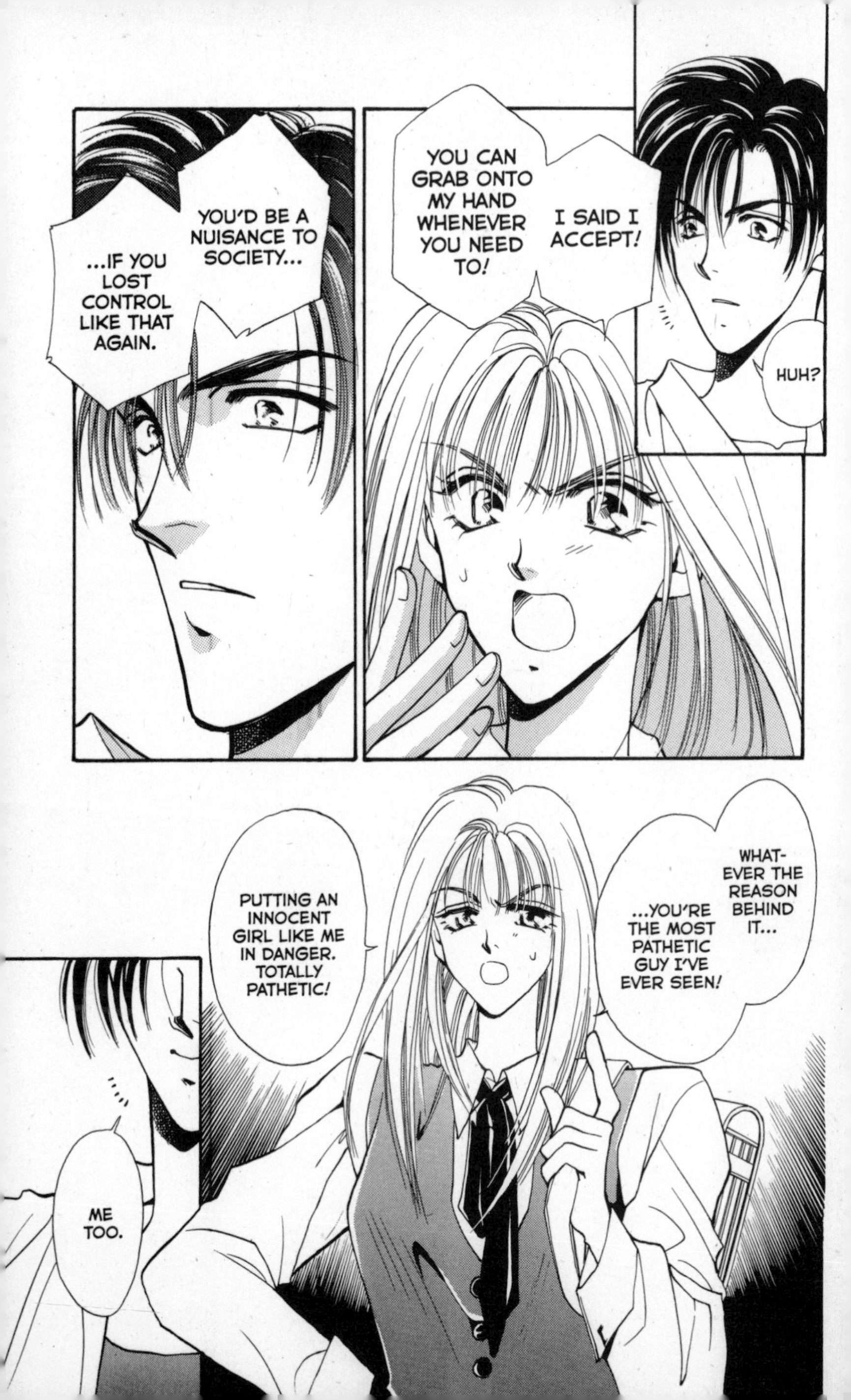

HUH?
I SAID I ACCEPT!
YOU CAN GRAB ONTO MY HAND WHENEVER YOU NEED TO!
YOU'D BE A NUISANCE TO SOCIETY...
...IF YOU LOST CONTROL LIKE THAT AGAIN.
WHAT-EVER THE REASON BEHIND IT...
...YOU'RE THE MOST PATHETIC GUY I'VE EVER SEEN!
PUTTING AN INNOCENT GIRL LIKE ME IN DANGER. TOTALLY PATHETIC!
ME TOO.

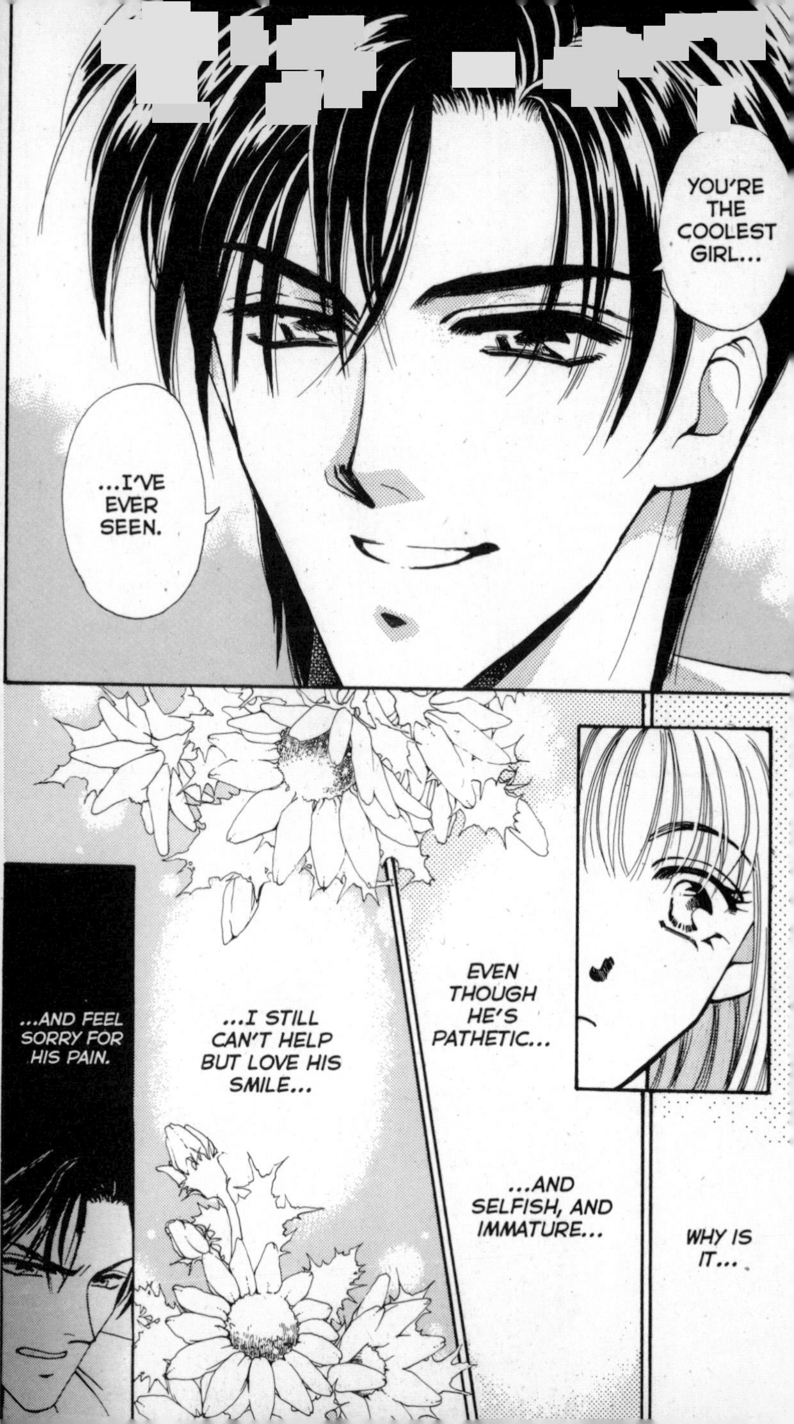
YOU'RE THE COOLEST GIRL...
...I'VE EVER SEEN.
WHY IS IT...
EVEN THOUGH HE'S PATHETIC...
...AND SELFISH, AND IMMATURE...
...I STILL CAN'T HELP BUT LOVE HIS SMILE...
...AND FEEL SORRY FOR HIS PAIN.

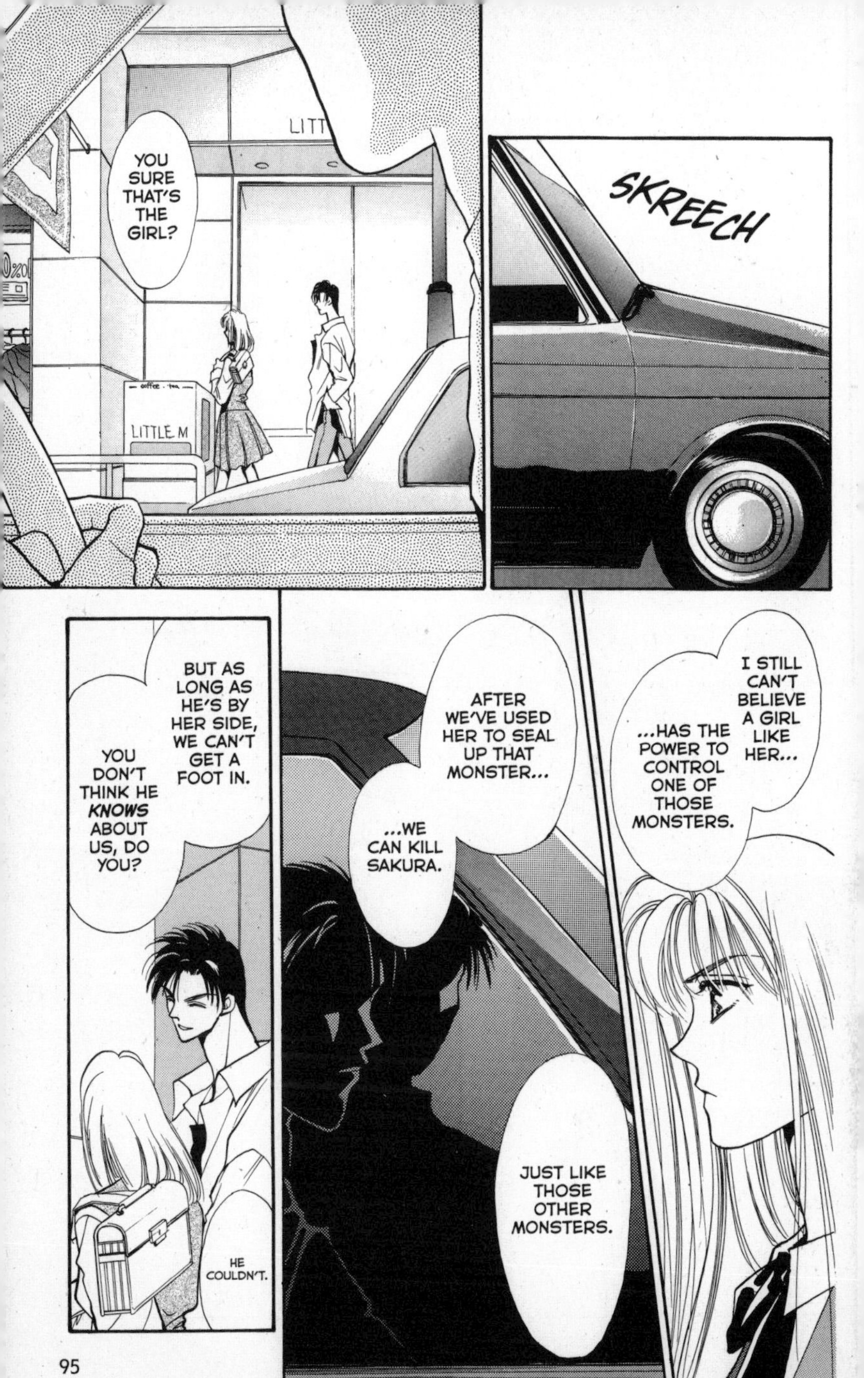
SKREECH
LITT
YOU SURE THAT'S THE GIRL?
coffee · tea
LITTLE M
I STILL CAN'T BELIEVE A GIRL LIKE HER...
...HAS THE POWER TO CONTROL ONE OF THOSE MONSTERS.
AFTER WE'VE USED HER TO SEAL UP THAT MONSTER...
...WE CAN KILL SAKURA.
JUST LIKE THOSE OTHER MONSTERS.
BUT AS LONG AS HE'S BY HER SIDE, WE CAN'T GET A FOOT IN.
YOU DON'T THINK HE *KNOWS* ABOUT US, DO YOU?
HE COULDN'T.

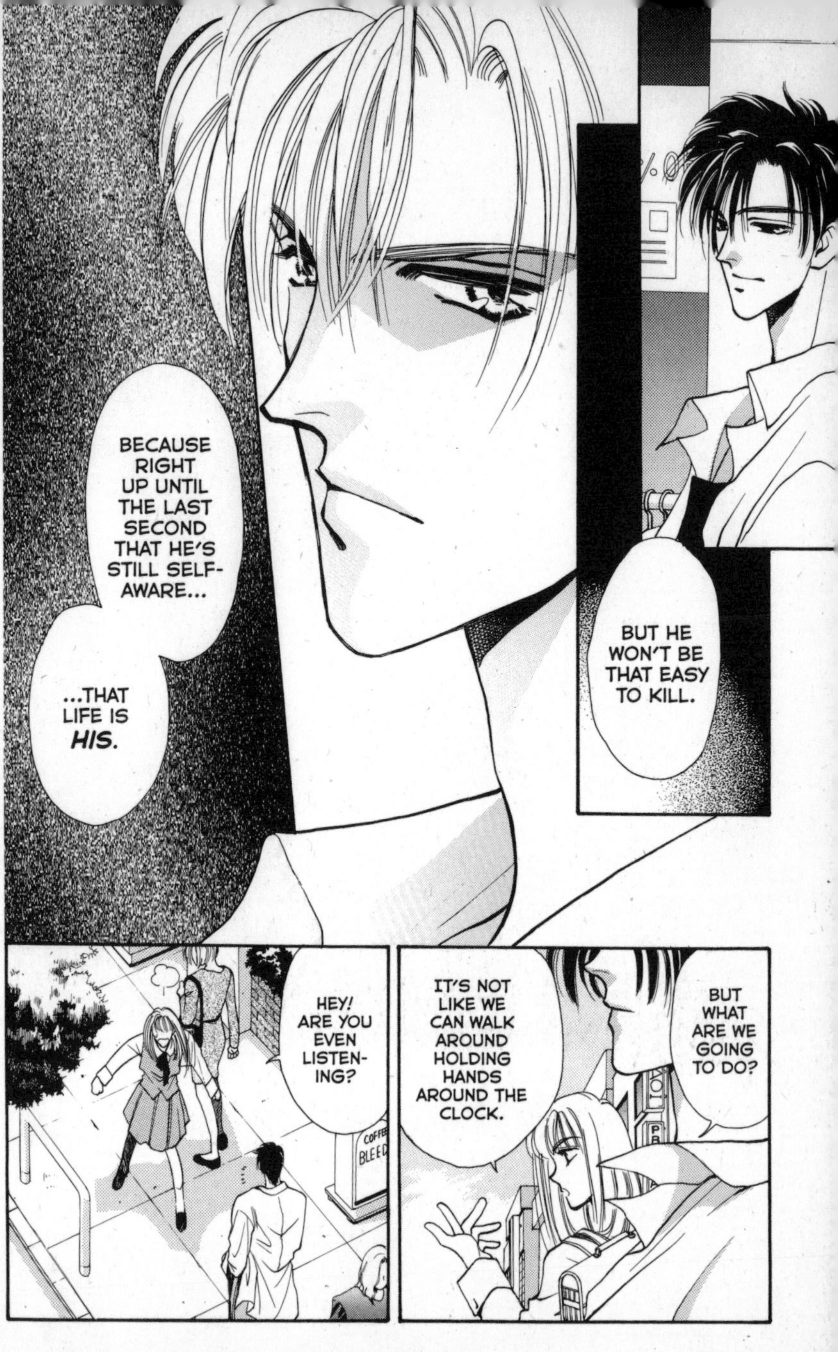
BUT HE WON'T BE THAT EASY TO KILL.
BECAUSE RIGHT UP UNTIL THE LAST SECOND THAT HE'S STILL SELF-AWARE...
...THAT LIFE IS ***HIS***.
BUT WHAT ARE WE GOING TO DO?
IT'S NOT LIKE WE CAN WALK AROUND HOLDING HANDS AROUND THE CLOCK.
HEY! ARE YOU EVEN LISTENING?

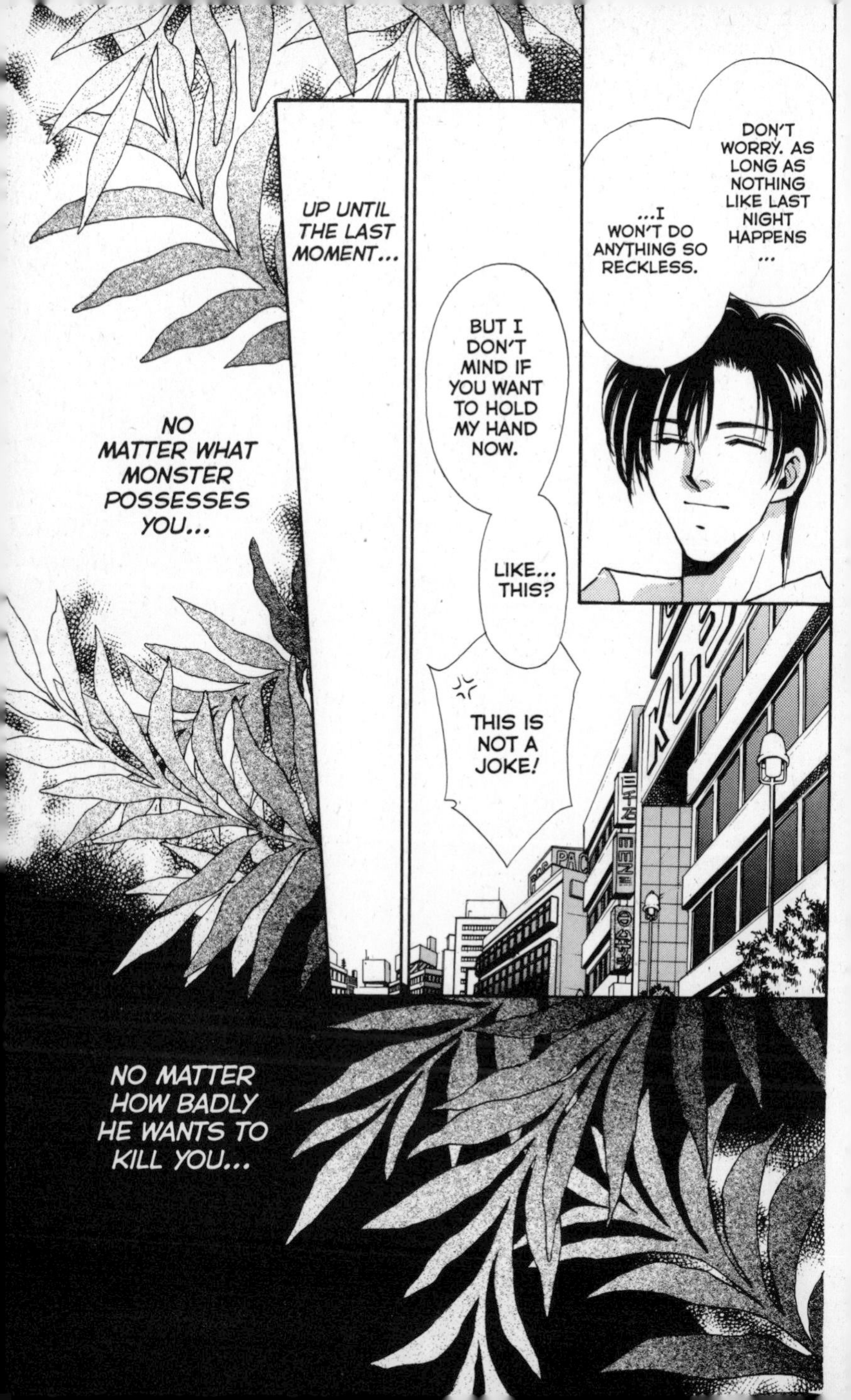

DON'T WORRY. AS LONG AS NOTHING LIKE LAST NIGHT HAPPENS...
...I WON'T DO ANYTHING SO RECKLESS.
BUT I DON'T MIND IF YOU WANT TO HOLD MY HAND NOW.
LIKE... THIS?
THIS IS NOT A JOKE!
UP UNTIL THE LAST MOMENT...
NO MATTER WHAT MONSTER POSSESSES YOU...
NO MATTER HOW BADLY HE WANTS TO KILL YOU...

獣たちの夜

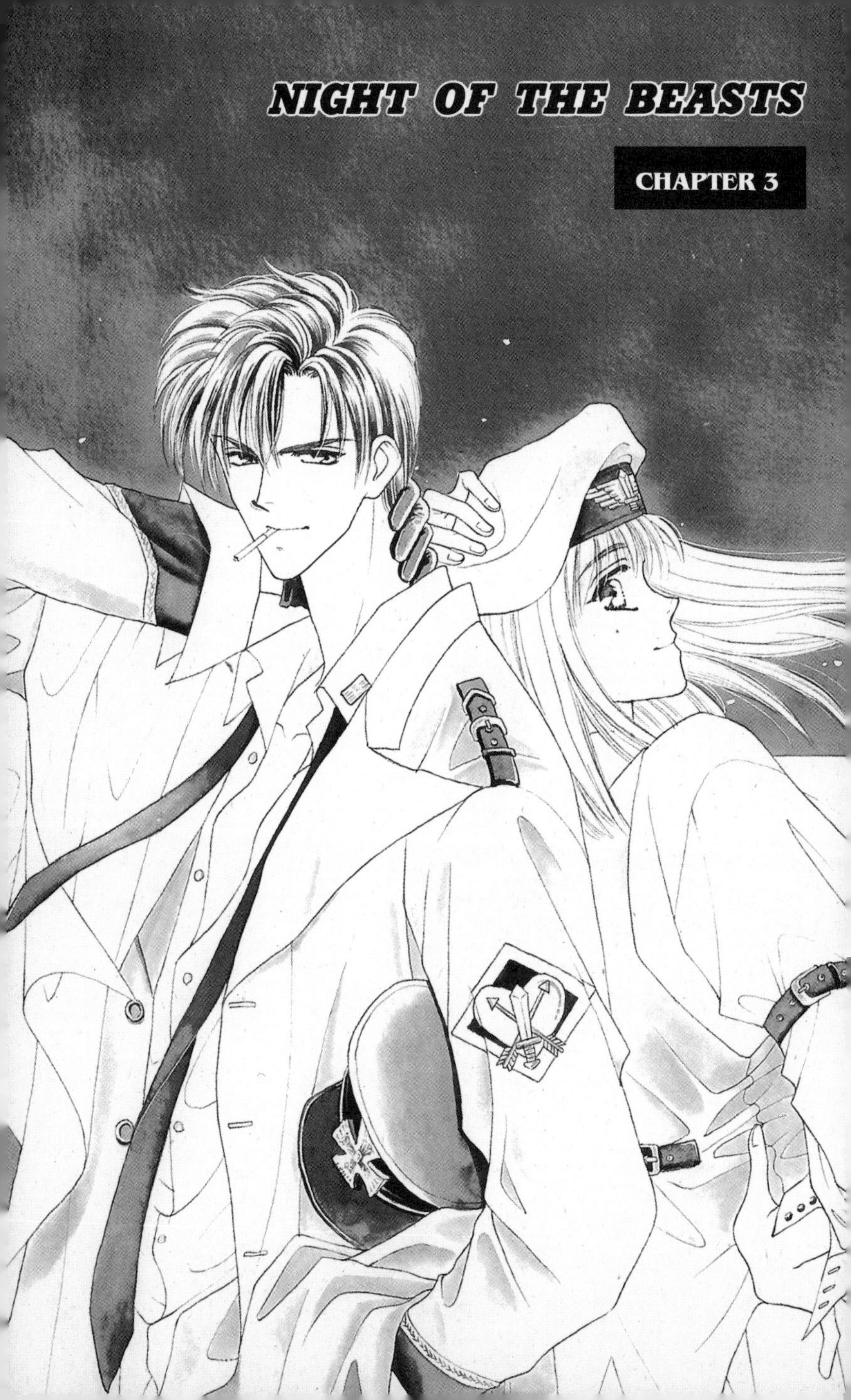
NIGHT OF THE BEASTS
CHAPTER 3

獣たちの夜

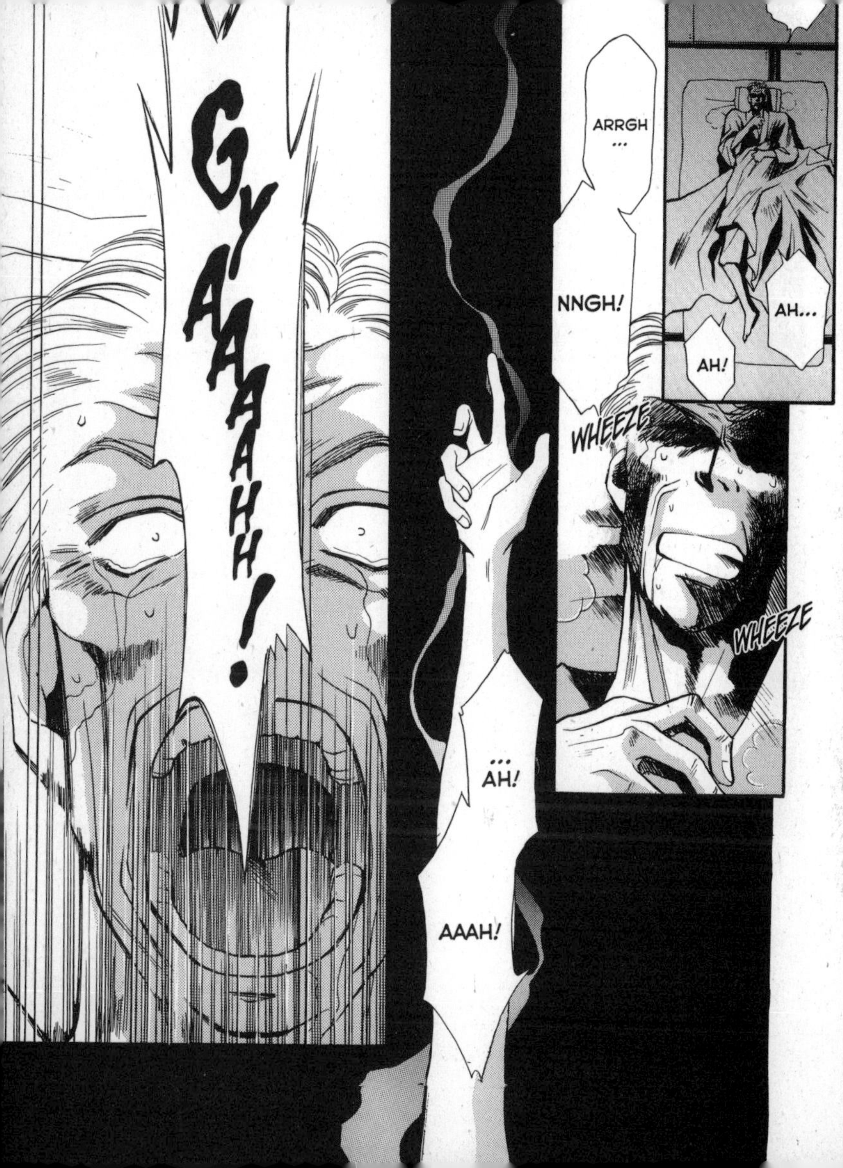
AH...
AH!
ARRGH ...
NNGH!
WHEEZE
WHEEZE
...AH!
AAAH!
GYAAAAHH!!

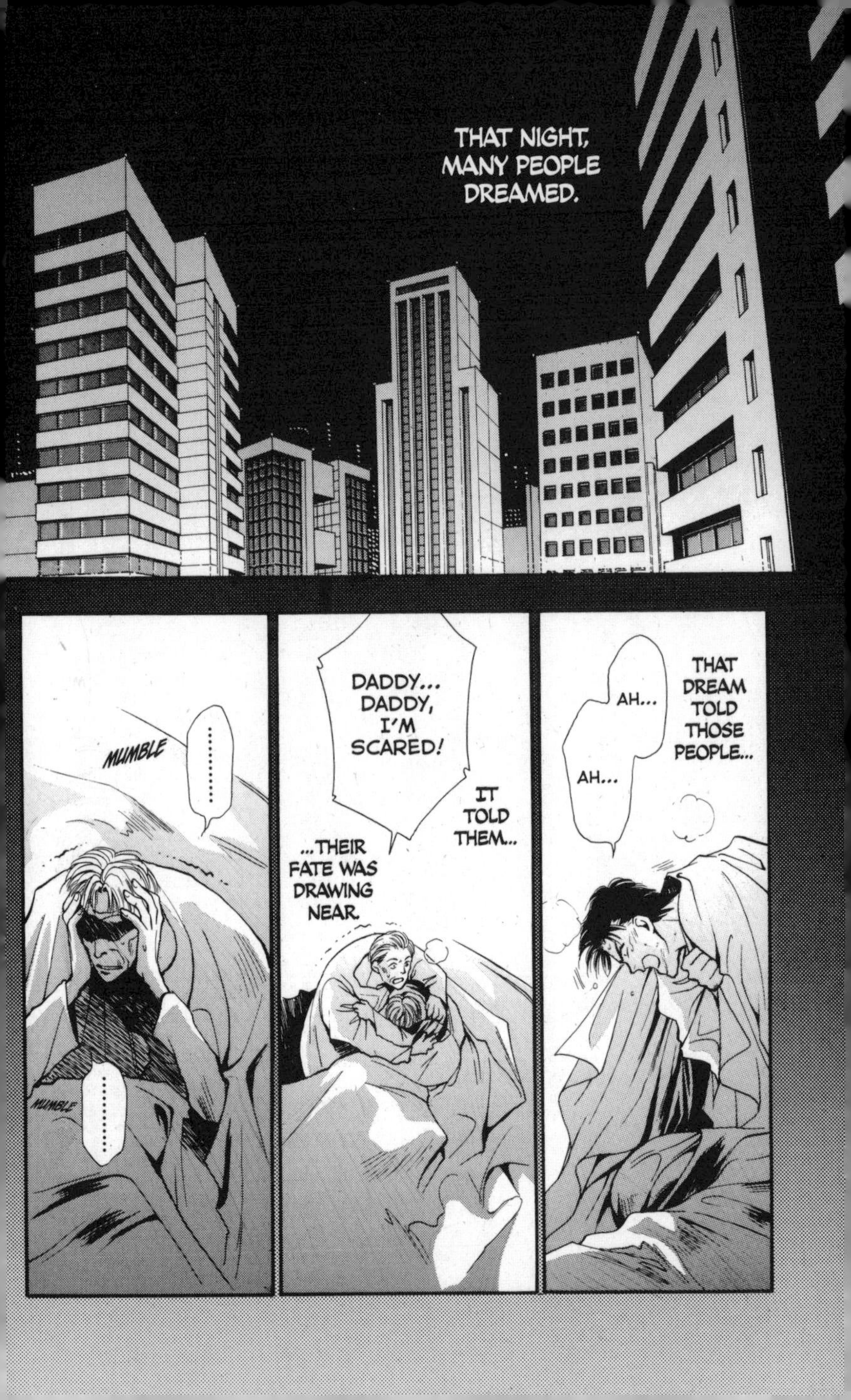
THAT NIGHT, MANY PEOPLE DREAMED.
THAT DREAM TOLD THOSE PEOPLE...
AH...
AH...
DADDY... DADDY, I'M SCARED!
IT TOLD THEM...
...THEIR FATE WAS DRAWING NEAR.
MUMBLE
....
MUMBLE
....

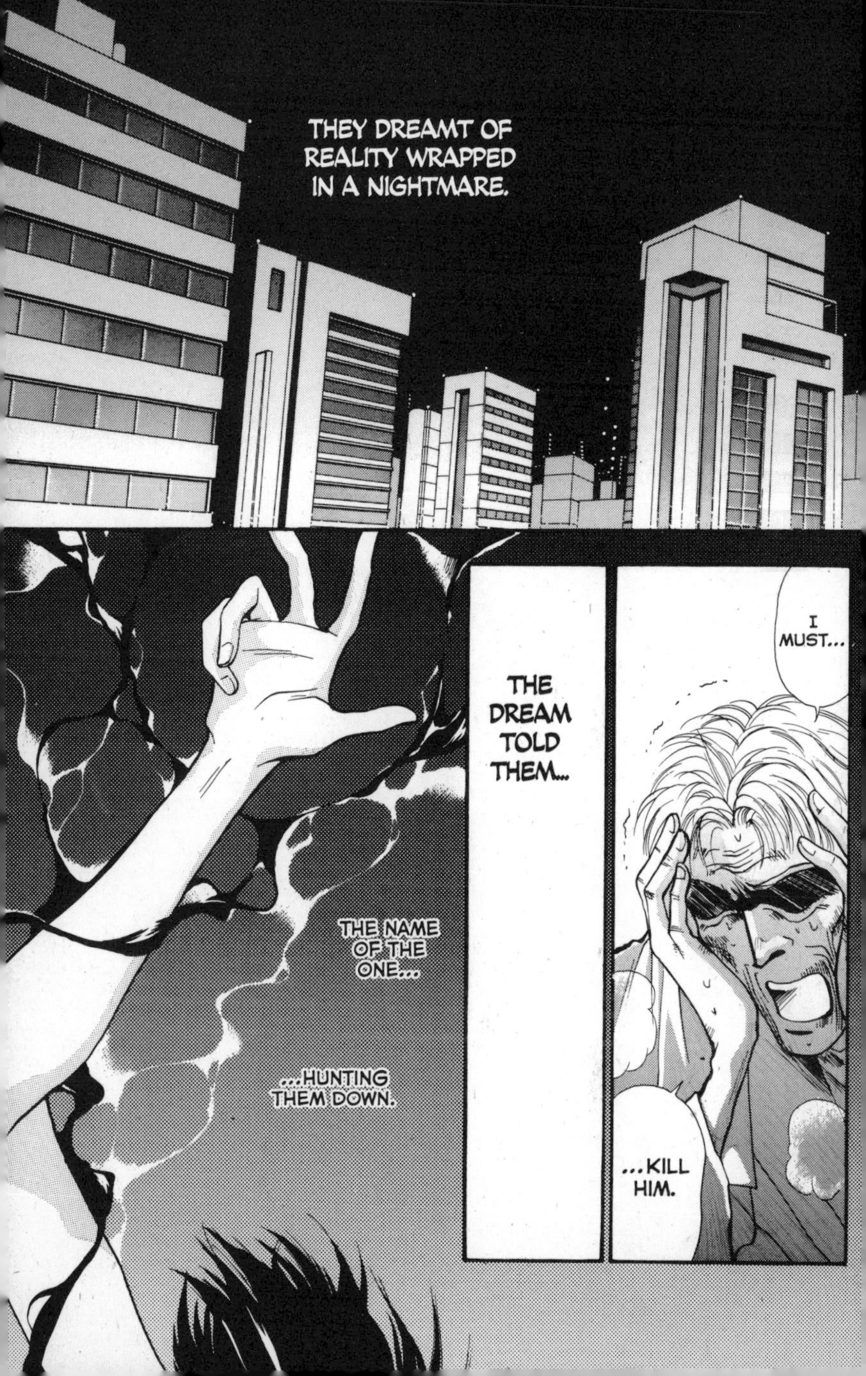
THEY DREAMT OF REALITY WRAPPED IN A NIGHTMARE.
I MUST...
...KILL HIM.
THE DREAM TOLD THEM...
THE NAME OF THE ONE...
...HUNTING THEM DOWN.

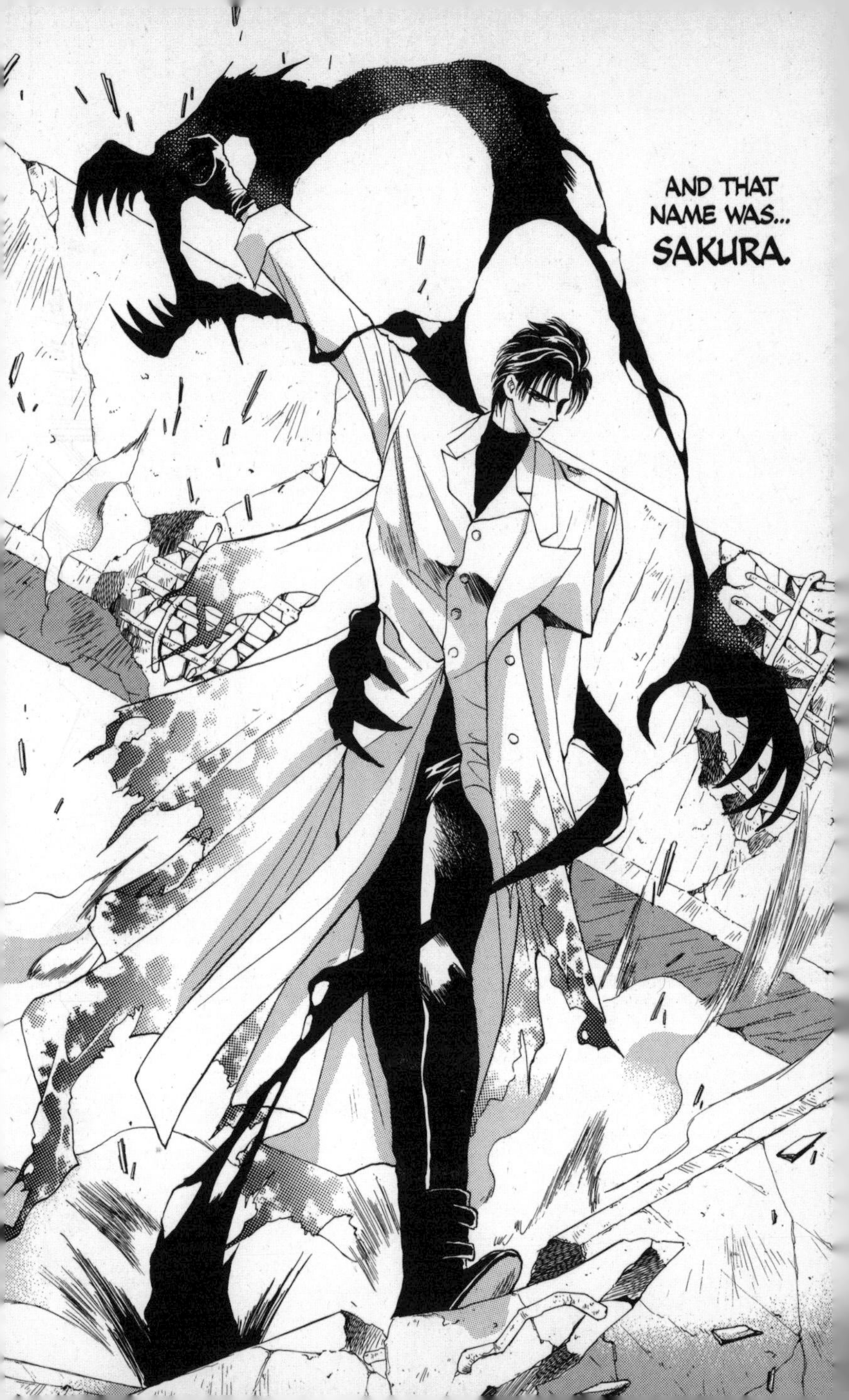
AND THAT NAME WAS... SAKURA.

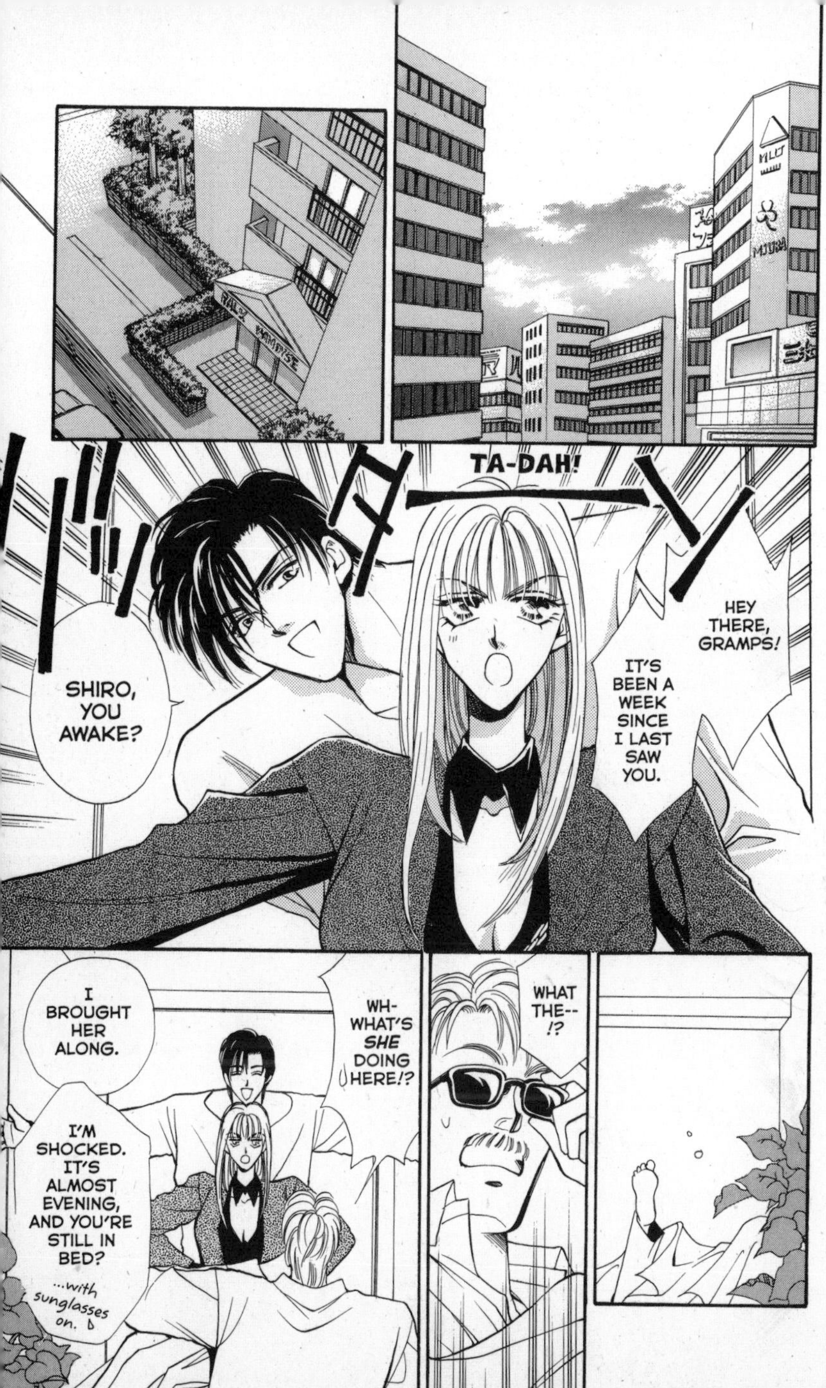
TA-DAH!
HEY THERE, GRAMPS!
IT'S BEEN A WEEK SINCE I LAST SAW YOU.
SHIRO, YOU AWAKE?
WHAT THE--!?
WH-WHAT'S *SHE* DOING HERE!?
I BROUGHT HER ALONG.
I'M SHOCKED. IT'S ALMOST EVENING, AND YOU'RE STILL IN BED?
...with sunglasses on.

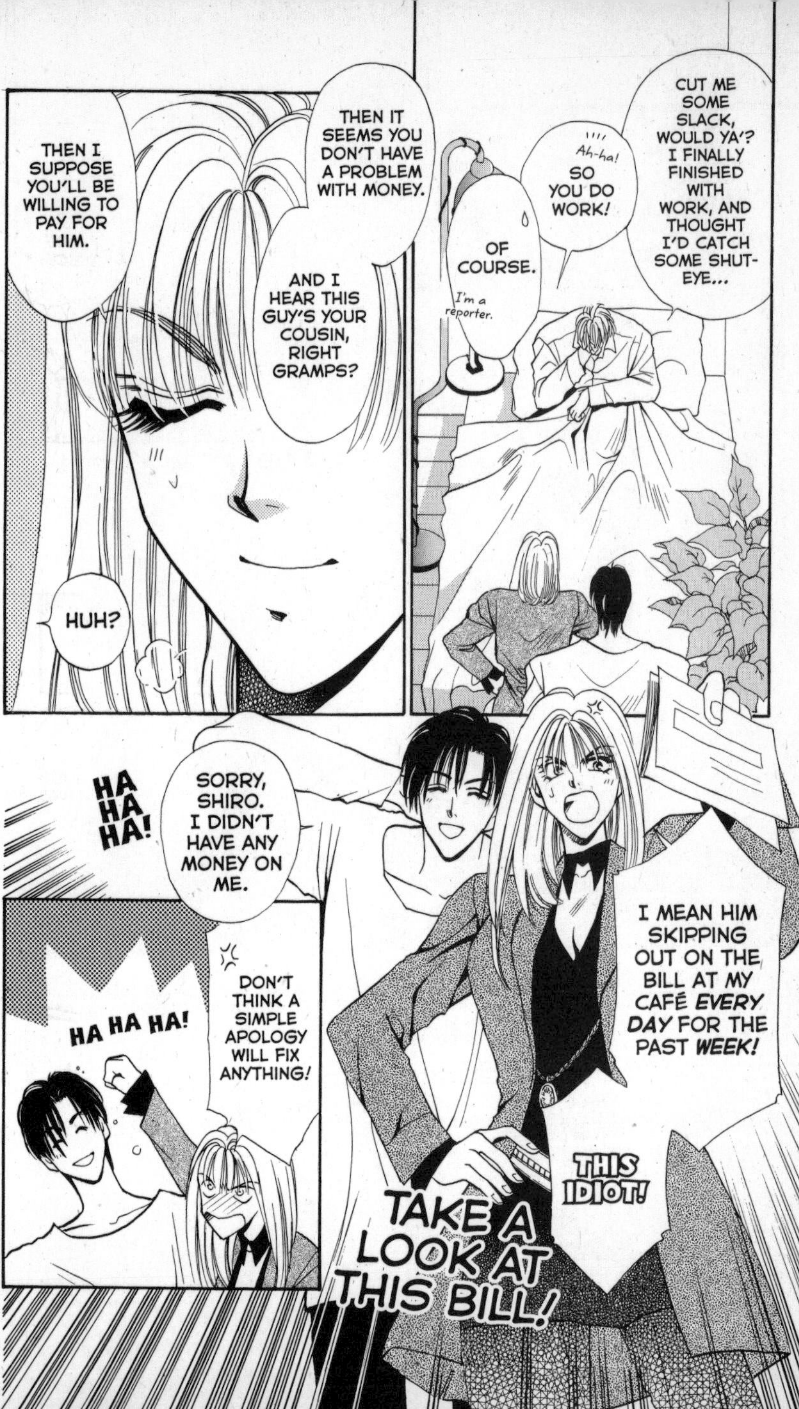
CUT ME SOME SLACK, WOULD YA'? I FINALLY FINISHED WITH WORK, AND THOUGHT I'D CATCH SOME SHUT-EYE...
Ah-ha! SO YOU DO WORK!
OF COURSE. I'm a reporter.
THEN IT SEEMS YOU DON'T HAVE A PROBLEM WITH MONEY.
AND I HEAR THIS GUY'S YOUR COUSIN, RIGHT GRAMPS?
THEN I SUPPOSE YOU'LL BE WILLING TO PAY FOR HIM.
HUH?
TAKE A LOOK AT THIS BILL!
THIS IDIOT!
I MEAN HIM SKIPPING OUT ON THE BILL AT MY CAFÉ EVERY DAY FOR THE PAST WEEK!
SORRY, SHIRO. I DIDN'T HAVE ANY MONEY ON ME.
HA HA HA!
DON'T THINK A SIMPLE APOLOGY WILL FIX ANYTHING!
HA HA HA!

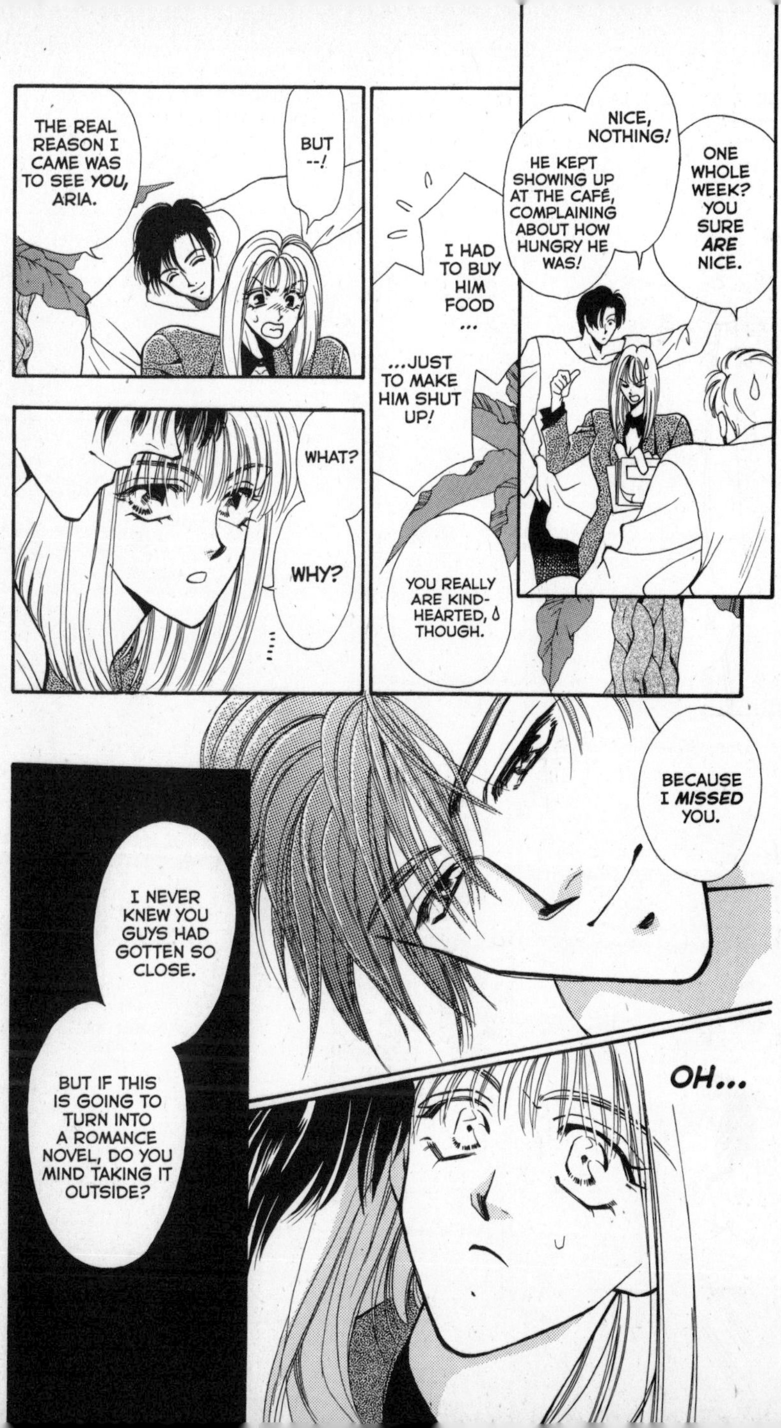
ONE WHOLE WEEK? YOU SURE ARE NICE.
NICE, NOTHING!
HE KEPT SHOWING UP AT THE CAFÉ, COMPLAINING ABOUT HOW HUNGRY HE WAS!
I HAD TO BUY HIM FOOD...
...JUST TO MAKE HIM SHUT UP!
YOU REALLY ARE KIND-HEARTED, THOUGH.
BUT --!
THE REAL REASON I CAME WAS TO SEE *YOU*, ARIA.
WHAT?
WHY?
...
BECAUSE I *MISSED* YOU.
OH...
I NEVER KNEW YOU GUYS HAD GOTTEN SO CLOSE.
BUT IF THIS IS GOING TO TURN INTO A ROMANCE NOVEL, DO YOU MIND TAKING IT OUTSIDE?

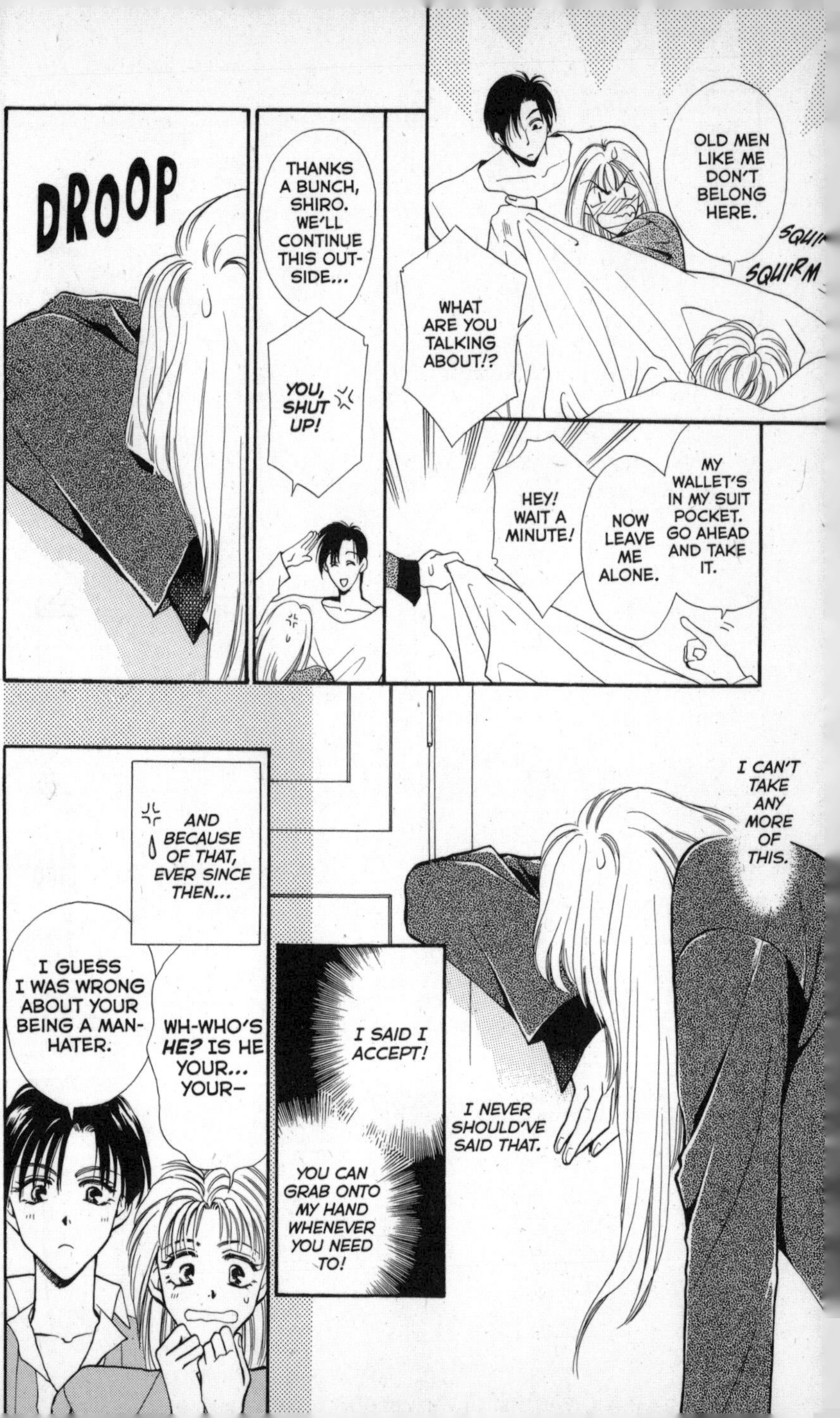
OLD MEN LIKE ME DON'T BELONG HERE.
SQUI
SQUIRM
WHAT ARE YOU TALKING ABOUT!?
MY WALLET'S IN MY SUIT POCKET. GO AHEAD AND TAKE IT.
NOW LEAVE ME ALONE.
HEY! WAIT A MINUTE!
THANKS A BUNCH, SHIRO. WE'LL CONTINUE THIS OUT-SIDE...
YOU, SHUT UP!
DROOP
I CAN'T TAKE ANY MORE OF THIS.
I NEVER SHOULD'VE SAID THAT.
I SAID I ACCEPT!
YOU CAN GRAB ONTO MY HAND WHENEVER YOU NEED TO!
AND BECAUSE OF THAT, EVER SINCE THEN...
WH-WHO'S HE? IS HE YOUR... YOUR–
I GUESS I WAS WRONG ABOUT YOUR BEING A MAN-HATER.

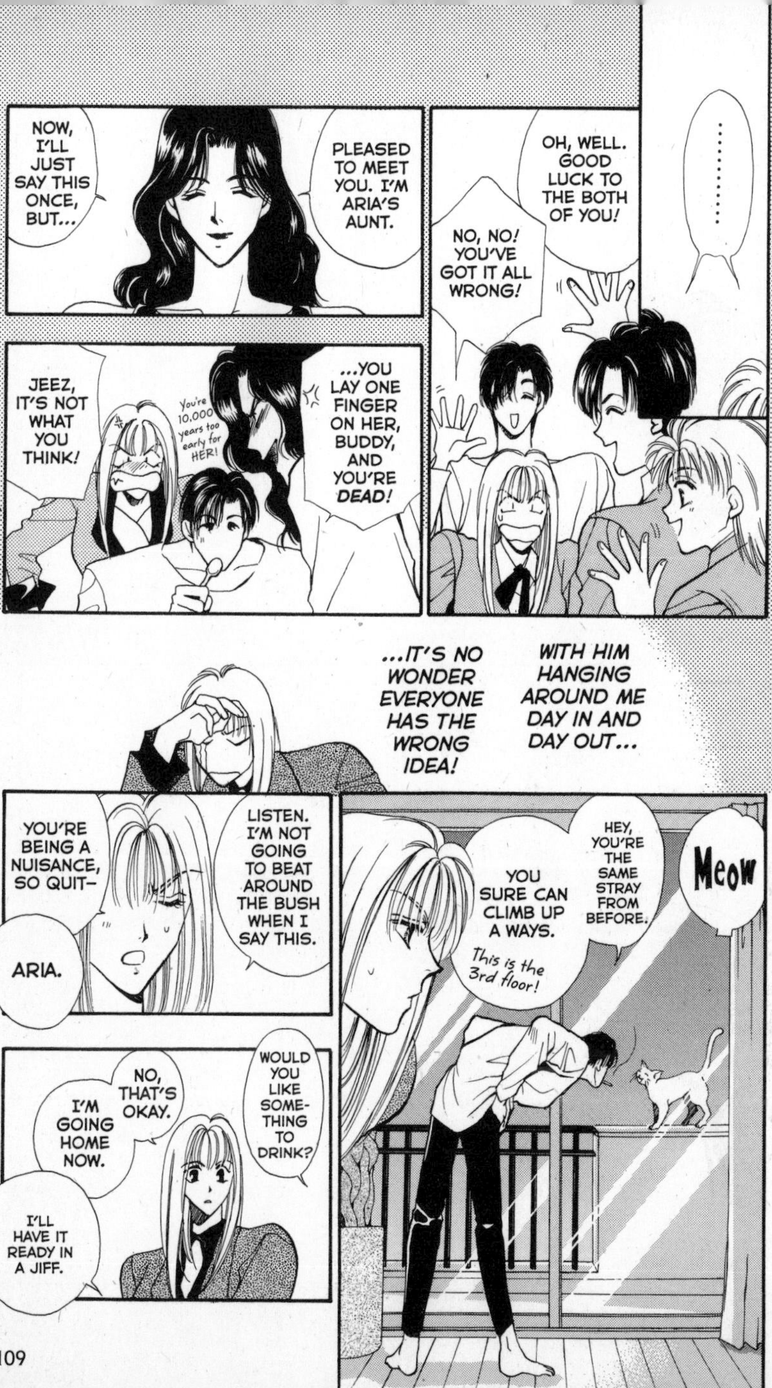
......
OH, WELL. GOOD LUCK TO THE BOTH OF YOU!
NO, NO! YOU'VE GOT IT ALL WRONG!
PLEASED TO MEET YOU. I'M ARIA'S AUNT.
NOW, I'LL JUST SAY THIS ONCE, BUT...
...YOU LAY ONE FINGER ON HER, BUDDY, AND YOU'RE DEAD!
You're 10,000 years too early for HER!
JEEZ, IT'S NOT WHAT YOU THINK!
WITH HIM HANGING AROUND ME DAY IN AND DAY OUT...
...IT'S NO WONDER EVERYONE HAS THE WRONG IDEA!
Meow
HEY, YOU'RE THE SAME STRAY FROM BEFORE.
YOU SURE CAN CLIMB UP A WAYS.
This is the 3rd floor!
LISTEN. I'M NOT GOING TO BEAT AROUND THE BUSH WHEN I SAY THIS.
YOU'RE BEING A NUISANCE, SO QUIT—
ARIA.
WOULD YOU LIKE SOMETHING TO DRINK?
NO, THAT'S OKAY.
I'M GOING HOME NOW.
I'LL HAVE IT READY IN A JIFF.

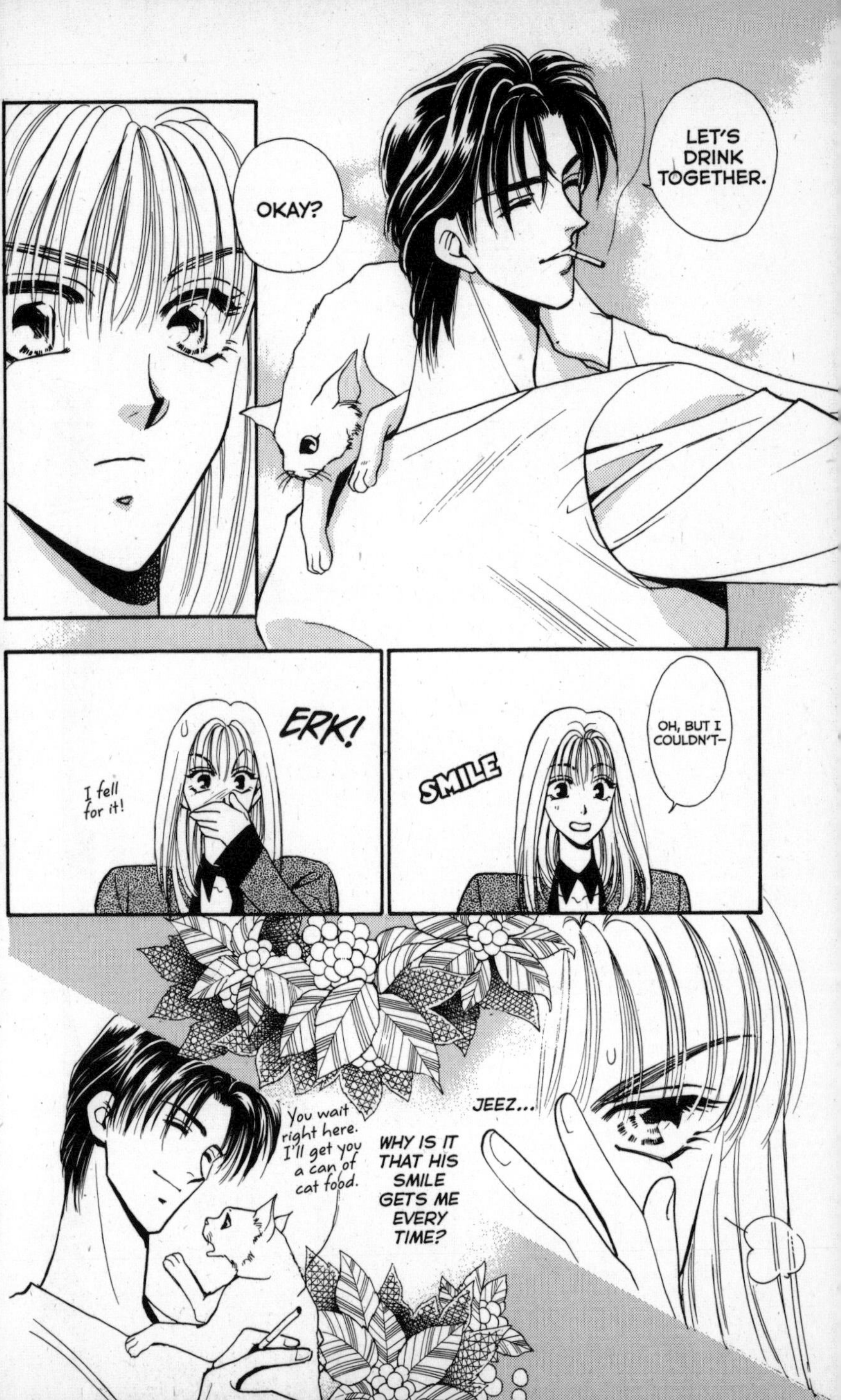
LET'S DRINK TOGETHER.
OKAY?
OH, BUT I COULDN'T—
SMILE
ERK!
I fell for it!
JEEZ...
WHY IS IT THAT HIS SMILE GETS ME EVERY TIME?
You wait right here. I'll get you a can of cat food.

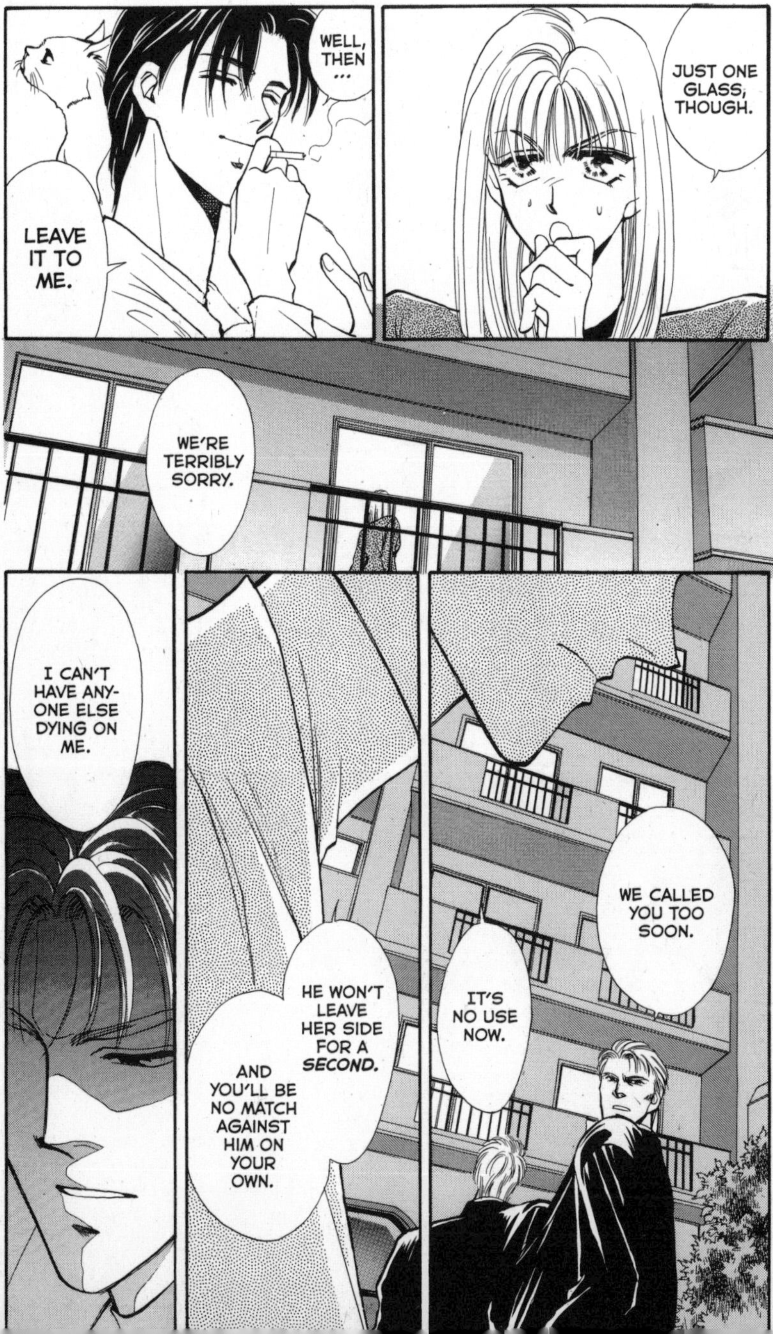
JUST ONE GLASS, THOUGH.
WELL, THEN ...
LEAVE IT TO ME.
WE'RE TERRIBLY SORRY.
WE CALLED YOU TOO SOON.
IT'S NO USE NOW.
HE WON'T LEAVE HER SIDE FOR A *SECOND.*
AND YOU'LL BE NO MATCH AGAINST HIM ON YOUR OWN.
I CAN'T HAVE ANY-ONE ELSE DYING ON ME.

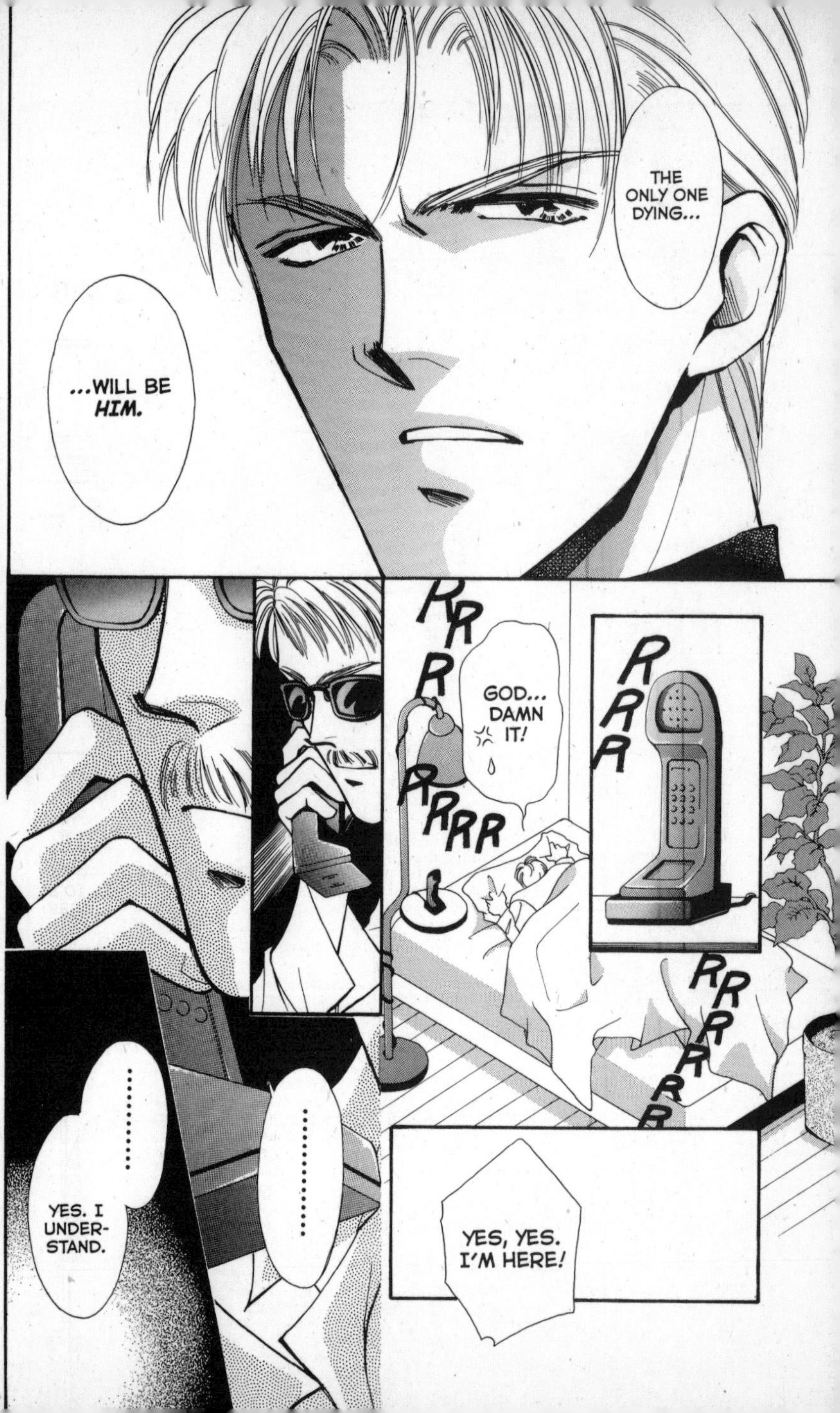
THE ONLY ONE DYING...
...WILL BE HIM.
RRR
RRRRRRRR
GOD... DAMN IT!
RRRRRRR
YES, YES. I'M HERE!
......
......
YES. I UNDERSTAND.

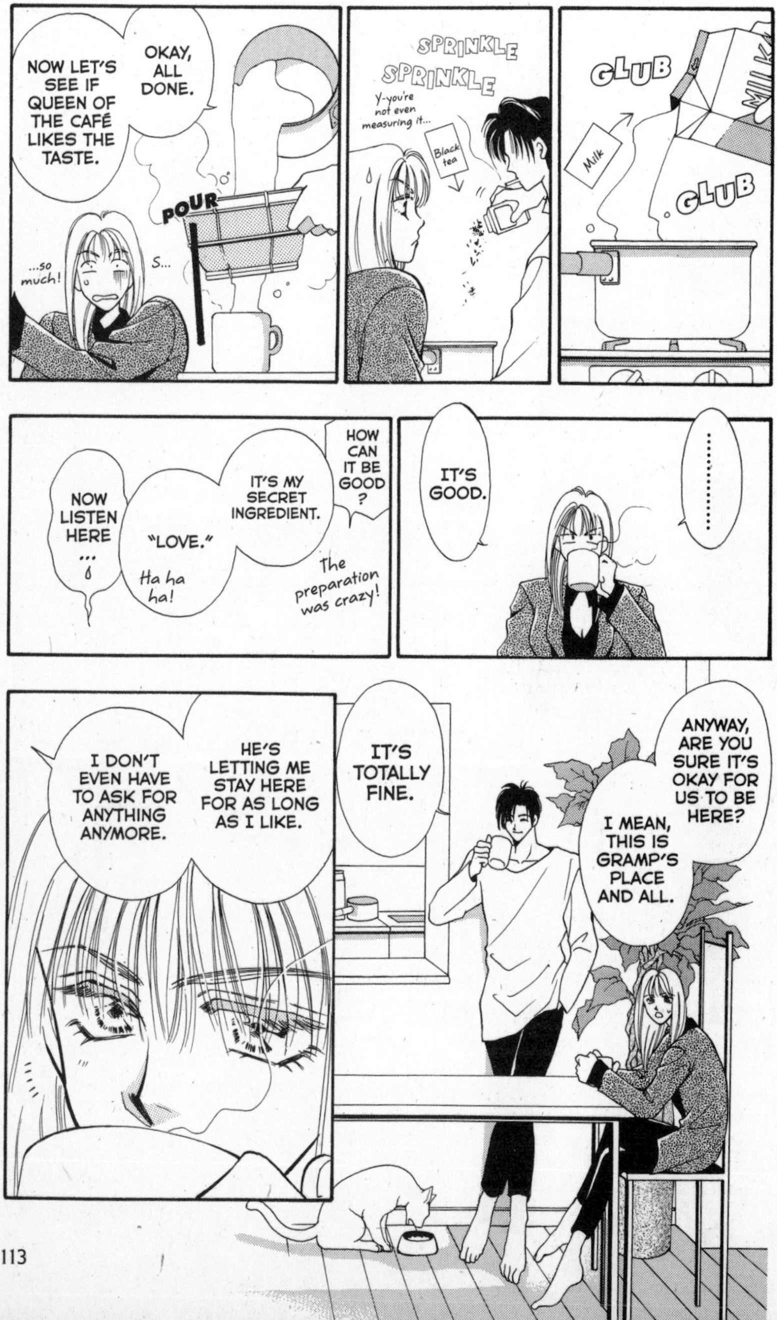
MILK
GLUB
Milk
GLUB
SPRINKLE
SPRINKLE
Y-you're not even measuring it...
Black tea
OKAY, ALL DONE.
NOW LET'S SEE IF QUEEN OF THE CAFÉ LIKES THE TASTE.
POUR
S...
...so much!
....
IT'S GOOD.
HOW CAN IT BE GOOD?
IT'S MY SECRET INGREDIENT.
"LOVE."
Ha ha ha!
The preparation was crazy!
NOW LISTEN HERE...
ANYWAY, ARE YOU SURE IT'S OKAY FOR US TO BE HERE?
I MEAN, THIS IS GRAMP'S PLACE AND ALL.
IT'S TOTALLY FINE.
HE'S LETTING ME STAY HERE FOR AS LONG AS I LIKE.
I DON'T EVEN HAVE TO ASK FOR ANYTHING ANYMORE.

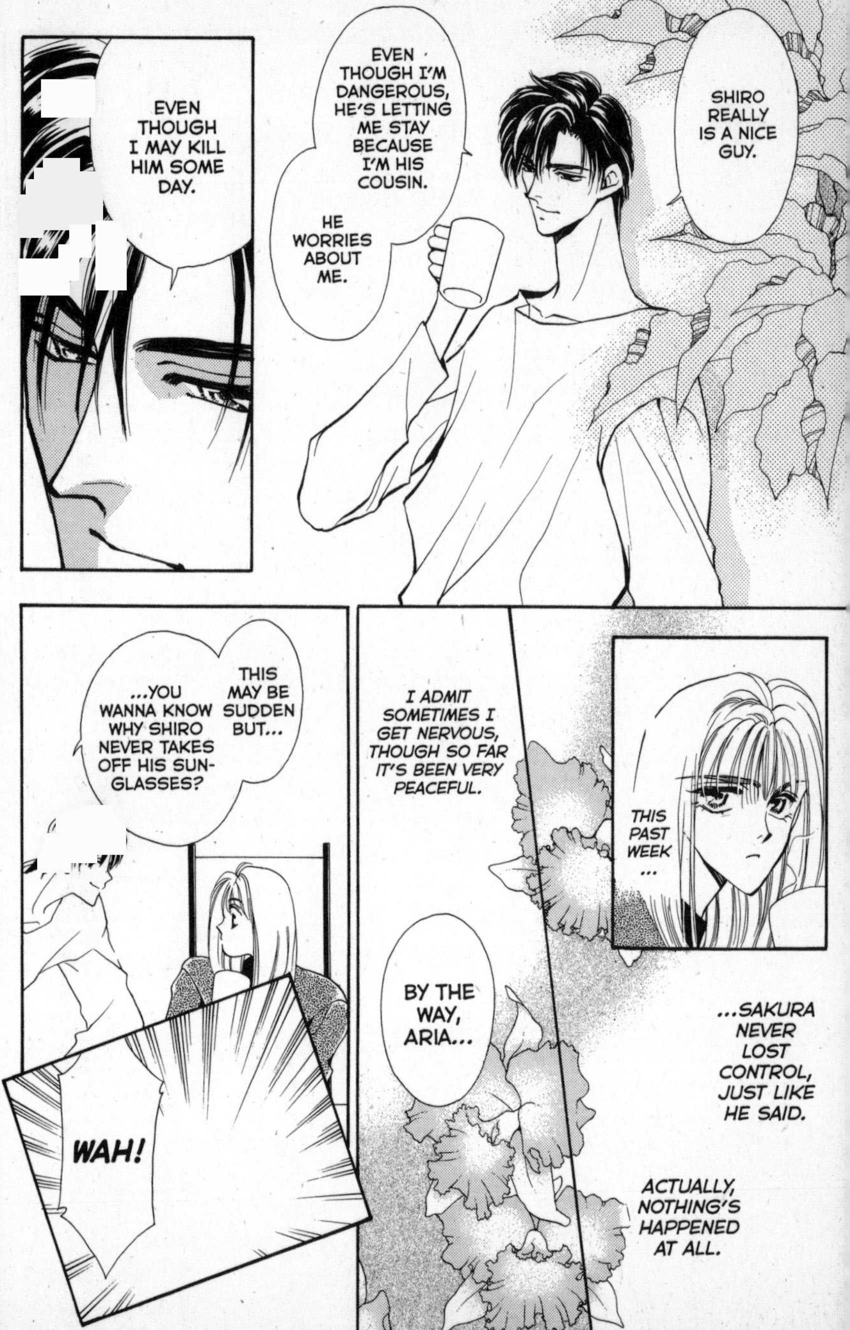
SHIRO REALLY IS A NICE GUY.
EVEN THOUGH I'M DANGEROUS, HE'S LETTING ME STAY BECAUSE I'M HIS COUSIN.
HE WORRIES ABOUT ME.
EVEN THOUGH I MAY KILL HIM SOME DAY.
THIS PAST WEEK ...
...SAKURA NEVER LOST CONTROL, JUST LIKE HE SAID.
ACTUALLY, NOTHING'S HAPPENED AT ALL.
I ADMIT SOMETIMES I GET NERVOUS, THOUGH SO FAR IT'S BEEN VERY PEACEFUL.
BY THE WAY, ARIA...
THIS MAY BE SUDDEN BUT...
...YOU WANNA KNOW WHY SHIRO NEVER TAKES OFF HIS SUN-GLASSES?
WAH!

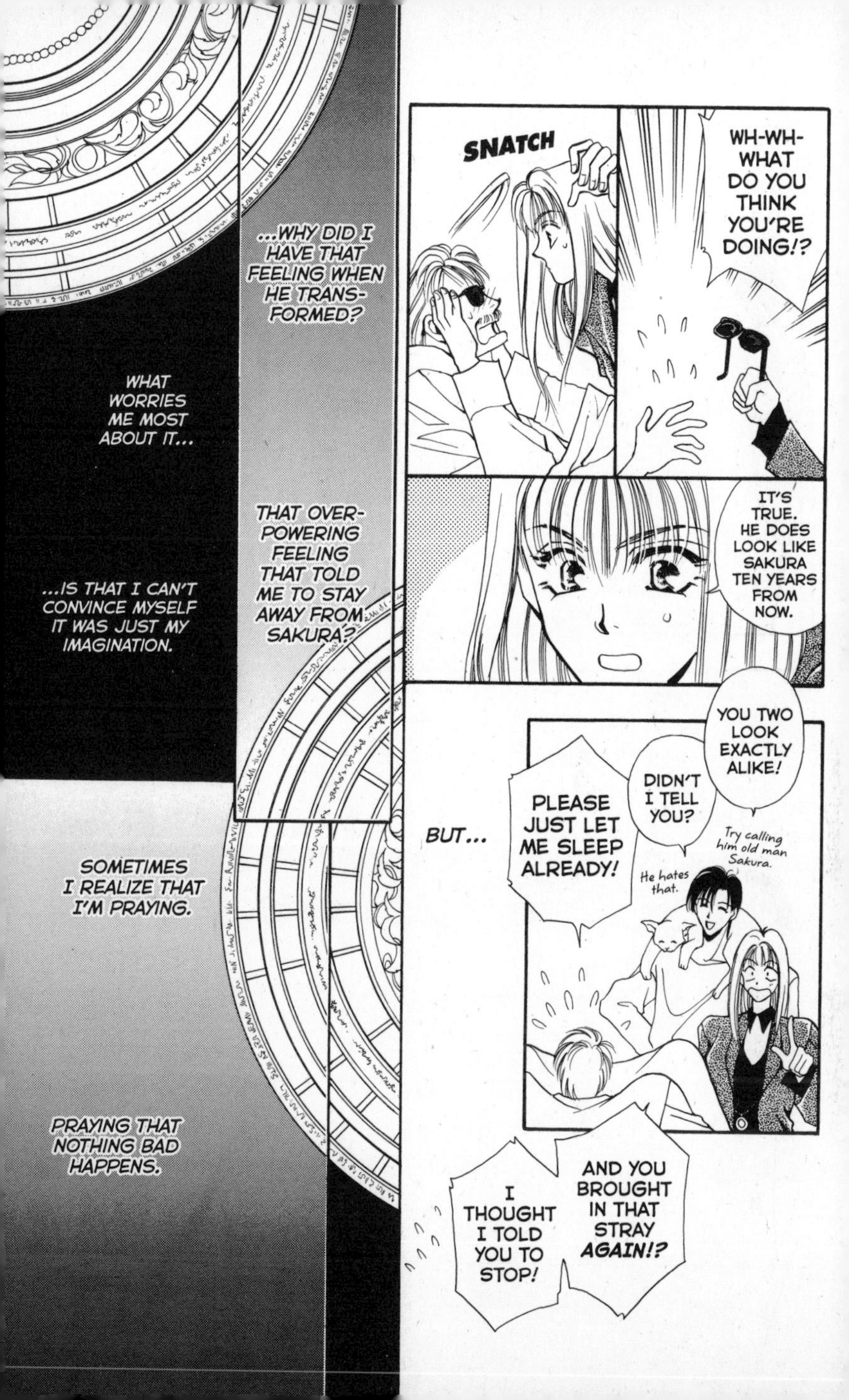
WH-WH-WHAT DO YOU THINK YOU'RE DOING!?
SNATCH
IT'S TRUE. HE DOES LOOK LIKE SAKURA TEN YEARS FROM NOW.
YOU TWO LOOK EXACTLY ALIKE!
DIDN'T I TELL YOU?
Try calling him old man Sakura.
He hates that.
PLEASE JUST LET ME SLEEP ALREADY!
BUT...
AND YOU BROUGHT IN THAT STRAY AGAIN!?
I THOUGHT I TOLD YOU TO STOP!
...WHY DID I HAVE THAT FEELING WHEN HE TRANS-FORMED?
THAT OVER-POWERING FEELING THAT TOLD ME TO STAY AWAY FROM SAKURA?
WHAT WORRIES ME MOST ABOUT IT...
...IS THAT I CAN'T CONVINCE MYSELF IT WAS JUST MY IMAGINATION.
SOMETIMES I REALIZE THAT I'M PRAYING.
PRAYING THAT NOTHING BAD HAPPENS.

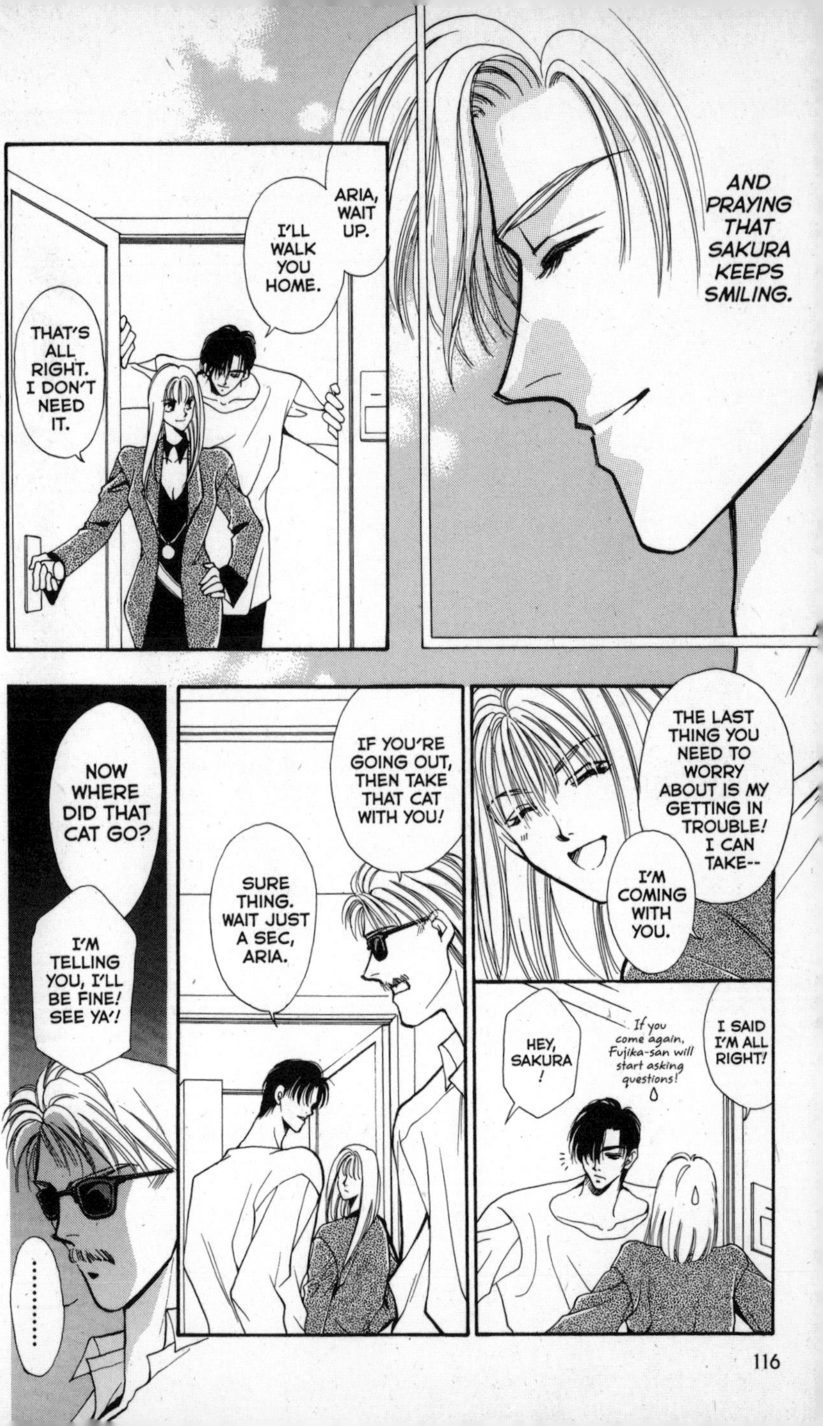
AND PRAYING THAT SAKURA KEEPS SMILING.
ARIA, WAIT UP.
I'LL WALK YOU HOME.
THAT'S ALL RIGHT. I DON'T NEED IT.
THE LAST THING YOU NEED TO WORRY ABOUT IS MY GETTING IN TROUBLE! I CAN TAKE--
I'M COMING WITH YOU.
I SAID I'M ALL RIGHT!
If you come again, Fujika-san will start asking questions!
HEY, SAKURA!
IF YOU'RE GOING OUT, THEN TAKE THAT CAT WITH YOU!
SURE THING. WAIT JUST A SEC, ARIA.
NOW WHERE DID THAT CAT GO?
I'M TELLING YOU, I'LL BE FINE! SEE YA'!
....

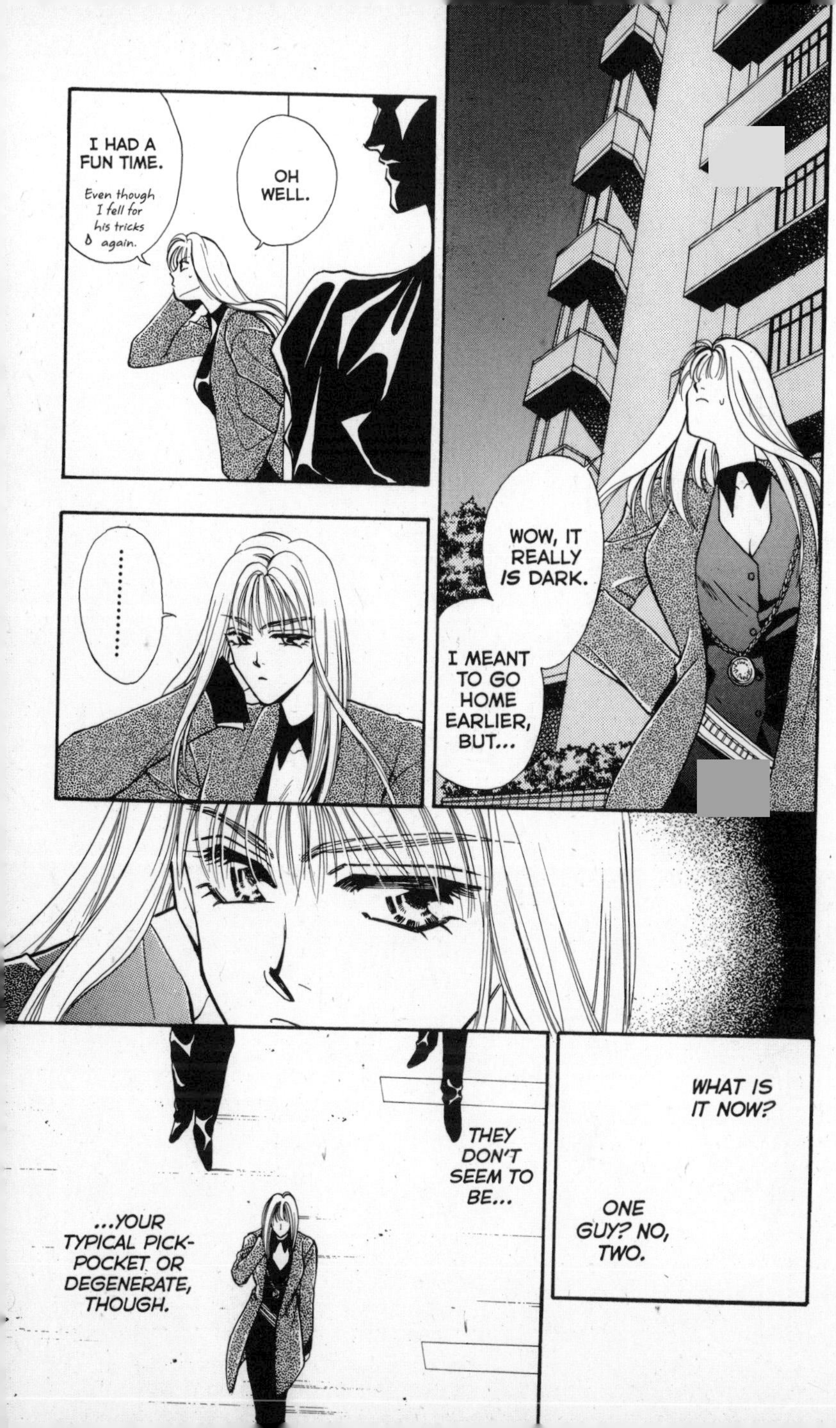
WOW, IT REALLY IS DARK.
I MEANT TO GO HOME EARLIER, BUT...
OH WELL.
I HAD A FUN TIME.
Even though I fell for his tricks again.
....
WHAT IS IT NOW?
ONE GUY? NO, TWO.
THEY DON'T SEEM TO BE...
...YOUR TYPICAL PICK-POCKET OR DEGENERATE, THOUGH.

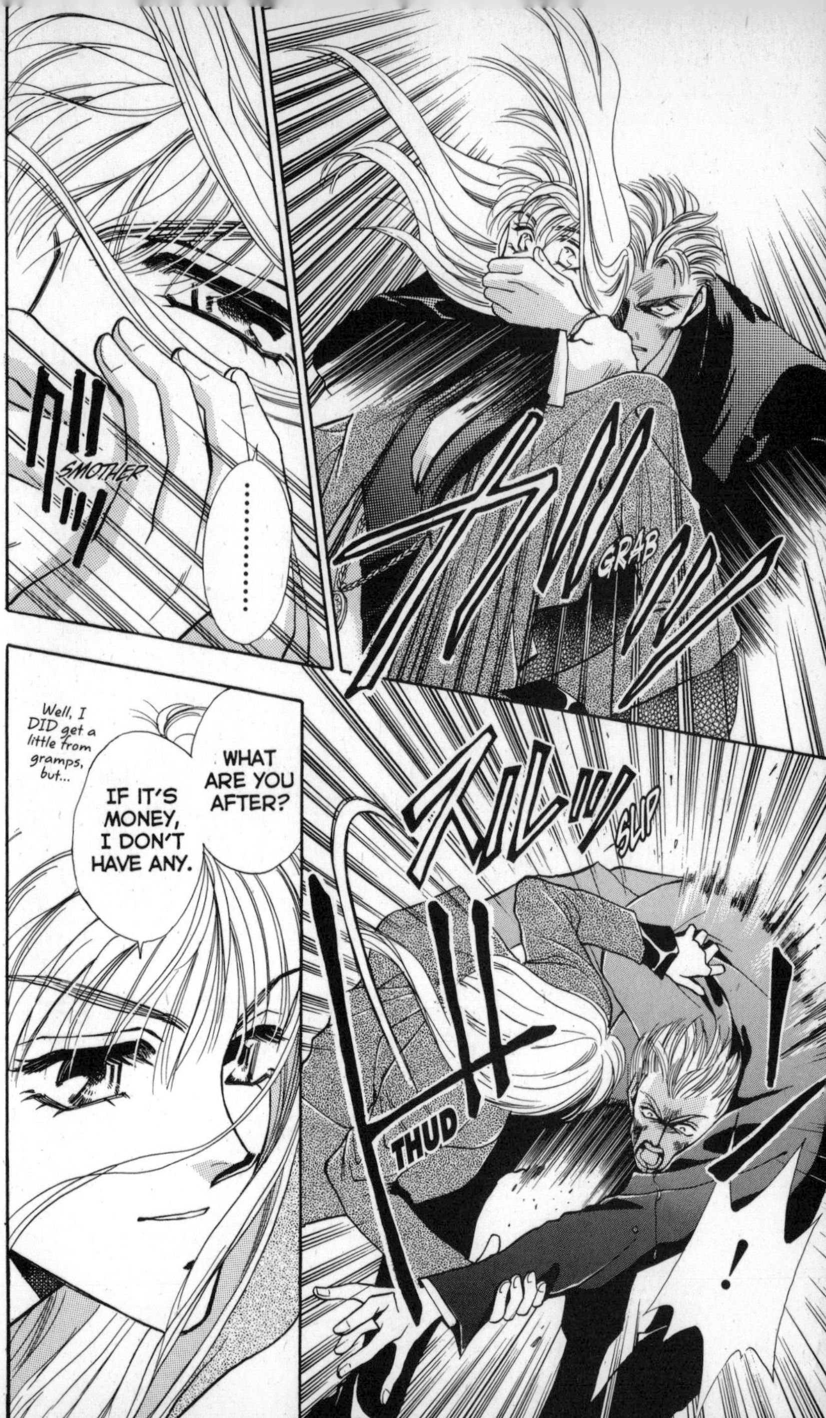
GRAB
SMOTHER
......
SLIP
THUD
!
!
WHAT ARE YOU AFTER?
IF IT'S MONEY, I DON'T HAVE ANY.
Well, I DID get a little from gramps, but...

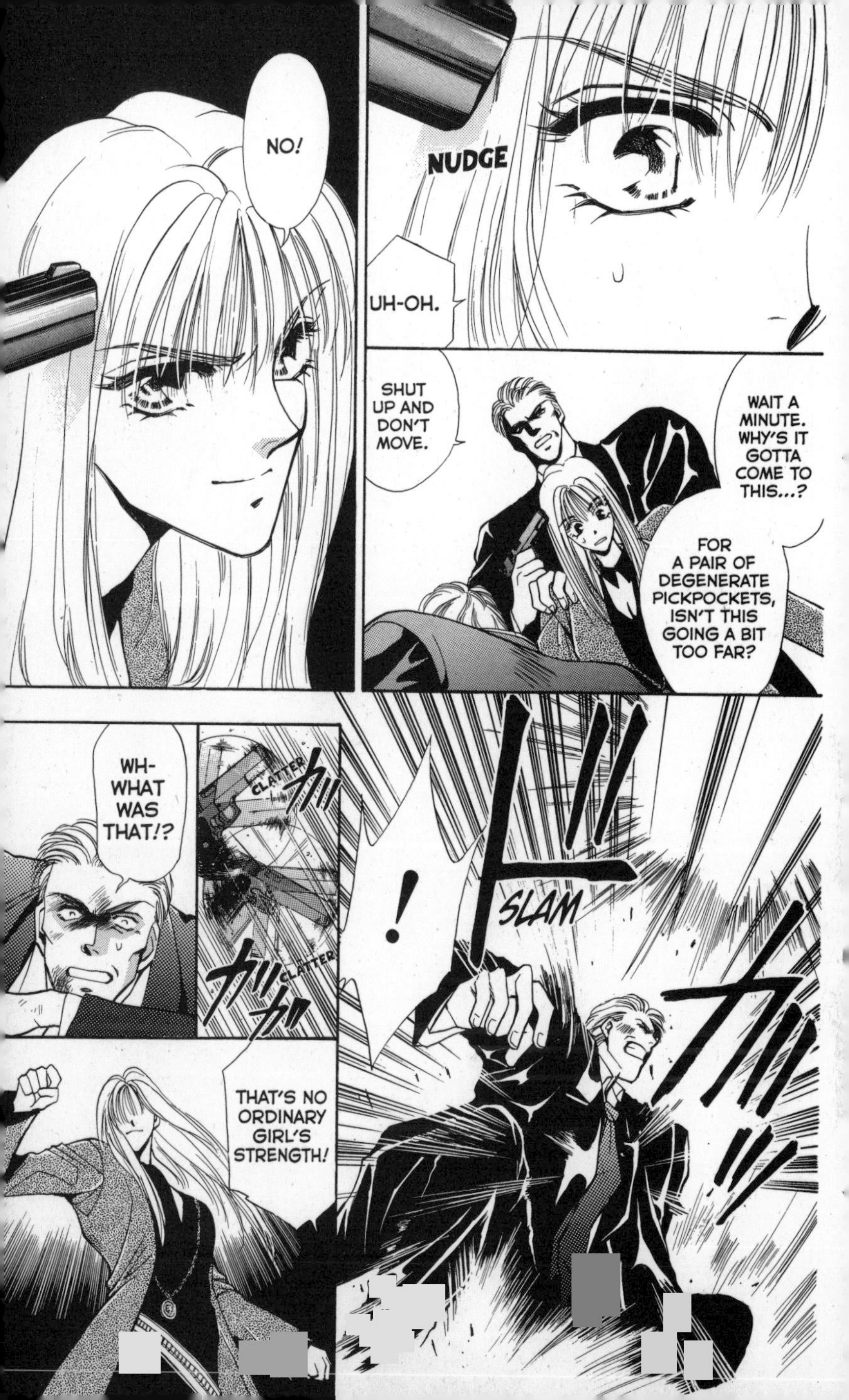
NUDGE
UH-OH.
WAIT A MINUTE. WHY'S IT GOTTA COME TO THIS...?
FOR A PAIR OF DEGENERATE PICKPOCKETS, ISN'T THIS GOING A BIT TOO FAR?
SHUT UP AND DON'T MOVE.
NO!
!
SLAM
CLATTER
CLATTER
WH-WHAT WAS THAT!?
THAT'S NO ORDINARY GIRL'S STRENGTH!

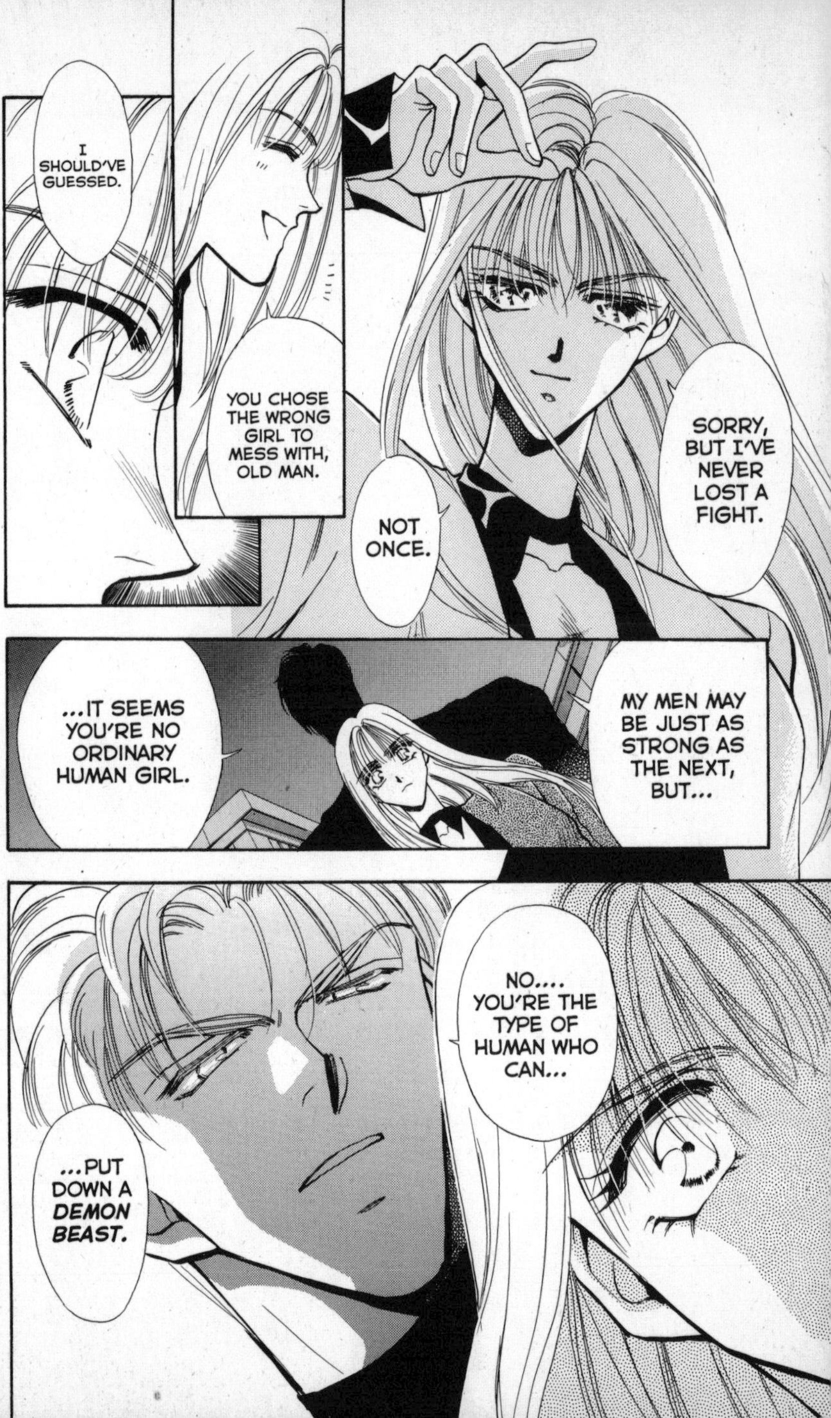
SORRY, BUT I'VE NEVER LOST A FIGHT.
NOT ONCE.
YOU CHOSE THE WRONG GIRL TO MESS WITH, OLD MAN.
I SHOULD'VE GUESSED.
MY MEN MAY BE JUST AS STRONG AS THE NEXT, BUT...
...IT SEEMS YOU'RE NO ORDINARY HUMAN GIRL.
NO.... YOU'RE THE TYPE OF HUMAN WHO CAN...
...PUT DOWN A *DEMON BEAST.*

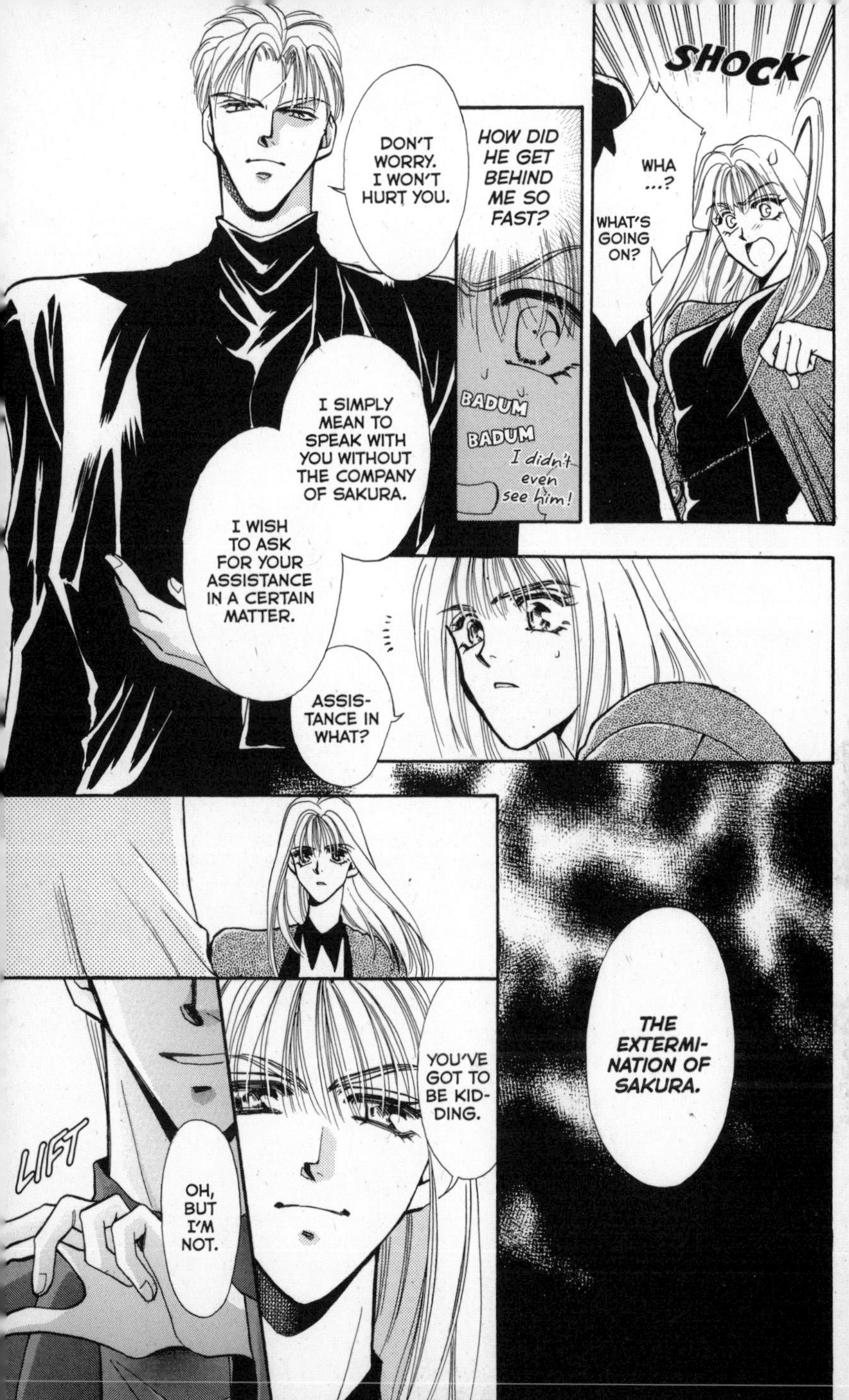
SHOCK
WHA ...?
WHAT'S GOING ON?
HOW DID HE GET BEHIND ME SO FAST?
BADUM
BADUM
I didn't even see him!
DON'T WORRY. I WON'T HURT YOU.
I SIMPLY MEAN TO SPEAK WITH YOU WITHOUT THE COMPANY OF SAKURA.
I WISH TO ASK FOR YOUR ASSISTANCE IN A CERTAIN MATTER.
ASSISTANCE IN WHAT?
THE EXTERMINATION OF SAKURA.
YOU'VE GOT TO BE KIDDING.
LIFT
OH, BUT I'M NOT.

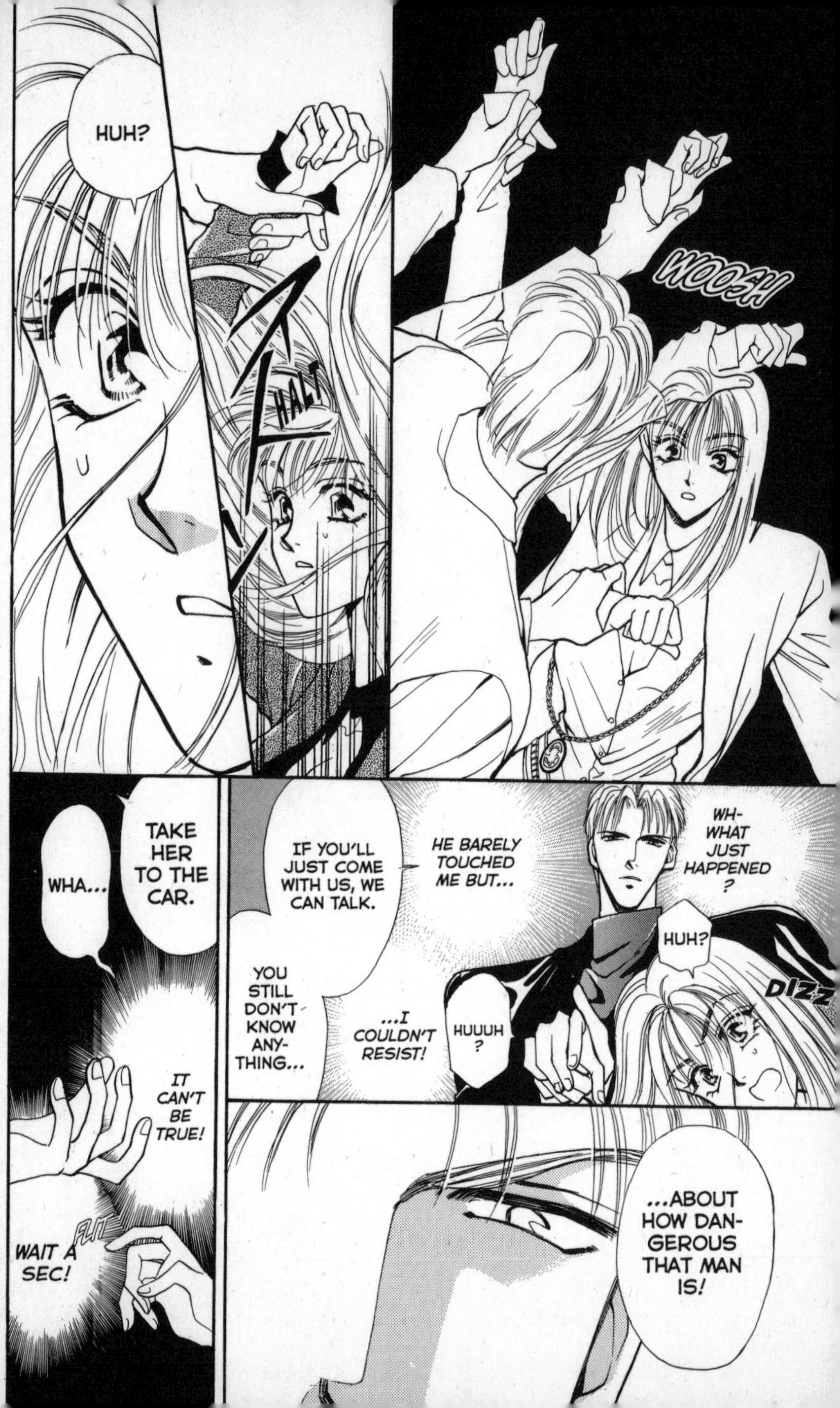
WOOSH
HUH?
HALT
WH-WHAT JUST HAPPENED?
HE BARELY TOUCHED ME BUT...
IF YOU'LL JUST COME WITH US, WE CAN TALK.
HUH?
DIZZ
HUUUH?
...I COULDN'T RESIST!
YOU STILL DON'T KNOW ANYTHING...
...ABOUT HOW DANGEROUS THAT MAN IS!
TAKE HER TO THE CAR.
WHA...
IT CAN'T BE TRUE!
FLIT
WAIT A SEC!

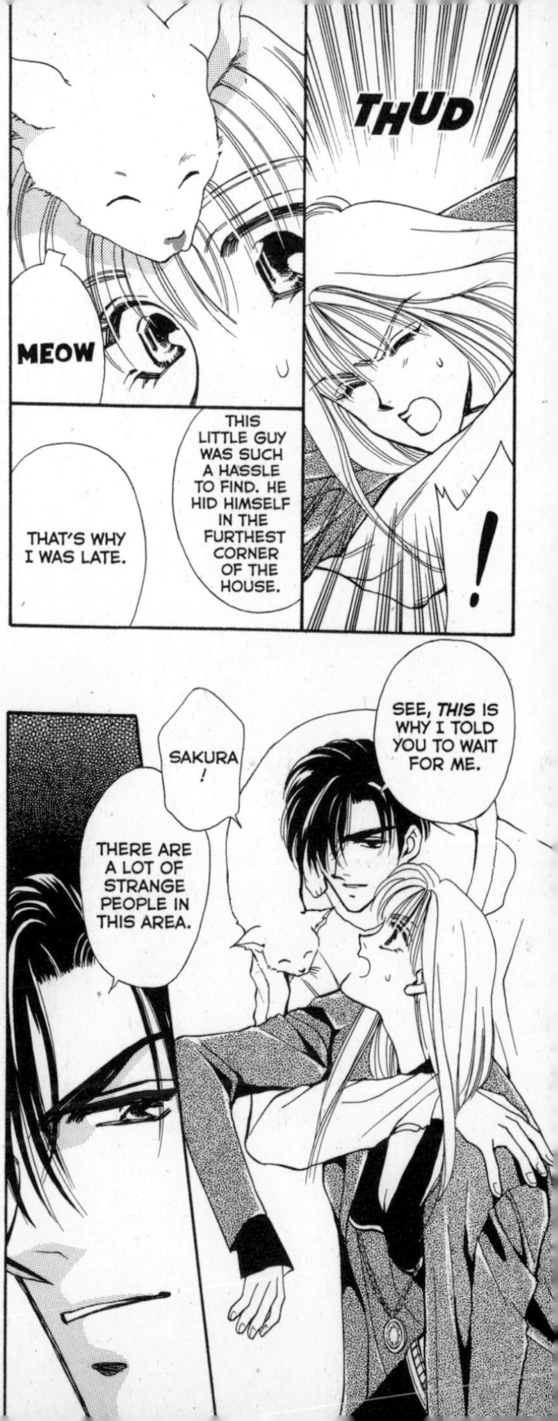

THUD
!
MEOW
THIS LITTLE GUY WAS SUCH A HASSLE TO FIND. HE HID HIMSELF IN THE FURTHEST CORNER OF THE HOUSE.
THAT'S WHY I WAS LATE.
SEE, *THIS* IS WHY I TOLD YOU TO WAIT FOR ME.
SAKURA!
THERE ARE A LOT OF STRANGE PEOPLE IN THIS AREA.

Here's a question I get asked a lot in my fan letters. "What music do you listen to while you draw?" Usually I just leave the radio on while I work, but I mainly listen to my assistants talking.

I swear, their conversations make me keel over with laughter. It's pretty amusing.

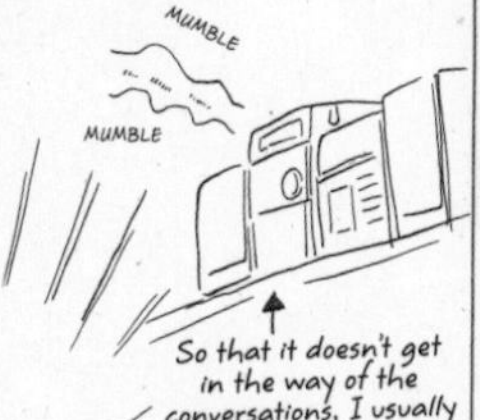

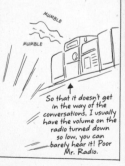

MUMBLE
MUMBLE

So that it doesn't get in the way of the conversations, I usually have the volume on the radio turned down so low, you can barely hear it! Poor Mr. Radio.

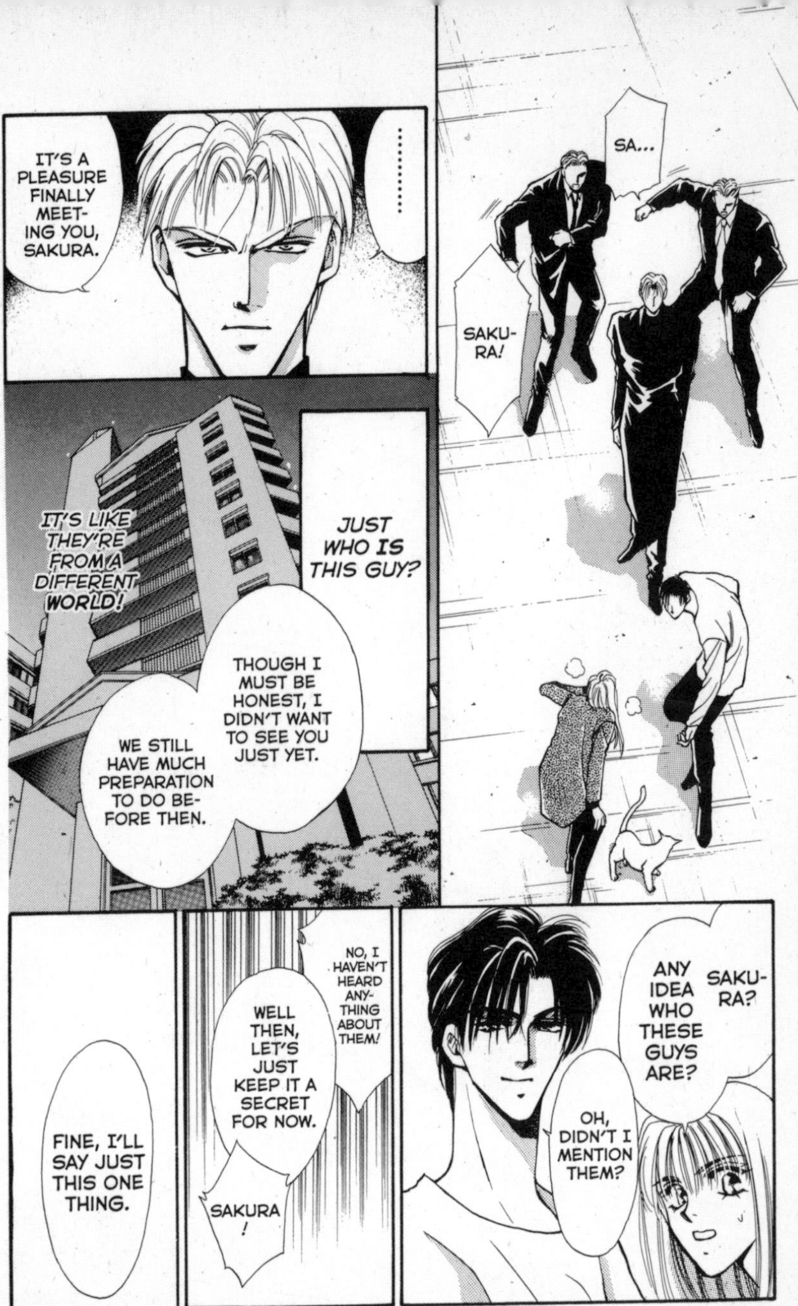
SA...
SAKU-RA!
......
IT'S A PLEASURE FINALLY MEET-ING YOU, SAKURA.
JUST WHO *IS* THIS GUY?
IT'S LIKE THEY'RE FROM A DIFFERENT WORLD!
THOUGH I MUST BE HONEST, I DIDN'T WANT TO SEE YOU JUST YET.
WE STILL HAVE MUCH PREPARATION TO DO BE-FORE THEN.
SAKU-RA?
ANY IDEA WHO THESE GUYS ARE?
OH, DIDN'T I MENTION THEM?
NO, I HAVEN'T HEARD ANY-THING ABOUT THEM!
WELL THEN, LET'S JUST KEEP IT A SECRET FOR NOW.
SAKURA!
FINE, I'LL SAY JUST THIS ONE THING.

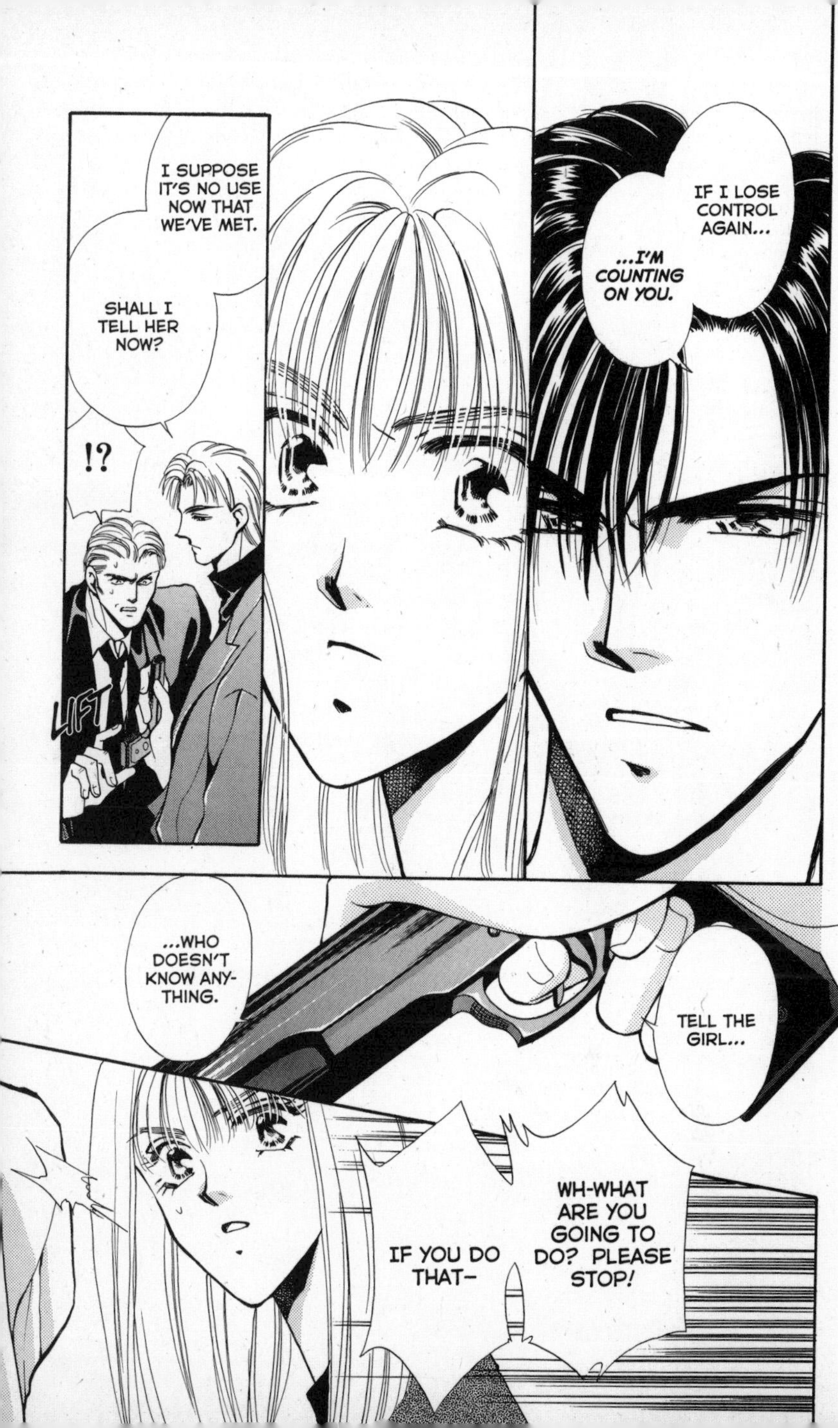
IF I LOSE CONTROL AGAIN...
...I'M COUNTING ON YOU.
I SUPPOSE IT'S NO USE NOW THAT WE'VE MET.
SHALL I TELL HER NOW?
!?
LIFT
TELL THE GIRL...
...WHO DOESN'T KNOW ANYTHING.
WH-WHAT ARE YOU GOING TO DO? PLEASE STOP!
IF YOU DO THAT–

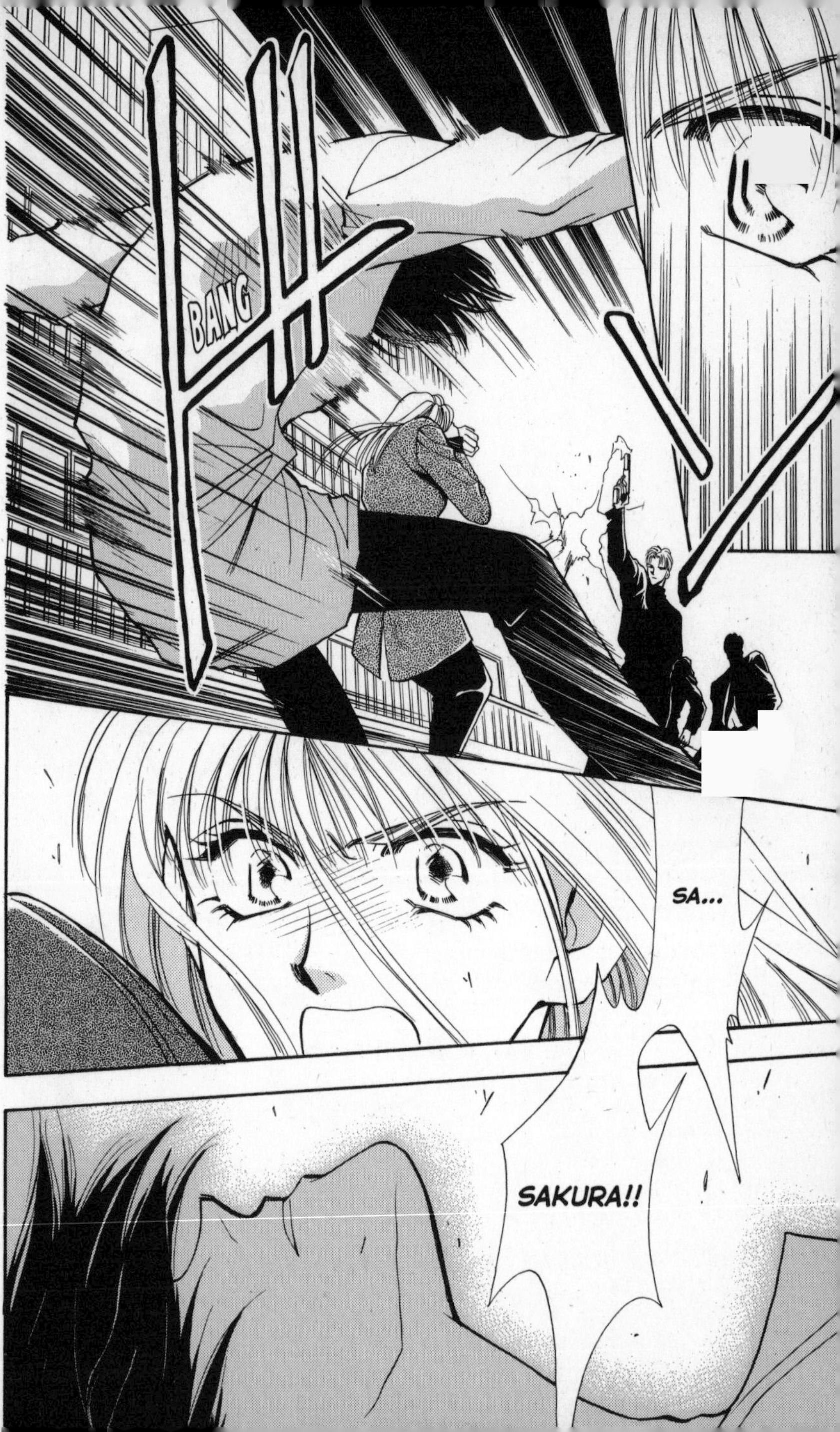
BANG
SA...
SAKURA!!

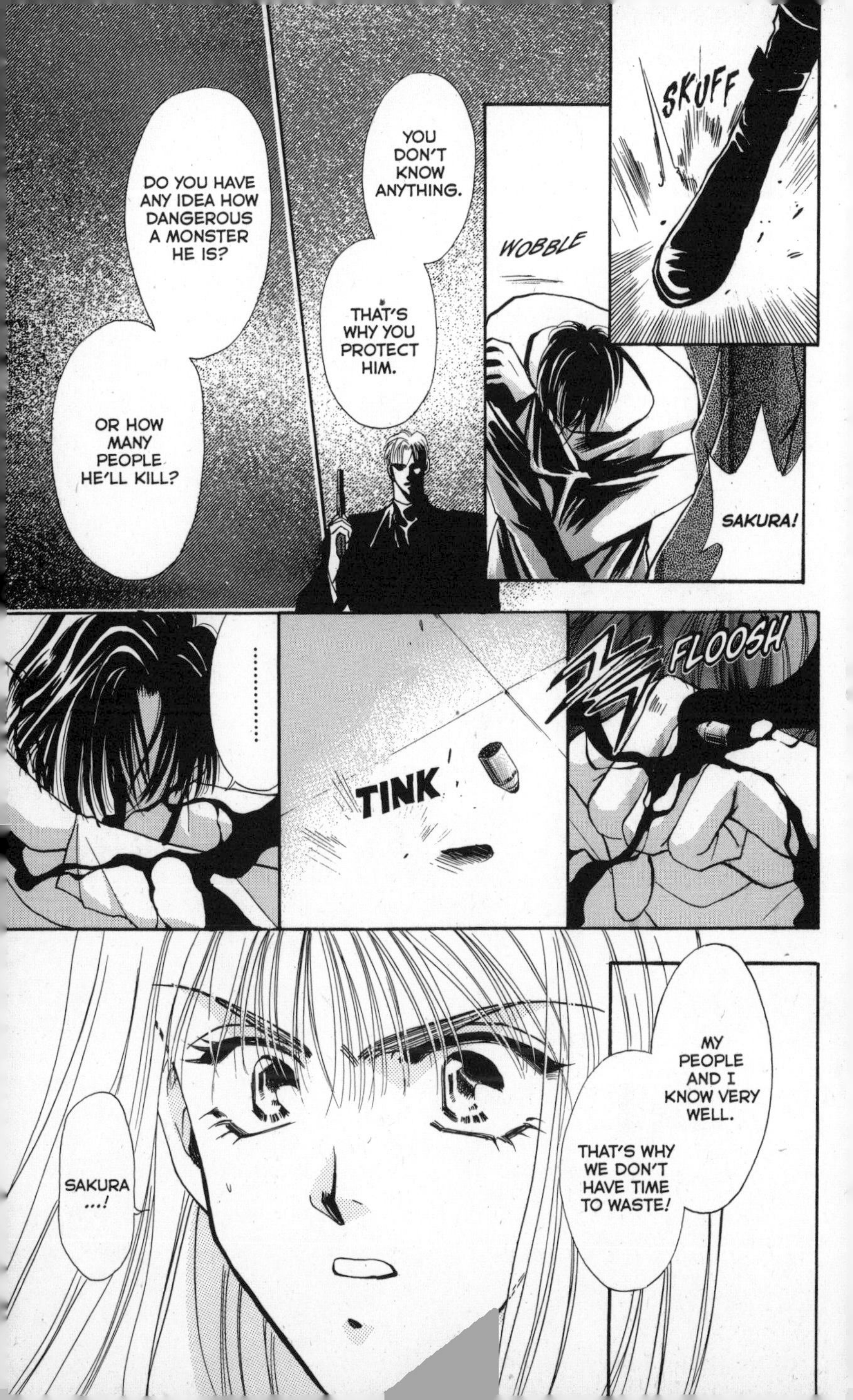
SKUFF
WOBBLE
SAKURA!
YOU DON'T KNOW ANYTHING.
THAT'S WHY YOU PROTECT HIM.
DO YOU HAVE ANY IDEA HOW DANGEROUS A MONSTER HE IS?
OR HOW MANY PEOPLE HE'LL KILL?
FLOOSH
TINK
……
MY PEOPLE AND I KNOW VERY WELL.
THAT'S WHY WE DON'T HAVE TIME TO WASTE!
SAKURA …!

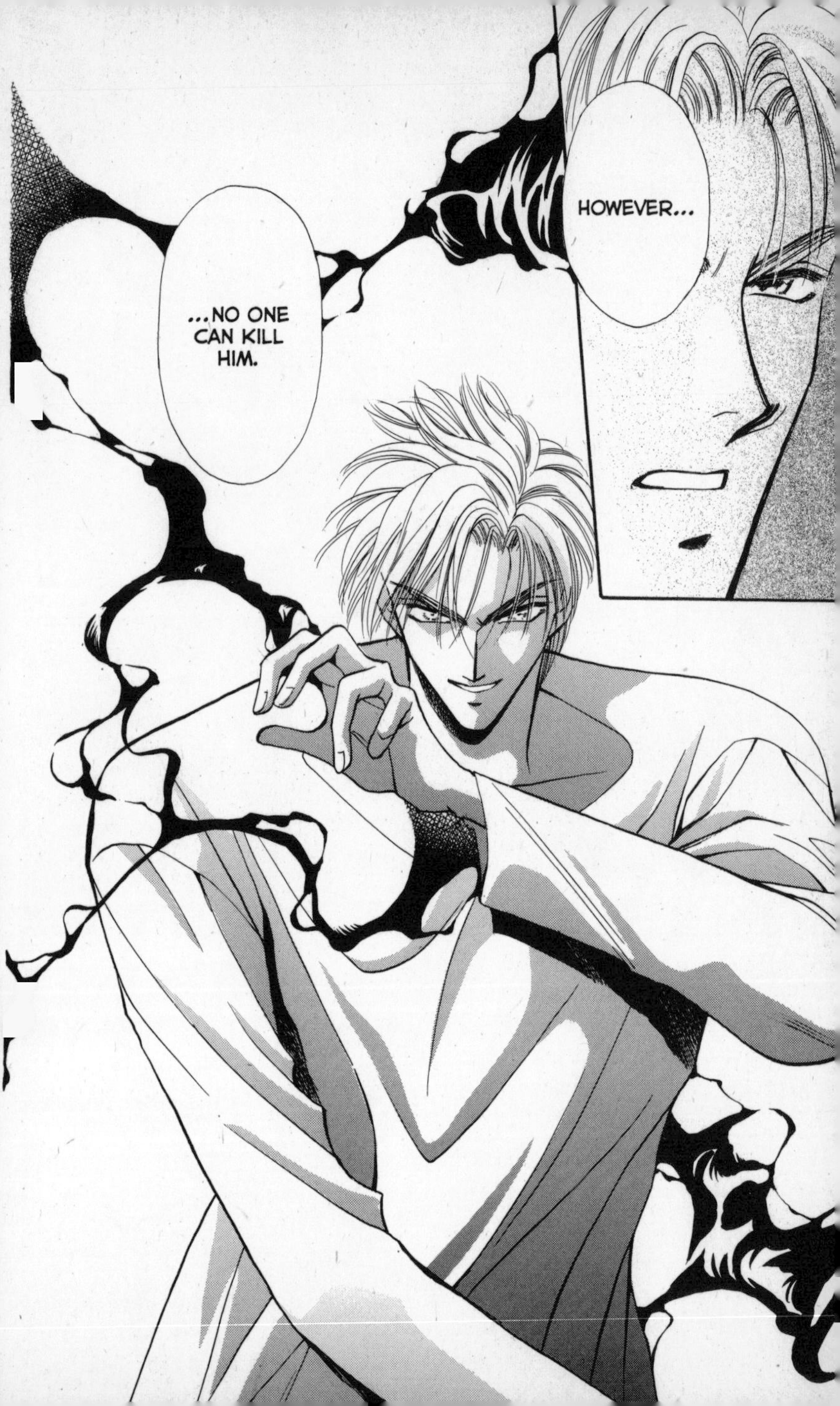
HOWEVER...
...NO ONE CAN KILL HIM.

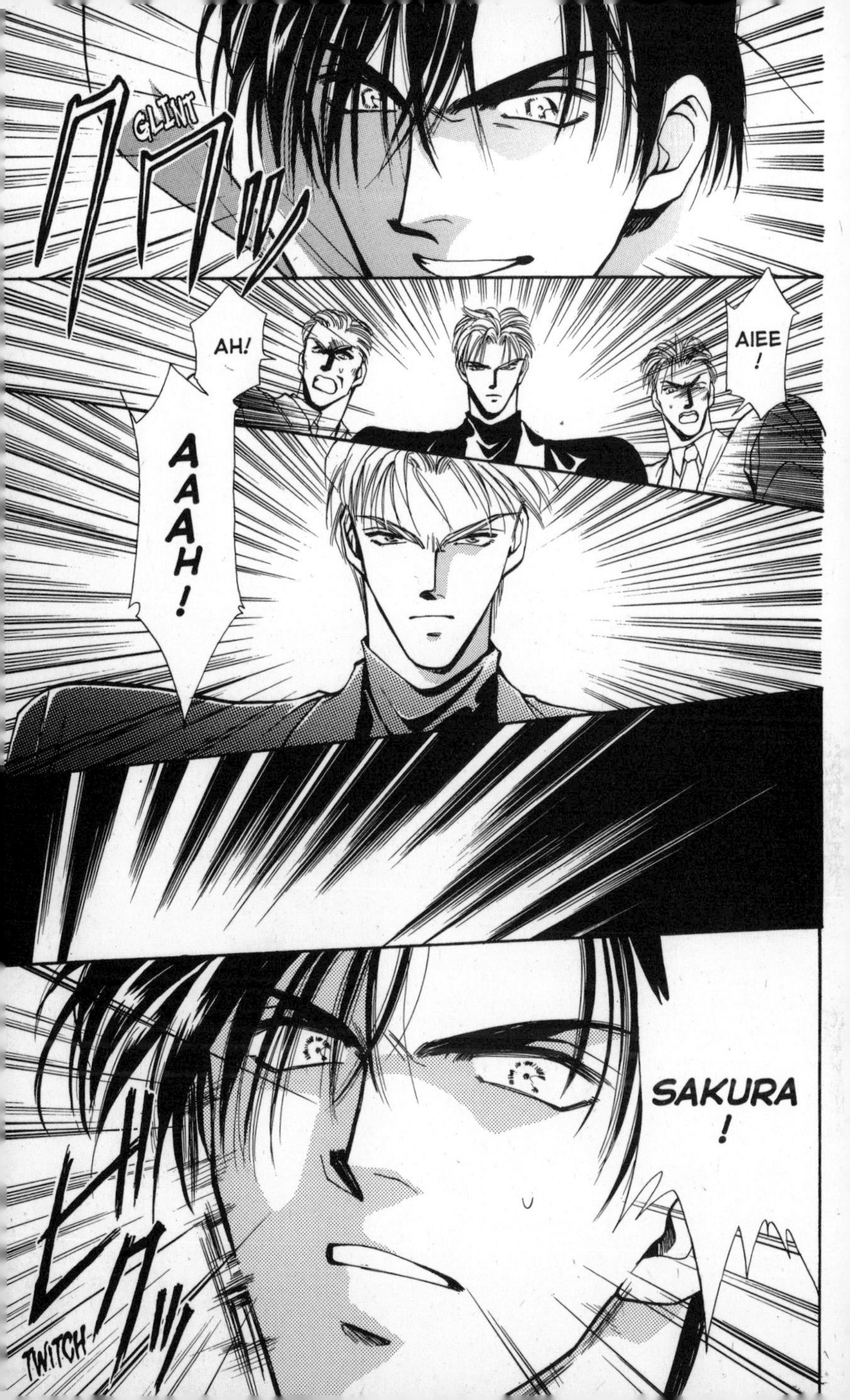
GLINT
AIEE!
AH!
AAAAH!
SAKURA!
TWITCH

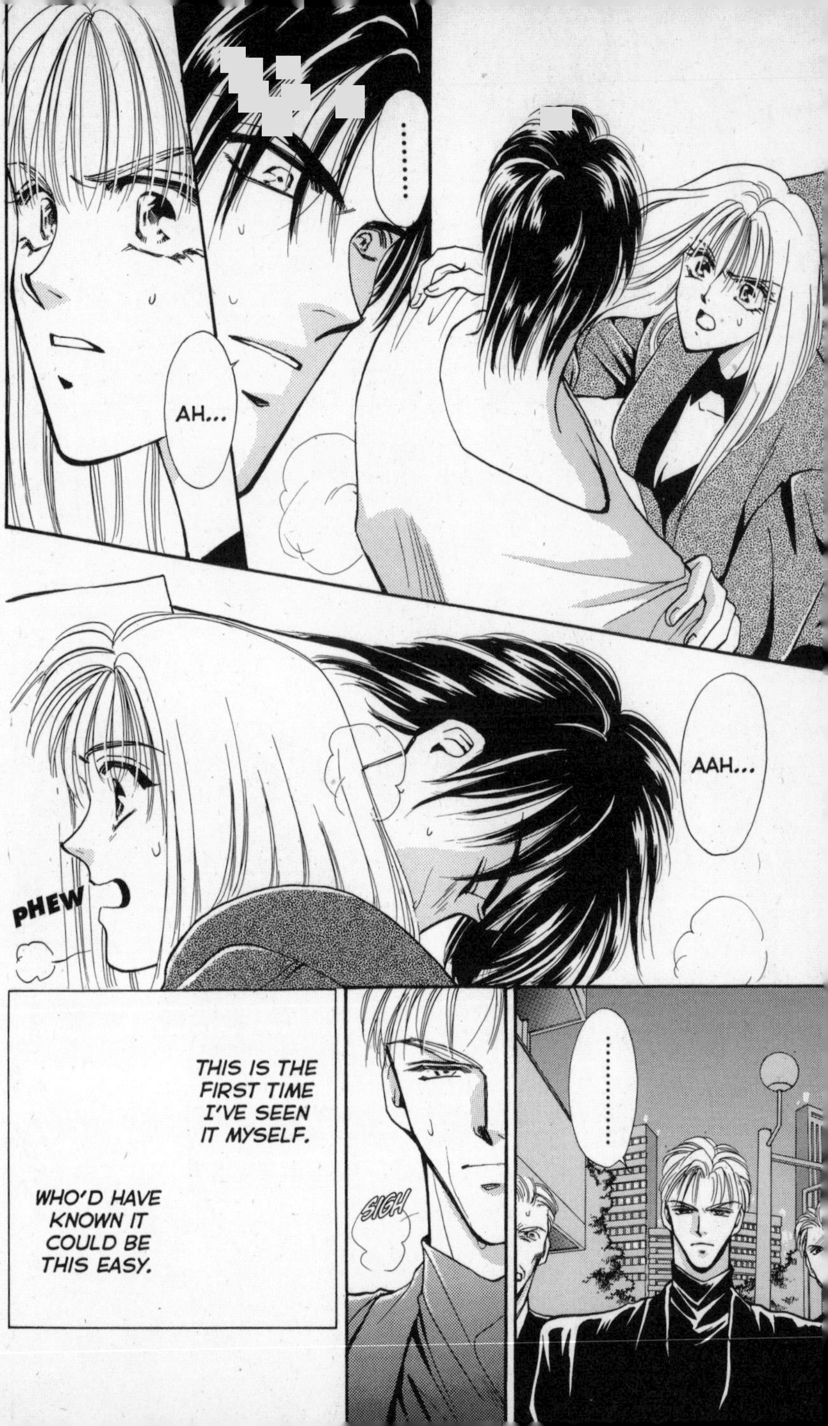
......
AH...
AAH...
PHEW
......
SIGH
THIS IS THE FIRST TIME I'VE SEEN IT MYSELF.
WHO'D HAVE KNOWN IT COULD BE THIS EASY.

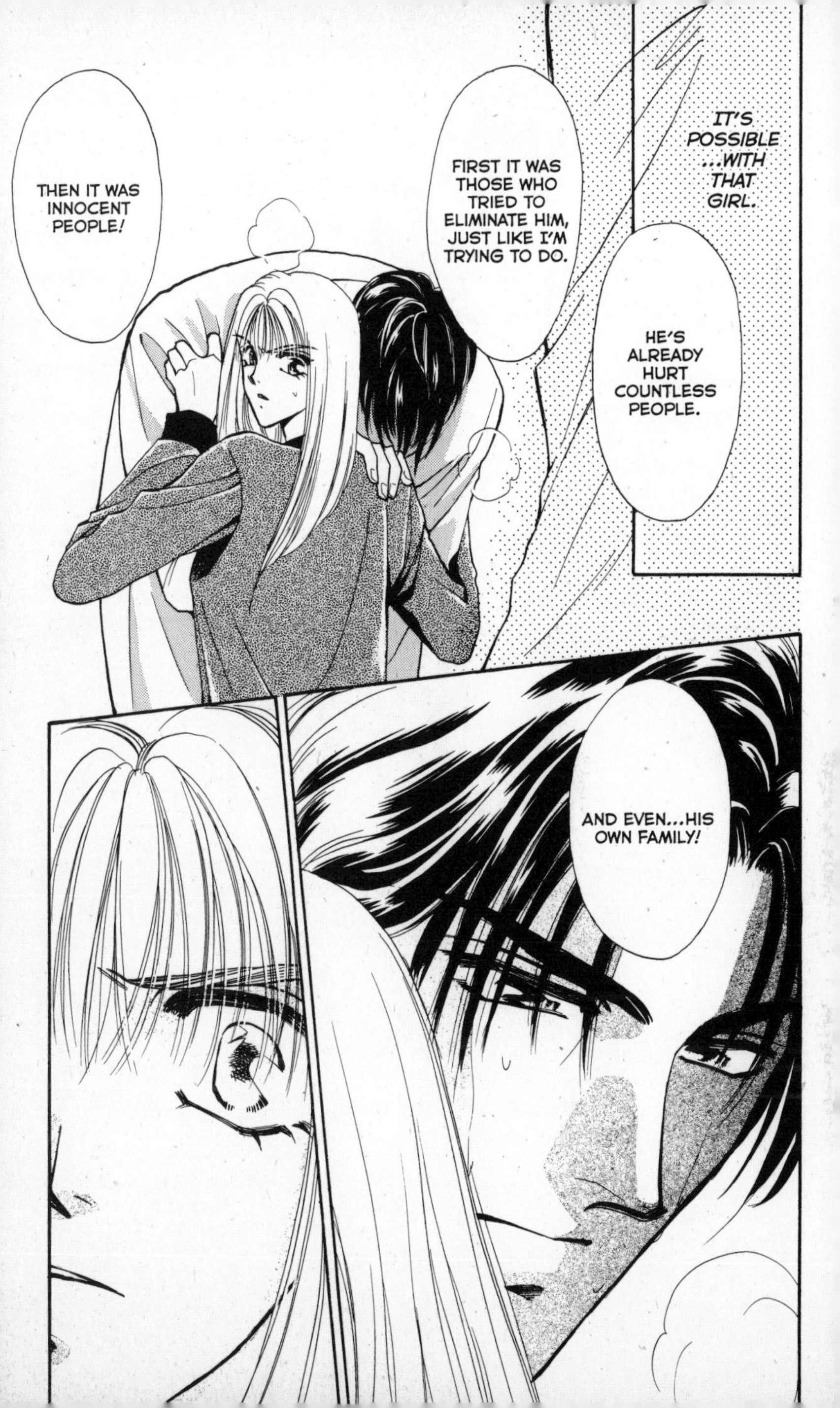
IT'S POSSIBLE ...WITH THAT GIRL.
HE'S ALREADY HURT COUNTLESS PEOPLE.
FIRST IT WAS THOSE WHO TRIED TO ELIMINATE HIM, JUST LIKE I'M TRYING TO DO.
THEN IT WAS INNOCENT PEOPLE!
AND EVEN...HIS OWN FAMILY!

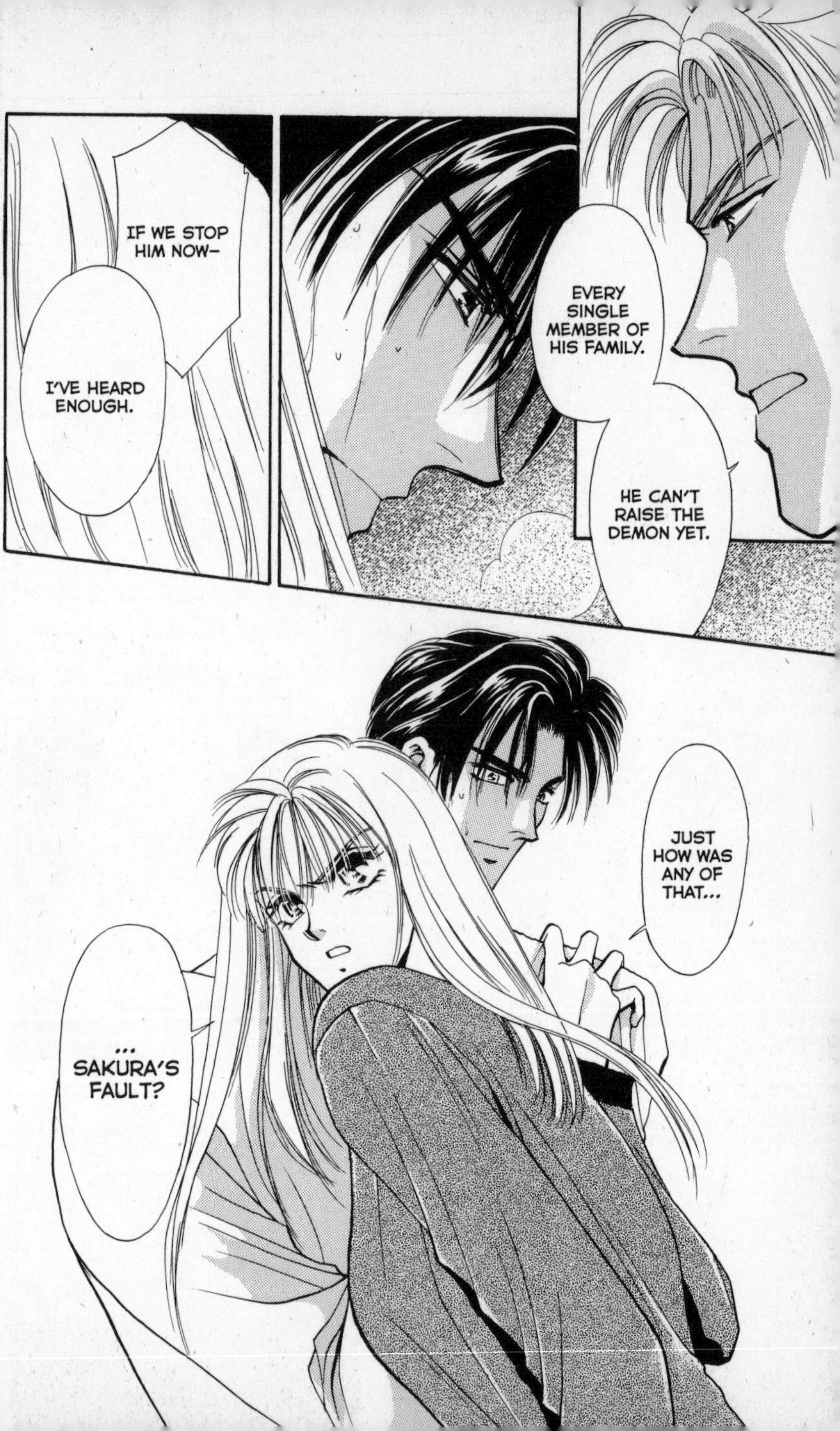
EVERY SINGLE MEMBER OF HIS FAMILY.
HE CAN'T RAISE THE DEMON YET.
IF WE STOP HIM NOW—
I'VE HEARD ENOUGH.
JUST HOW WAS ANY OF THAT...
... SAKURA'S FAULT?

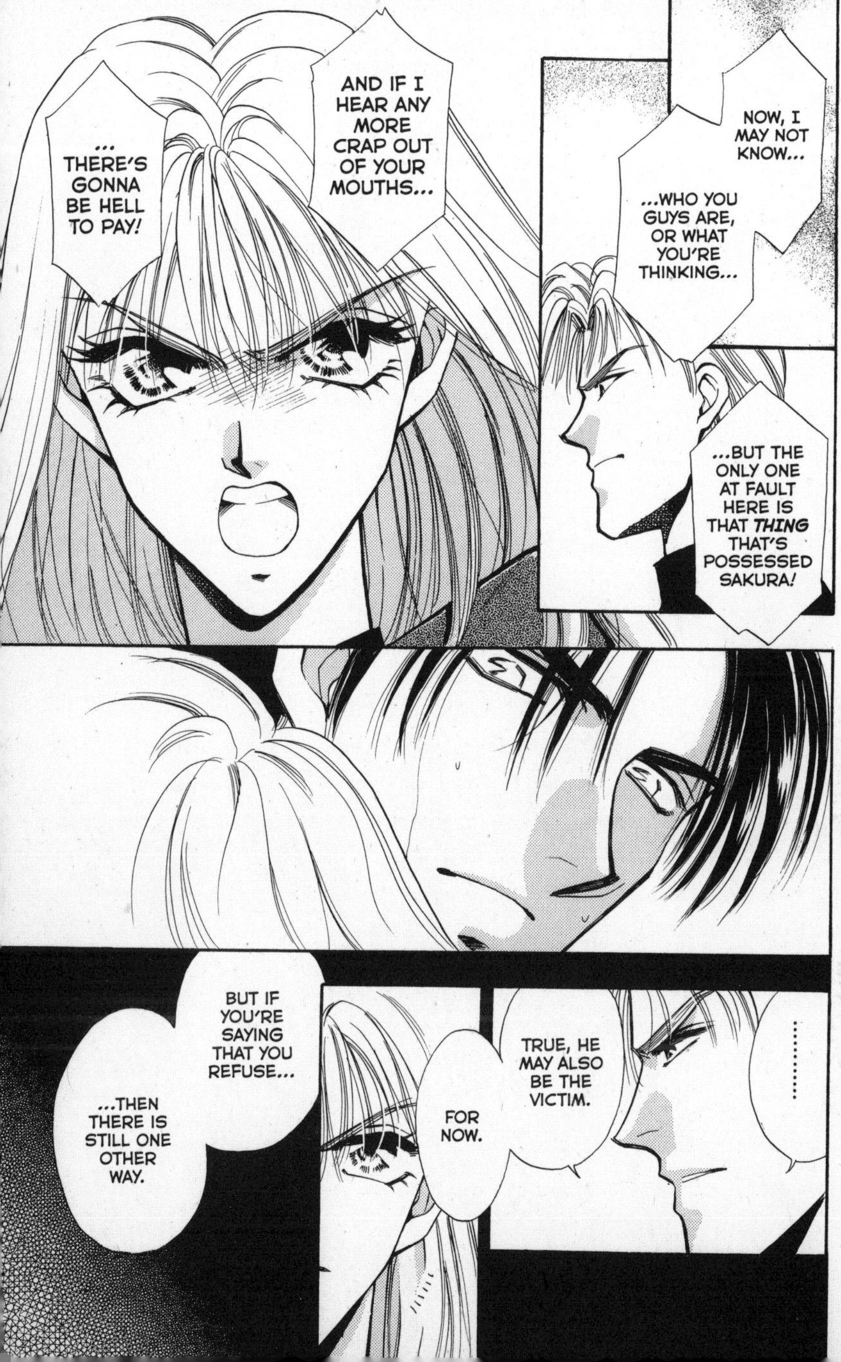
NOW, I MAY NOT KNOW...
...WHO YOU GUYS ARE, OR WHAT YOU'RE THINKING...
...BUT THE ONLY ONE AT FAULT HERE IS THAT *THING* THAT'S POSSESSED SAKURA!
AND IF I HEAR ANY MORE CRAP OUT OF YOUR MOUTHS...
...THERE'S GONNA BE HELL TO PAY!
......
TRUE, HE MAY ALSO BE THE VICTIM.
FOR NOW.
BUT IF YOU'RE SAYING THAT YOU REFUSE...
...THEN THERE IS STILL ONE OTHER WAY.

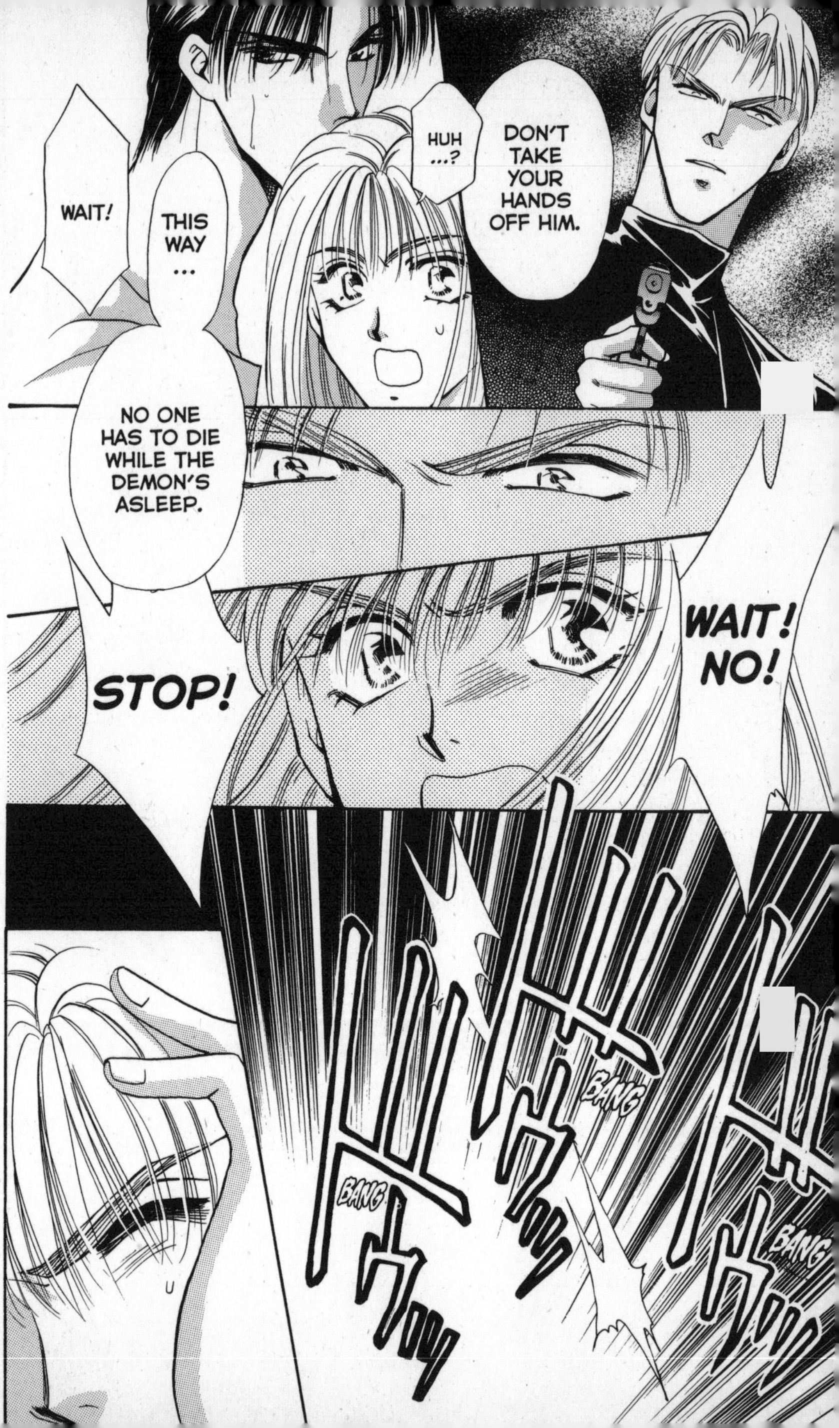
DON'T TAKE YOUR HANDS OFF HIM.
HUH ...?
THIS WAY ...
WAIT!
NO ONE HAS TO DIE WHILE THE DEMON'S ASLEEP.
WAIT! NO!
STOP!
BANG
BANG
BANG

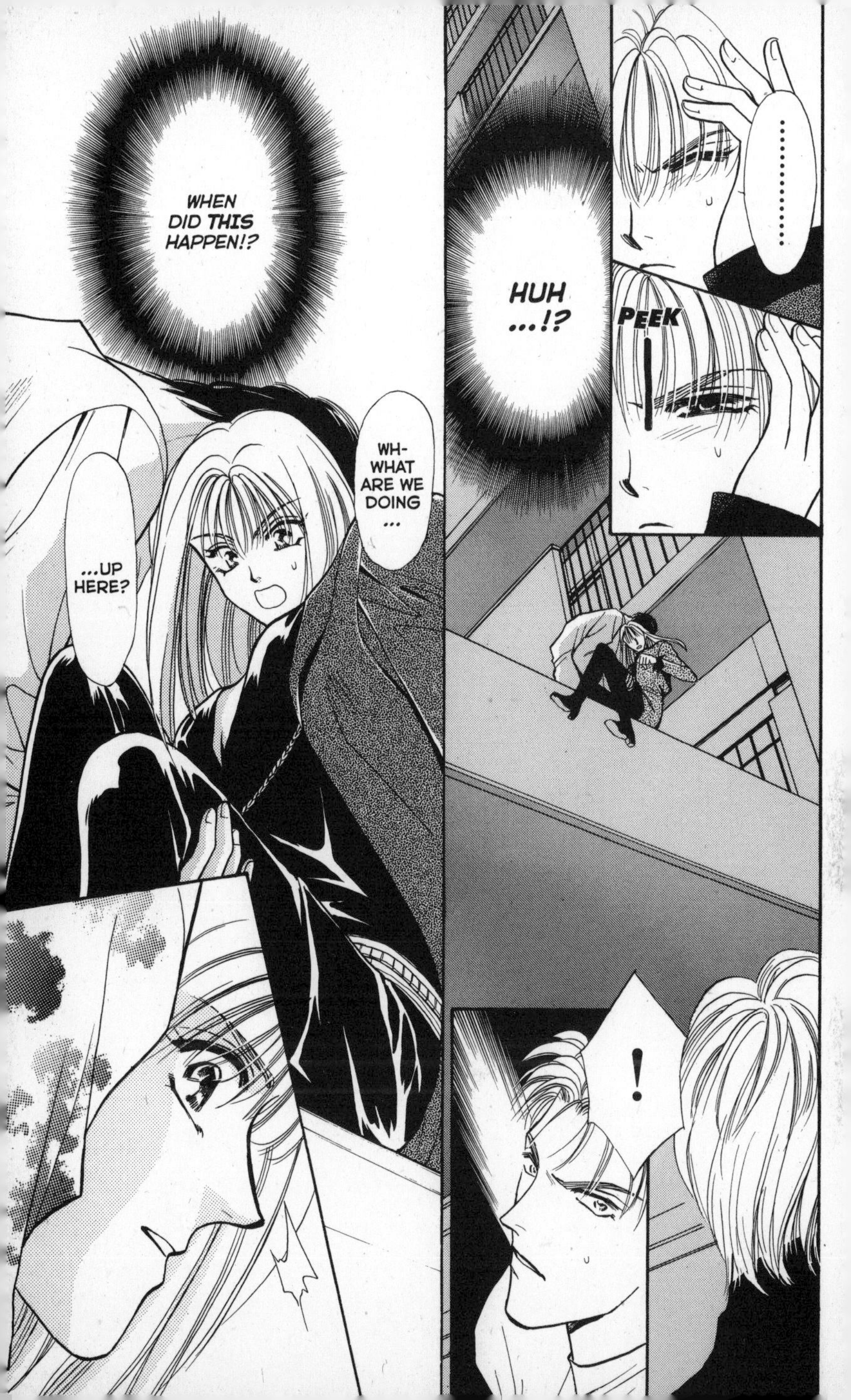

......
PEEK
HUH ...!?
!
WHEN DID THIS HAPPEN!?
WH- WHAT ARE WE DOING ...
...UP HERE?

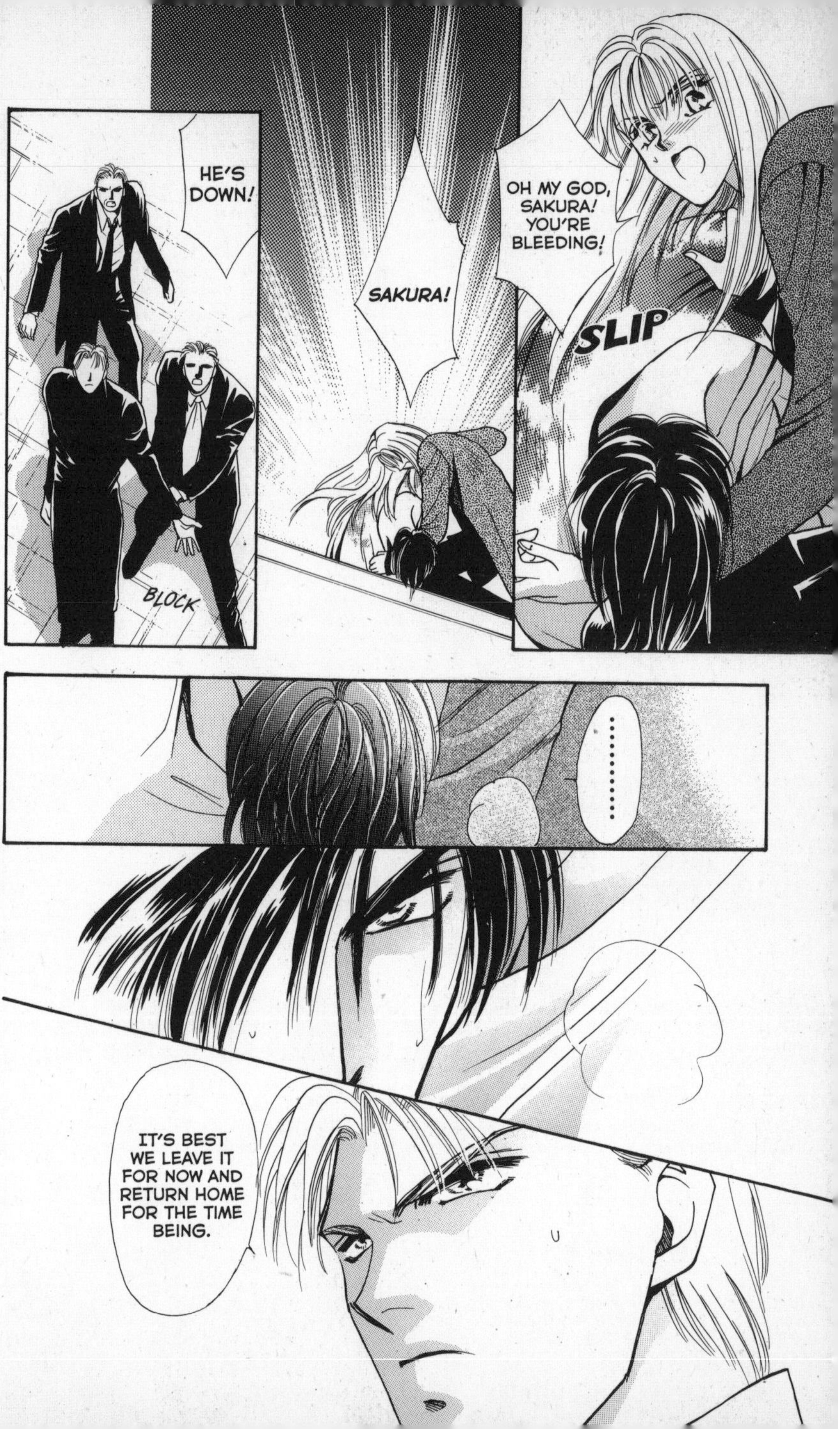
OH MY GOD, SAKURA! YOU'RE BLEEDING!
SLIP
SAKURA!
HE'S DOWN!
BLOCK
....
IT'S BEST WE LEAVE IT FOR NOW AND RETURN HOME FOR THE TIME BEING.

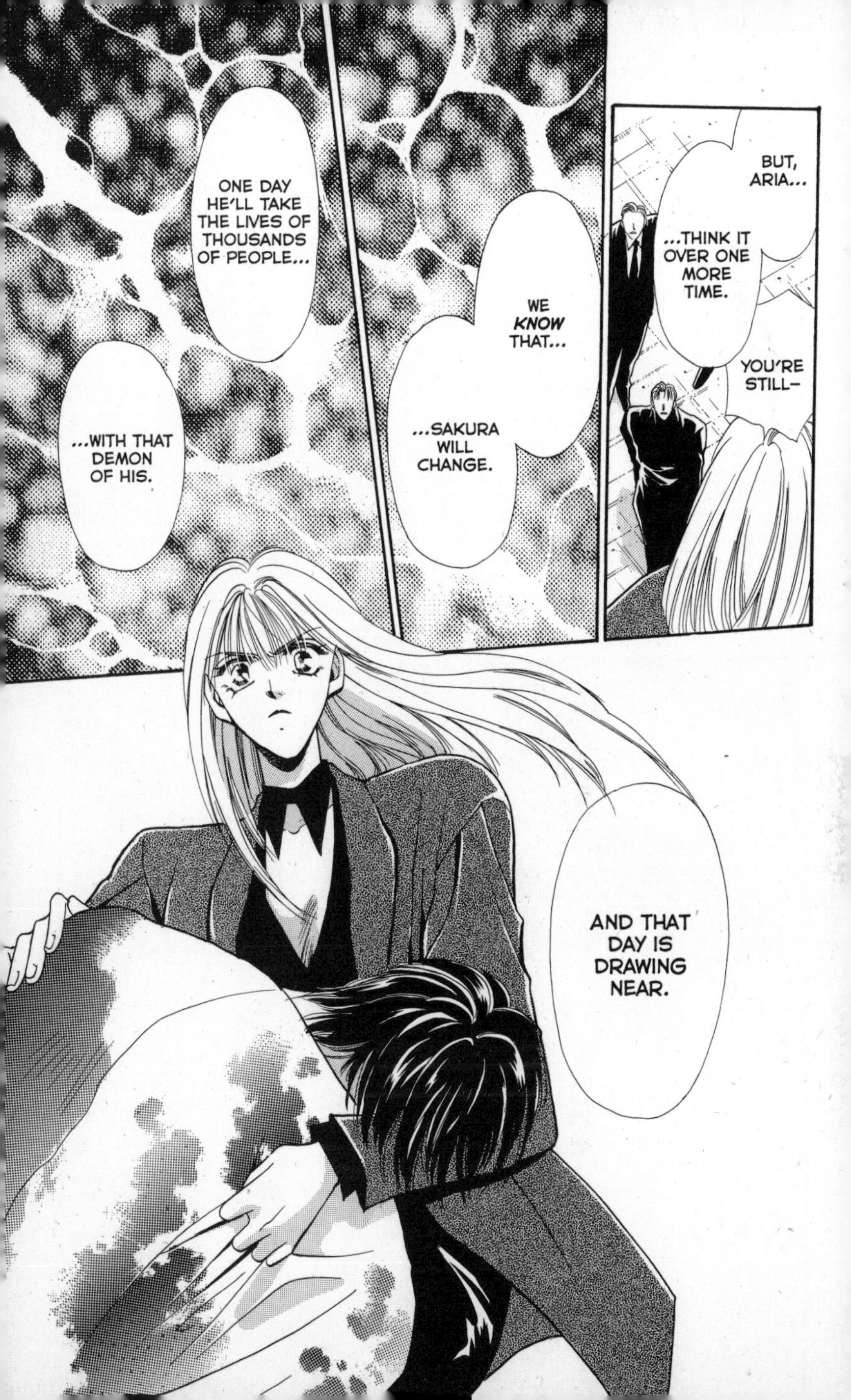
BUT, ARIA...
...THINK IT OVER ONE MORE TIME.
YOU'RE STILL–
WE *KNOW* THAT...
...SAKURA WILL CHANGE.
ONE DAY HE'LL TAKE THE LIVES OF THOUSANDS OF PEOPLE...
...WITH THAT DEMON OF HIS.
AND THAT DAY IS DRAWING NEAR.

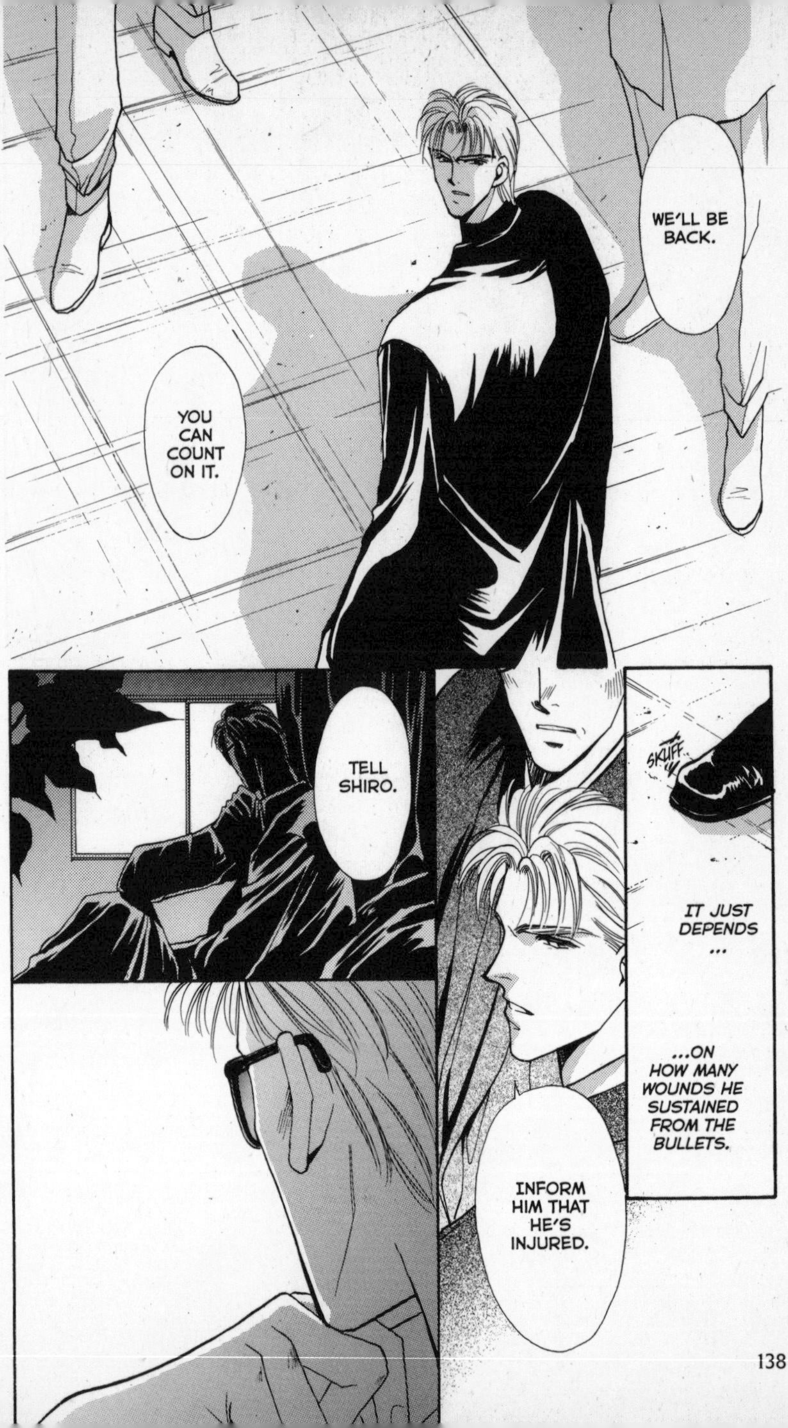
WE'LL BE BACK.
YOU CAN COUNT ON IT.
SKUFF
IT JUST DEPENDS ...
...ON HOW MANY WOUNDS HE SUSTAINED FROM THE BULLETS.
INFORM HIM THAT HE'S INJURED.
TELL SHIRO.

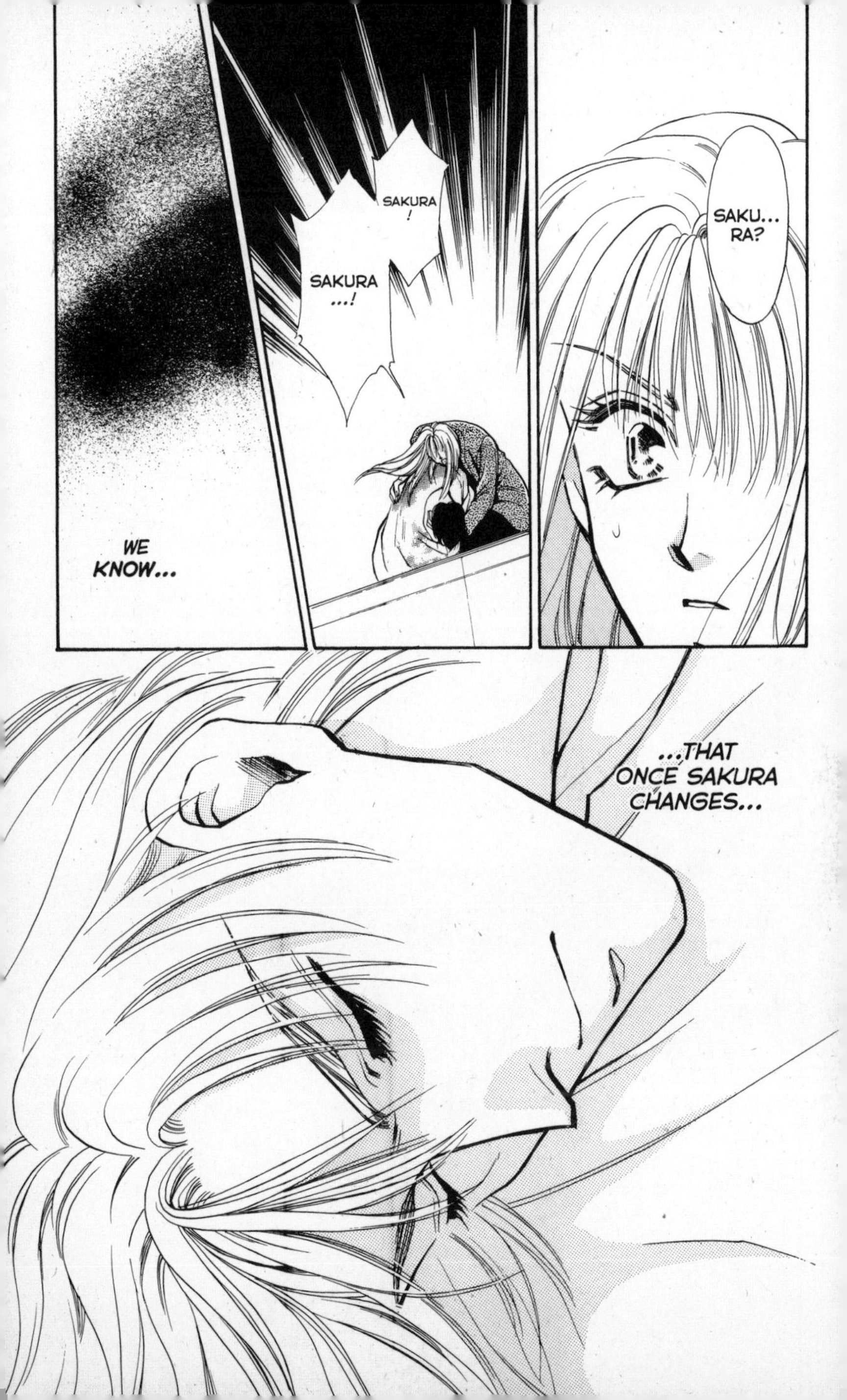
SAKU... RA?
SAKURA!
SAKURA...!
WE KNOW...
...THAT ONCE SAKURA CHANGES...

NIGHT OF THE BEASTS

CHAPTER 4

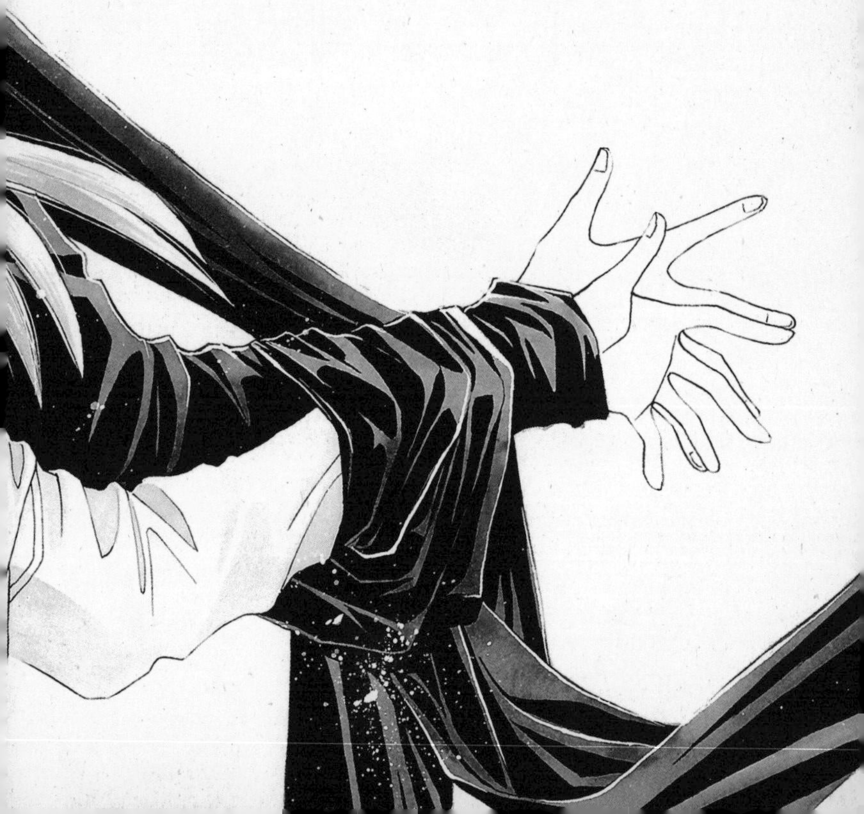

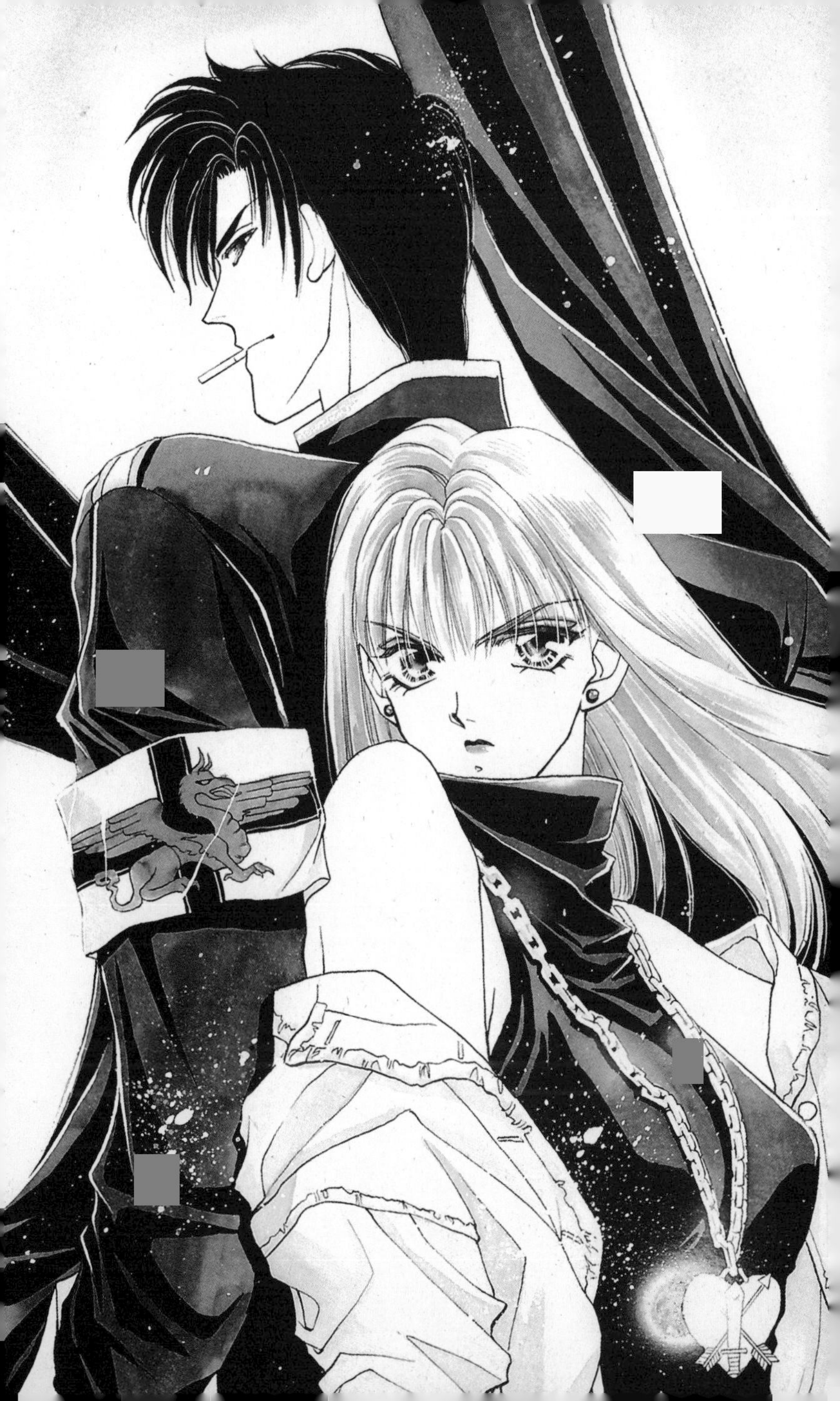

獣たちの夜

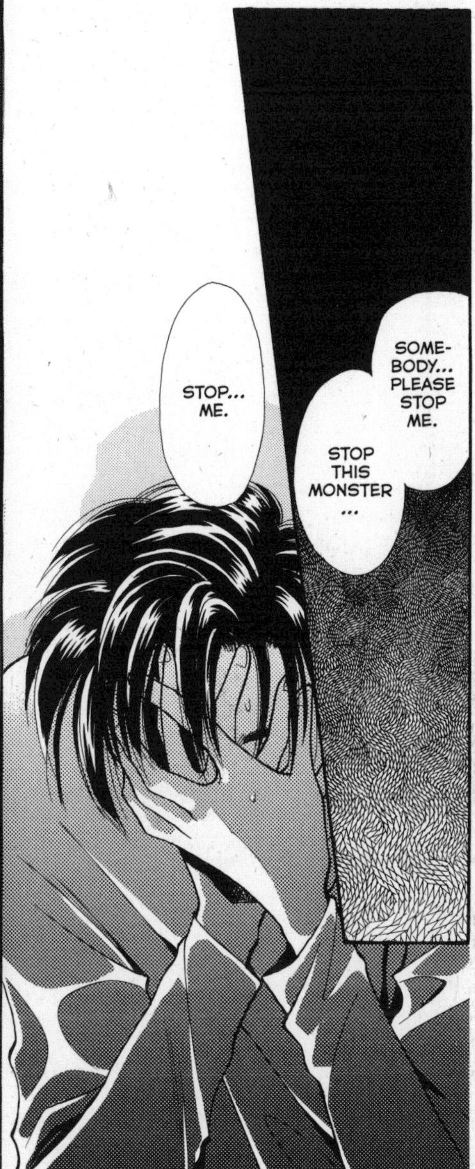
SOME-BODY... PLEASE STOP ME.
STOP THIS MONSTER ...
STOP... ME.

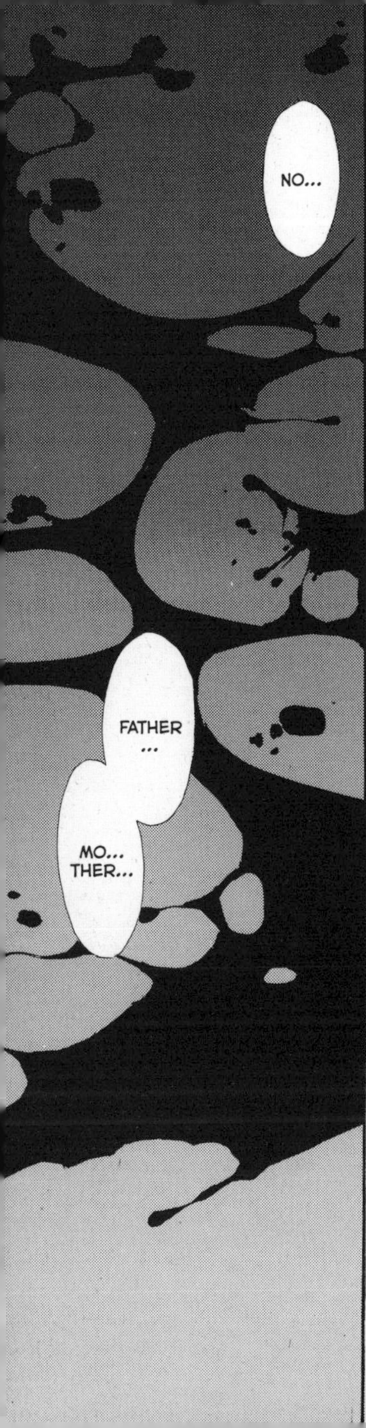
NO...
FATHER ...
MO... THER...

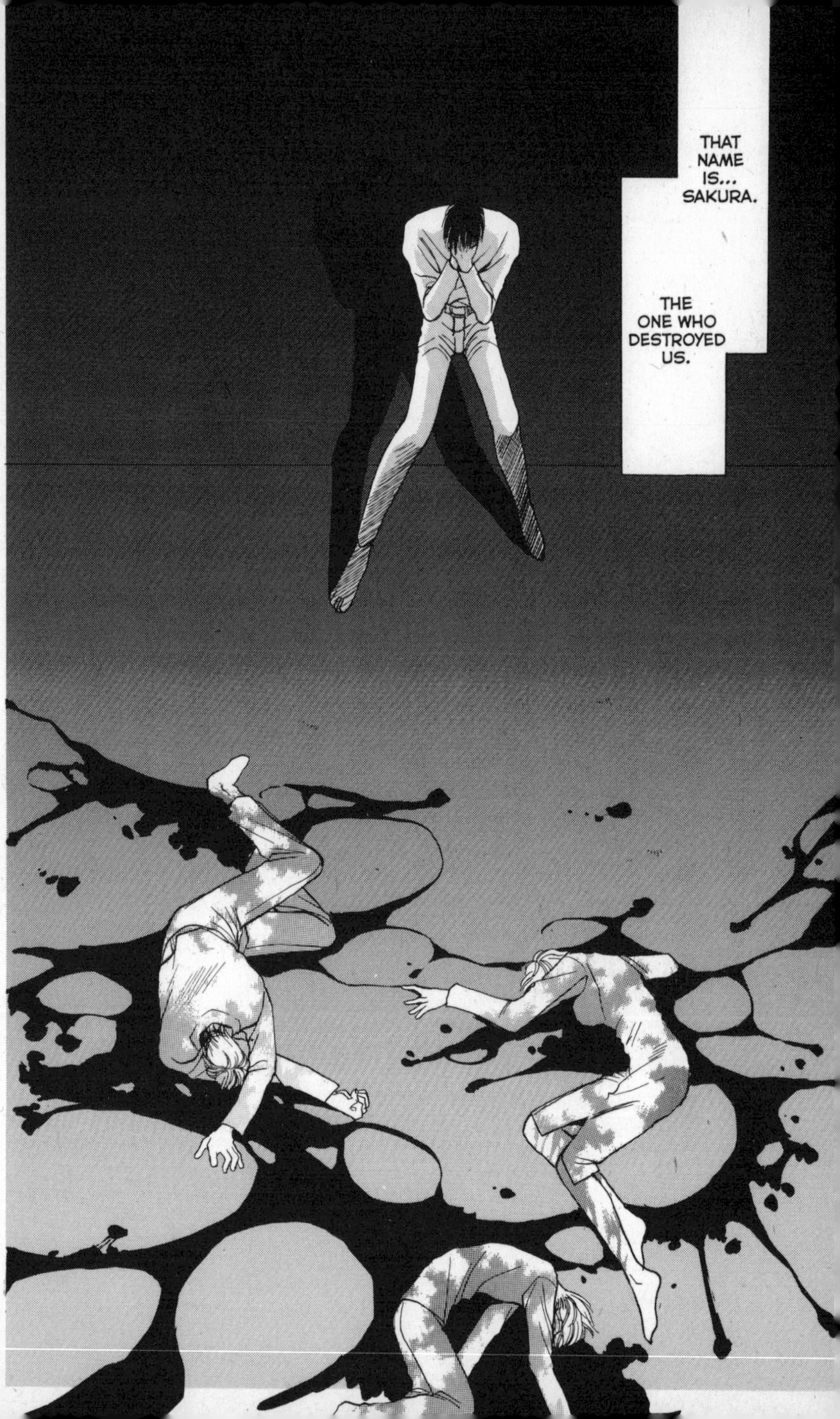
THAT NAME IS... SAKURA.
THE ONE WHO DESTROYED US.

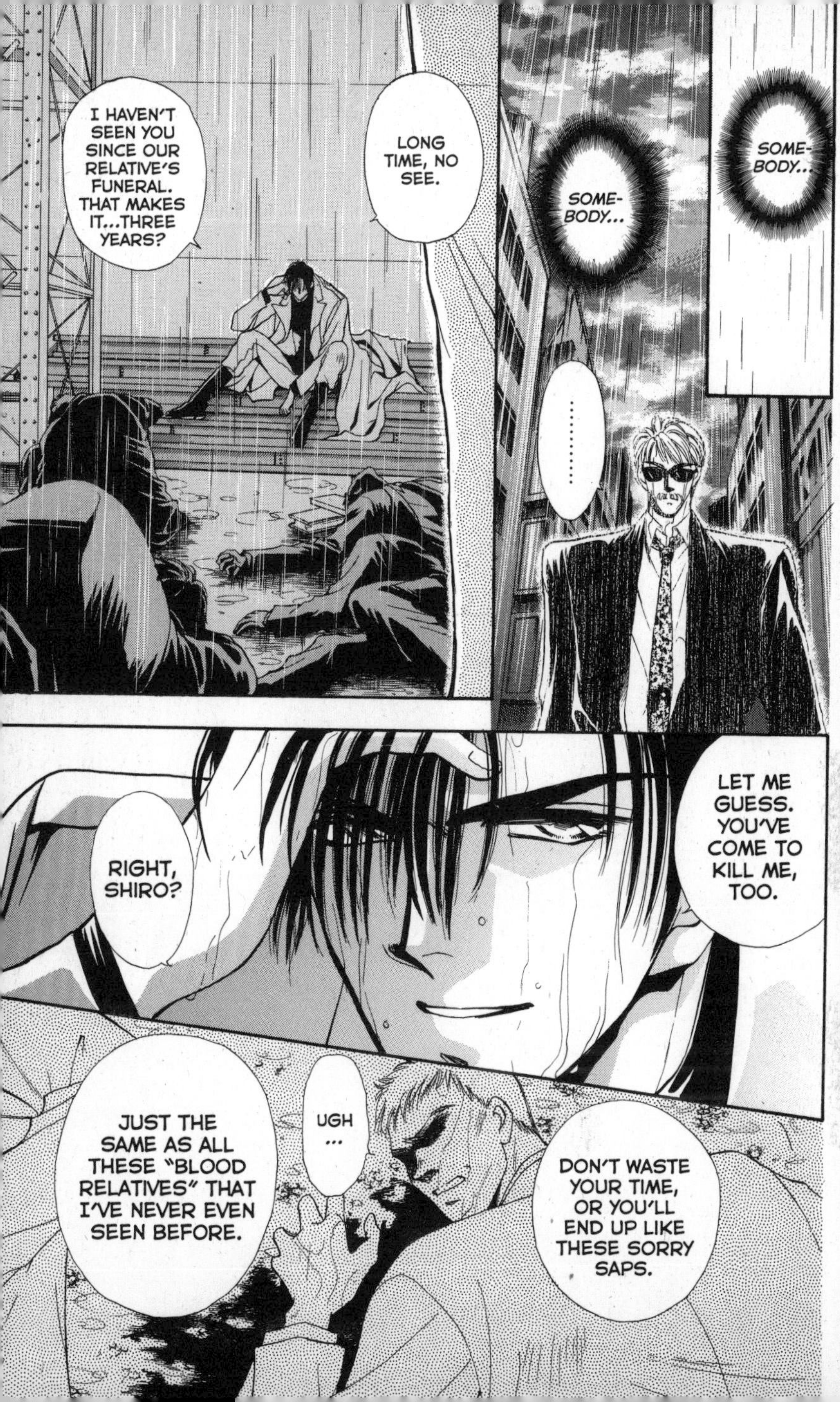
SOME-BODY...
SOME-BODY...
......
LONG TIME, NO SEE.
I HAVEN'T SEEN YOU SINCE OUR RELATIVE'S FUNERAL. THAT MAKES IT...THREE YEARS?
LET ME GUESS. YOU'VE COME TO KILL ME, TOO.
RIGHT, SHIRO?
UGH...
JUST THE SAME AS ALL THESE "BLOOD RELATIVES" THAT I'VE NEVER EVEN SEEN BEFORE.
DON'T WASTE YOUR TIME, OR YOU'LL END UP LIKE THESE SORRY SAPS.

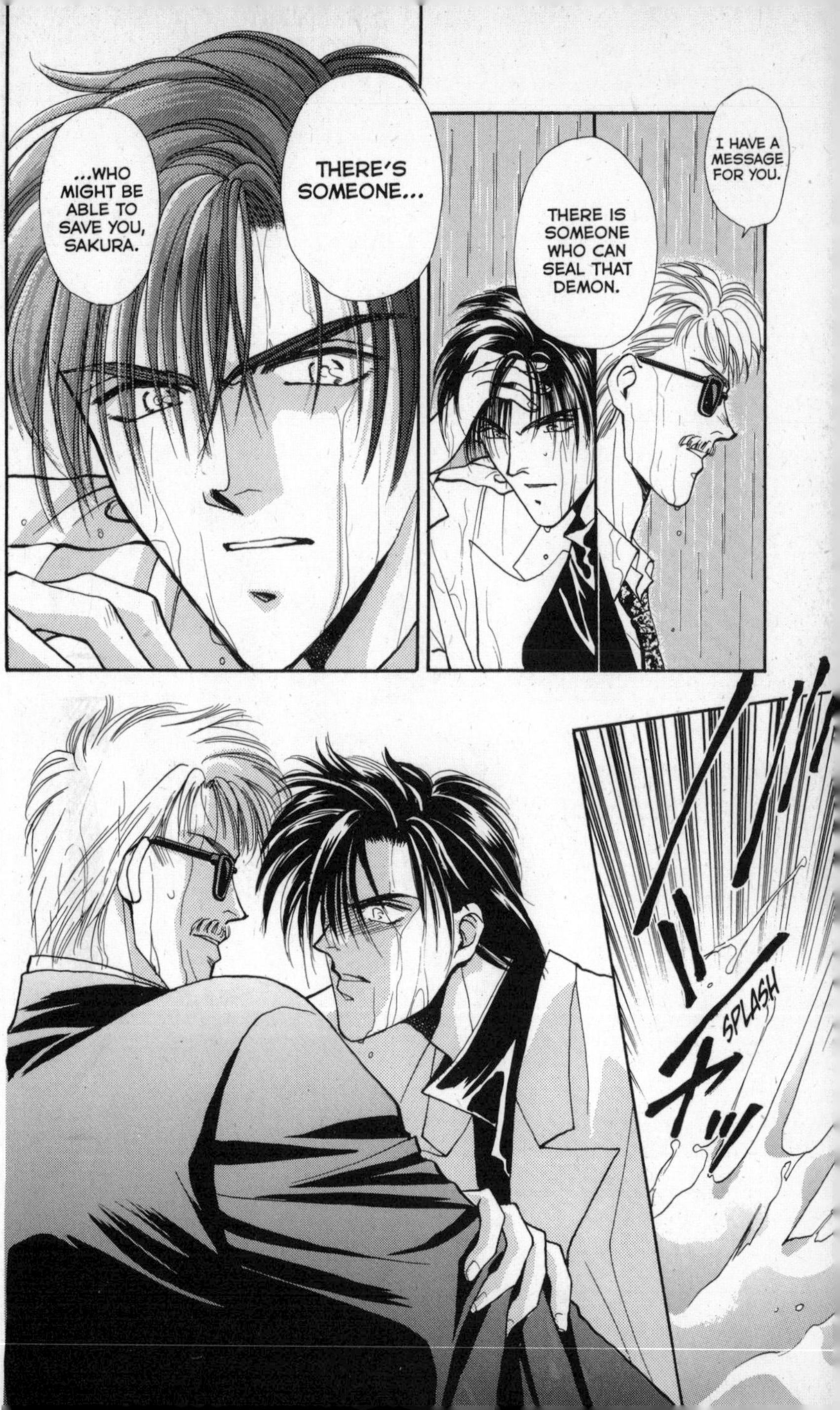
I HAVE A MESSAGE FOR YOU.
THERE IS SOMEONE WHO CAN SEAL THAT DEMON.
THERE'S SOMEONE...
...WHO MIGHT BE ABLE TO SAVE YOU, SAKURA.
SPLASH

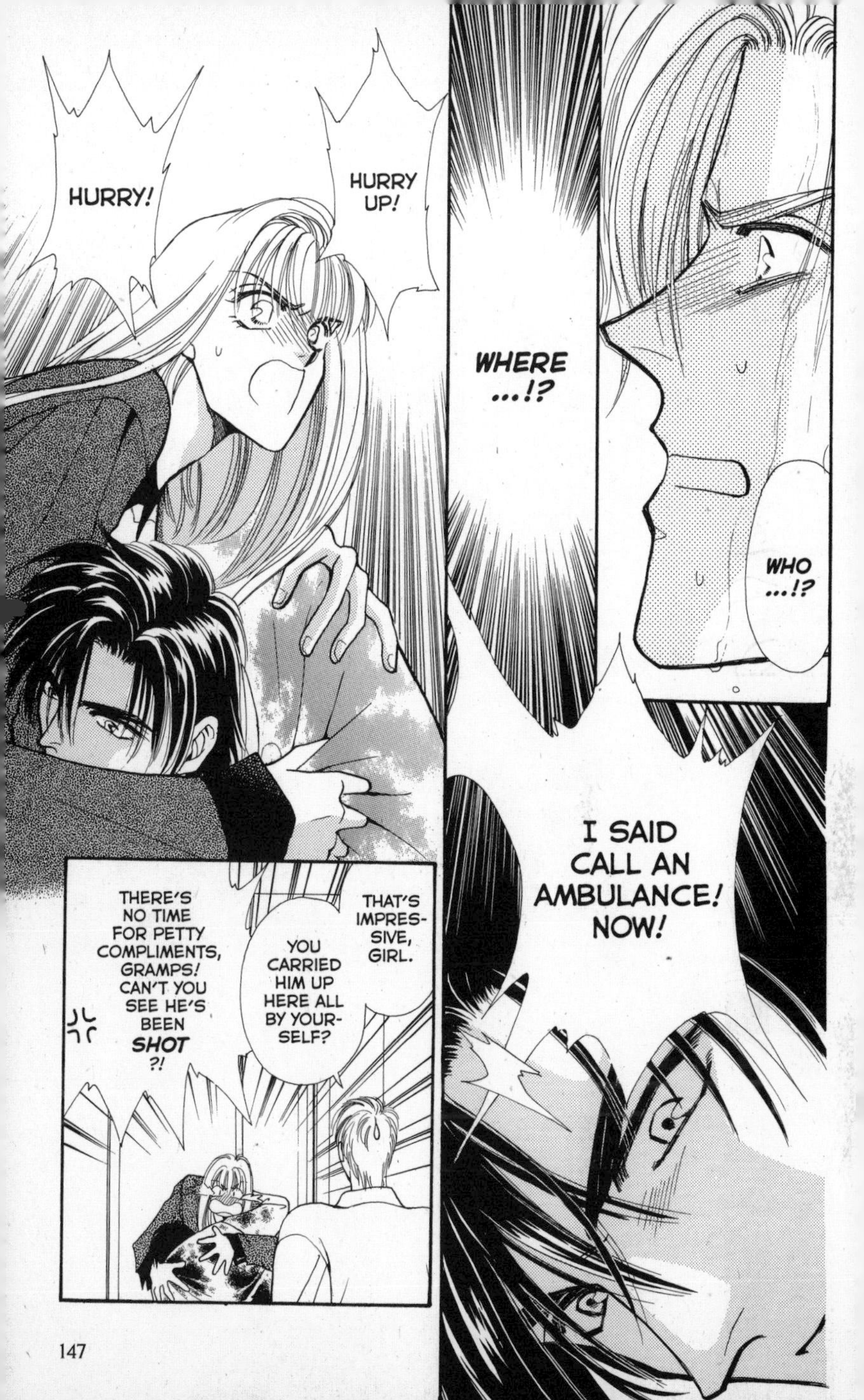
WHO ...!?
WHERE ...!?
HURRY UP!
HURRY!
THAT'S IMPRESSIVE, GIRL.
YOU CARRIED HIM UP HERE ALL BY YOURSELF?
THERE'S NO TIME FOR PETTY COMPLIMENTS, GRAMPS! CAN'T YOU SEE HE'S BEEN **SHOT** ?!
I SAID CALL AN AMBULANCE! NOW!

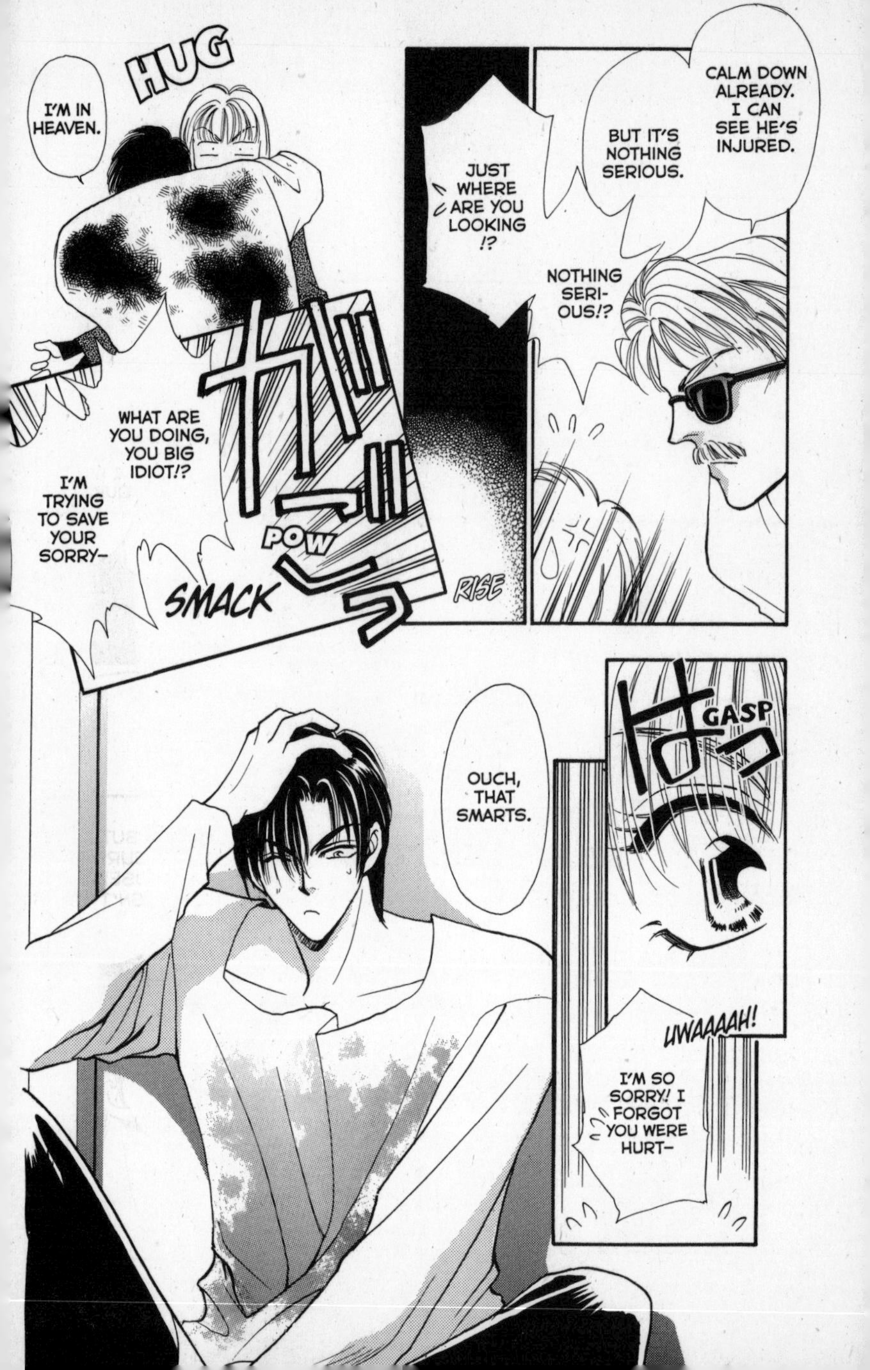
CALM DOWN ALREADY. I CAN SEE HE'S INJURED.
BUT IT'S NOTHING SERIOUS.
NOTHING SERI-OUS!?
JUST WHERE ARE YOU LOOKING !?
RISE
HUG
I'M IN HEAVEN.
WHAT ARE YOU DOING, YOU BIG IDIOT!?
POW
SMACK
I'M TRYING TO SAVE YOUR SORRY–
はっ
GASP
UWAAAAH!
I'M SO SORRY! I FORGOT YOU WERE HURT–
OUCH, THAT SMARTS.

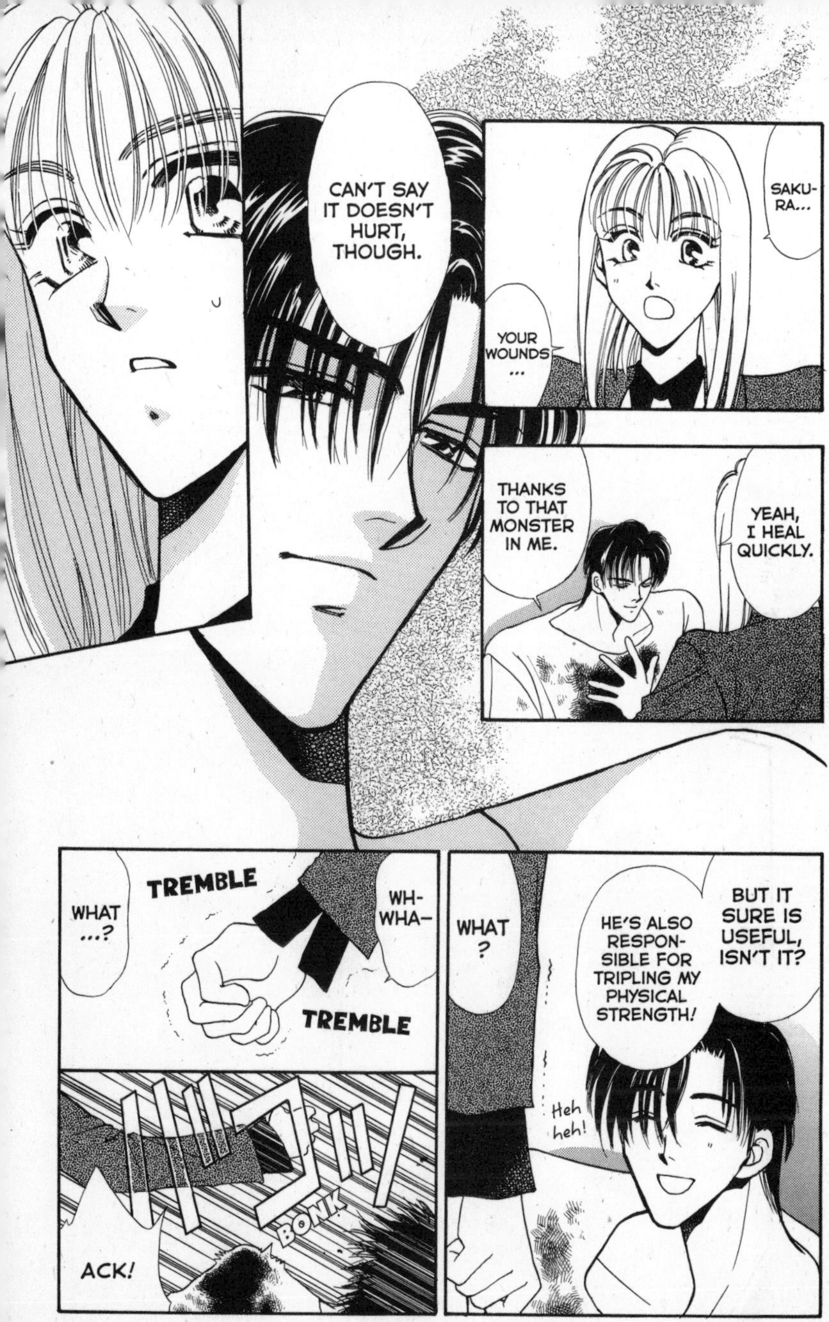
SAKU-RA...
YOUR WOUNDS ...
YEAH, I HEAL QUICKLY.
THANKS TO THAT MONSTER IN ME.
CAN'T SAY IT DOESN'T HURT, THOUGH.
BUT IT SURE IS USEFUL, ISN'T IT?
HE'S ALSO RESPON-SIBLE FOR TRIPLING MY PHYSICAL STRENGTH!
WHAT ?
Heh heh!
WH-WHA-
TREMBLE
WHAT ...?
TREMBLE
BONK
ACK!

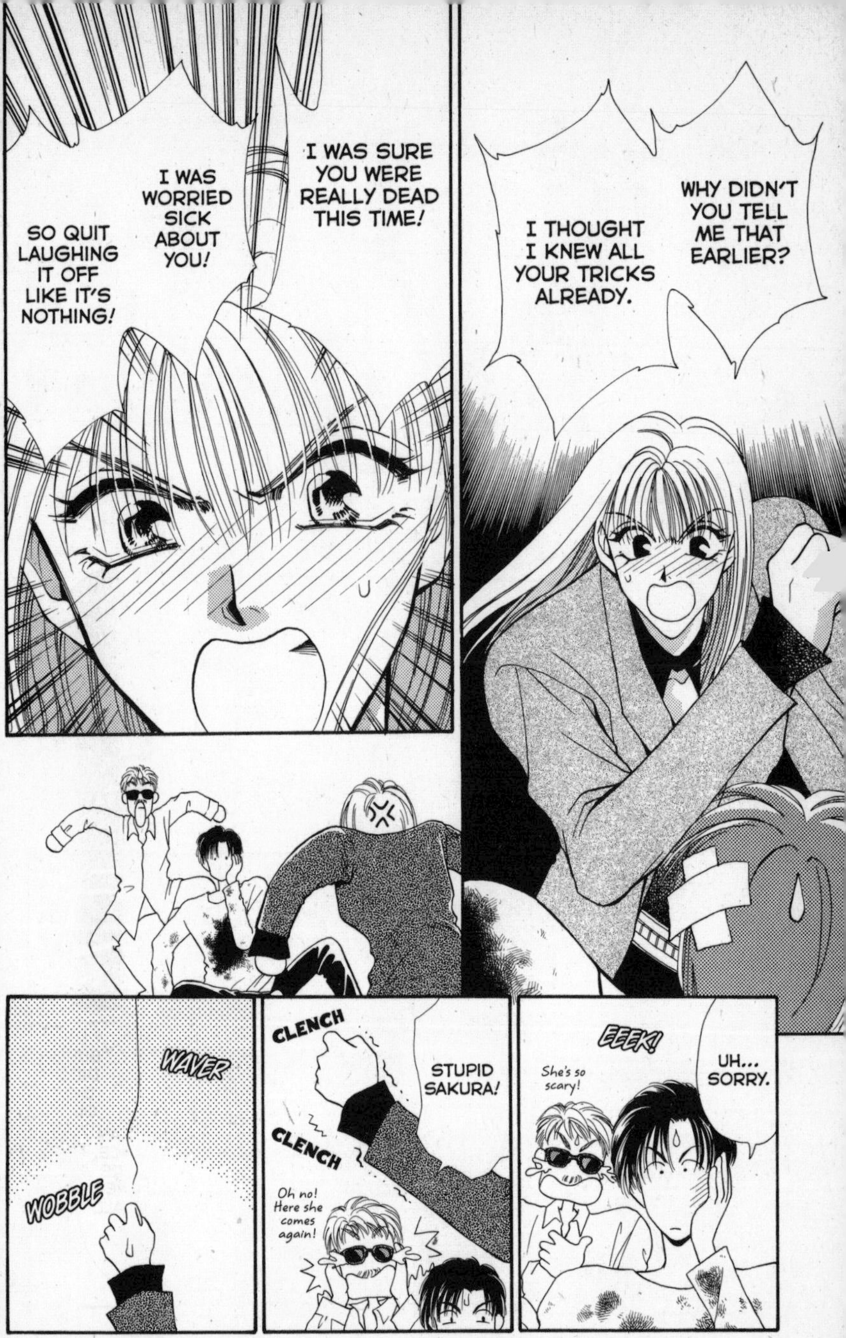
WHY DIDN'T YOU TELL ME THAT EARLIER?
I THOUGHT I KNEW ALL YOUR TRICKS ALREADY.
I WAS SURE YOU WERE REALLY DEAD THIS TIME!
I WAS WORRIED SICK ABOUT YOU!
SO QUIT LAUGHING IT OFF LIKE IT'S NOTHING!
UH... SORRY.
EEEK!
She's so scary!
STUPID SAKURA!
CLENCH
CLENCH
Oh no! Here she comes again!
WAVER
WOBBLE

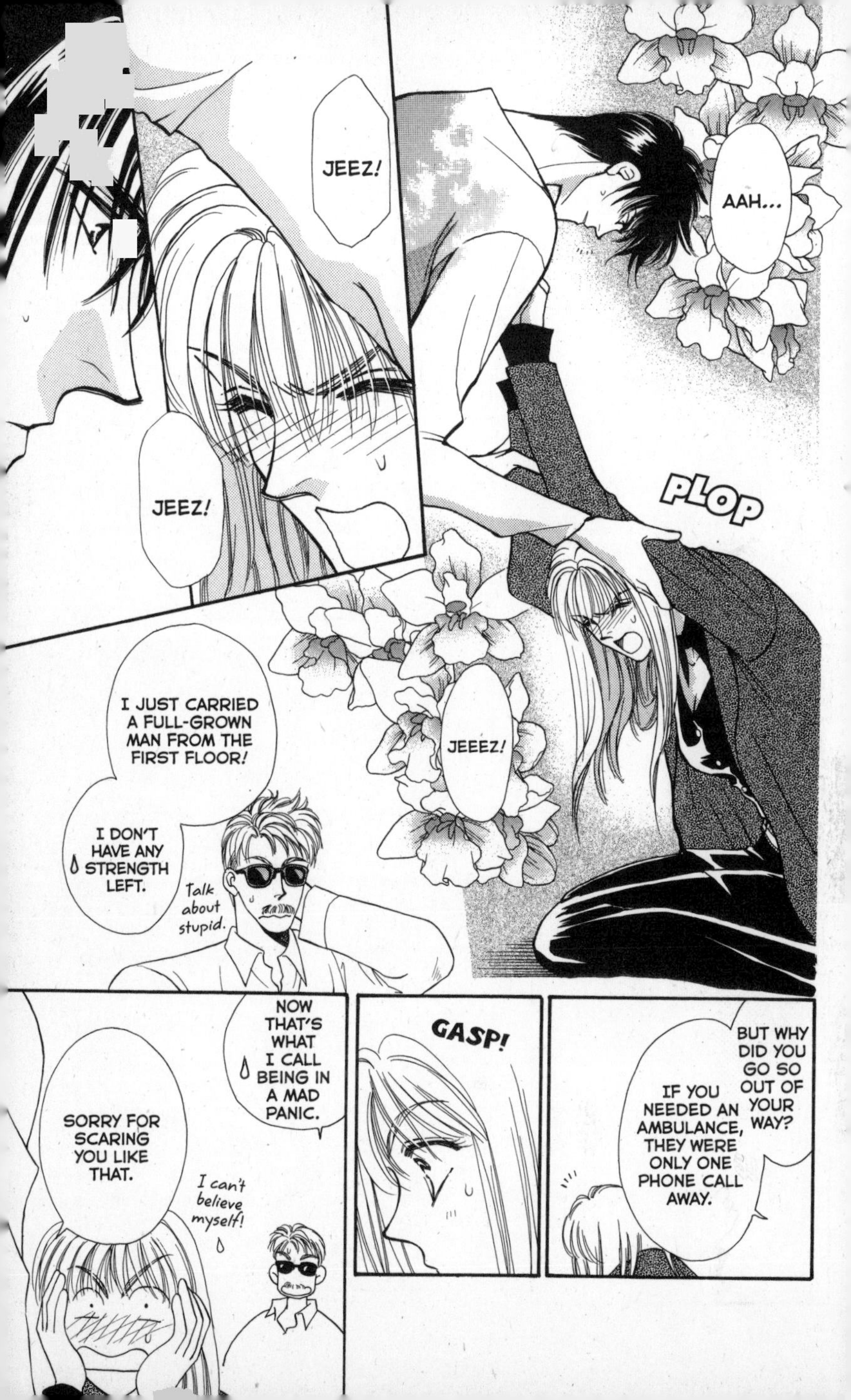
AAH...
PLOP
JEEEZ!
JEEZ!
JEEZ!
I JUST CARRIED A FULL-GROWN MAN FROM THE FIRST FLOOR!
I DON'T HAVE ANY STRENGTH LEFT.
Talk about stupid.
BUT WHY DID YOU GO SO OUT OF YOUR WAY?
IF YOU NEEDED AN AMBULANCE, THEY WERE ONLY ONE PHONE CALL AWAY.
GASP!
NOW THAT'S WHAT I CALL BEING IN A MAD PANIC.
SORRY FOR SCARING YOU LIKE THAT.
I can't believe myself!

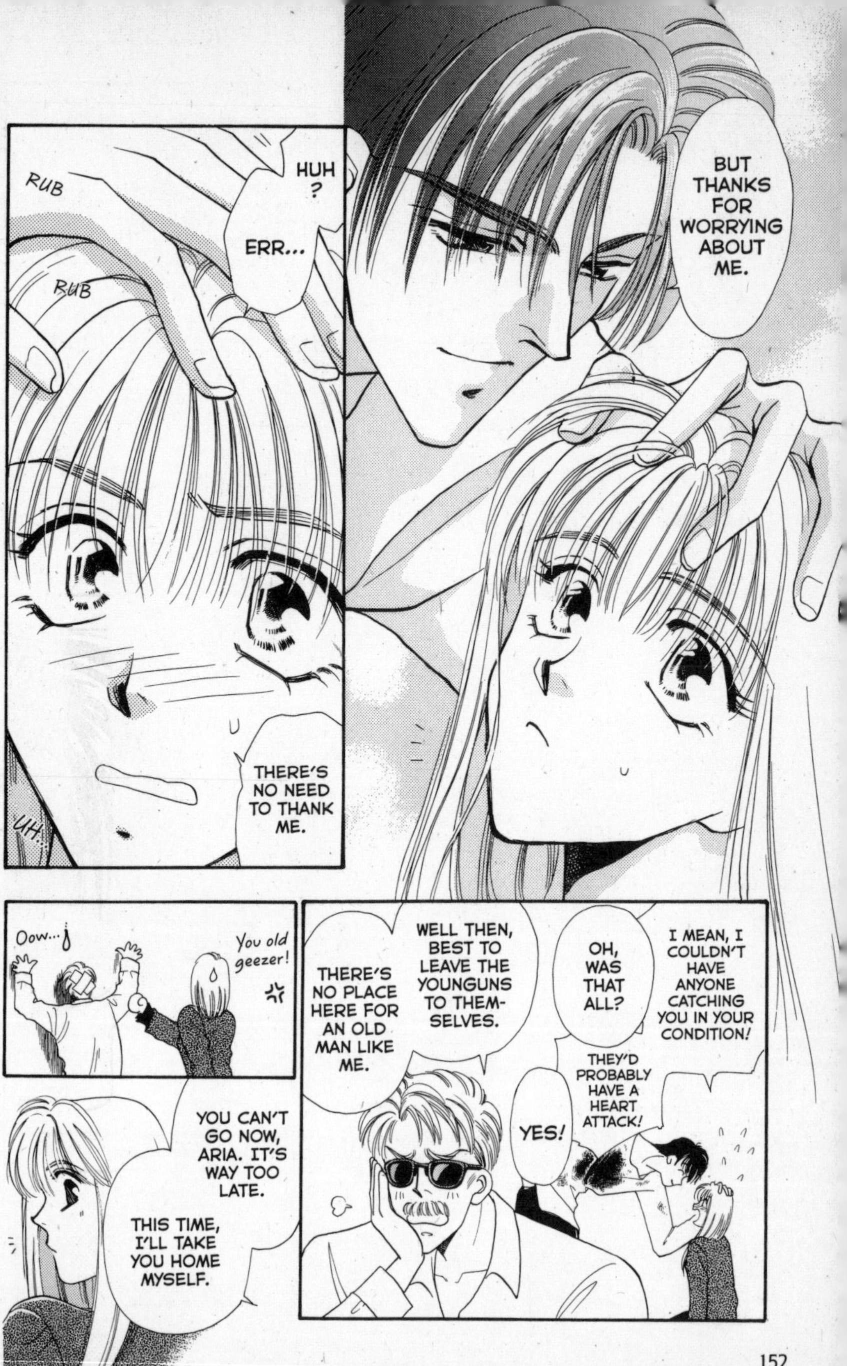
BUT THANKS FOR WORRYING ABOUT ME.
RUB
HUH?
ERR...
RUB
THERE'S NO NEED TO THANK ME.
UH..
I MEAN, I COULDN'T HAVE ANYONE CATCHING YOU IN YOUR CONDITION!
THEY'D PROBABLY HAVE A HEART ATTACK!
OH, WAS THAT ALL?
YES!
WELL THEN, BEST TO LEAVE THE YOUNGUNS TO THEMSELVES.
THERE'S NO PLACE HERE FOR AN OLD MAN LIKE ME.
You old geezer!
Oow...
YOU CAN'T GO NOW, ARIA. IT'S WAY TOO LATE.
THIS TIME, I'LL TAKE YOU HOME MYSELF.

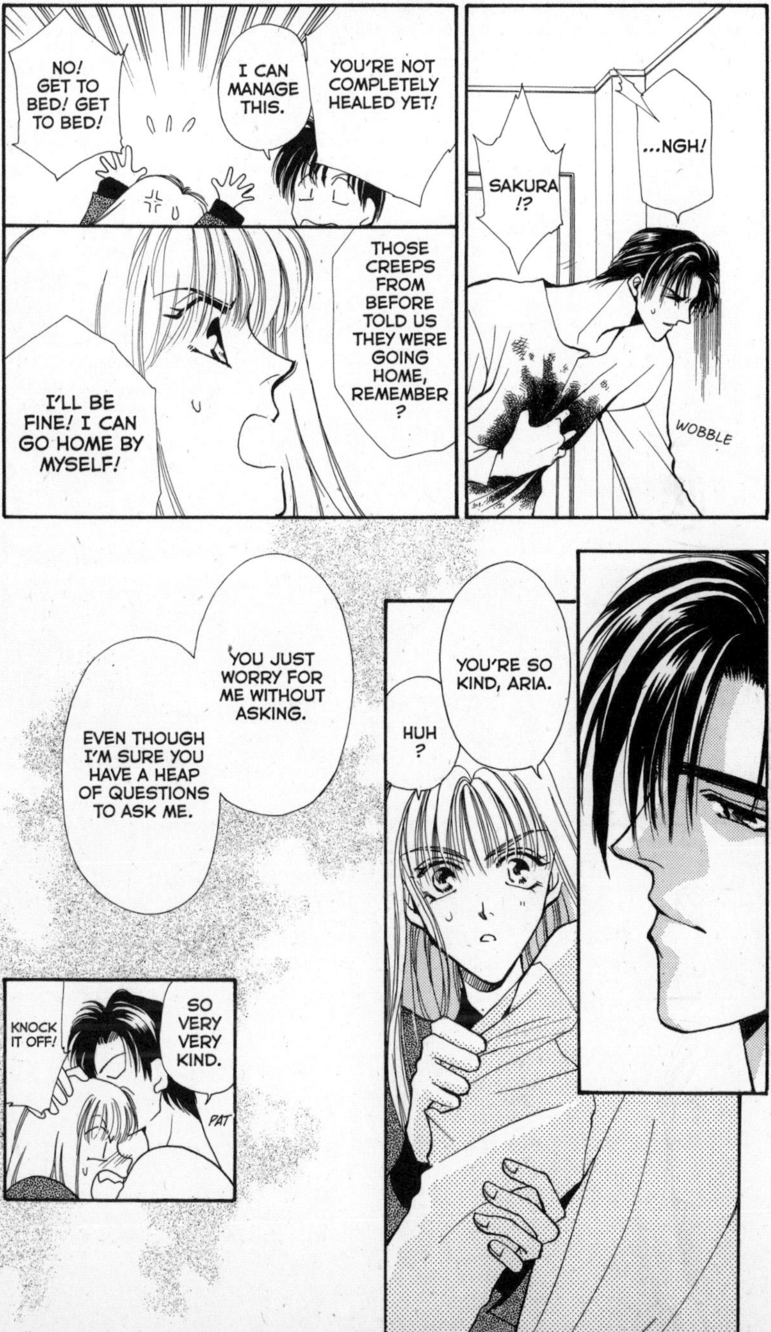
...NGH!
SAKURA!?
WOBBLE
YOU'RE NOT COMPLETELY HEALED YET!
I CAN MANAGE THIS.
NO! GET TO BED! GET TO BED!
THOSE CREEPS FROM BEFORE TOLD US THEY WERE GOING HOME, REMEMBER?
I'LL BE FINE! I CAN GO HOME BY MYSELF!
YOU'RE SO KIND, ARIA.
HUH?
YOU JUST WORRY FOR ME WITHOUT ASKING.
EVEN THOUGH I'M SURE YOU HAVE A HEAP OF QUESTIONS TO ASK ME.
SO VERY VERY KIND.
PAT
KNOCK IT OFF!

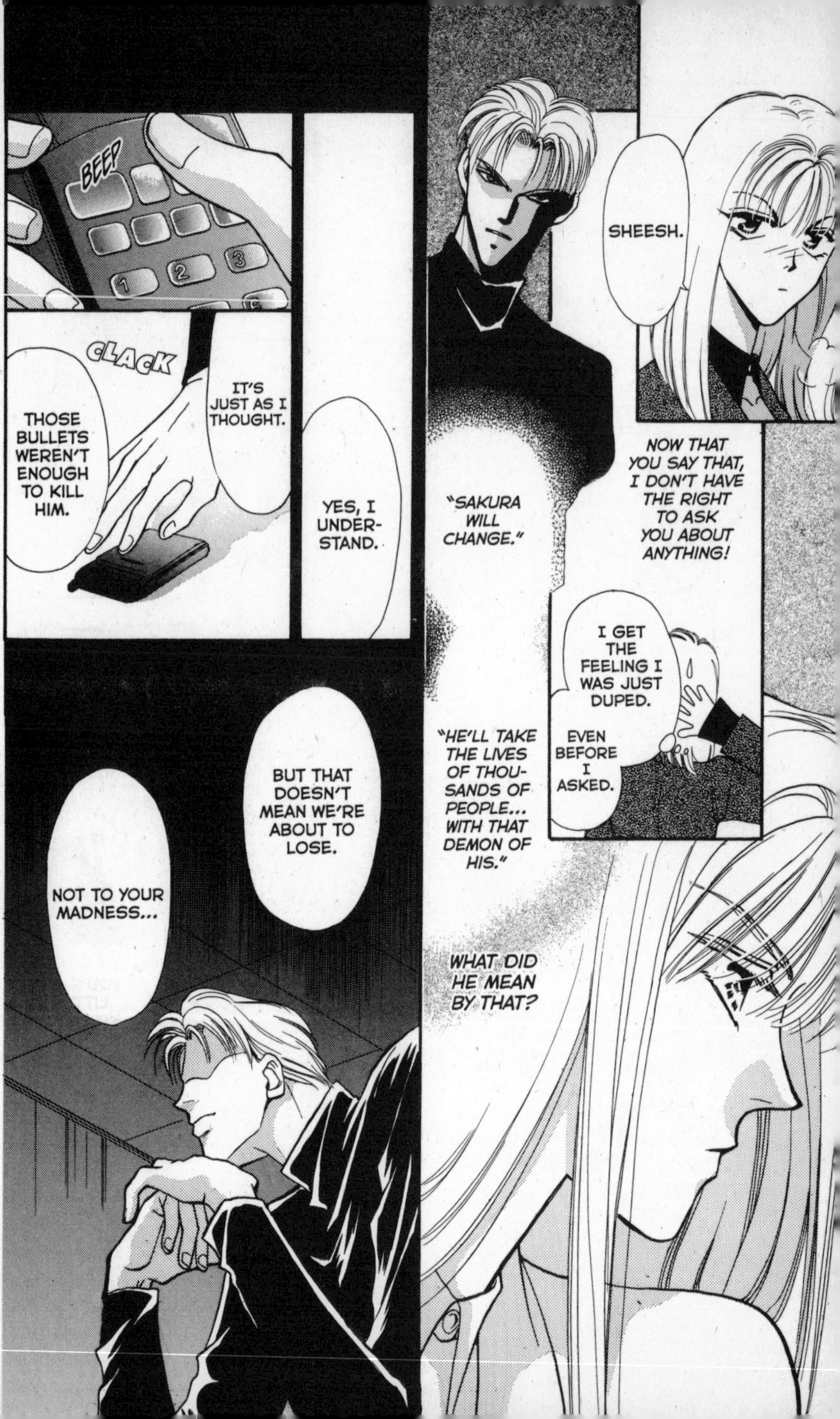
SHEESH.
NOW THAT YOU SAY THAT, I DON'T HAVE THE RIGHT TO ASK YOU ABOUT ANYTHING!
I GET THE FEELING I WAS JUST DUPED.
EVEN BEFORE I ASKED.
"SAKURA WILL CHANGE."
"HE'LL TAKE THE LIVES OF THOU-SANDS OF PEOPLE... WITH THAT DEMON OF HIS."
WHAT DID HE MEAN BY THAT?
YES, I UNDER-STAND.
BEEP
CLACK
IT'S JUST AS I THOUGHT.
THOSE BULLETS WEREN'T ENOUGH TO KILL HIM.
BUT THAT DOESN'T MEAN WE'RE ABOUT TO LOSE.
NOT TO YOUR MADNESS...

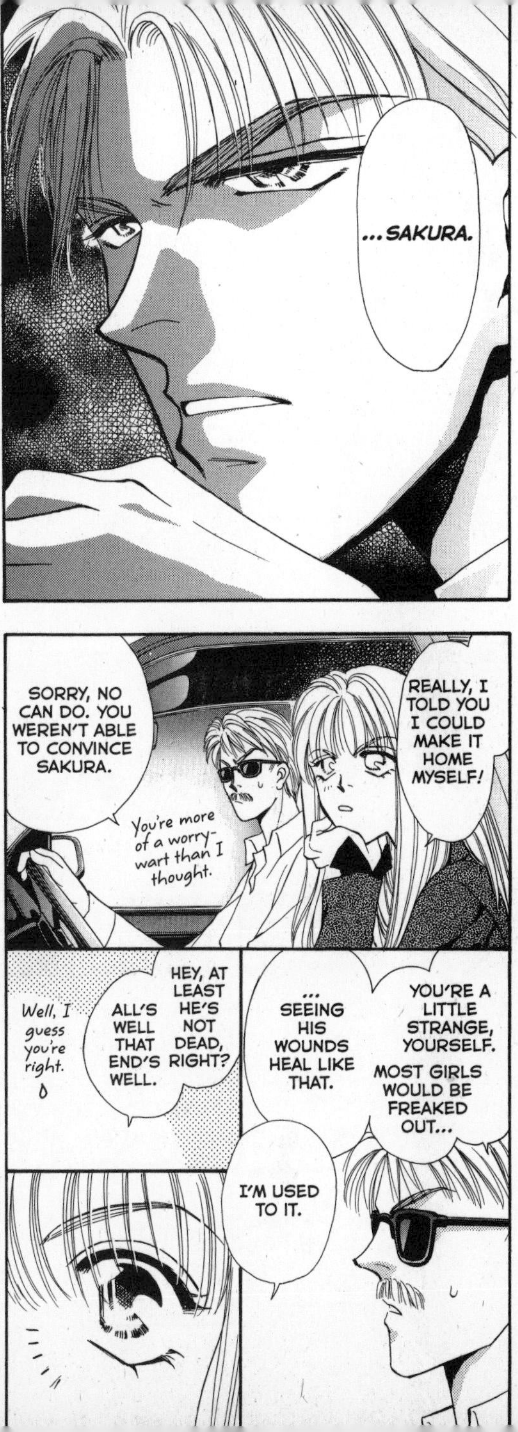
...SAKURA.
REALLY, I TOLD YOU I COULD MAKE IT HOME MYSELF!
SORRY, NO CAN DO. YOU WEREN'T ABLE TO CONVINCE SAKURA.
You're more of a worry-wart than I thought.
YOU'RE A LITTLE STRANGE, YOURSELF.
MOST GIRLS WOULD BE FREAKED OUT...
... SEEING HIS WOUNDS HEAL LIKE THAT.
HEY, AT LEAST HE'S NOT DEAD, RIGHT?
ALL'S WELL THAT END'S WELL.
Well, I guess you're right.
I'M USED TO IT.

Here's another question I get asked a lot in my letters: "Who's your favorite musician?" Recently I've really gotten into "Enya." I just love her beautiful songs. Only problem is, if I'm not paying attention, I may actually be lulled to sleep by the music!

That's why, whenever I'm working alone, I make sure to listen to really peppy Japanese songs. B'z, or trf, or sometimes even the nostalgic TM Network.

Oh, but King Show is also good, too.

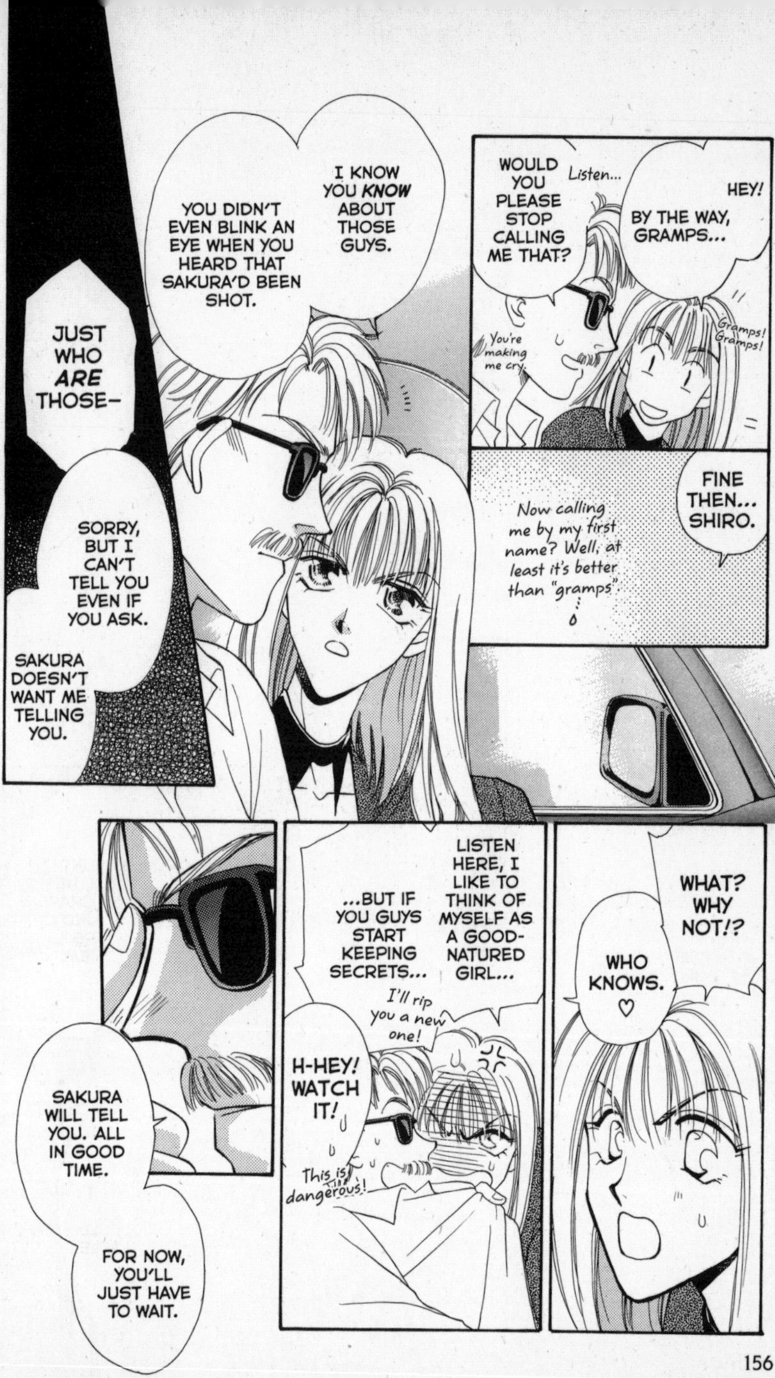
HEY! BY THE WAY, GRAMPS...
Gramps! Gramps!
WOULD YOU PLEASE STOP CALLING ME THAT?
Listen...
You're making me cry.
FINE THEN... SHIRO.
Now calling me by my first name? Well, at least it's better than "gramps".
I KNOW YOU KNOW ABOUT THOSE GUYS.
YOU DIDN'T EVEN BLINK AN EYE WHEN YOU HEARD THAT SAKURA'D BEEN SHOT.
JUST WHO ARE THOSE–
SORRY, BUT I CAN'T TELL YOU EVEN IF YOU ASK.
SAKURA DOESN'T WANT ME TELLING YOU.
WHAT? WHY NOT!?
WHO KNOWS. ♡
LISTEN HERE, I LIKE TO THINK OF MYSELF AS A GOOD-NATURED GIRL...
...BUT IF YOU GUYS START KEEPING SECRETS...
I'll rip you a new one!
H-HEY! WATCH IT!
This is dangerous!
SAKURA WILL TELL YOU. ALL IN GOOD TIME.
FOR NOW, YOU'LL JUST HAVE TO WAIT.

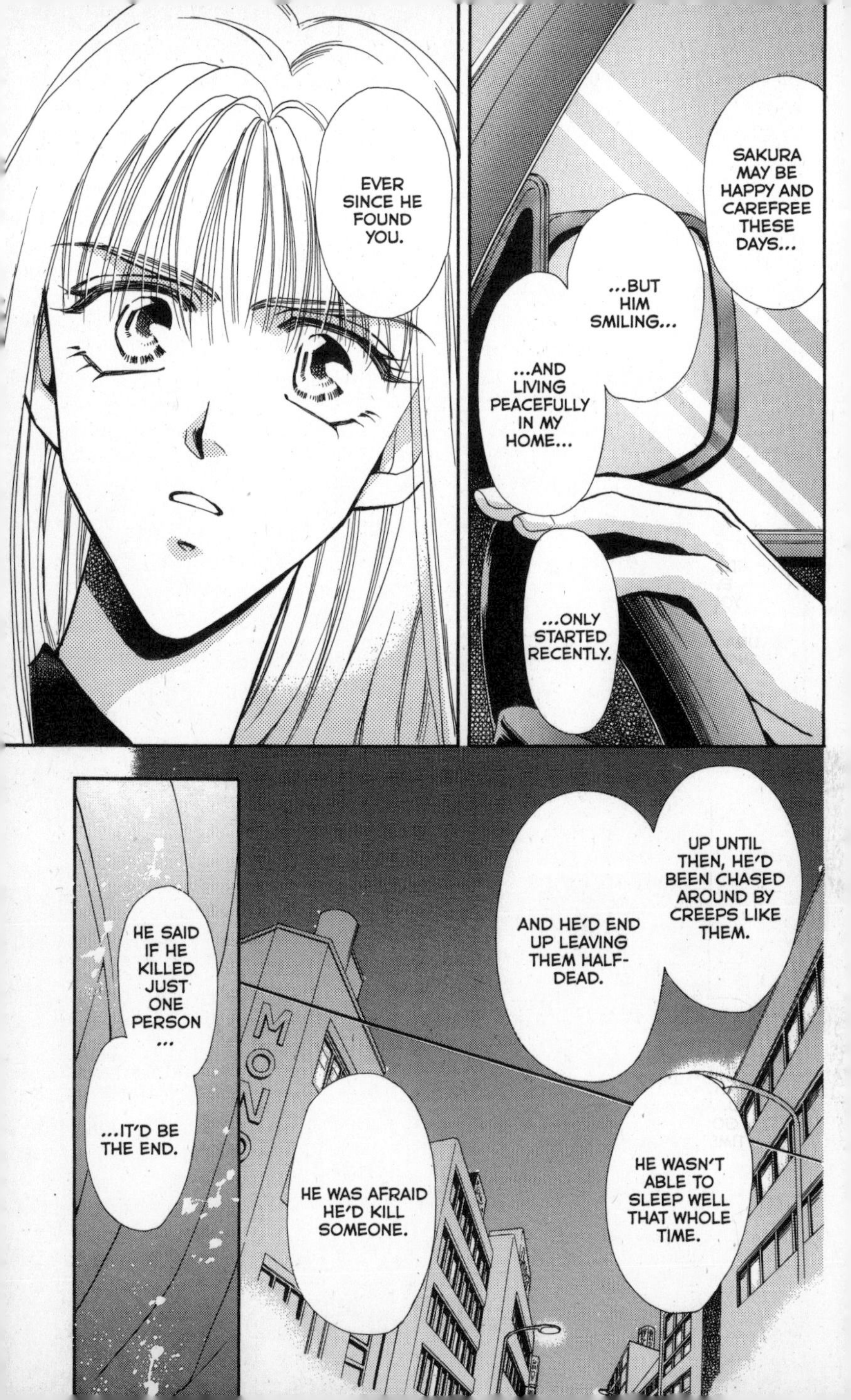
SAKURA MAY BE HAPPY AND CAREFREE THESE DAYS...
...BUT HIM SMILING...
...AND LIVING PEACEFULLY IN MY HOME...
...ONLY STARTED RECENTLY.
EVER SINCE HE FOUND YOU.
UP UNTIL THEN, HE'D BEEN CHASED AROUND BY CREEPS LIKE THEM.
AND HE'D END UP LEAVING THEM HALF-DEAD.
HE WASN'T ABLE TO SLEEP WELL THAT WHOLE TIME.
HE WAS AFRAID HE'D KILL SOMEONE.
HE SAID IF HE KILLED JUST ONE PERSON...
...IT'D BE THE END.

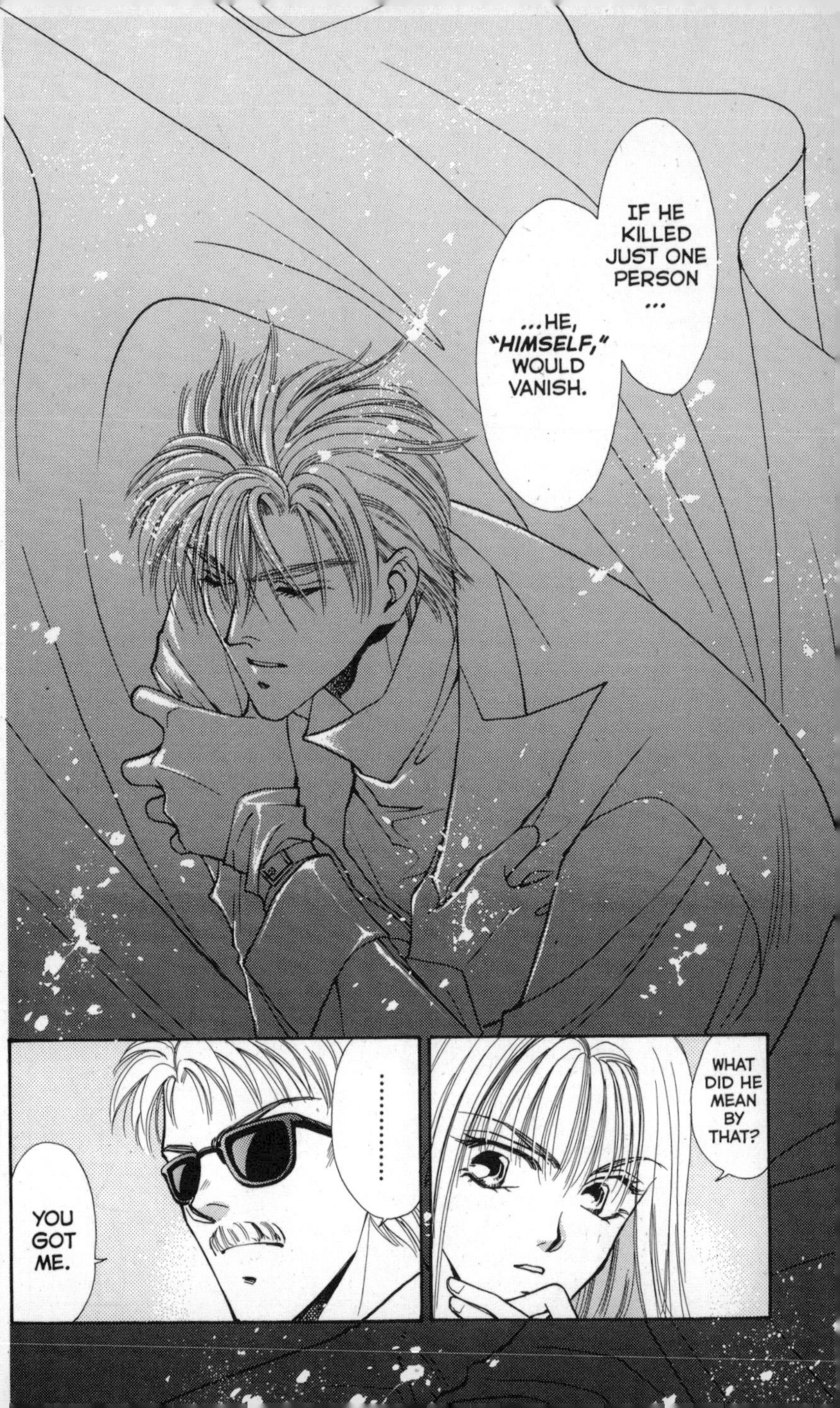
IF HE KILLED JUST ONE PERSON ...
...HE, "HIMSELF," WOULD VANISH.
WHAT DID HE MEAN BY THAT?
......
YOU GOT ME.

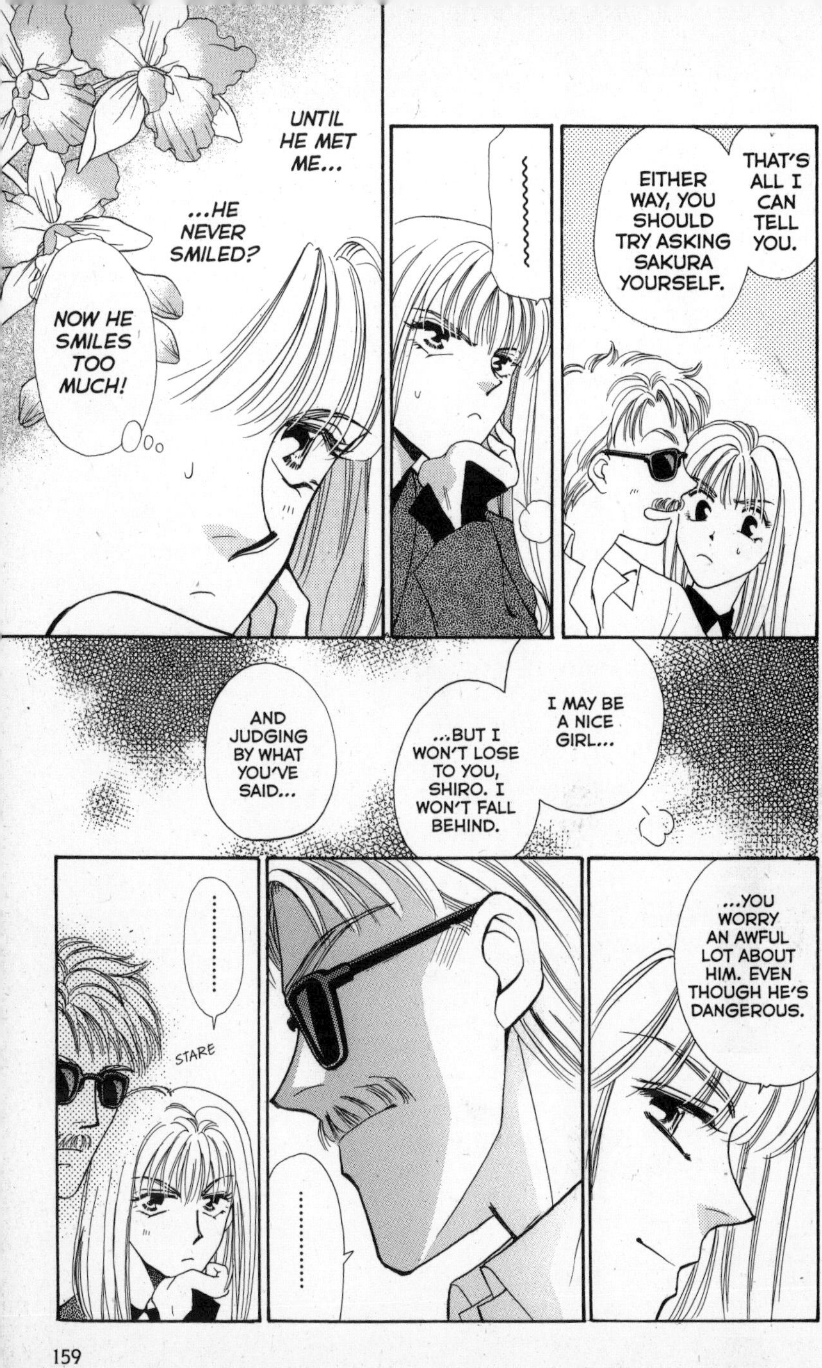
THAT'S ALL I CAN TELL YOU.
EITHER WAY, YOU SHOULD TRY ASKING SAKURA YOURSELF.
UNTIL HE MET ME...
...HE NEVER SMILED?
NOW HE SMILES TOO MUCH!
I MAY BE A NICE GIRL...
...BUT I WON'T LOSE TO YOU, SHIRO. I WON'T FALL BEHIND.
AND JUDGING BY WHAT YOU'VE SAID...
...YOU WORRY AN AWFUL LOT ABOUT HIM. EVEN THOUGH HE'S DANGEROUS.
......
......
STARE

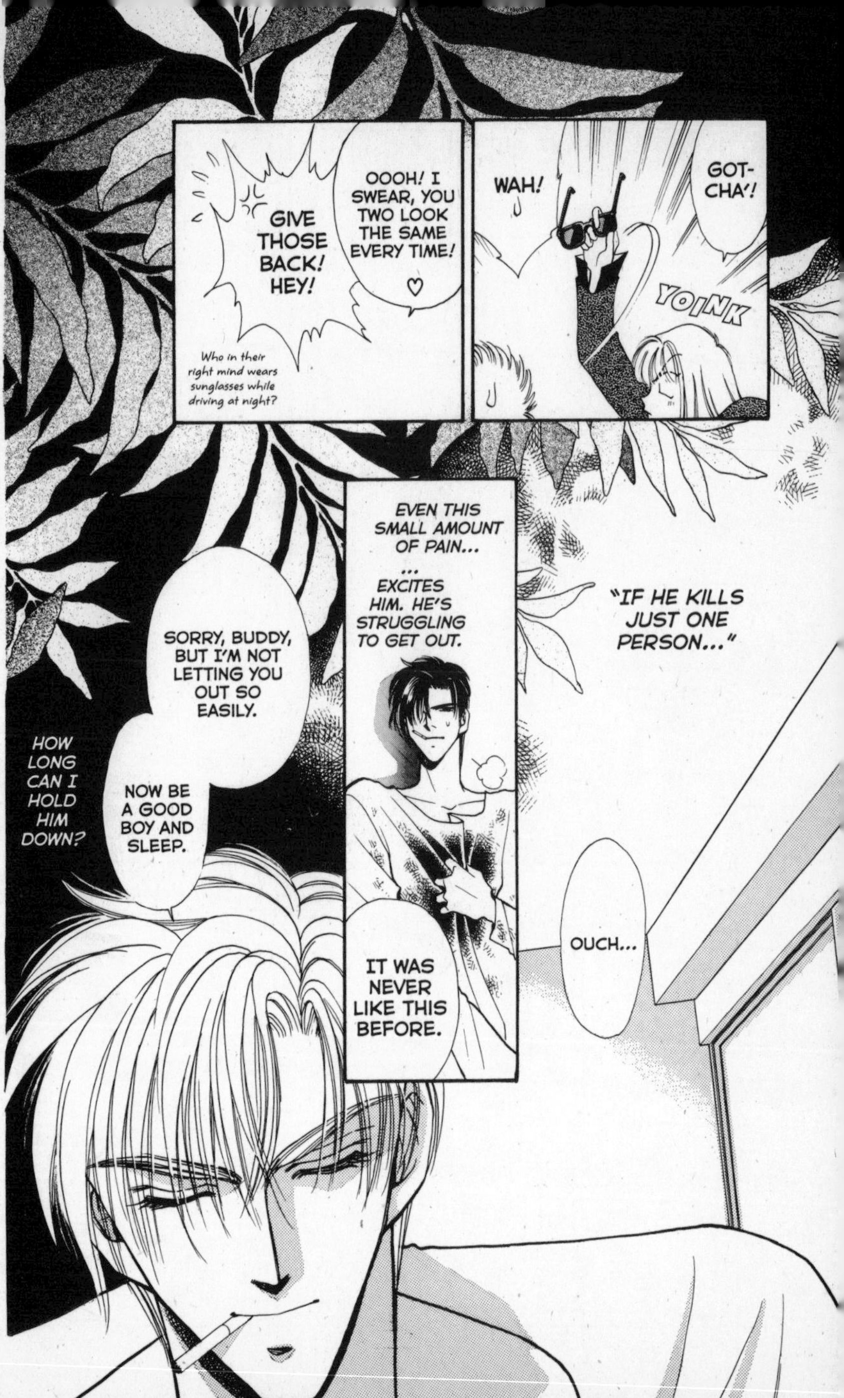
GOT-CHA'!
WAH!
YOINK
OOOH! I SWEAR, YOU TWO LOOK THE SAME EVERY TIME! ♡
GIVE THOSE BACK! HEY!
Who in their right mind wears sunglasses while driving at night?
"IF HE KILLS JUST ONE PERSON..."
OUCH...
EVEN THIS SMALL AMOUNT OF PAIN... ...EXCITES HIM. HE'S STRUGGLING TO GET OUT.
IT WAS NEVER LIKE THIS BEFORE.
SORRY, BUDDY, BUT I'M NOT LETTING YOU OUT SO EASILY.
NOW BE A GOOD BOY AND SLEEP.
HOW LONG CAN I HOLD HIM DOWN?

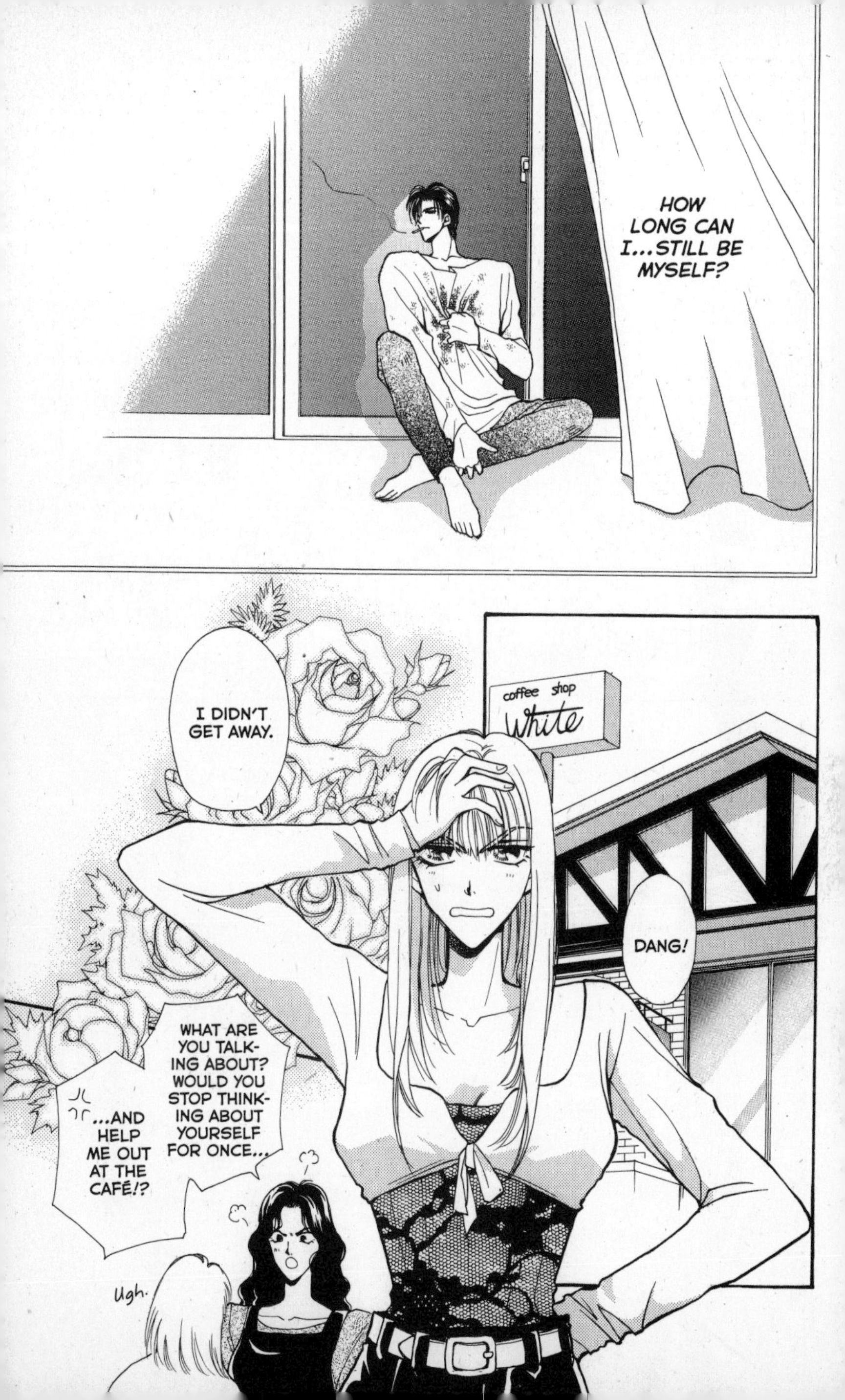
HOW LONG CAN I...STILL BE MYSELF?
coffee shop White
DANG!
I DIDN'T GET AWAY.
WHAT ARE YOU TALKING ABOUT? WOULD YOU STOP THINKING ABOUT YOURSELF FOR ONCE...
...AND HELP ME OUT AT THE CAFÉ!?
Ugh.

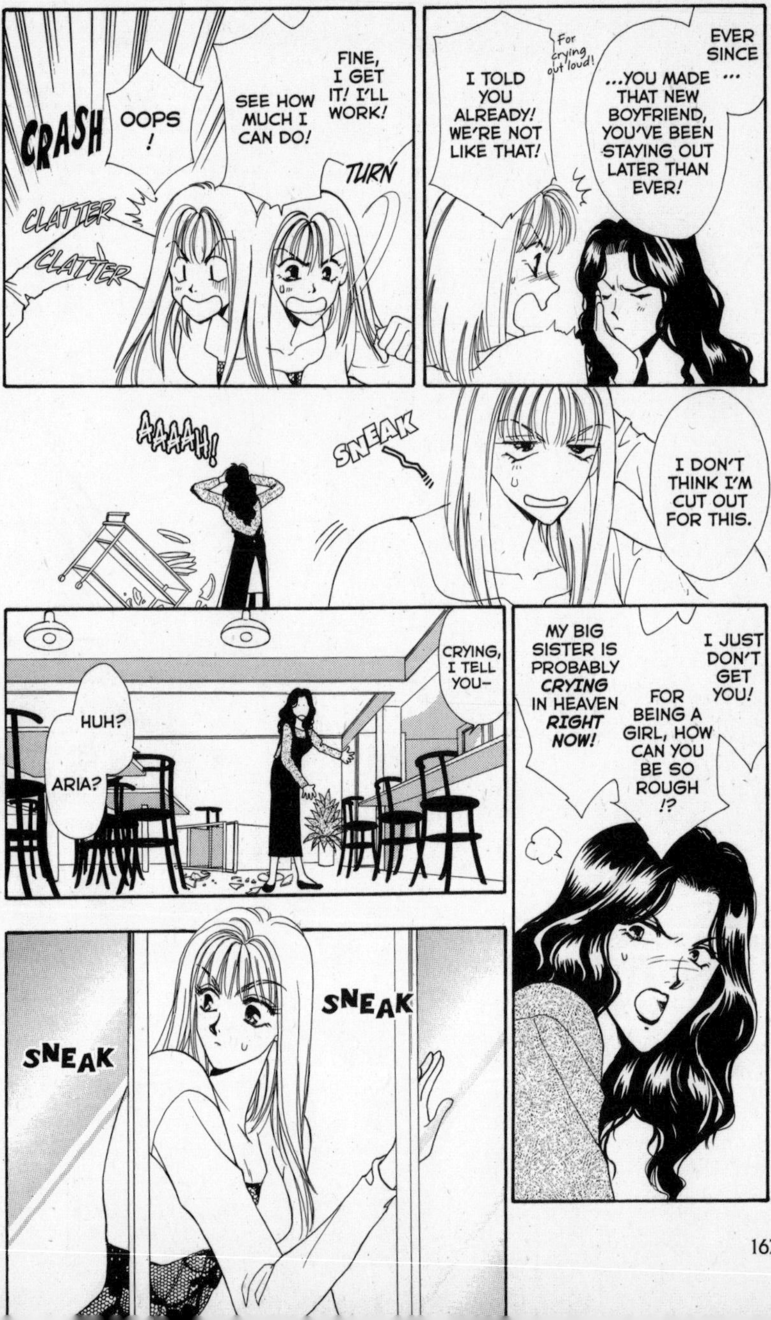
EVER SINCE ...
...YOU MADE THAT NEW BOYFRIEND, YOU'VE BEEN STAYING OUT LATER THAN EVER!
For crying out loud!
I TOLD YOU ALREADY! WE'RE NOT LIKE THAT!
FINE, I GET IT! I'LL WORK!
SEE HOW MUCH I CAN DO!
TURN
OOPS !
CRASH
CLATTER
CLATTER
I DON'T THINK I'M CUT OUT FOR THIS.
SNEAK
AAAAH!
I JUST DON'T GET YOU!
FOR BEING A GIRL, HOW CAN YOU BE SO ROUGH !?
MY BIG SISTER IS PROBABLY CRYING IN HEAVEN RIGHT NOW!
CRYING, I TELL YOU–
HUH?
ARIA?
SNEAK
SNEAK

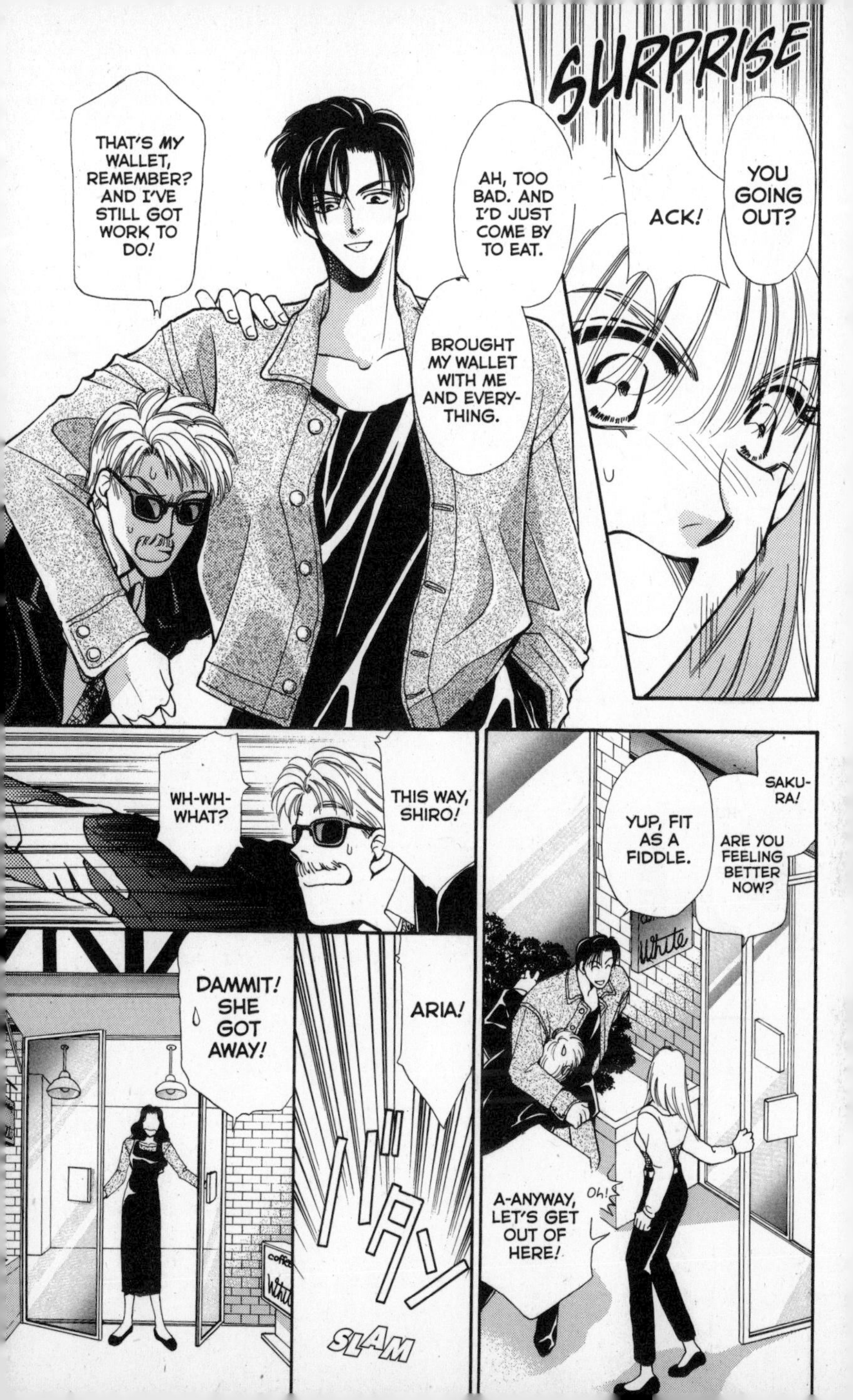
SURPRISE
YOU GOING OUT?
ACK!
AH, TOO BAD. AND I'D JUST COME BY TO EAT.
BROUGHT MY WALLET WITH ME AND EVERYTHING.
THAT'S *MY* WALLET, REMEMBER? AND I'VE STILL GOT WORK TO DO!
SAKURA!
ARE YOU FEELING BETTER NOW?
YUP, FIT AS A FIDDLE.
Oh!
A-ANYWAY, LET'S GET OUT OF HERE!
THIS WAY, SHIRO!
WH-WH-WHAT?
ARIA!
SLAM
DAMMIT! SHE GOT AWAY!

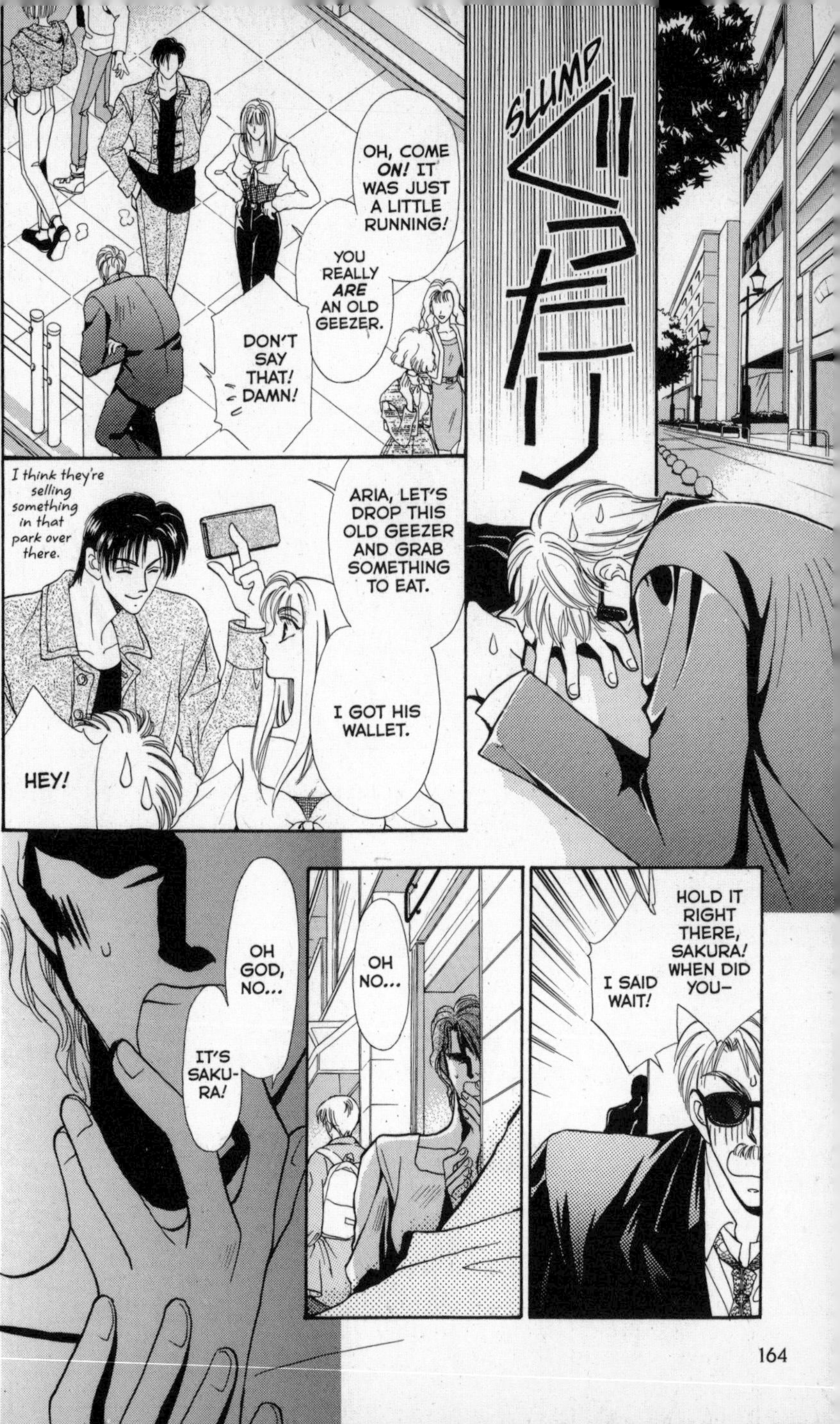
SLUMP
OH, COME ON! IT WAS JUST A LITTLE RUNNING!
YOU REALLY ARE AN OLD GEEZER.
DON'T SAY THAT! DAMN!
ARIA, LET'S DROP THIS OLD GEEZER AND GRAB SOMETHING TO EAT.
I think they're selling something in that park over there.
I GOT HIS WALLET.
HEY!
HOLD IT RIGHT THERE, SAKURA! WHEN DID YOU—
I SAID WAIT!
OH NO...
OH GOD, NO...
IT'S SAKU-RA!

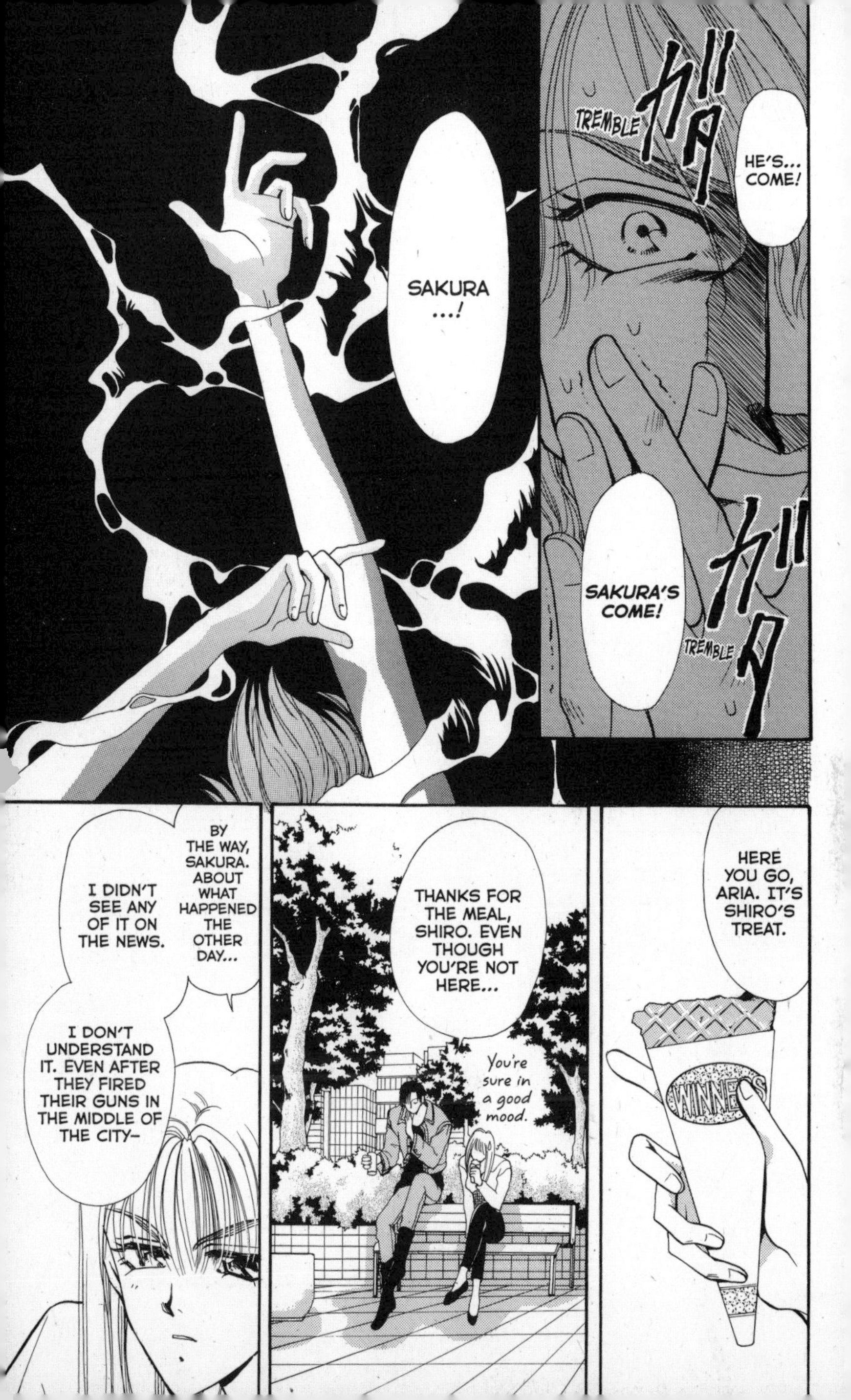
TREMBLE
HE'S... COME!
SAKURA'S COME!
TREMBLE
SAKURA ...!
HERE YOU GO, ARIA. IT'S SHIRO'S TREAT.
THANKS FOR THE MEAL, SHIRO. EVEN THOUGH YOU'RE NOT HERE...
You're sure in a good mood.
BY THE WAY, SAKURA. ABOUT WHAT HAPPENED THE OTHER DAY...
I DIDN'T SEE ANY OF IT ON THE NEWS.
I DON'T UNDERSTAND IT. EVEN AFTER THEY FIRED THEIR GUNS IN THE MIDDLE OF THE CITY–

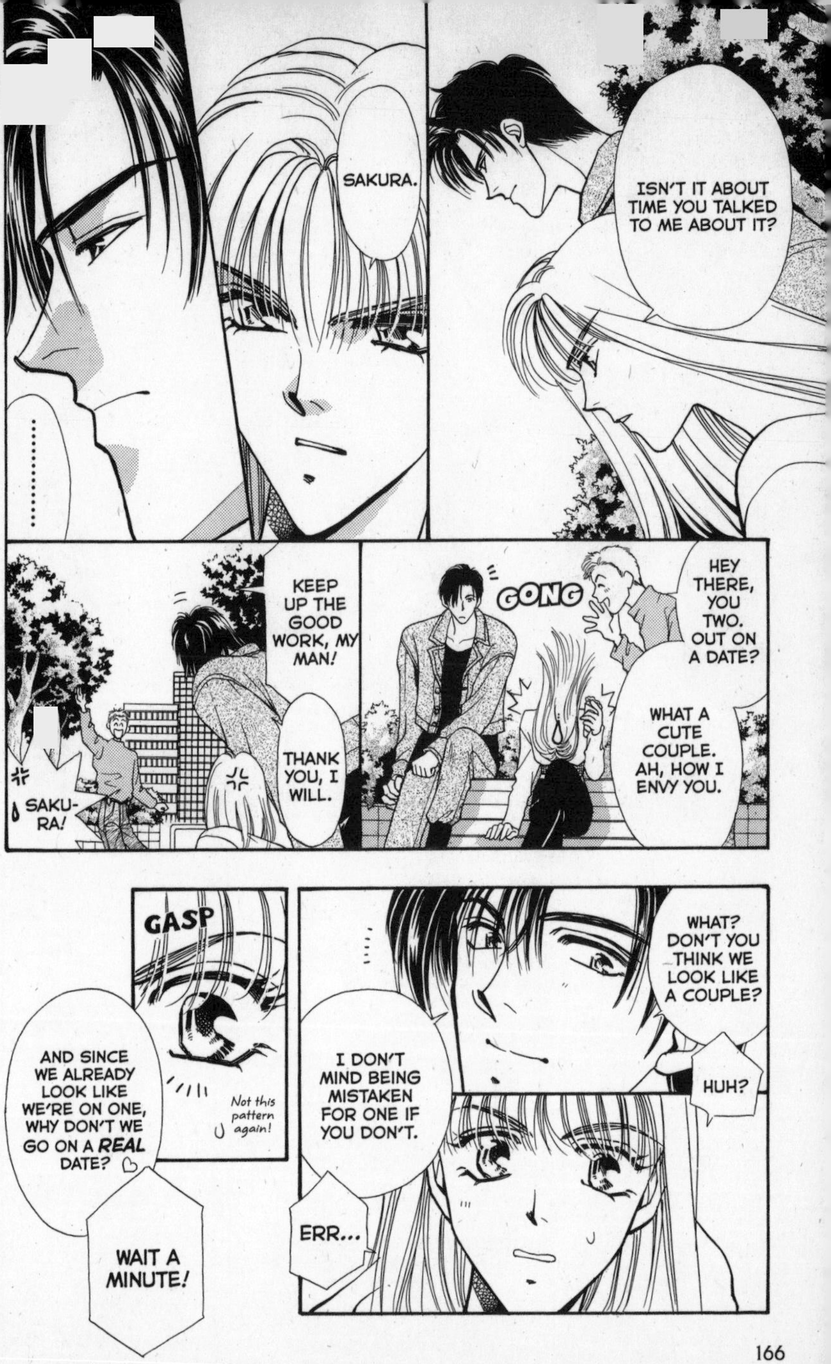
ISN'T IT ABOUT TIME YOU TALKED TO ME ABOUT IT?
SAKURA.
......
HEY THERE, YOU TWO. OUT ON A DATE?
GONG
WHAT A CUTE COUPLE. AH, HOW I ENVY YOU.
KEEP UP THE GOOD WORK, MY MAN!
THANK YOU, I WILL.
SAKU-RA!
WHAT? DON'T YOU THINK WE LOOK LIKE A COUPLE?
HUH?
I DON'T MIND BEING MISTAKEN FOR ONE IF YOU DON'T.
ERR...
GASP
Not this pattern again!
AND SINCE WE ALREADY LOOK LIKE WE'RE ON ONE, WHY DON'T WE GO ON A REAL DATE?
WAIT A MINUTE!

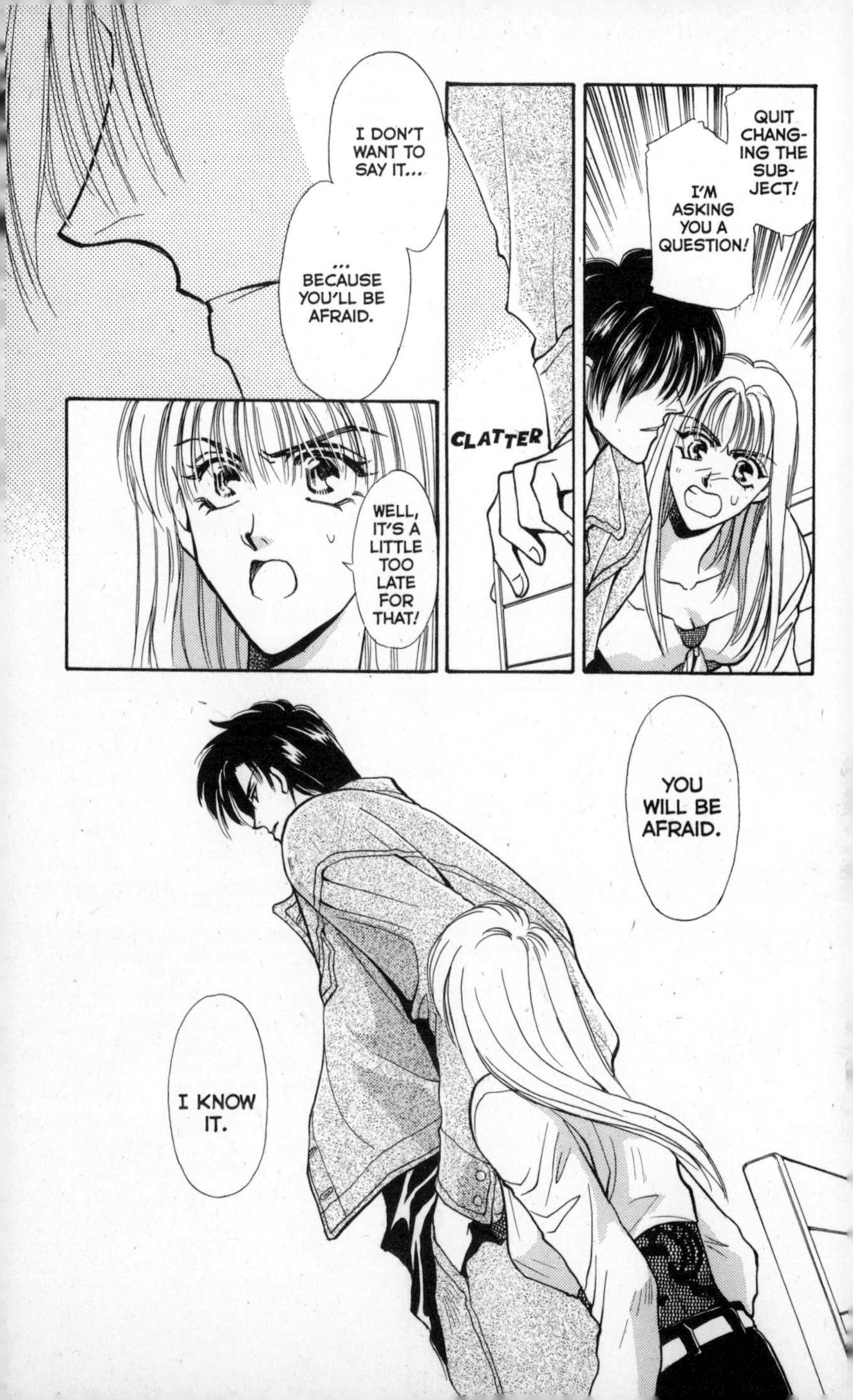
QUIT CHANGING THE SUBJECT!
I'M ASKING YOU A QUESTION!
CLATTER
I DON'T WANT TO SAY IT...
... BECAUSE YOU'LL BE AFRAID.
WELL, IT'S A LITTLE TOO LATE FOR THAT!
YOU WILL BE AFRAID.
I KNOW IT.

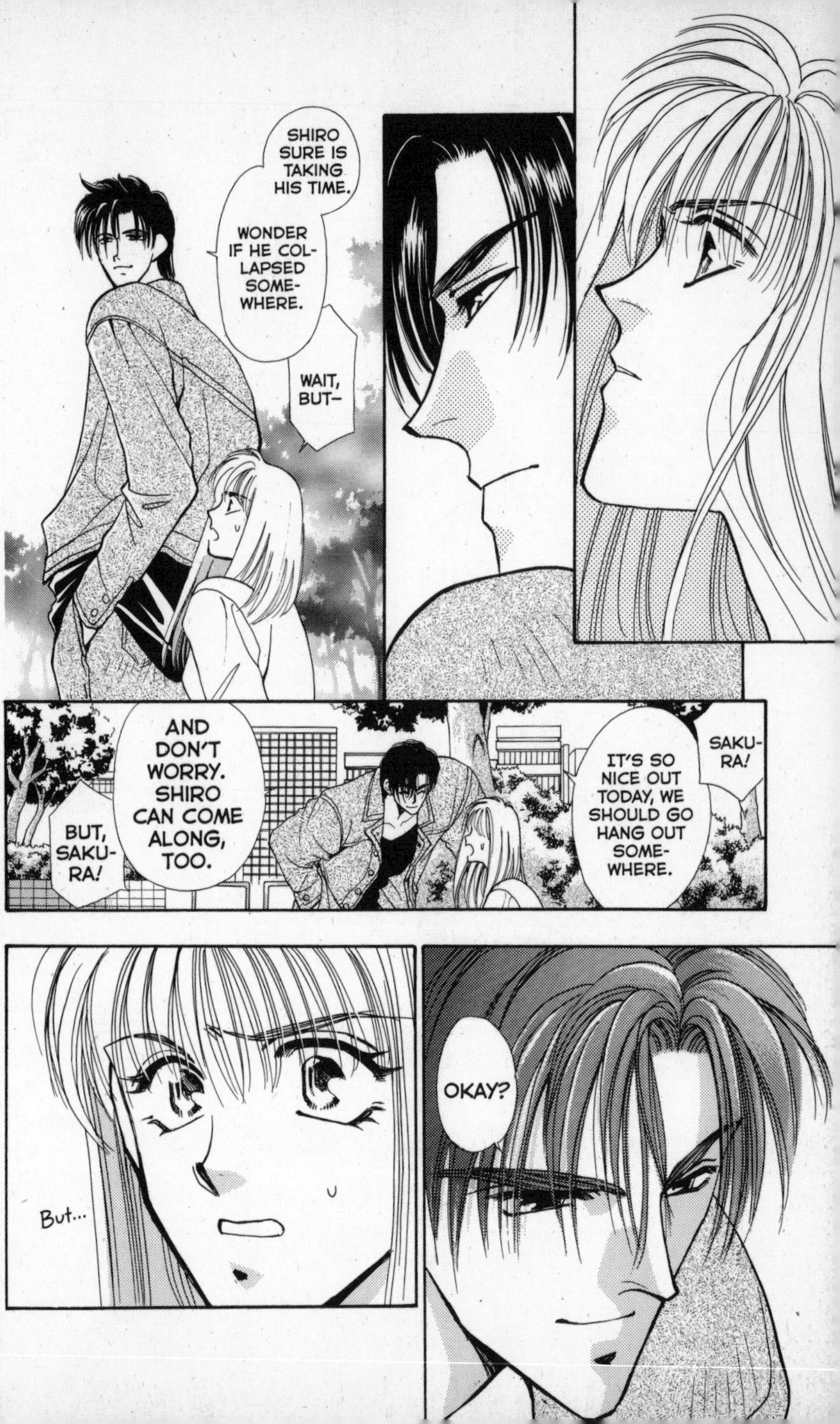
SHIRO SURE IS TAKING HIS TIME.
WONDER IF HE COL-LAPSED SOME-WHERE.
WAIT, BUT–
SAKU-RA!
IT'S SO NICE OUT TODAY, WE SHOULD GO HANG OUT SOME-WHERE.
AND DON'T WORRY. SHIRO CAN COME ALONG, TOO.
BUT, SAKU-RA!
OKAY?
But...

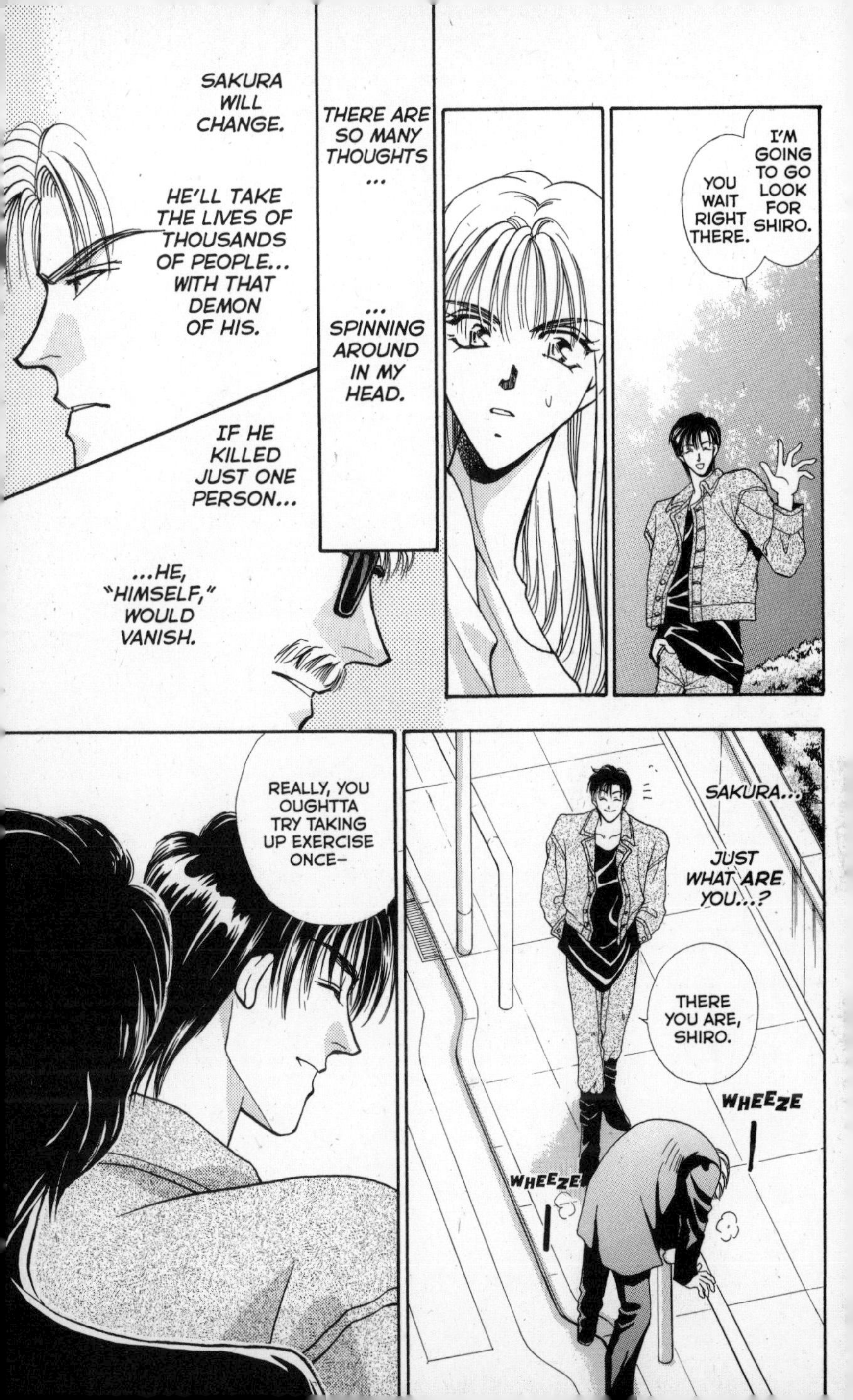
I'M GOING TO GO LOOK FOR SHIRO.
YOU WAIT RIGHT THERE.
THERE ARE SO MANY THOUGHTS...
...SPINNING AROUND IN MY HEAD.
SAKURA WILL CHANGE.
HE'LL TAKE THE LIVES OF THOUSANDS OF PEOPLE... WITH THAT DEMON OF HIS.
IF HE KILLED JUST ONE PERSON...
...HE, "HIMSELF," WOULD VANISH.
SAKURA...
JUST WHAT ARE YOU...?
THERE YOU ARE, SHIRO.
WHEEZE
WHEEZE
REALLY, YOU OUGHTTA TRY TAKING UP EXERCISE ONCE–

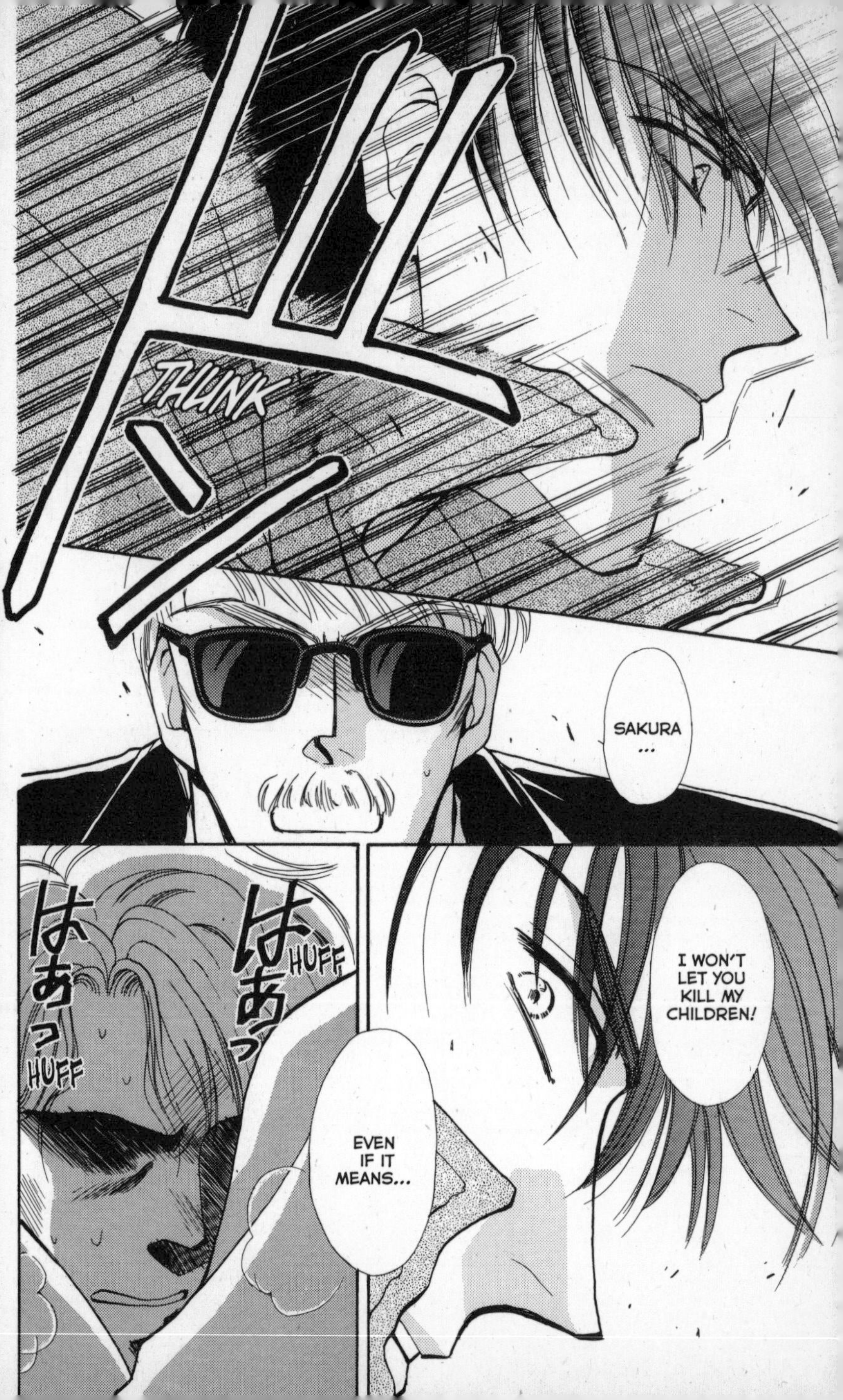
THUNK
SAKURA ...
I WON'T LET YOU KILL MY CHILDREN!
EVEN IF IT MEANS...
はあっ
HUFF
はあっ
HUFF

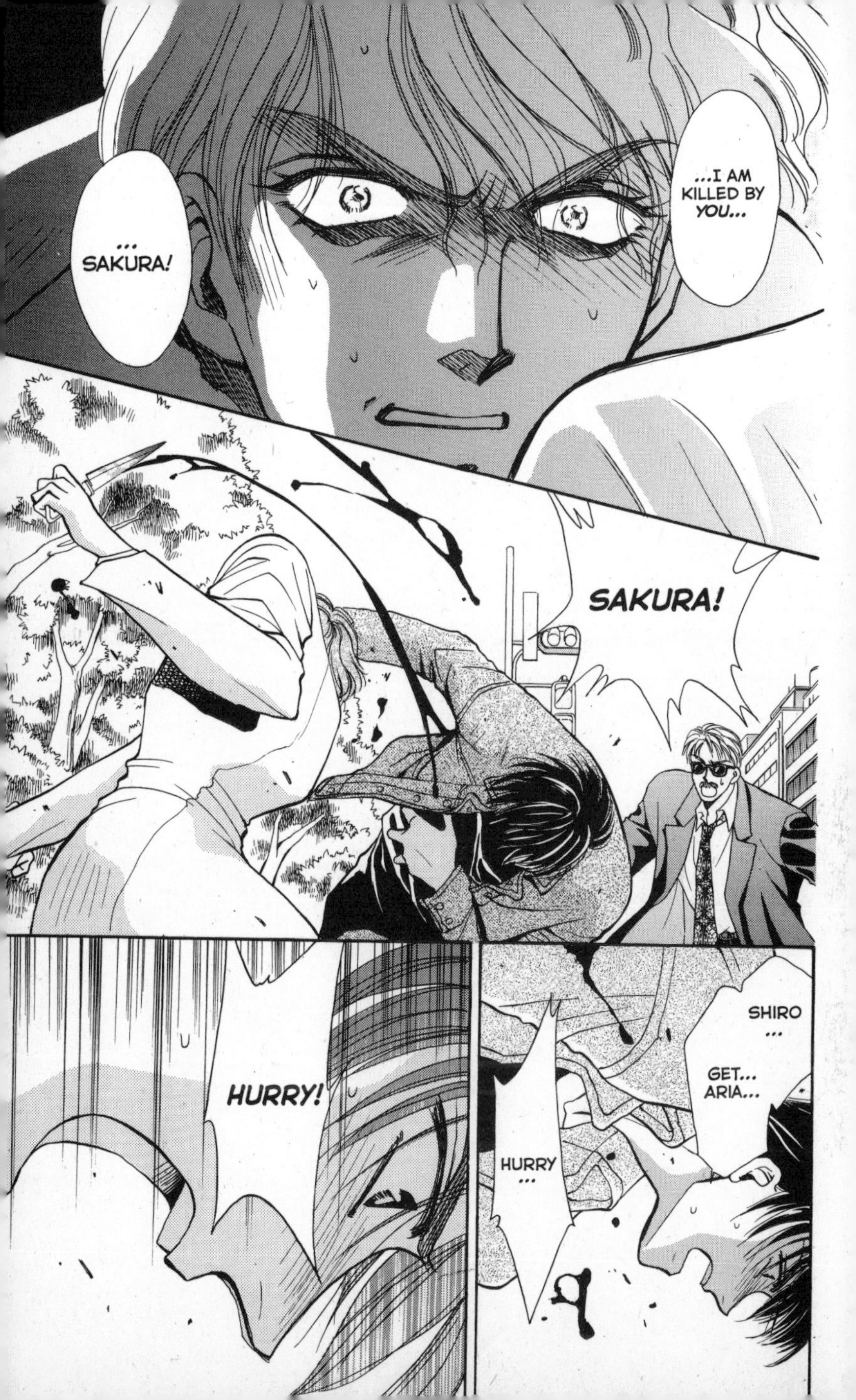
...I AM KILLED BY YOU...
... SAKURA!
SAKURA!
SHIRO ...
GET... ARIA...
HURRY ...
HURRY!

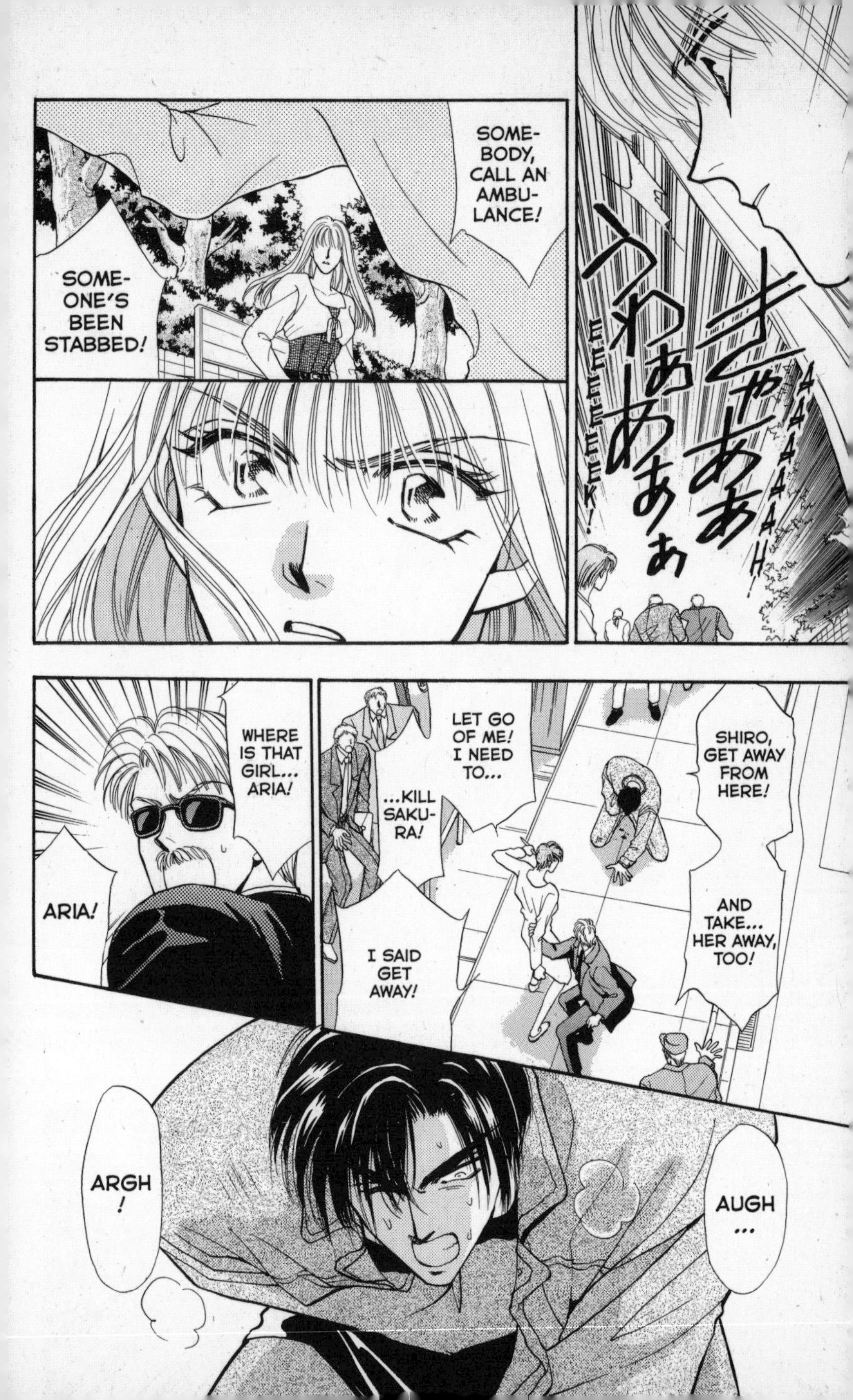
きゃあああ
AAAAAAH!
うわあああぁ
EEEEEEK!
SOME-BODY, CALL AN AMBU-LANCE!
SOME-ONE'S BEEN STABBED!
SHIRO, GET AWAY FROM HERE!
LET GO OF ME! I NEED TO...
...KILL SAKU-RA!
AND TAKE... HER AWAY, TOO!
I SAID GET AWAY!
WHERE IS THAT GIRL... ARIA!
ARIA!
AUGH...
ARGH!

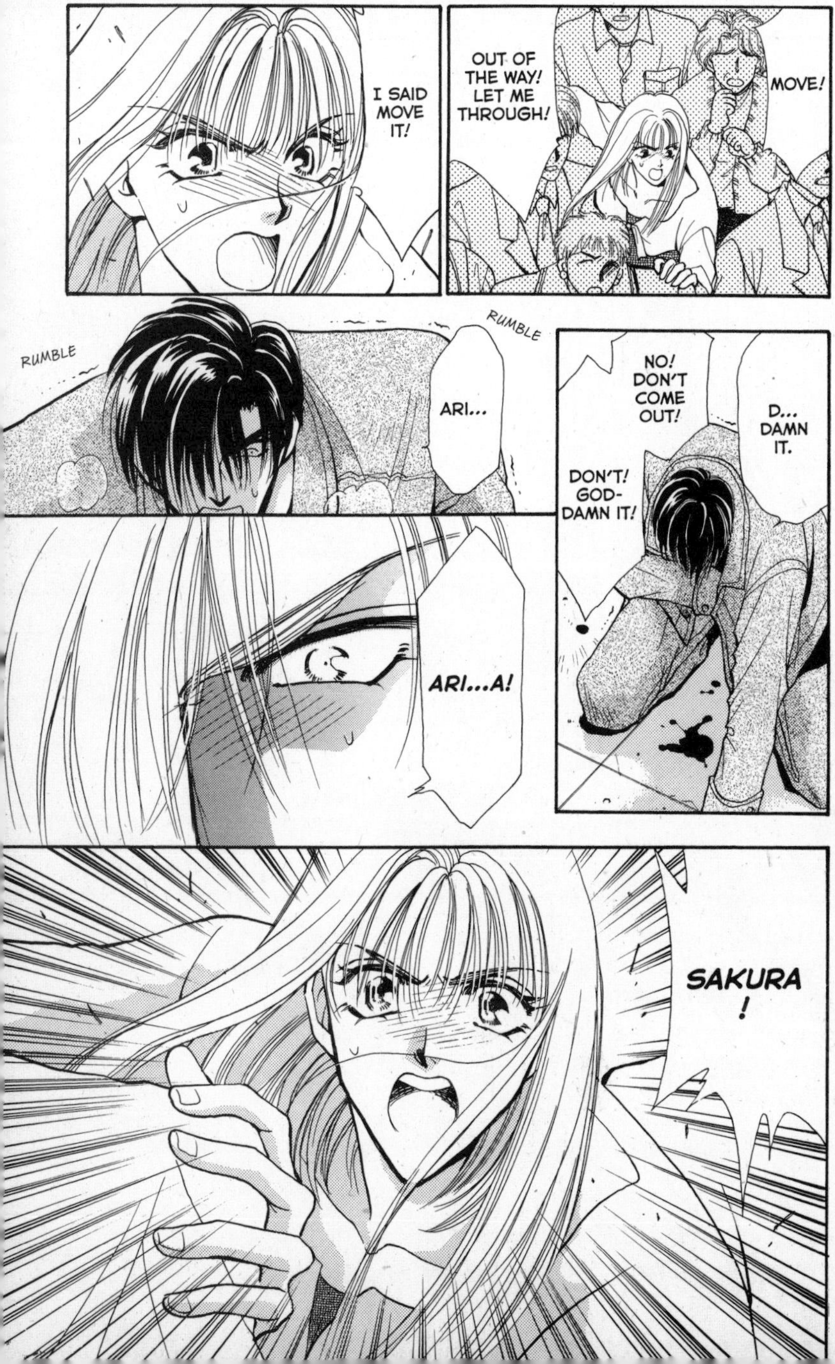
MOVE!
OUT OF THE WAY! LET ME THROUGH!
I SAID MOVE IT!
D... DAMN IT.
NO! DON'T COME OUT!
DON'T! GOD-DAMN IT!
RUMBLE
ARI...
RUMBLE
ARI...A!
SAKURA!

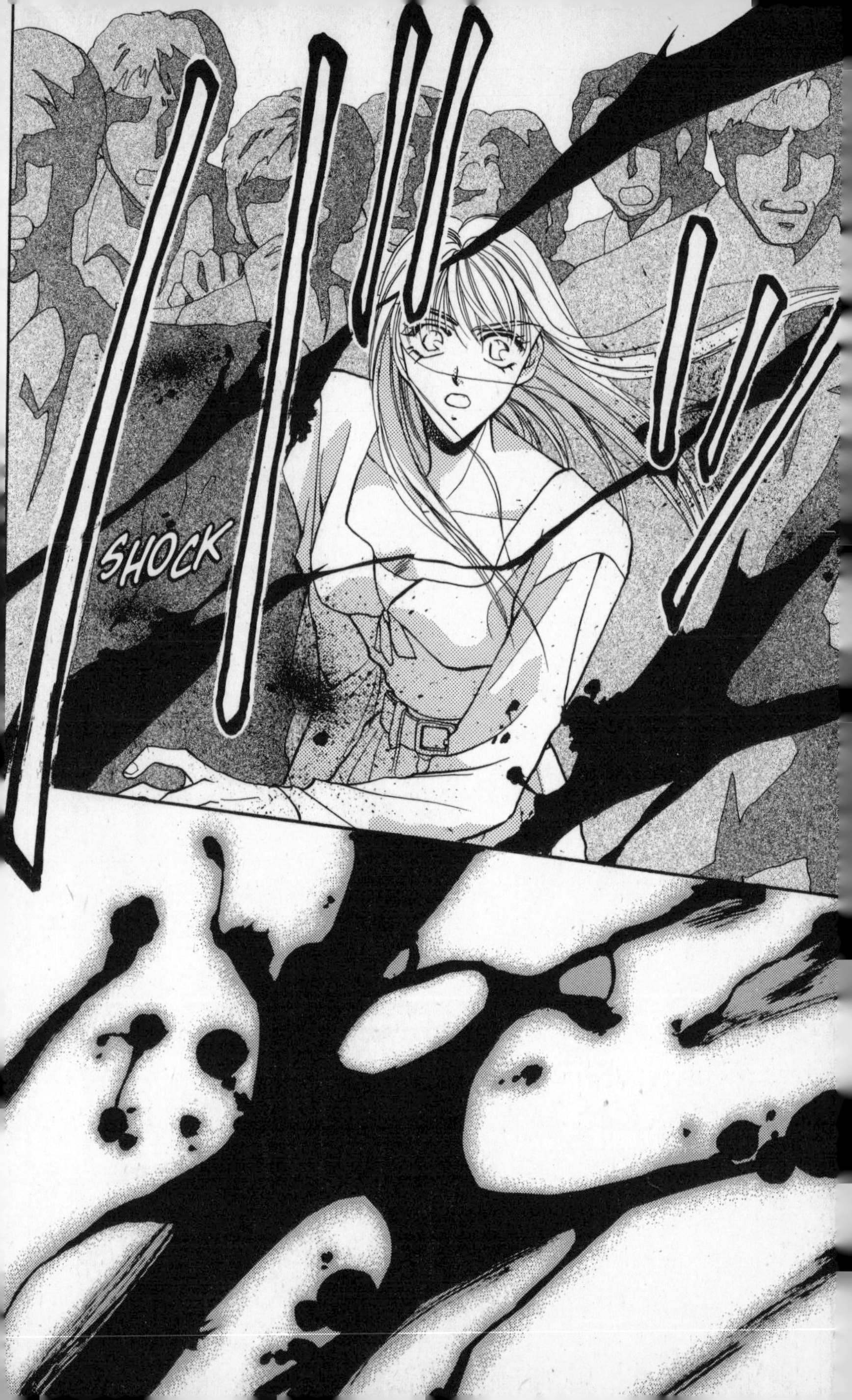
SHOCK

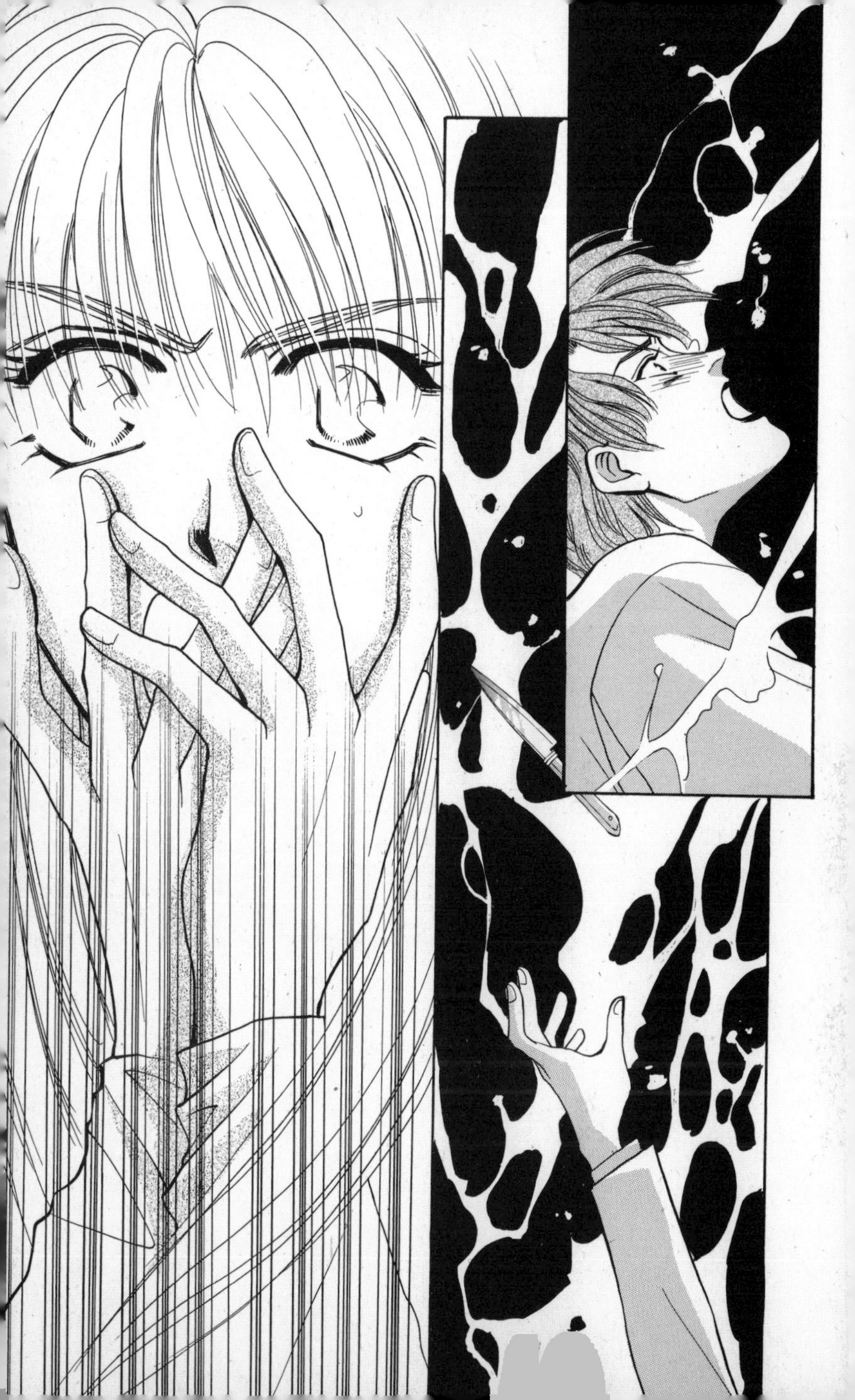

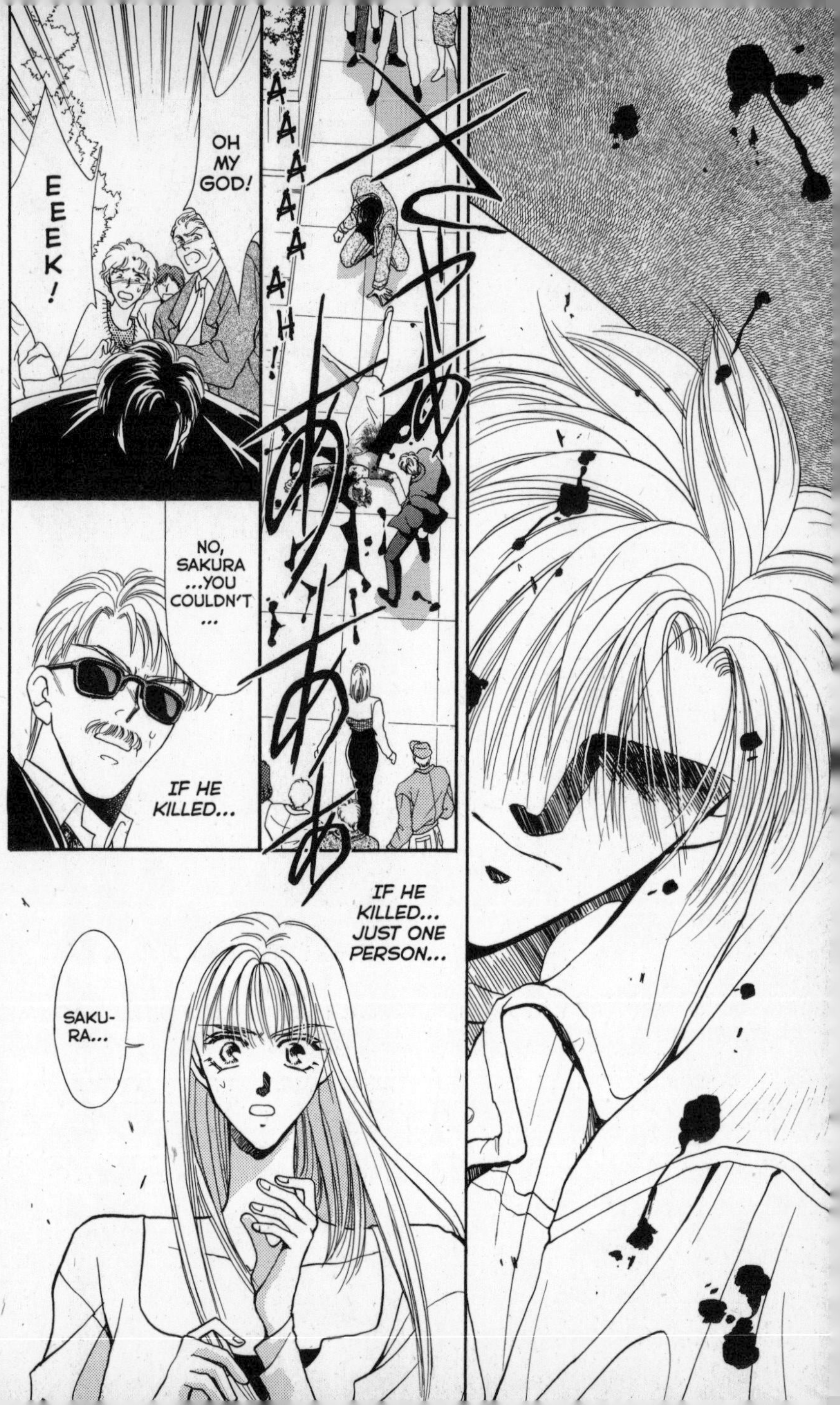
きゃあああ
AAAAAH!
OH MY GOD!
EEEK!
NO, SAKURA ...YOU COULDN'T ...
IF HE KILLED...
IF HE KILLED... JUST ONE PERSON...
SAKU-RA...

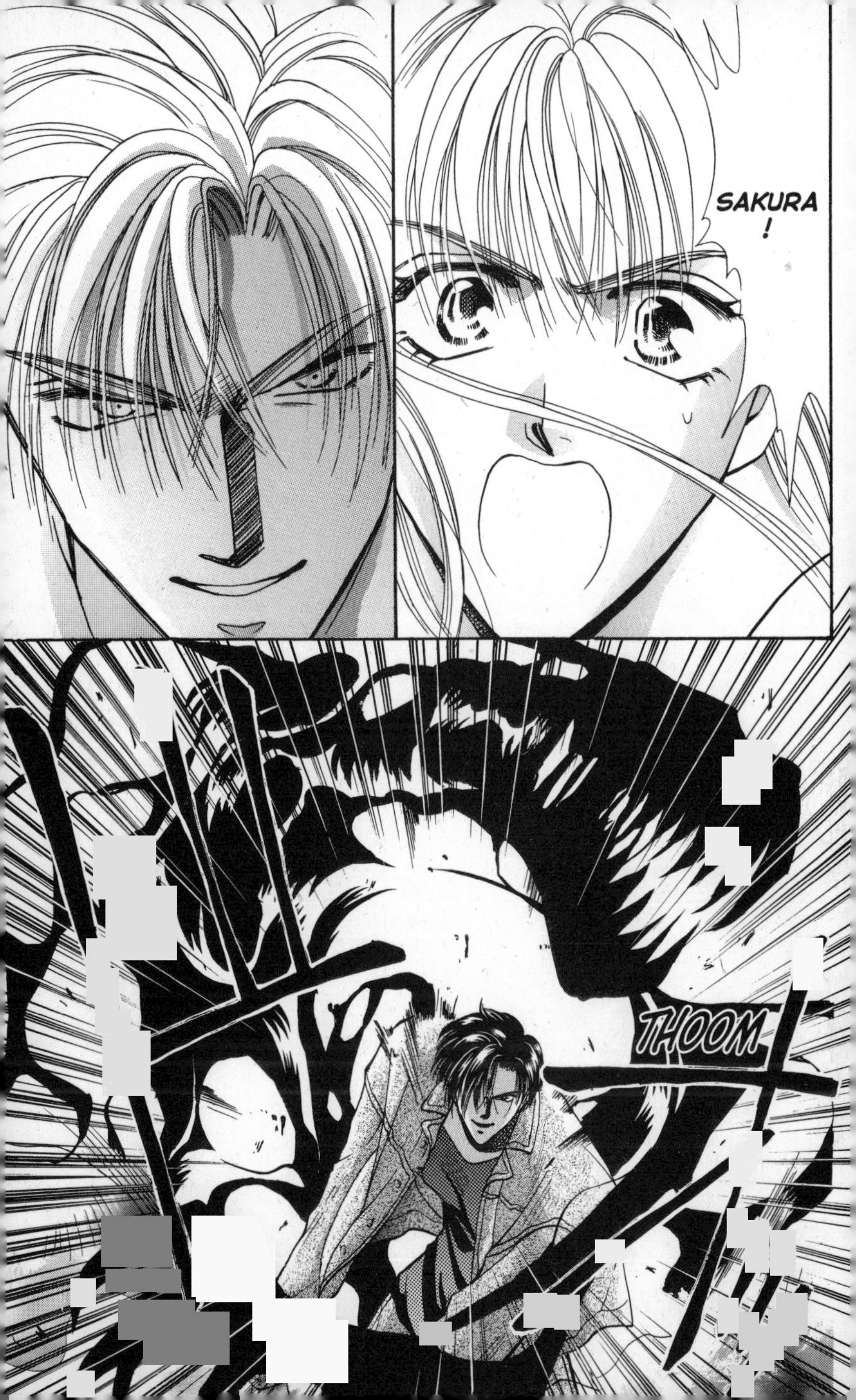
SAKURA !
THOOM

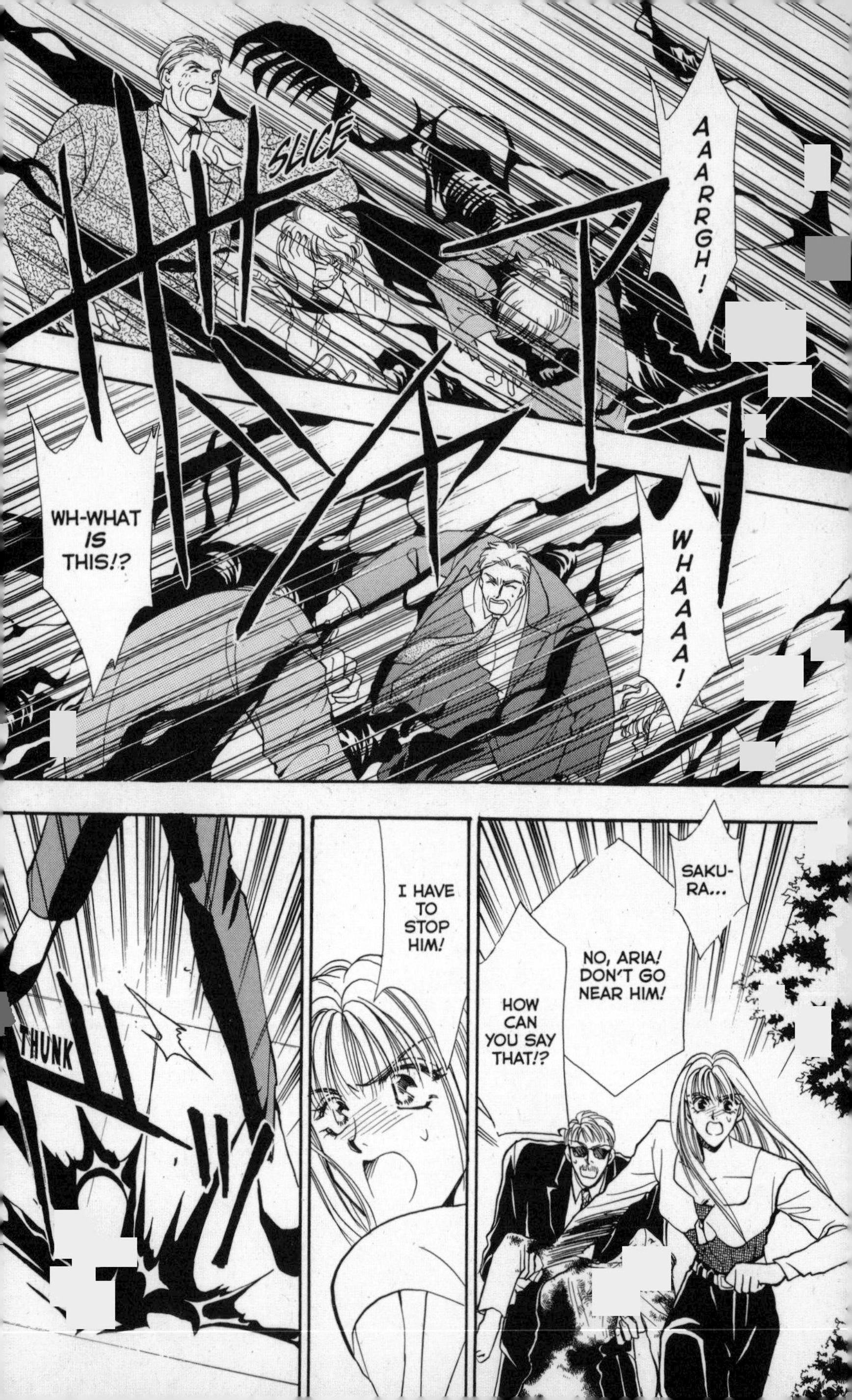
AAARRGH!
SLICE
WHAAAAA!
WH-WHAT *IS* THIS!?
SAKU-RA...
NO, ARIA! DON'T GO NEAR HIM!
HOW CAN YOU SAY THAT!?
I HAVE TO STOP HIM!
THUNK

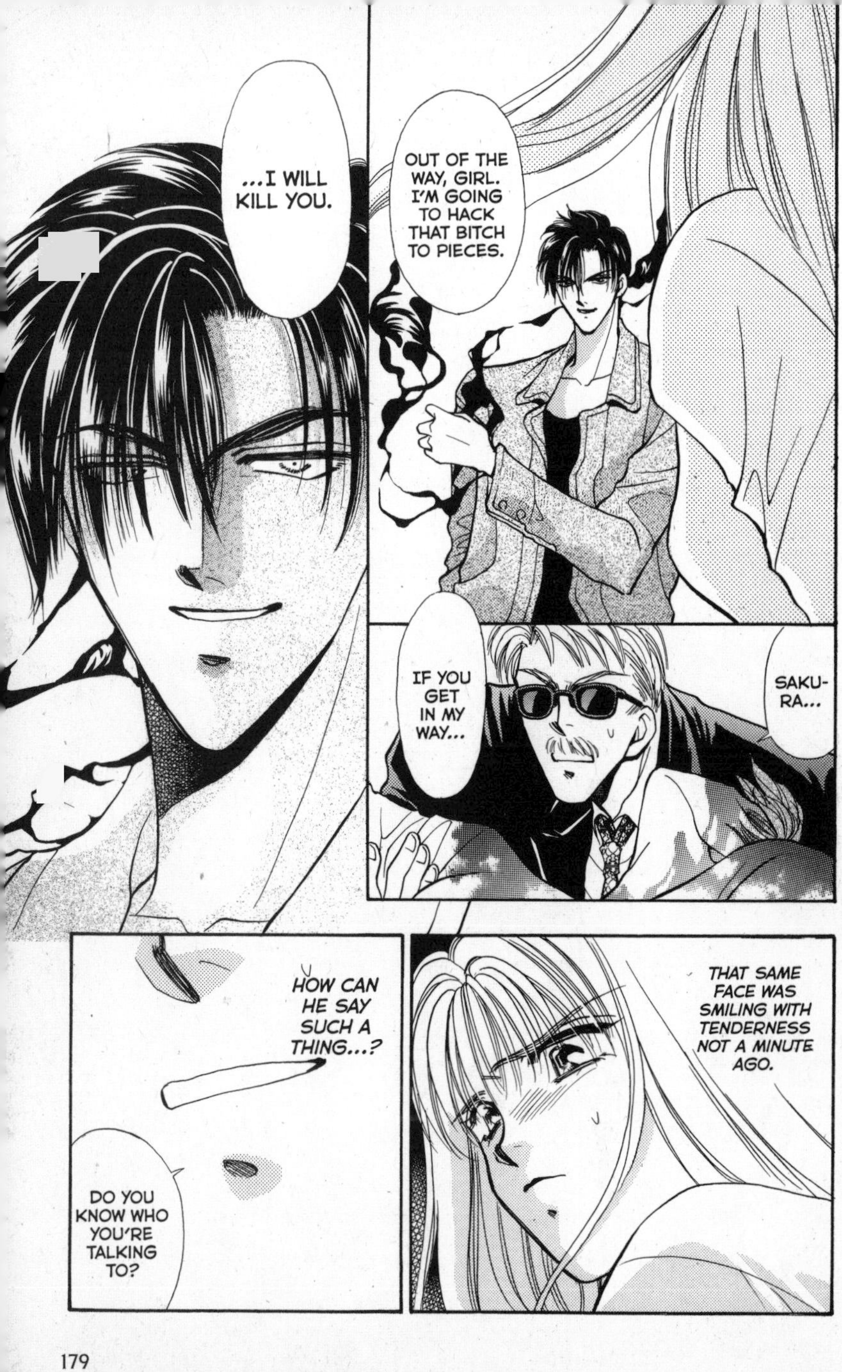
OUT OF THE WAY, GIRL. I'M GOING TO HACK THAT BITCH TO PIECES.
SAKU-RA...
IF YOU GET IN MY WAY...
...I WILL KILL YOU.
THAT SAME FACE WAS SMILING WITH TENDERNESS NOT A MINUTE AGO.
HOW CAN HE SAY SUCH A THING...?
DO YOU KNOW WHO YOU'RE TALKING TO?

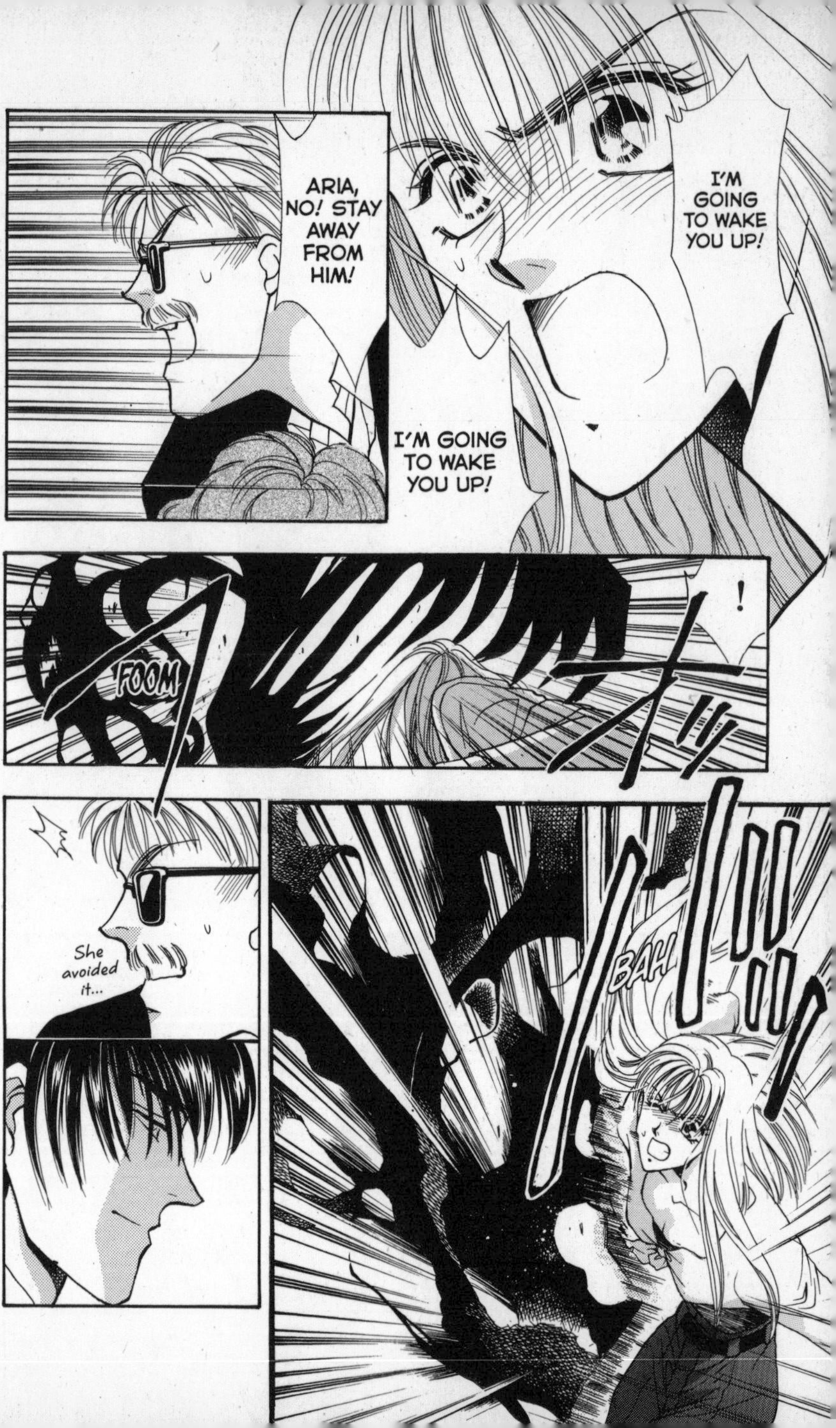
I'M GOING TO WAKE YOU UP!
I'M GOING TO WAKE YOU UP!
ARIA, NO! STAY AWAY FROM HIM!
!
FOOM
BAH
She avoided it...

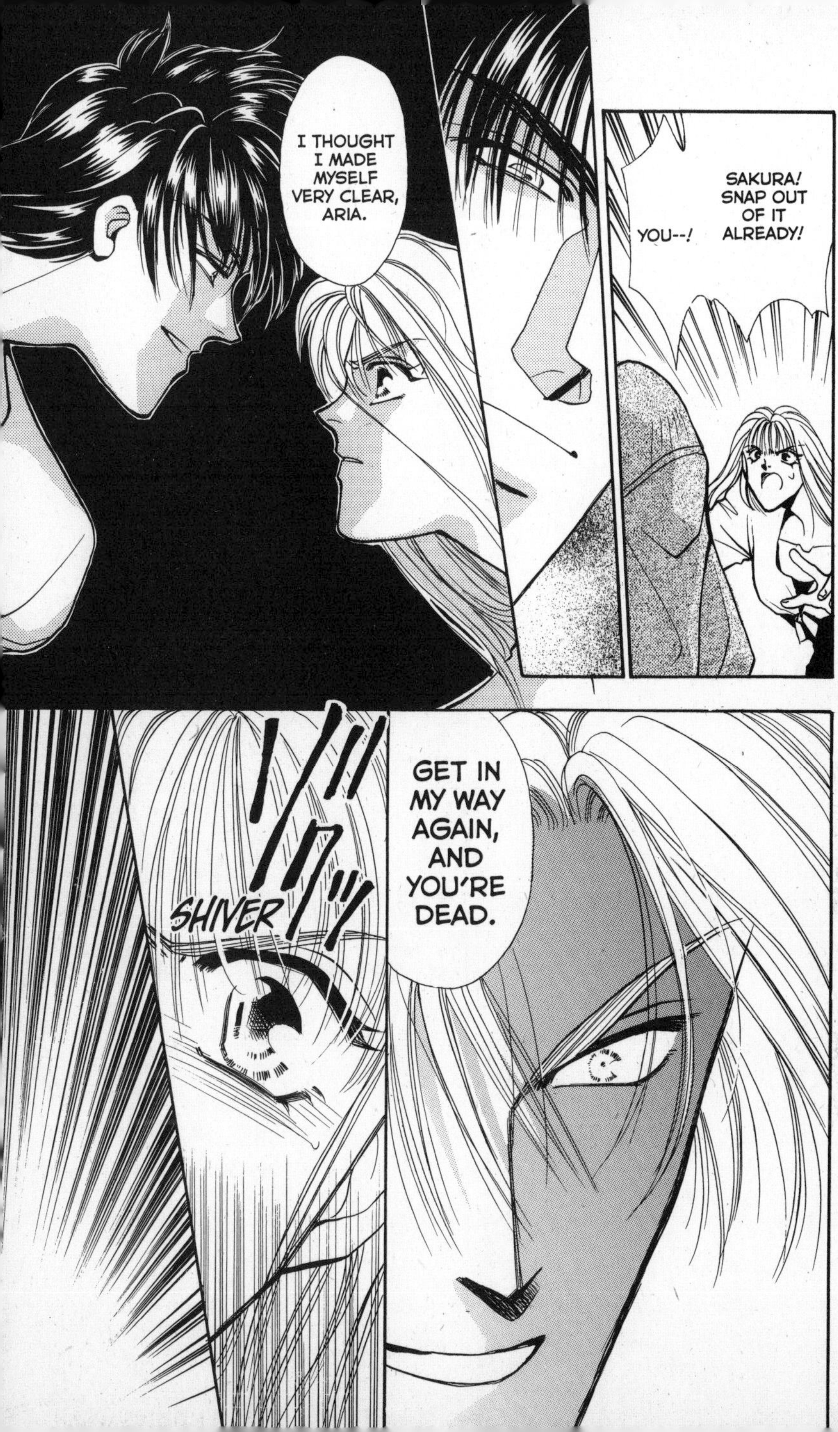
SAKURA! SNAP OUT OF IT ALREADY!
YOU--!
I THOUGHT I MADE MYSELF VERY CLEAR, ARIA.
GET IN MY WAY AGAIN, AND YOU'RE DEAD.
SHIVER

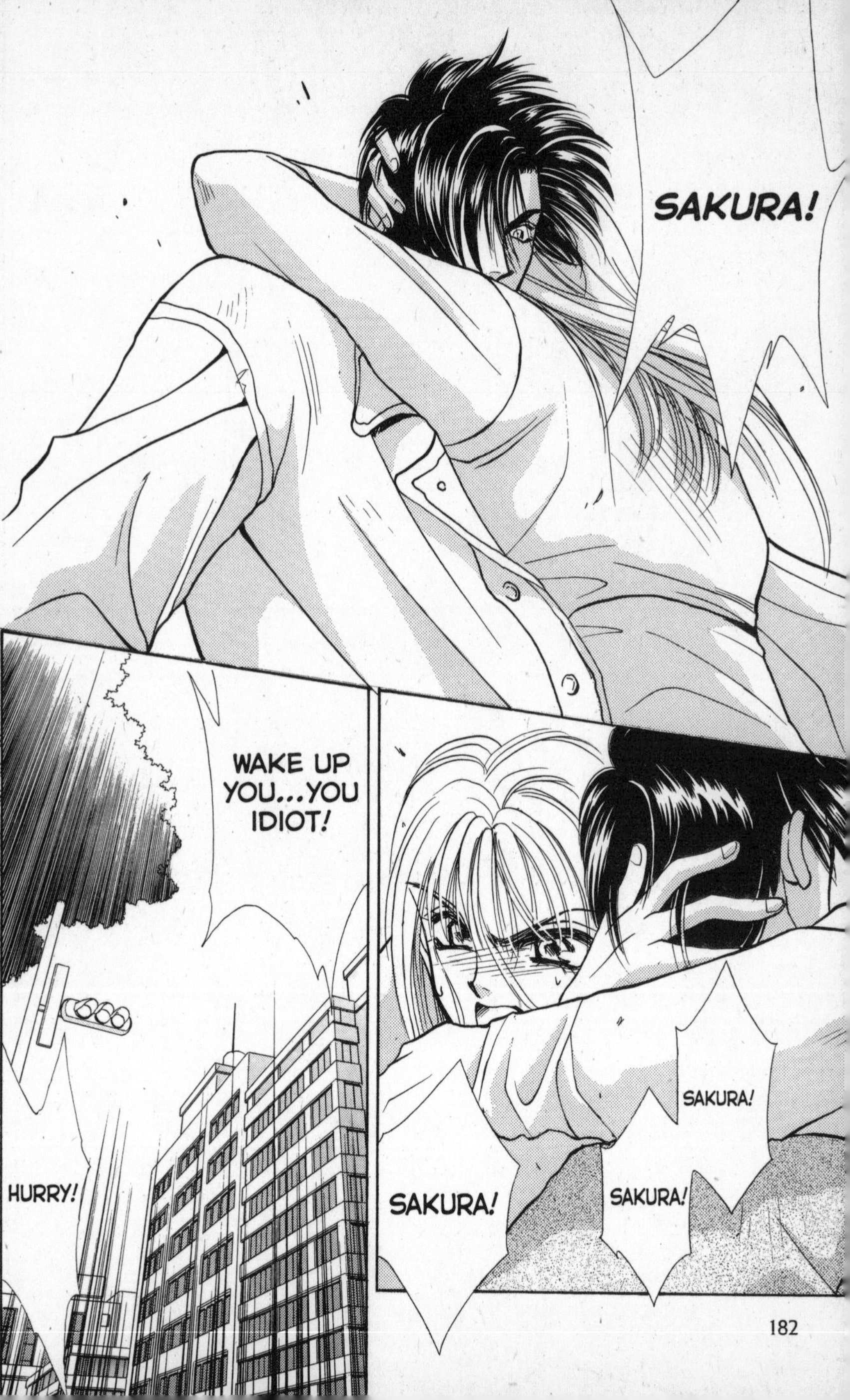
SAKURA!
SAKURA!
SAKURA!
SAKURA!
WAKE UP YOU...YOU IDIOT!
HURRY!

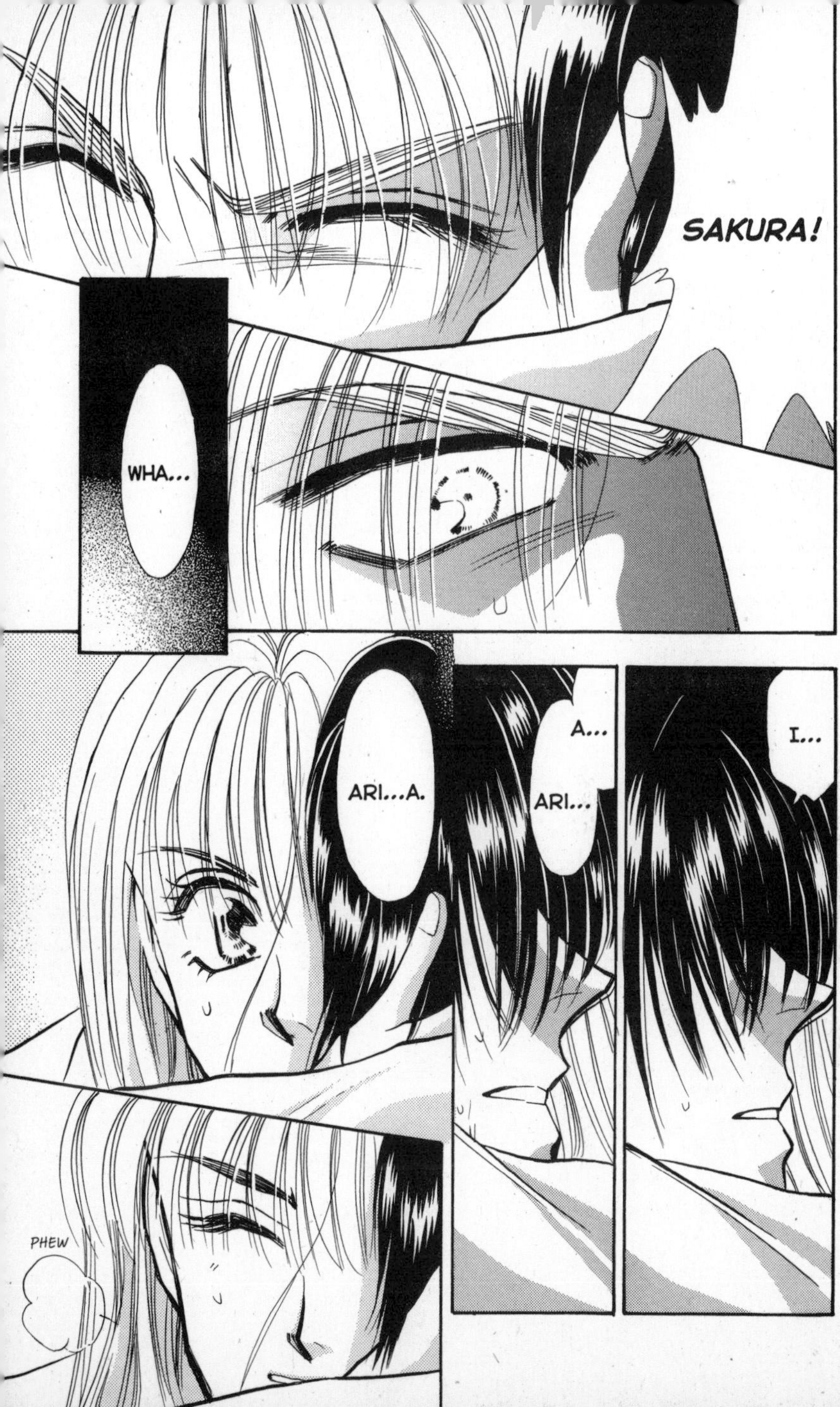
SAKURA!
WHA...
I...
A...
ARI...
ARI...A.
PHEW

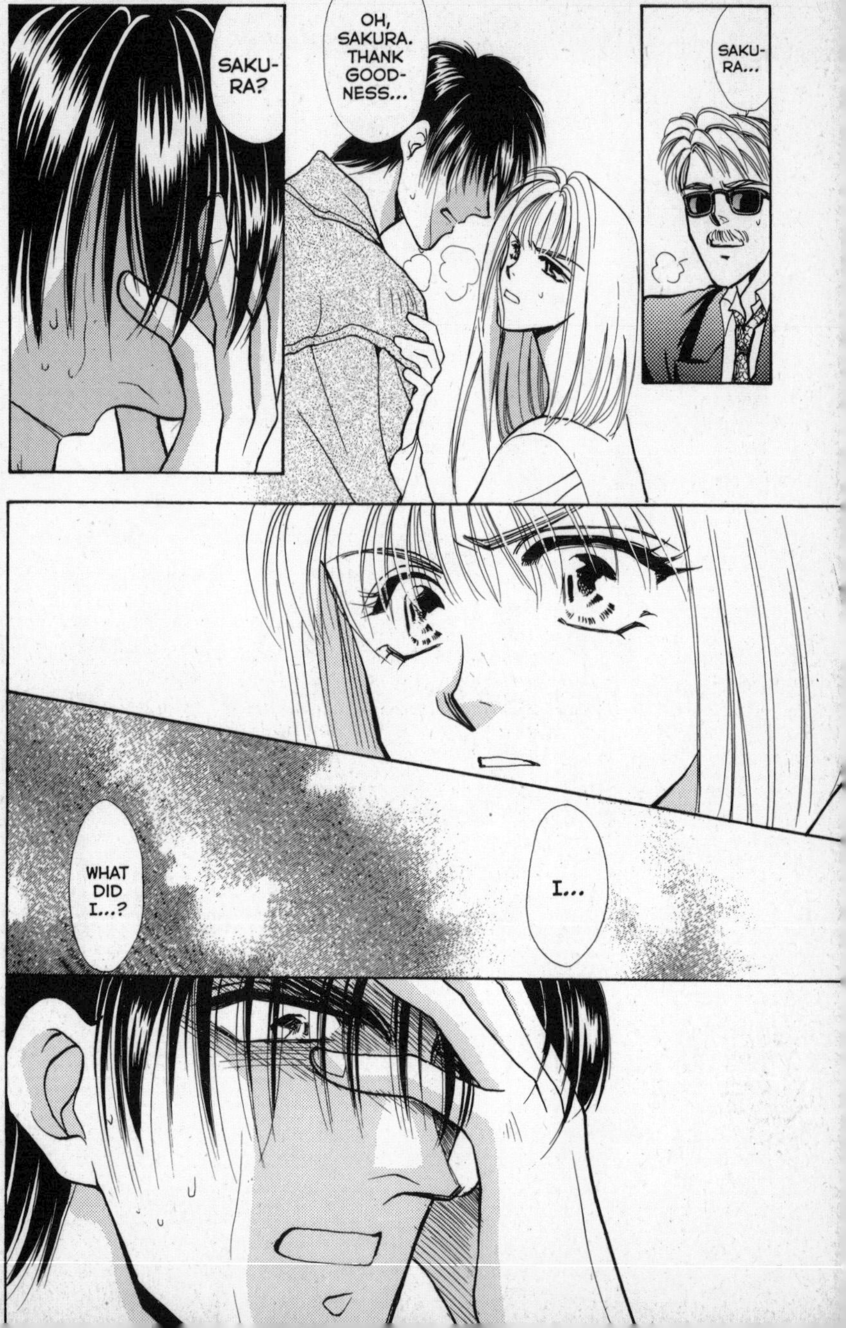
SAKU-RA...
OH, SAKURA. THANK GOODNESS...
SAKU-RA?
I...
WHAT DID I...?

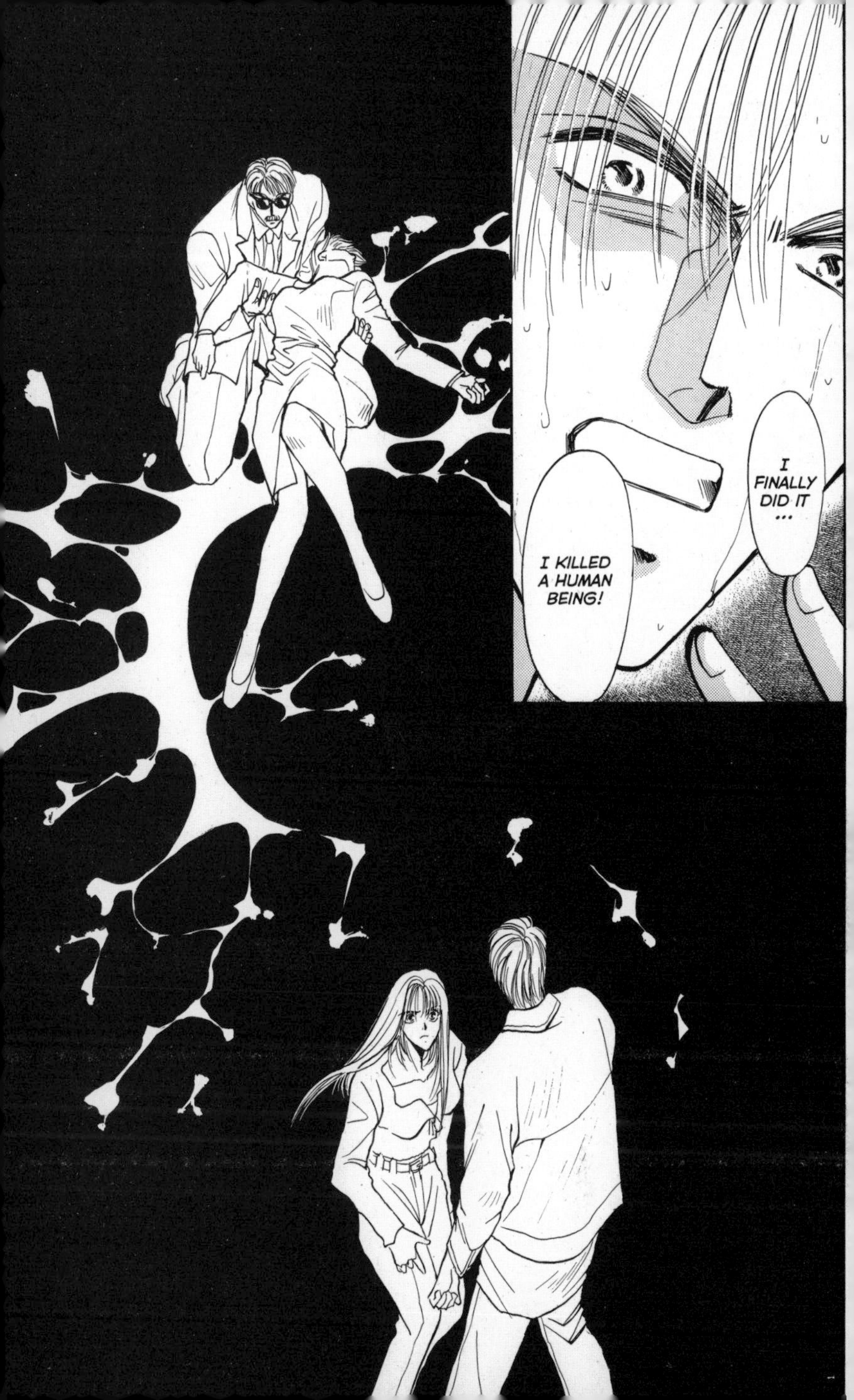
I FINALLY DID IT ...
I KILLED A HUMAN BEING!

獣たちの夜

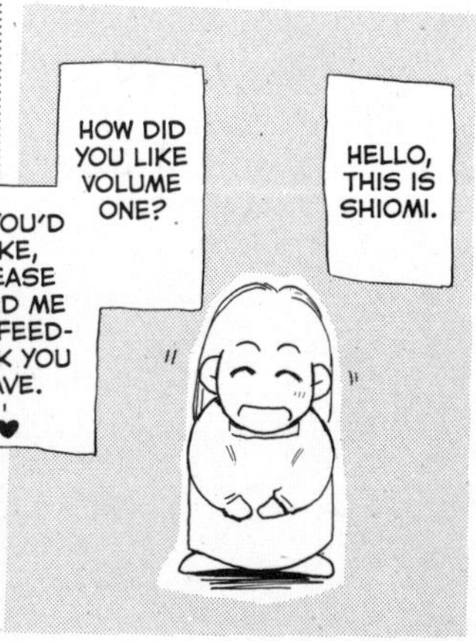
HELLO, THIS IS SHIOMI.
HOW DID YOU LIKE VOLUME ONE?
IF YOU'D LIKE, PLEASE SEND ME ANY FEED-BACK YOU HAVE.

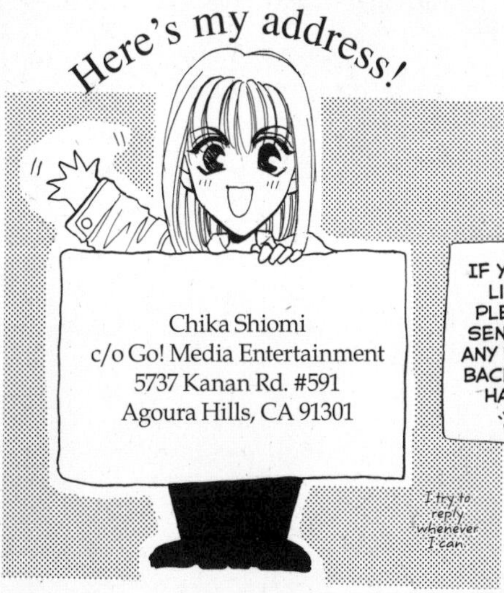
Here's my address!
Chika Shiomi
c/o Go! Media Entertainment
5737 Kanan Rd. #591
Agoura Hills, CA 91301
I try to reply whenever I can.

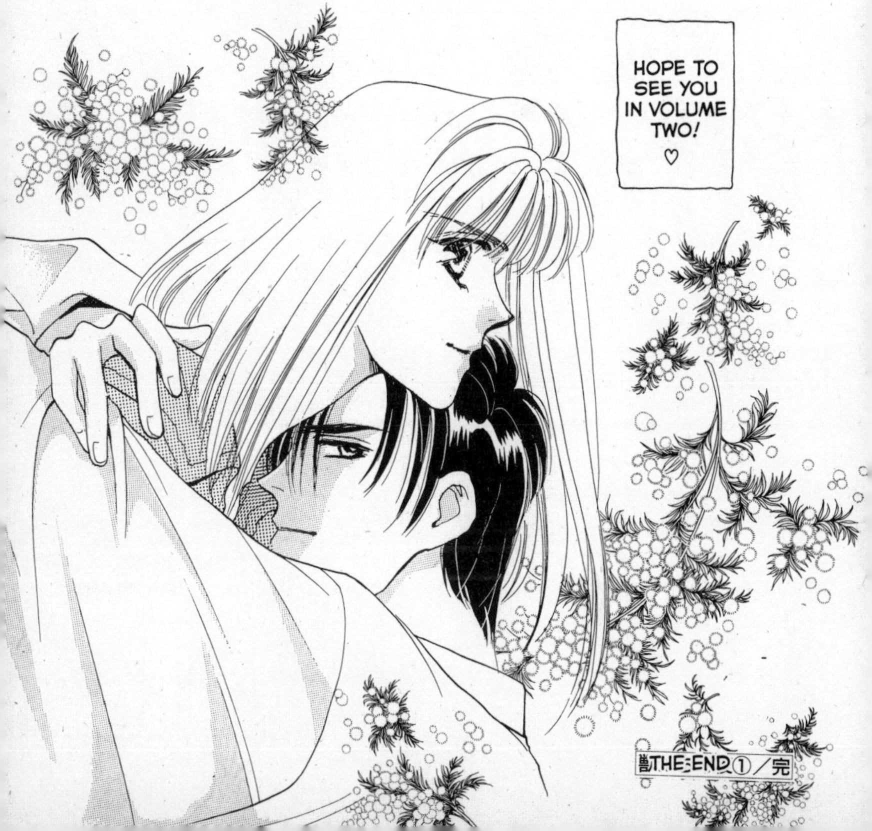
HOPE TO SEE YOU IN VOLUME TWO!
THE END ① /完

IN THE NEXT VOLUME...

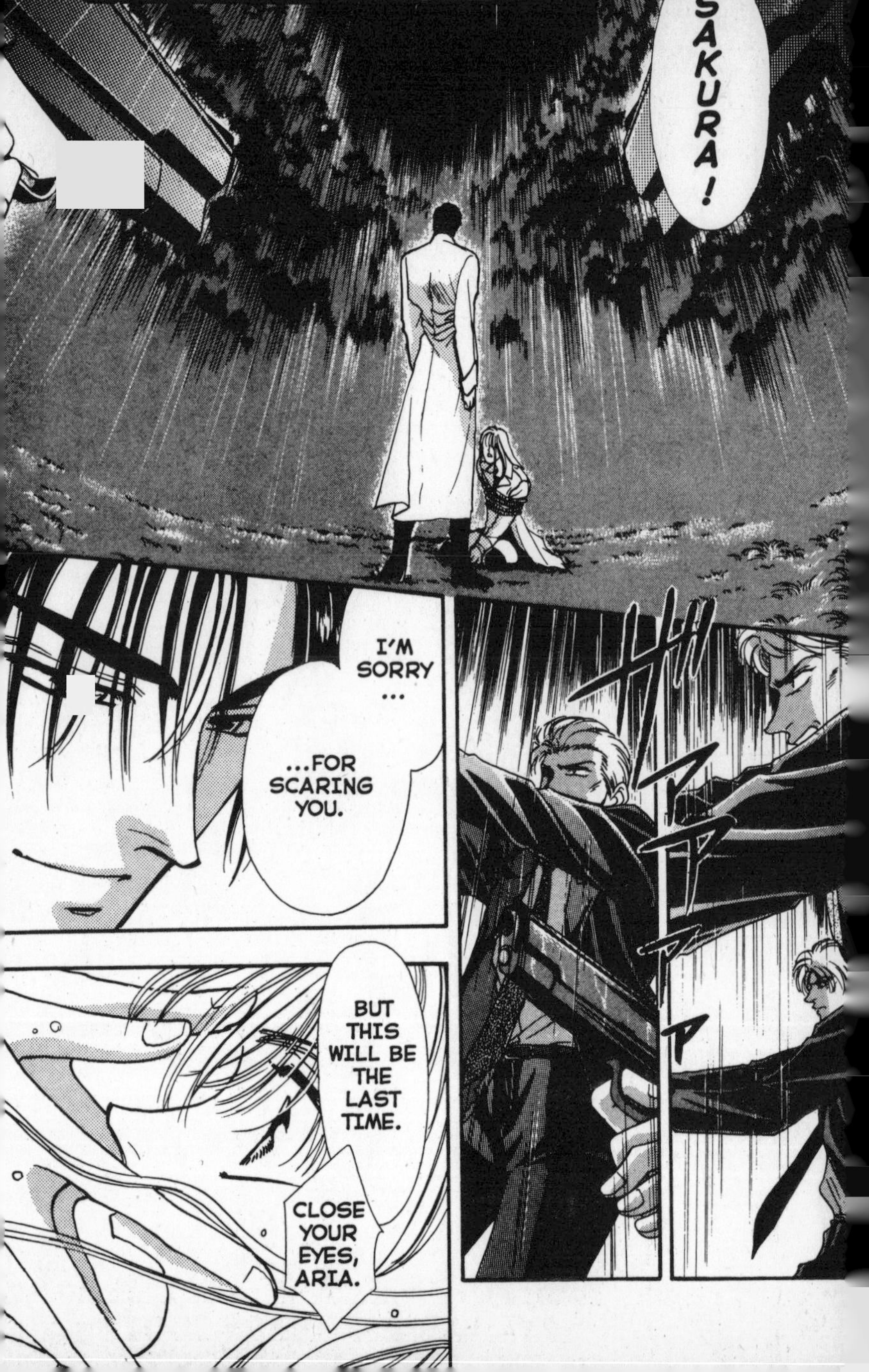
SAKURA!
I'M SORRY...
...FOR SCARING YOU.
BUT THIS WILL BE THE LAST TIME.
CLOSE YOUR EYES, ARIA.

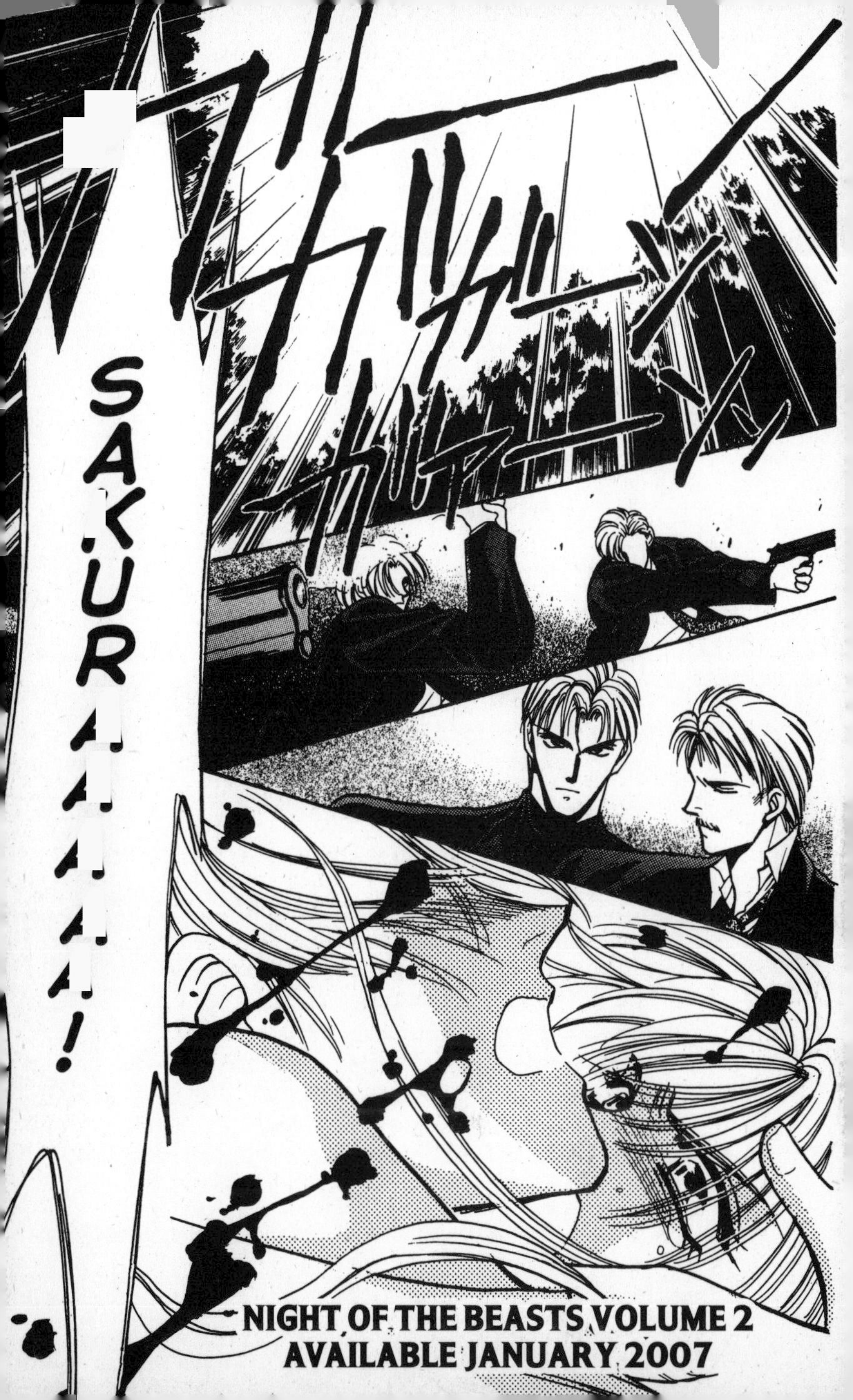
SAKURAAAAA!
NIGHT OF THE BEASTS VOLUME 2
AVAILABLE JANUARY 2007

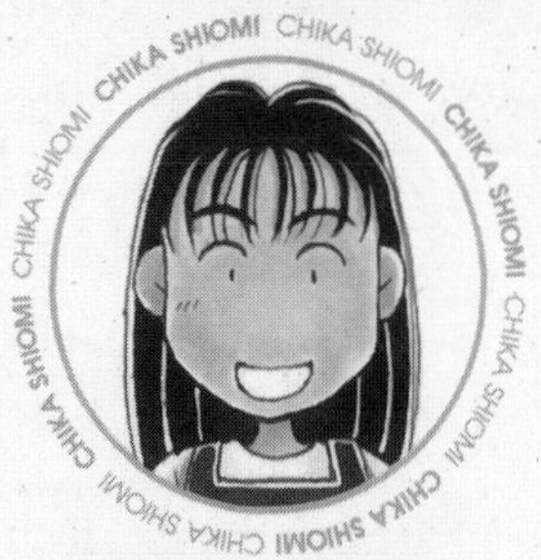
CHIKA SHIOMI

CHIKA SHIOMI

This is my first series released monthly, and being that I'm slow at drawing, I'm always in a pinch at the end of every month. Please cheer me on, everybody!

I was born February 21st. I live alone in Aichi Prefecture. I'm a Pisces, and my blood type is AB. My hobbies are skiing and going to hot water springs.

ABOUT THE MANGA-KA

Chika Shiomi has an amazing talent for depicting chilling and provocative horror stories that appeal to both shojo and shonen readers. Having created manga since 1993, starting with short stories in Akita Shoten's *Mystery Bonita* magazine, she has had a bountiful career of publishing both long-running series and short stories that have become popular both in Japan and abroad. Shiomi-sensei was born on February 21st and loves to travel and listen to Guns 'n Roses.

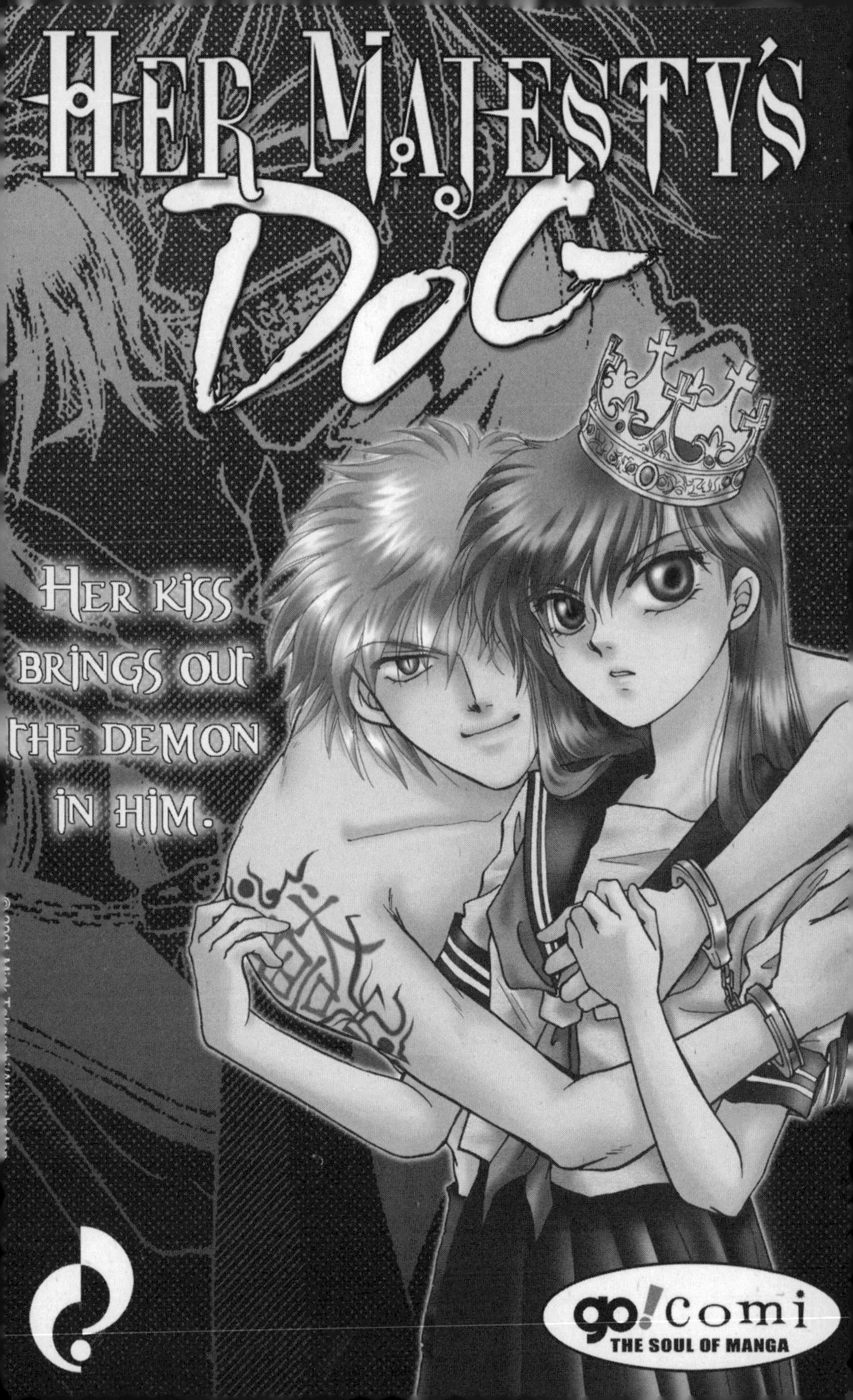

HER MAJESTY'S DOG
HER KISS BRINGS OUT THE DEMON IN HIM.
go!comi
THE SOUL OF MANGA